Mine Towns

Mine Towns
Buildings for Workers in Michigan's Copper Country

Alison K. Hoagland

University of Minnesota Press
Minneapolis • London

Portions of this book were previously published in "The Boardinghouse Murders: Housing and American Ideals in Michigan's Copper Country in 1913," *Perspectives in Vernacular Architecture: The Journal of the Vernacular Architecture Forum* 11 (2004): 1–18.

Unless otherwise credited, photographs and plans were created by the author.

Published by the University of Minnesota Press
111 Third Avenue South, Suite 290
Minneapolis, MN 55401-2520
http://www.upress.umn.edu

Printed in the United States of America on acid-free paper

The University of Minnesota is an equal-opportunity educator and employer.

Library of Congress Cataloging-in-Publication Data

Hoagland, Alison K.
Mine towns : buildings for workers in Michigan's Copper Country /
Alison K. Hoagland.
p. cm.
Includes bibliographical references and index.
ISBN 978-0-8166-6566-2 (hc : alk. paper)
ISBN 978-0-8166-6567-9 (pb : alk. paper)
1. Company town architecture—Michigan—Keweenaw Peninsula.
2. Architecture, Domestic—Michigan—Keweenaw Peninsula.
3. Architecture and society—Michigan—Keweenaw Peninsula—History—19th century.
4. Architecture and society—Michigan—Keweenaw Peninsula—History—20th century.
I. Title. II. Title: Buildings for workers in Michigan's Copper Country.
  NA9053.C57H63 2010
  728.09774'99—dc22

                    2009047051

17 16 15 14 13 12 11 10   10 9 8 7 6 5 4 3 2 1

Contents

Acknowledgments

My first acknowledgment goes to my father, George Stewart Hoagland, and it involves baseball. One of my favorite childhood memories is of attending games with him. We—father, mother, my brother, and I—would board a train in Wilmington, Delaware, and get off at the North Philadelphia station. Then we would walk several blocks to Connie Mack Stadium and watch the Phillies play. When the games were over, sometimes late into the night, our train would be waiting. These were DuPont Nights at the ballpark.

My grandfather, father, and brother worked for DuPont for more than one hundred years combined. Most families become entangled with their breadwinner's employer, but DuPont employees in Delaware were perhaps an extreme example; in the 1950s and 1960s, when I was growing up, the company dominated the state. When an actress I knew got her big break in Wilmington, moving from understudy to the lead in a traveling theater production, she was told not to worry about the reviews. The DuPont Company owned the playhouse, and the DuPont Company owned the newspaper. The review would be good.

Perhaps because as a child I was so oblivious to the extreme influence of the company, I later became fascinated with these questions of employer influence and control. The Copper Country of Michigan has proven an excellent place to explore these issues. I am grateful to Larry Lankton for persuading me to come here, for encouraging me to focus on this place, and for having written a model history of the area, *Cradle to Grave*. I thank other colleagues at Michigan Technological University, especially Carol MacLennan, Terry Reynolds, Mary Durfee, Bruce Seely, Hugh Gorman, and Bill Gale, for encouragement and support over the years.

It is customary to thank various archives and libraries where historians did research, but the cooperation I received from local archives was truly outstanding. Erik Nordberg at the Michigan Technological University Archives helped this project all along the way, not only responding to my requests but also flagging items of interest that he came across. I also thank Julie Blair, Christine Holland, and Cathy Grier of his staff. Thanks, too, to Tim O'Neil for sharing a cache of newspaper articles; to Dick Taylor for flagging correspondence at the Houghton County

Historical Society; to Deb Oyler at the Calumet Public Library; to Paul Sintkowski for making Houghton County deed books available; to Mark Schara for help with CAD; and to Mark Wisti for sharing an important collection of legal papers. I am grateful to Jeremiah Mason, Abby Sue Fisher, and Brian Hoduski of the Keweenaw National Historical Park for helping me and thinking of me when they found relevant items. Lynn Bjorkman, also at the park, has been a valued and generous colleague, sharing material and serving as a sounding board.

I would like to acknowledge my Vernacular Architecture Forum colleagues nationwide. I presented parts of this book at various conferences, and I appreciate my colleagues' comments. I learned from VAFers who shared their places, such as when Kingston Heath took us to New Bedford, Arne Alanen led us to the Iron Range of Minnesota, and Tom Hubka and Judith Kenny gave us a tour of Milwaukee. Similarly, I learned when I showed the Copper Country to visitors: I thank Mark Schara, Betty Bird, Tom Hubka, Neil Larson, Jill Fisher, Mike Chiarappa, Kristin Szylvian, Ann Smart Martin, and Carolyn Torma for their perceptive questions and willingness to come so far, and thanks, too, to Lynn Bjorkman and Arne Alanen for cohosting some of those visits.

In order to study houses, it is necessary to get inside them, and I am indebted to the many homeowners, organizations, and others who made this possible: Bob Ball, Calumet Township, City of Houghton, Copper Country Habitat for Humanity, Donald Currey, Adele Destrampe, Kevin Freeman, Frederick Guenther, Cheryl Harter, Joe Kaplan and Keren Tischler, Keweenaw County Historical Society, Mike Kezele, Corinne Koski, Ronald Moen, Craig Nuottila, Marcia Primeau, Brian Rendel, John Rosemurgy, Quincy Mine Hoist Association, Quincy Development Corporation, and Robert Stites. Thirteen classes of graduate students in Michigan Tech's Industrial Archaeology Program helped me document these workers' houses and also helped develop my thinking on this topic. These students are too numerous to mention, but I thank them all.

Finally, I would particularly like to thank Joe and Elaine Putrich of Cuba, Illinois. Our meeting was almost happenstance and could not have been more rewarding for me. They shared their family history and welcomed me into their home. They patiently watched the story of Joe's grandparents take on new dimensions and have been enthusiastic about my work. They make me proud to be a historian.

Introduction
Negotiating Paternalism in the Copper Country

In the Copper Country of Michigan, the combination of a remote location and a highly profitable industry fostered the development of a relationship between management and labor that extended beyond the workplace. The location was the Keweenaw Peninsula, which projects seventy-five miles into Lake Superior from the western end of the Upper Peninsula (Figure I.1). The industry was the mining, milling, and smelting of copper, a material used for kettles, stills, ordnance, and sheathing for ships' hulls even before the intense demands for it by the electrical industry beginning in the 1880s. Between the 1840s and the 1880s, this region produced three quarters of the nation's copper. In the 1880s its output was exceeded by Butte, Montana, and then the American Southwest, but Michigan's copper industry continued to thrive until after World War I.

Eastern capital, American managers, and immigrant miners developed the resource and built a community that approached a population of one hundred thousand by 1910. Needing to attract workers to this remote location, and to keep them once they got here, the companies offered not only adequate wages but also houses, health care, schools, and a host of other amenities. Not all of these benefits were distributed equally, though, and this fundamental inequality marred the companies' attempts at benevolence.

The Copper Country offers both historical and architectural resources that make it an ideal place to study the manifestations of corporate paternalism. Historically, the Copper Country was developed by a variety of companies that offered a range of living arrangements to their workers—company housing, ground rents, commercial towns—so that employees had options; why they made the choices they did and how they negotiated these arrangements with the companies illustrates the complexity of paternalism. A large number of workers' houses and other buildings survive. Soundly built, they were not consumed by expanding pits, as was often the case in other mining towns. With little new development after copper mining ceased in Houghton and Keweenaw counties in the late 1960s, the built environment has survived by default, providing a wealth of material evidence.

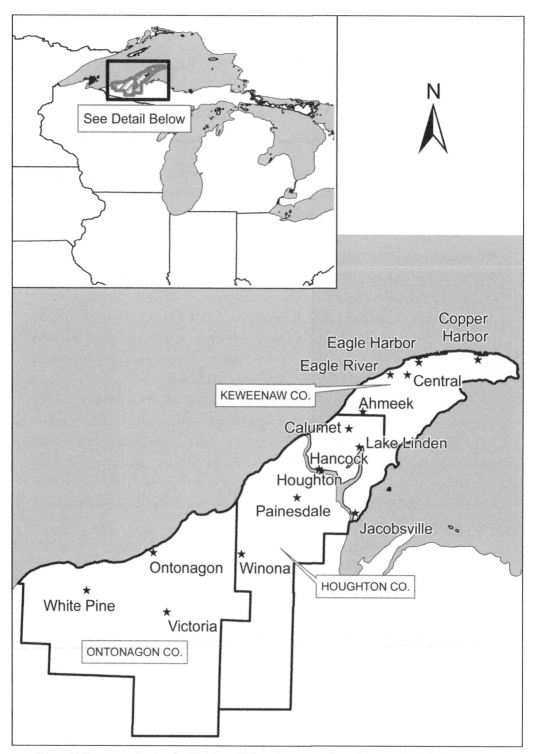

Figure I.1 Keweenaw Peninsula, Michigan. Rich native copper deposits gave this Lake Superior land mass the name "Copper Country." Map by Timothy A. Goddard, 2008.

The Copper Country

In 1843 the United States acquired rights to this land through a treaty with the Ojibway. State geologist Douglass Houghton had published the results of his 1840 survey identifying native copper—pure copper unalloyed with other metals—as the primary resource. The copper-mining potential of the region was known, and a mining land rush was on. Early discoveries in the north end of the district in present-day Keweenaw County and in the south in what is now Ontonagon County directed much of the pre–Civil War development to those places. The long-term successes, though, proved to be in the middle, in Houghton County.[1]

The early workings in Ontonagon and Keweenaw counties focused on mass copper, large pieces of native copper. Mass copper tended to be distributed unevenly and run out quickly, though, and early successful mines expired by 1870. In Houghton County, successful companies concentrated on amygdaloidal and conglomerate copper, both of which are embedded in rock. Producing copper for market required three basic processes: mining, milling, and smelting. Mining involved drilling and blasting to loosen the rock, then using trams, or carts on rails, to move it horizontally toward a shaft, then hoisting it to the surface (Figure I.2). Dedicated railroads or incline trams transported the rock to the stamp mill, which was located adjacent to a body of water because a considerable amount of water was needed to separate rock from copper after the rock was stamped to a fine consistency. Railroads then took the copper to a smelter where it was further refined in furnaces. These processes required a great deal of capital, most of which came from East Coast investors.[2]

The processes also required a labor force, something that was absent in the virtually unsettled Keweenaw. Both skilled and unskilled workers, employed underground as well as on the surface, found their way to the Copper Country. In 1870 57 percent of Houghton County's population was foreign-born, making it the county with the third-greatest number of ethnic groups in the country. By 1880, American-born people held a slim majority. Englishmen from Cornwall, bringing mining experience and fleeing a depression in their homeland, particularly dominated the mines, rising to supervisory positions. Germans and Irishmen were also in the first wave of immigrants to work underground. Americans tended to work on the surface and quickly assumed managerial posts. French Canadians also stayed on the surface, preferring lumbering jobs. By the end of the nineteenth century, Finns composed a sizable immigrant group, along with Italians and Eastern Europeans, especially Slovenians and Croatians.[3]

Figure I.2 Calumet, looking north on Mine Street, 1888. In the core of Calumet & Hecla's works, shafthouses are on the left, the tall stack serves the Superior Engine House, and the large building is the Central School. At the bottom right, the railroad roundhouse is under construction. Company houses are interspersed among the industrial buildings. Courtesy of Keweenaw National Historical Park.

The work was hard, particularly underground. Mining custom from Cornwall, adopted here, had miners work in small teams, bidding on particular pieces of the underground and receiving contracts that rewarded skill and work. Miners generally worked ten-hour shifts, with Sundays off. Unskilled jobs included trammers, who loaded the tram cars with three tons of rock and pushed the laden cars on rails to the shafts. This job particularly gained the sympathy of government investigators in the early twentieth century: "The worst working conditions here have been those of the trammers. . . . The trammers not only load but push the cars, pushing them to the shafts, 300 to 1,500 feet. It is almost unbelievable that men are required to do such work."[4] At the surface, workers sorted rock for the mill. A sizable support system was also necessary: machinists, carpenters, molders, patternmakers, blacksmiths, railroad workers, and so on (Figure I.3).

Perhaps thirty companies were in operation at any one time, and about twenty by the early twentieth century, but three companies dominated. The earliest of these was the Quincy Mining Company, founded in 1846, which turned a profit in

Figure I.3 Quincy Mine, looking southwest toward No. 2 Shaft-Rockhouse, mid-1920s. Quincy's 1918 hoist house, on the far left, accommodated the largest steam hoist in the world, as the company's shafts exceeded nine thousand feet on an angle (five thousand vertical feet). The landscape is cluttered with small purpose-built buildings such as the three small buildings on the lower right (the mine captain's office, oil house, and timbermen's change house), with the residential area across the road to the right. Courtesy of Keweenaw National Historical Park.

1862 and produced dividends for its East Coast investors for fifty-seven of the next fifty-nine years, gaining the nickname "Old Reliable." Quincy was located just north of Portage Lake, the body of water that separated Houghton and Hancock. After the Civil War, Calumet & Hecla (C&H) formed by combining two marginally profitable companies. Alexander Agassiz, son of the Harvard naturalist Louis Agassiz, provided the leadership that turned C&H into the most profitable company in the region, producing more than half of all Copper Country dividends over a century. Located ten miles north of Portage Lake in the town called Calumet, C&H dominated the industry, paying its workers slightly better, employing more people, and offering more perquisites to workers, so that company was able to set the tone and parameters of paternalism in the Copper Country. Last on the scene was Copper Range, located about ten miles south of Portage Lake. Founded in 1899, Copper Range soon acquired Champion, Baltic, and Trimountain mining companies and by 1905 had surpassed Quincy as the second-leading producer in the region.[5] Beginning so late, Copper Range had the opportunity to learn from the other companies' experiences in the way it established the worker–management relationship, but it tended to follow precedent rather than break it.

To the companies, land was an important and perhaps profit-generating resource, so they were loath to part with it. Building housing for workers on company land aided their efforts to attract and retain workers. By 1913, Copper Country companies owned 3,525 houses that they rented to workers. In addition, workers owned 1,751 houses on land they leased from the companies.[6] While these "householders," as the companies termed these two kinds of tenants, constituted only about a third of the workforce, another quarter to a third of the workers boarded with them, so houses on company land accommodated a significant portion of the mine-related labor.

The Copper Country thrived, with its mines increasing production until 1917. Because of the military's need for copper—which went into brass that made shells and bullets—the industry flourished particularly in wartime, with both the Civil War and World War I causing high prices and high employment. The recessions of the 1870s and 1890s produced slight downturns, but basically output increased steadily until the first decade of the twentieth century. Ultimately, mines in other regions could extract copper more cheaply than the ever-deeper mines here, so the Copper Country could not compete. After World War I, the region went into a long decline. Production slowed drastically in the 1920s and 1930s, then ceased finally in 1968.[7] Regionally, mining activity shifted to White Pine, a copper sulfide mine in western Ontonagon County, which operated into the 1990s, but for the bulk of the Copper Country, mining ceased in the 1960s.

Rather than a conventional history of local architecture through time, this book will focus on the Copper Country's boom years of about 1890 to 1918. The early twentieth century was a period of great change in the Copper Country. The workforce—which exceeded fourteen thousand men on the eve of a major strike in 1913–14—was increasingly Finnish, Austrian (Croatian and Slovenian), and Italian, nationalities for which English was not the primary language. Local management was changing too, as general managers (also called superintendents and agents, depending on the company and the time) who had begun their careers in the mines were replaced by college-educated mining engineers, such as Charles Lawton at Quincy and James MacNaughton at C&H.[8] At Copper Range, founded only in 1899, hard-driving Frederick Denton pushed out popular geologist Lucius L. Hubbard as general manager in 1905. The distant management changed as well. In New York, Thomas F. Mason, who was president of Quincy for twenty-four years, died in 1899, succeeded, after a three-year interregnum, by William R. Todd, who had been treasurer for twenty-nine years and would be president for twenty-two years. In Boston, C&H's Alexander Agassiz died in 1910 after having been president for thirty-nine years. His nephew, Quincy A. Shaw Jr., picked up the reins, but General Manager MacNaughton became increasingly powerful. The new leadership had less sympathy for the workers, less interest in benevolent paternalism, and more interest in efficiency and the bottom line.

The 1890–1918 period represents the mature phase of the mining district. Between 1890 and 1905, mine employment as well as overall population doubled. Profits for most active companies peaked. Population in the three-county region also peaked at this time, reaching almost a hundred thousand in 1910.[9] Most of the housing that survives is from this era, so this is where the material evidence concentrates. In addition, documentary evidence, especially architectural drawings and photographs, dates mostly from this period. In 1913 workers throughout the Copper Country went on strike in an attempt to gain recognition for a union. The strike lasted for eight-and-a-half months and garnered national attention. Government investigations, magazine articles, and the propaganda of pro- and anti-union forces all shed light on paternalistic practices, so the year 1913 is a particularly well-documented one.

The story does not end in the 1910s, however, although most company-financed construction did. The Michigan copper industry's decline is hardly unusual, but the buildings have additional stories to tell. How homeowners changed their houses, particularly when they acquired houses that had been built and owned by the company, reveals the failings of the original house as well as rising expectations. And, while the survival or loss of many buildings is serendipitous, some survive or suffer demolition because of the legacy associated with them. Accordingly, these buildings offer insights into Copper Country residents' attitudes about the companies after the companies have ceased to exist.

Some sense of the topography is necessary for understanding the operations of the mines and communities. The district is a linear one, with copper lodes stretching lengthwise close to the center of the Keweenaw Peninsula. The mining companies naturally located here, but each of them depended upon water to the east or west for milling and transportation. Thus the early mining towns of Cliff, Phoenix, and Central received supplies through Eagle River and Eagle Harbor on the northwest side of the Peninsula, and the Copper Range mines south of Houghton put their milling sites on the west side, at Freda, Beacon Hill, and Redridge. Calumet & Hecla and Quincy built their mills and smelters on Portage Lake and its offshoot, Torch Lake. Situated at the base of the Keweenaw Peninsula, Portage Lake was enlarged with canals at either end to form the Portage Waterway, which provided easy water access to Houghton, Hancock, and the mines of Houghton County.

Because of the Copper Country's northern latitude and location on Lake Superior, winter is long and water access is not year-round. The Copper Country also receives, on average, more than two hundred inches of snow. The railroad arrived in 1883, providing year-round access and further cementing the importance of the communities of Houghton, the county seat on the south side of the Portage; Hancock on the north side, which incorporated as a city in 1903; and Calumet ten miles north.

The creation of these villages, as well as many other smaller ones, is important because their lots were platted and sold to private individuals; these were not company towns in the strictest sense. In 1859 the Quincy Mining Company hired two hundred new employees (nearly doubling its workforce) and, apparently facing a housing shortage, decided to let the private market fill the void. Using some of its extensive landholdings, the company laid out the village of Hancock and sold off the lots. The founder of the Calumet and Hecla companies did the same in 1868 with the village of Red Jacket, which was later named Calumet. Much later, in 1903, South Range was platted to serve Copper Range's communities. The rationale for incorporated villages outside of the company's domain was articulated in 1856, when the Phoenix Copper Company began selling lots in the lakeshore community of Eagle River. The company recognized that a town would grow there and the land would become more valuable, but not until its mine did: "Our object is to make money by mining and not to speculate in house lots."[10] The company opted to sell off its village lots and concentrate on mining. Quincy managers made a similar decision in creating Hancock. Later mine managers might have regretted that these communities formed so close to their works, but it relieved them of having to provide a full range of commercial services to their mining camps. It also lessened their control over their environs, however, and bars, brothels, and unionist activity also inhabited these platted lands.

Total control of the landscape was never possible for the mining companies. It is this lack of complete dominion that is so intriguing. The companies did not strategize an autocratic, paternalistic environment; in fact, their ventures into paternalism seemed to lack a strategy. Housing was needed to attract workers. Good housing, the companies found, along with other perquisites, could also retain workers. And soon the company was running a paternalistic real estate enterprise and struggling with its parameters. Thus in one location, in 1896, the Quincy Mining Company decided to lease land to workers rather than sell it to them, because, as the agent wrote, it "will *give us the practical control* all the time." Just four years later, about a mile away, Quincy elected to build houses and sell them, with their lots, to workers. That same year, the company also built thirty-six houses to rent to workers.[11] There is no rational explanation for these varied strategies, unless it was to provide their employees with a range of options.

Meanwhile, workers had their own strategies, which varied according to personal situations. Some found that company housing was cheap, convenient, and allowed them to build a nest egg. Some believed that only on their own land would it make sense to invest in a house. Others moved through jobs so quickly that seemingly any housing situation would suit; they had no investment in the job or place. Exploring these and other strategies will enable an understanding of paternalism as a two-way street. Not only did managers give, but workers took, and crediting workers with making rational choices is one of the purposes of this book.

The gender reference inherent in the term *paternalism* is not accidental; on many levels, it was a male world. The managers who instituted and operated the system were all male, as were the workers. In 1913 C&H employed just twenty-eight women out of a workforce of more than four thousand. The women, employed in the hospital, library, and bathhouse, were all daughters and granddaughters of C&H employees. Quincy employed a woman in its office in the early twentieth century—Ethel Fisher, a stenographer—so Quincy had at least one female employee out of a workforce that exceeded sixteen hundred people.[12]

Although most Copper Country women did not have a formal relationship with the mining company, they nevertheless were deeply enmeshed in the paternalistic system. Their houses were theirs only because their husbands or sons worked for the company; if that male relative died, they could lose their house. Few married women worked outside the home but many of them kept boarders to increase the family income. Less visibly, they also took in laundry or sewing or sold eggs or milk. The quality of the housing that resulted from the paternalistic deal between husband and employer mattered greatly to them; a house with running water was a much easier workplace for them than one without. Looking at houses inevitably becomes an examination of women's work.

Another important distinction in the Copper Country populace was ethnicity. Most residents were immigrants or the first generation to have been born in the United States, and their origins mattered. Americans, Scots, and English quickly rose to the top of the company hierarchy, with Germans not far behind. By the early twentieth century, immigrants from eastern and southern Europe, along with Finns, had assumed the lowest rungs of the ladder. While each nation's immigrants remained separate by speaking their own language, living in houses together, worshipping at their own churches, publishing their own newspapers, and forming their own fraternal organizations, their self-segregation was not absolute. They also crossed these boundaries to find common cause. Finns, Italians, and Eastern Europeans lived in the same neighborhoods and united to form the core of the union. Companies tended to view these more recent immigrants as the same, hiring them for the same hard jobs and assigning company houses to them sparingly. Ethnicity divided and united in equal measure.

In his 1943 history of Michigan's Copper Country, Angus Murdoch quoted the wife of a former trammer as saying, "The company was wonderful—a man always came and fixed the toilet." Of course, not all company houses had toilets, even in the 1940s. More importantly, the mining company's interest in the inner workings of her house indicates an involvement far greater than the workplace. The title of Murdoch's chapter "Benevolent Octopus" characterizes the extent of that involvement, but a more common term was *paternalism*.[13]

Corporate Paternalism

Management's provision of buildings for workers constitutes a form of paternalism, which includes any sort of involvement by management in the lives of its workers, especially outside of the job. This system, in which both company and worker participated, albeit unequally, is the subject of this book. The buildings stand as evidence of the complex relationship between company and employee. Set mostly in the early twentieth century, when that relationship was being challenged nationwide, this book examines a place in which autocratic managers used buildings as both a method of control and a medium of persuasion. Workers, for their part, used the same buildings for their own ends.

Although the term *paternalism* is rarely used to describe management's actions today, companies still involve themselves in their employees' home lives in myriad ways, for usually well-intentioned purposes. They generally provide health insurance and sometimes company doctors. In remote places they might provide housing. When a company fires a worker for smoking off the job (which occurred recently at the Scotts Company in Boston), though, it is clear that the boundary of how far into home lives companies should extend is still contested.[14]

With its image of a benevolent father protecting and guiding his children, paternalism was a strategy for developing a loyal workforce. In the nineteenth century, this guidance pertained particularly to the moral sphere, so that the benevolent employer would provide a church for his workers, see to the education of their children, and generally concern himself with the whole family. Provision of housing was not only a way to attract workers but also a way to ensure that this wholesome environment extended to their home lives. When industrial companies were small and the owner or manager knew his workers personally, this was regarded as a benevolent approach.[15]

The growth of industry and the immigration of a workforce that seemed ever more foreign broke down these personal relationships, but the structure of paternalism remained.[16] Enlightened employers provided housing, facilitated churches and schools, banned saloons, and generally controlled their workers' environment. Company towns in which the company owned all the buildings were the most extreme expression of this arrangement.

A severe jolt to this system occurred at Pullman, Illinois, a company town built in the early 1880s by the railroad-car manufacturer George Pullman. Initially heralded for its architecture and plan—"unity of design and an unexpected variety"—it was also criticized for its interest in profit and for the totality of its control. A violent strike in 1894—workers rising up against the benevolent father who had provided so much for them—sent a chill through the spines of other industrialists who were contemplating similar arrangements. One observer noted that "the experience of Pullman and similar efforts has not encouraged others to do much toward building towns owned and controlled by the company." Another reformer identified Pullman "as a justification for a 'do-as-little-as-you-have-to' policy in shaping town conditions."[17] Suddenly, arrangements beyond the workplace seemed suspect to industrialists.

The Pullman strike also presaged increasingly strike-prone labor relations. As many industrial corporations grew larger and the workplace became more impersonal in the early twentieth century, workers resorted to strikes more frequently. Industrialists continued to explore ways to deter labor organizing, to gain an edge in the competition for workers, and to create loyal ones. At the same time, progressive reformers concerned about the plight of industrial workers looked for ways to better their conditions. Provision of services appealed to both industrialists and reformers—"what more than wages?" as one article put it. Reformers recast this relationship as "welfare work" or "industrial betterment"; historians generally refer to it as "welfare capitalism." What was different about the new paternalism was the language that suggested the worker be consulted. In 1902 Richard Ely, a professor of political economy at the University of Wisconsin, described two types of benevolence: "the paternal, the absolutistic," which is imposed from above, and "the democratic," which arises from below. Although few employers actually polled workers as to their desires, at least a new egalitarianism entered the rhetoric. As a writer for *The Engineering Magazine* noted, "Reason, justice, and sympathetic comprehension must be the elements of the relations—not patronage on the one side, nor unmanly dependency on the other." Reformers urged lunchrooms, baseball teams, landscaped grounds, and night classes, among many other things. Justifying it was not a problem: a happy, well-provided-for workforce was an effective one; welfare work paid. As one observer said, "Enlightened self-interest demands that the employer shall consider the welfare and comfort of his men."[18]

Through much of the nineteenth century, mining company towns had been marked by straight streets and identical wood-frame houses. Some of the houses were cheaply built, such as the plank houses in Windber, Pennsylvania, whose walls were, literally, two inches thick. Some coal-mining regions, such as southern Appalachia and the Rocky Mountains, built simple one-story houses, while southwestern Pennsylvania coal towns favored two-story double houses. Regardless of their location, company houses tended to be unornamented, often unpainted, poorly equipped, and minimally designed. Coal smoke from the nearby industry cast a dreary pall over the monotonous landscape.[19]

As part of the new welfare capitalism, a new company town emerged in the early twentieth century, one with curvilinear streets and varied architecture. Architects and city planners developed communities that, as much as possible, differentiated the home from the industrial workplace. Neat cottages in the latest architectural styles occupied curving streets that provided variety and interesting views. For example, Boston-based landscape architect Warren Manning designed Gwinn, Michigan, an iron-mining company town about a hundred miles west of the Copper Country, in 1906–7. Gwinn's irregular plan focused on a small commercial area framing a public park; a variety of plans characterized the houses. New "model towns" such as these, taking advantage of professional expertise, were heralded for their attractive house designs, cleanliness, and orderly layouts.[20]

This, then, is the arena in which Copper Country managers ruled their communities in the early twentieth century: new ideas were afloat, but these "model towns" remained exceptional. Not everyone jumped on the progressive bandwagon, even those establishing new company towns in 1899, as the Copper Range Company did. In their interest in progressive managers and well-designed towns, historians have tended to overlook the conservative community-builders who held onto old models of corporate paternalism, yet their impact was certainly greater in the short term, associated as they were with often-violent industrial conflict. Copper Country managers stubbornly persisted in older ways of doing things, remaining convinced that their autocratic yet benevolent guidance over a community was best. Rather than help invent a new kind of worker–management relationship, these traditional managers preferred to follow set patterns. To some extent, their desire for control seemed more embedded in their personalities than in any explicit strategy. A "father knows best" kind of arrogance characterized company managers in the Copper Country and in many other industrial communities in this period.

As top-down and autocratic as this paternalism was, no control was absolute. Workers were participants in this system—perhaps not entirely willingly, constrained by opportunity as they were—but nonetheless they played an important part in guiding and influencing this relationship. Some historians refer to this as workers' *agency*—workers took *action* and were not passive recipients of the company's benevolence. A better approach might be to see it as a *negotiation,* in which workers were active participants, although it did not take place at a bargaining table. Negotiation of managerial authority involved compromise and concessions on the part of management as well as influence and gains on the part of workers. Management could build houses that workers refused to inhabit. Tenants could demand central heating and get it. Management could raise rents on company houses, and workers could threaten to strike until management backed down. Each of these three situations occurred in the Copper Country.[21] Paternalism was a tangled web; neither side could act as freely as it wished, and each was involved in the other's strategies and plans.

The vehicle for understanding this complex relationship is the architecture built or facilitated by the companies. Many of management's paternalistic actions concerned buildings, especially company-owned houses, but also institutions such as libraries, churches, schools, hospitals, and more. The architecture is not only an element of this negotiation but also a rich source for understanding it. Rather than looking at what managers advertised, reformers analyzed, or workers said about their situations, an examination of the architecture reveals, often unintentionally, the parameters of the relationship. As scholars of material culture have claimed, by looking at the *things* surrounding a people, new insights can be gained. Particularly for large segments of society that were nonliterate, material culture serves as an important source for understanding their lives.[22] The same could also be said for people who do not control the written documentation of their lives, such as the working class. Workers and their families rarely left diaries or letters, rarely undertook to study their own society, and rarely photographed themselves. Instead, those documents were produced by others and filtered through others' perceptions. The material culture of the working class is less filtered—even, as we shall see, company-built houses.

Landscapes and buildings in particular can help explain how someone, or a class of people, lived. Because architecture defines relationships, it is an ideal medium for examining the relationship between management and workers. The hierarchy of personnel represented by the housing in a company town is unequivocal. Not only did the size of the house increase as the paycheck did, but the quality, location, and conveniences were better too. Buildings also prescribe relationships *inside* a house, such as whose path will be intersecting with whose. In elite housing, this is illustrated by servants' circulation spaces, well separated from the family's. In worker housing, the lack of circulation space is often the most striking element; many houses had no halls and thus offered little privacy to their inhabitants.

Beyond looking at how these company-fostered buildings defined interactions, this book will also examine how the architecture shaped the negotiation inherent in the paternalistic relationship. The landscape and architecture framed the relationship between management and worker, putting managers in houses on spacious lots in one neighborhood, placing workers in another area in smaller houses on smaller lots. Their understanding of each other was shaped by these spatial parameters. Further, the architecture became a tool in the negotiation process, which requires a multidisciplinary approach to understand. Documents inform the financial, legal, political, and business parameters of the complex interactions between employer and employee. Management paid its workers according to a set scale, but it could use its company housing with partiality to reward its preferred workers. It could also use the housing to threaten eviction and maintain loyalty during the strike, although the housing functioned even more effectively as propaganda to outsiders. The workers might have accepted the housing as their due, but they also used the five- or six-room single-family houses as boardinghouses to generate income, not as expressions of middle-class domesticity.

How workers and managers used these buildings for their own ends suggests the kinds of meanings the buildings held for them. This analysis shifts the attention away from the design and construction of the buildings to how they functioned after they were built.[23] Again, the impact is both internal and external: climbing the stairs to the Calumet & Hecla library's spacious reading room, book in hand, a patron would have one experience of the building; from his house directly across the street, C&H President Alexander Agassiz might experience the imposing stone façade of the library with a self-satisfied nod to his own benevolence.

Control is the key to the negotiation; what freedoms did the workers give up by accepting a company house or using the library? For most of the Copper Country's history, corporate control was administered lightly. Companies might ban liquor sales on company property, for instance, but it is clear that their employees drank beer and made wine in company houses without interference from the company. Even though the company owned most of the land, employees traversed it defiantly, as will be seen in chapter 2. The *threat* of the company exerting its privilege through eviction of company-house tenants, through declining to recompense injured workers, through interference in school curricula, or through myriad other ways was always there, though, and that is the power of corporate control. One reformer questioned "whether these employers do not have a power over their employees greater than any men, no matter how well-meaning or human, may safely trust themselves to wield."[24] Corporate control, though, was balanced by the provision of goods and services. This was the social contract inherent in a corporate paternalistic system: the worker will remain loyal to the company (stay in his job, not unionize, not strike) in return for which he will receive certain rewards beyond his paycheck (housing, schools, churches, medical care, aid in the event of misfortune).

In some places, companies invaded the domain of the house, as in the 1910s and 1920s when the Ford Company's Sociological Department sent home inspectors to verify that the employee was thrifty and sober. In the Copper Country there was never such a systematic program, but managers did remain aware of such things as how workers maintained their houses and yards and if widows were willing to work. In 1913 Calumet & Hecla employed a sociologist, Nathaniel Lloyd, but his duties apparently involved assessing working conditions rather than home life. He stayed for less than a year—during the turbulent months of the strike—and was not replaced.[25]

As a system in which the company involved itself in the worker's life beyond the workplace, paternalism could be extremely harsh; the coalfields of West Virginia were particularly autocratic, with 80 percent of the employees living in company housing and receiving payment in scrip redeemable at the company store, which kept the workers in debt.[26] It could also be somewhat more benign, such as in the Copper Country of Michigan, where the mining companies did not own all the land, where the majority of the workforce did not rent company houses, where company stores were rare, and where workers were free to come and go. What is striking about the companies' benevolence is that it was not universal; the companies could use their paternalism with partiality to favor the workers they most wanted to hire and keep. The Copper Country situation is intriguing because of the options it offered workers; with workers having an obvious choice, the interaction is more clearly a negotiation. But it was a complex interaction nonetheless; managers involved themselves in situations they regretted, and workers failed to gain recognition of a union.

This book is arranged to examine some of the issues of paternalism and the built environment as an unspoken negotiation between worker and management. The first chapter, "Saltboxes and T-Plans: Creating and Inhabiting the Company House," describes the company-built house leased to employees. It appealed to workers for many reasons; after all, in most cases, they *chose* that arrangement. For some, the cheap rent, proximity to work, and ready availability were the attraction. To management, company houses functioned to attract and retain workers. The second chapter, "The Spaces of a Strike: Company Buildings and Landscapes in a Time of Conflict," describes the unsuccessful struggle to obtain a union, marked by a long strike in 1913–14. Buildings were not ostensibly part of this negotiation, yet they played important roles. Eviction from company houses is always an implied threat, yet the lack of evictions during the strike complicates

Figure I.4 The Putrich family ca. 1925, after they had left the Copper Country. Antonia and Joseph are surrounded by their seven children: Fabian, Frank, Mary, and Paul (standing), and John, Sylvia, Josephine (sitting). Courtesy of Putrich Family.

the paternalistic picture. Management used company houses and other products of its benevolence as weapons in a propaganda war. Other building types, such as boardinghouses and armories, found particular application during the strike. Much of the conflict played out in public space, revealing management's and workers' attitudes toward the landscape.

Chapter 3, "'Home for the Working Man': Strategies for Homeownership," looks at several alternatives to company houses, including owning one's own house on one's own land or leasing a lot and building one's own house. Strategies for achieving homeownership often involved the company, even as homeowners gained independence from it. Even homeownership involved a negotiation with the company. The fourth chapter, "Acquiring Conveniences: Water, Heat, and Light," discusses the amenities that tenants demanded, such as household utilities.

Before attaining these conveniences, tenants pumped water, did laundry, stored firewood, and used the privy, all in their yards, revealing them as places of work as well as play. A set of correspondence in which tenants requested running water, indoor toilets, and electricity from the general manager of C&H provides a rare occasion in which workers wrote about their houses, showing to some extent how they thought about them. Similarly, the autocratic way in which management meted out these perquisites is revealing. Chapter 5, "Churches, Schools, Bathhouses: Building Community on Company Land," examines the institutional buildings that companies provided or facilitated: churches, libraries, bathhouses, schools, and hospitals. Companies were involved to varying extents in these places and organizations, helping to create viable communities but inevitably influencing them as well. Company office buildings, too, where men collected their paychecks, performed an important role of presenting the company to the community. Finally, the last chapter, "Preservation and Loss: Remembering through Buildings," looks at how the mining past is presented and valued in the buildings that the community chooses to preserve and lose.

In order to keep this analysis grounded in the tangible and personal, aspects of the story of Joseph and Antonia Putrich open each chapter (Figure I.4). Immigrants from Croatia, Joseph lived in the Copper Country for only twelve years, Antonia for ten. Their house does not survive, and they left no personal documents. But their chance involvement in a deadly shooting during the strike meant that more was recorded about their house in particular than any other worker's house in the Copper Country. Neither faceless nor anonymous, they are representative of Copper Country workers in many aspects of their immigration, work, and departure, but most of all in *how* they lived there.

1 Saltboxes and T-Plans
Creating and Inhabiting the Company House

On July 13, 1907, Joseph Putrich and Antonia Grubesich were married in Painesdale, Michigan. They set up housekeeping in a small dwelling—four rooms plus a kitchen. The wood-frame residence, which had been built five years earlier, was supposed to be temporary; it was set on posts, not a foundation, and had no siding other than horizontal planks over the studs. The Putriches began populating the house with children and boarders. Although their first child died an infant, Joseph and Antonia had seven more children over the next ten years. In 1910 they housed seven boarders, all male, all workers in the copper mine, like Joseph. In 1913 they accommodated ten boarders, again all copper-mine workers. They also had a live-in servant. All of the boarders and servants were, like the Putriches, born in Croatia. The house was crowded, cold in winter, poorly equipped, and shabby by most standards. It belonged to the Champion Copper Company.[1]

Company houses, built by companies to rent to employees, were a paternalistic extension of the workplace relationship, a visible incursion into the private lives of workers who were tied to the company not only by a paycheck but also by a home, thus making for a complex association. Workers clearly believed it to be advantageous, or at least worthwhile, to accept a company house, while the companies found that diverting important capital from industrial operations for this purpose paid off indirectly.

The worker–manager relationship created by company housing can be examined in several ways. The houses that the companies built for their workers can shed light on what the company thought of its worker and the value it placed on him. The attraction of company housing for the worker can be explained in terms of a structure's location, quality, layout, or size. Although the tenant, usually an immigrant, and company management were the most essential actors, others were significantly involved as well. Scrutinizing the activities of company employees responsible for assigning houses, for designing them, and for building them—or to whom those tasks were contracted—is crucial for understanding how these houses came to be. The terms of the unspoken negotiation that ensured both company and worker usually got what they wanted from the housing arrangement helps to explain why this paternalistic system persisted, long after Pullman's disastrous experience in his railroad-car town.

Architecture and Landscape

Over the seventy years (ca. 1848–1918) that Copper Country companies were building houses for their workers, they produced thousands of dwellings. In 1913 twenty-one companies owned 3,525 houses that they rented to employees. They built fancy houses for managers and plain ones for workers. They built them out of frame and logs and covered them with shingles and clapboards. Most were one-and-a-half or two stories; one-story houses were rare. Nearly all of them had gable roofs. What the companies built changed over time but not radically. Rising expectations meant that log houses were considered a lesser type and that, particularly after the turn of the twentieth century, workers' houses became larger and more complex. Some of the forms, though, were remarkably enduring, so a typology is more meaningful than a chronology. The types of houses did not differ much between the companies, either—at least not among the big three of Calumet & Hecla (804 company houses in 1913), Quincy (468), and Copper Range (607).[2]

Company houses in the Copper Country took various forms, but they were simply conceived. As historians Thomas C. Hubka and Judith T. Kenny have pointed out, before the reform movements and rising standard of living of the early twentieth century, workers' houses tended to have rooms that served multiple functions and were not architecturally differentiated; the houses were crowded and without privacy. In the early twentieth century the working class gained amenities previously reserved for the middle and upper classes: the three-fixture bathroom, the dining room, kitchen technologies (running water, hot water, means of refrigeration, washing machines), utilities (sewage, electricity, gas), the private bedroom, the storage closet, the front porch, and the car and garage.[3] Some of these amenities concern spaces and are revealed in the plan of a house; others concern conveniences that we now think of as utilities and will be addressed in chapter 4. Except for the dining room—an essential allocation of space in houses where there were many boarders—tenants of company houses in the Copper

Country gained these middle-class amenities slowly, usually as part of the negotiation involved in paternalism, and mostly not at all.

The most important aspect of these company houses was the number of rooms and their arrangement—in other words, the plan. The basic module of workers' houses in the Copper Country was a two-room plan. Whether these two rooms were oriented side-by-side or front-to-back made all the difference in their appearance and where additional rooms might be added, but their orientation probably did not make much difference in their use. One room would have been used for cooking, eating, and more public activities, while the other would have served as a bedroom. If a third room were added or if the building were originally three rooms, the kitchen would be in that third room. If there were any space in the attic, or if there were a full second story, it would be used for sleeping. The following typology of company houses in the Copper Country illustrates basic arrangements of two to six rooms, in which middle-class amenities are noticeably absent.

Two-Room Plan

A good example of a two-room, side-gable house survives on U.S. 41 in Ahmeek (Figure 1.1). One of a line of six once-identical houses, the 22-by-16-foot house is built of hewn logs, dovetailed at the corners. The house probably dates from the 1880s, when the Ahmeek Mining Company was in its exploratory phase. Entry

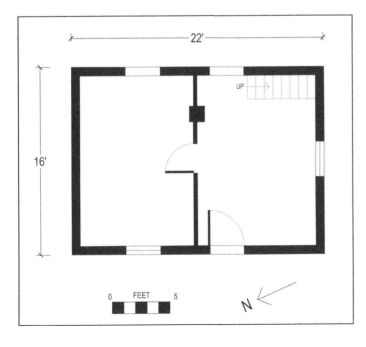

Figure 1.1 Log house in Ahmeek, conjectural plan based on physical evidence. Probably built in the 1880s, the house has a basic two-room plan. Measured by Mary Durfee and author in 2000; drawn by author.

was into the west room, which had a steep stairway along its back wall leading to the loft above. A "hung" chimney, supported on a wooden cabinet, interrupted the center partition wall and would have been available to stoves in both rooms. In both rooms, the logs were whitewashed and painted. The west room was red, and the east room, blue. Upstairs, the knee wall rose about four feet before the slope of the ceiling. The attic was partitioned and ceiled.[4]

This house also offers an illustration of how these two-room, side-gabled houses were upgraded and expanded. Over time, the interior walls were lathed and plastered, creating a more finished appearance. By 1913 the house had received a third room, constructed of wood frame, making an L plan (Figure 1.2). By the end of the twentieth century that third room had been expanded across the back. The gable roof changed angle slightly and extended to cover it, making

Figure 1.2 Log houses in Ahmeek, photographed August 23, 1913. A one-room addition is visible on the rear as well as a swing set in the yard. Courtesy of Archives of Michigan.

the saltbox form. In 2001 that extended addition was removed, and a one-room addition, with a footprint similar to the first addition, adorned the rear.

Saltbox

Saltboxes, comprising up to six rooms, are a familiar form in the Copper Country. They derive their name from a colonial table salt container, which had an asymmetrical hinged top. The saltbox house form, identified by an asymmetrical gable roof, developed in colonial New England, although its appearance in the Copper Country seems to be independent of any New England connections. Most likely, it developed as the Ahmeek house did, as a one-story addition to a two-room, side-gabled house. Extending the back half of the gable roof over the addition produced the saltbox effect. The term *saltbox* was not used by company officials but is commonly employed today.

Saltboxes seem to have been built as a whole, not in additions, quite early in the Copper Country's history. At Central, a Keweenaw County mine developed in the 1850s, saltboxes were built in the early 1860s. On the first floor of one such house, two rooms, 20 by 15 feet and 20 by 11½ feet, stretched across the width of the house. The straight-run stairway started in the kitchen and led upstairs to two small bedrooms and a tiny hall in the taller front portion of the house. The house had the familiar saltbox profile with an unbroken roofline.[5]

Mining companies continued to build saltboxes in the twentieth century. In 1905–7 Ahmeek Mining Company, by then mostly controlled by Calumet & Hecla (C&H), built twenty saltboxes as its first substantial housing at its new mine

RIGHT AND BOTTOM OF FACING PAGE: Figure 1.4 C&H plans and side elevation of a saltbox house, 1907. One expansion of the two-room plan resulted in an asymmetrical gable roof; this form was known as a saltbox. Courtesy of Michigan Technological University Archives and Copper Country Historical Collections.

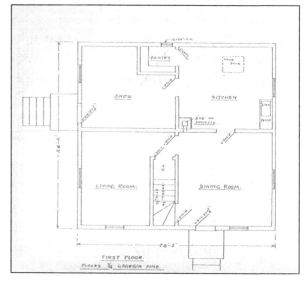

LEFT: Figure 1.3 Wood-frame houses in Ahmeek, built 1905–7, photographed 1913. Dozens of saltboxes line the road in Ahmeek, a mining location partly owned by Calumet & Hecla. Courtesy of Michigan Technological University Archives and Copper Country Historical Collections.

(Figures 1.3, 1.4). These wood-frame houses, covered with clapboards on the walls and wood shingles on the roof, measured approximately 28 by 26 feet. Wood-post foundations were replaced with stone foundations by 1916. The one-and-a-half-story portion in the front had a living room and dining room on the first floor, separated by a straight-run stair, and two bedrooms on the second floor. Behind the first-floor rooms were a kitchen and a shed; the gable roof extended in back to cover them without a break in its line. C&H classified these houses as having five rooms, apparently not counting the shed. This plan easily permitted closing off the "living room" to serve as a bedroom.[6]

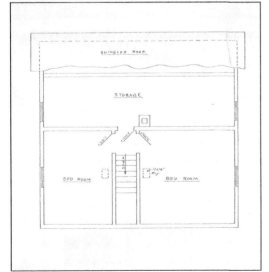

Figure 1.5 T-plan house in Limerick, built 1864, photographed by Jet Lowe in 1978. Quincy Mining Co. built about seventy T-plan houses during the profitable time of the Civil War. Courtesy of Historic American Engineering Record.

T-Plan

The other option for expansion of two-room, side-by-side plans was to build the addition in a T-shaped plan with the addition's gable roof perpendicular to that in the main block. Although houses could grow by additions into this shape, companies also built them as a whole in this configuration. Some of the earliest examples were built by Quincy Mining Company in 1864 in the location called Limerick (Figure 1.5). The 30 or so houses at Limerick and 40 or so at Hardscrabble were some of the 110 houses that Quincy built that year, in the boom time of the Civil War; 68 "frame tenement houses" cost the company $26,691.22. At Limerick, the

Figure 1.6 Quincy plans and elevation of a T-plan house, 1899. Quincy Mining Co. used the T-plan design for more than three decades; these drawings were for houses at Quincy's stamp mill in Mason. Because of the steep hillside there, the T-plan was rotated so that the stem of the T paralleled the road. Courtesy of Historic American Engineering Record.

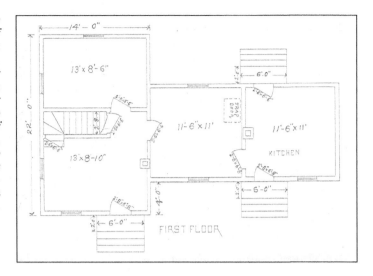

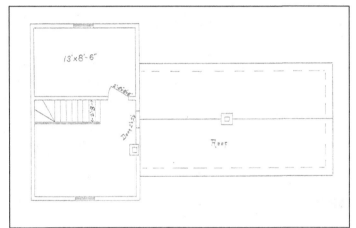

T-plans faced each other across one street, with a third, parallel row facing the mine. They were all built of wood frame, sided with clapboard, and roofed with shingles. Inside, they were lathed and plastered. The one-and-a-half-story front section, measuring about 22½ by 14½ feet, had a central door and was divided into two rooms. The stairway to the second floor was in the right-rear corner. Behind this front block extended a one-story section of two rooms, measuring about 13 by 26 feet. The six-room total was the same as a saltbox, and the square footage was about the same.[7]

The T-plan house proved to be a durable one for Quincy, which built houses in this form for the next thirty-five years. In the 1890s, in the stamp-mill community of Mason, Quincy turned the building sideways to accommodate the sloping site and adjusted the plan slightly (Figure 1.6). In 1899–1900 Quincy built a number of T-plan houses near Shaft No. 8, on land it had recently acquired from the Mesnard Mining Company. Similar to the Limerick houses, with three-bay fronts, these houses had an additional room on the second story, over the stem of the T, making them seven-room houses in a T-plan. These were sometimes referred to as "telescope" houses because of their decline in height in stages. They were a bit larger than the Limerick houses, not including the seventh room. The main block measured about 22 by 16 feet, while the stem of the T was 12 by 24 feet. The door was centered in the front, leading to the stairway that divided the two front rooms. The stem of the T was divided into two rooms, with an entrance into the rearmost, which served as the kitchen. There were three bedrooms on the second floor.[8]

Front-Gable

If the basic two rooms were arranged front-to-back, options for additions were different, as was the general appearance. With the ridge of the gable roof running perpendicular to the road, these houses offered front gables to the street (Figure 1.7). Their narrower frontage made them more appropriate for narrower, urban lots. At its most basic, this house would be just two rooms down and two up. The only variation was the placement of the stairway, which might divide the two rooms, as in a design from the Osceola Consolidated Mining Company in 1909, or run up a side wall in the rear room, as in Ahmeek, where seven four-room houses were built by 1907.[9] Additions to the two-room plan would generally consist of a third room attached to the rear as a single-story addition, and kitchen facilities would move to that room.

Figure 1.7 Front-gable houses in North Kearsarge, photographed 1913. Turning the two-room plan so that it was entered on the end resulted in these small gable-front houses with two rooms on each floor. Courtesy of Michigan Technological University Archives and Copper Country Historical Collections.

Side-Entry

There are always house forms that defy categorization, such as the side-gable house situated with its gable end to the street. The end on the street was two bays wide, with no door; entry was in the side, more than halfway to the rear. The plan of this house had the stairway in the rear corner closest to the door and the pantry and kitchen next to it. "Parlor" and "sitting room" were in the front, or street side, of the house. Upstairs were three bedrooms. The footprint of C&H's house in this mode measured 22 by 26 feet, while Copper Range's was 21 by 25 feet. The extra space allowed C&H's house two closets upstairs. Houses of this type were also pictured at South Kearsarge and LaSalle mines; it was a popular early-twentieth-century design. One variation, shown in South Kearsarge and Trimountain photographs, was the addition of a tall thin window to light the stairhall, next to the door (Figure 1.8).[10]

Figure 1.8 Side-entry house at Trimountain, photographed 1920s. James and Janie Williams, their eight children, and James's brother lived in this Copper Range house in which the gable end faces the street but the main entrance is on the side. Courtesy of Michigan Technological University Archives and Copper Country Historical Collections.

Gambrel Roof

One interesting variation of the front-gable plan was the gambrel-roofed one produced by Calumet & Hecla in 1899 (Figures 1.9, 1.10). C&H was the only company that used this design; no other is so identified with a specific company. Company drawings call it a "mansard roof," using the British term for what Americans, by then, generally called gambrel. Previously, Americans called it a Dutch roof, associating it with colonial Dutch forms, and its reappearance at this time is often associated with the Dutch Colonial Revival style. Local residents called them "trunk houses," though, because of their resemblance to the rounded top of a steamer trunk. Around 1900, C&H built at least seventy-four of them in Albion, Hecla, and Red Jacket shaft locations.[11] The gambrel roofs increased headroom, producing a

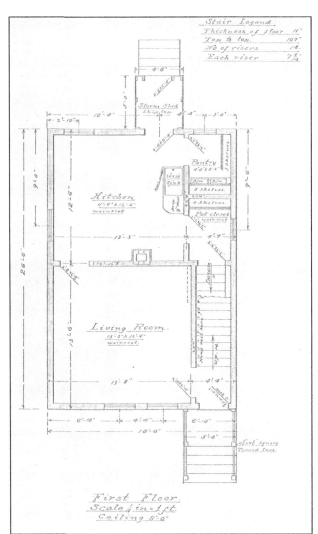

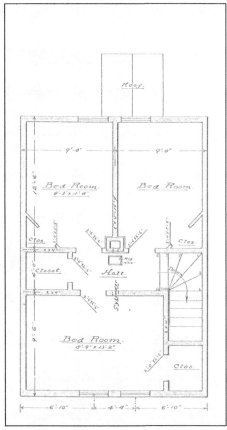

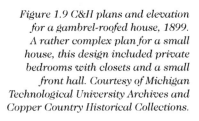

Figure 1.9 C&H plans and elevation for a gambrel-roofed house, 1899. A rather complex plan for a small house, this design included private bedrooms with closets and a small front hall. Courtesy of Michigan Technological University Archives and Copper Country Historical Collections.

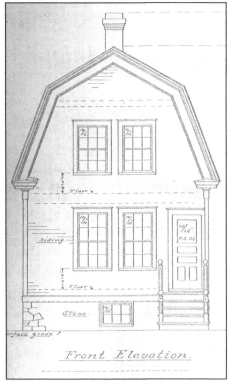

Figure 1.10 Gambrel-roofed houses in Calumet, photographed 1913. The gambrel roof allowed additional headroom on the second floor. Courtesy of Michigan Technological University Archives and Copper Country Historical Collections.

floor-to-ceiling height of eight feet on the second floor, except within twenty inches of the side walls. The first-floor plan offered just two rooms in an 18-by-26-foot rectangle. But there were additional spaces, such as a landing with turned posts at the front door, a storm shed at the back door, a foyer upon entry, a pantry off the kitchen, and a pot closet at the head of the basement stairs. The second floor had three bedrooms, each with a closet, and an additional closet off the hall.

Closets, porches, and halls, the first amenities previously associated with the middle class that found their way into company houses, increased construction costs and might be viewed as wasted space because they did not increase the livable area, but they offered a bit of gentility.[12] Rather than allowing everyone to enter the house directly into a room, halls served as a place to sort out visitors and family. They also prevented cold outside air from flowing into the living area. Upstairs, halls meant that each bedroom could be reached directly. Middle-class reformers urged private bedrooms so that someone did not have to walk through another's bedroom to get to their own. Porches and storm sheds served as other liminal spaces where visitors could be dealt with before they were granted entry. Closets hid belongings and kitchenware and also suggested that occupants had material goods worth storing. The appearance of spaces such as these in workers' houses indicated a desire by the company to provide residents with amenities that they might find attractive.

As expectations rose in the early twentieth century, these amenities became more common in company houses. The front-gable house also became larger, with a bigger footprint and additional rooms. C&H produced a design in 1900 for a 20-by-36½-foot house with three rooms on the first floor—along with foyer, pot closet, and pantry—and five bedrooms on the second, four of them with closets (see Figures 4.6, 6.8). Charles W. Maass, a C&H draftsman, occupied one of these houses, at 1769 Cemetery Street in Calumet, from 1901 to 1907. After Maass left the company to start his own architectural firm, C&H engineer Christopher Tucker lived there with his wife, Mary, and their ten children.[13]

In 1900 C&H also produced a plan for a seven-room front-gable house, one that appears to have been widely used (Figure 1.11). The house measured about 21 by 24 feet, with a pantry projecting off the rear. It had three rooms on the first floor, along with a front hall; there was a cased opening between the sitting room

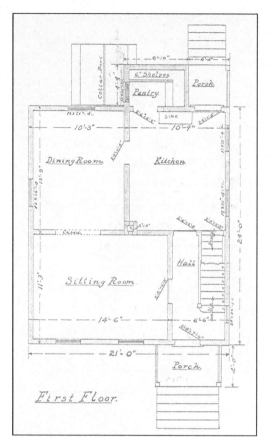
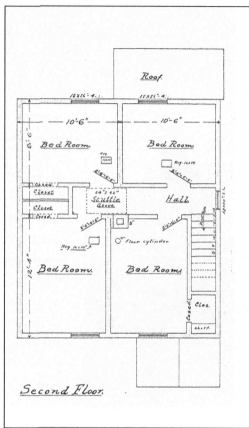

ABOVE AND FACING PAGE: Figure 1.11 C&H plans and elevation of a large front-gable house, 1900. This design provided several amenities: private bedrooms, closets, a front hall, a dining room, a pantry, and even a small front porch. Courtesy of Michigan Technological University Archives and Copper Country Historical Collections.

and dining room, preventing either of those rooms from being shut off as bed-rooms. Three of the four bedrooms on the second floor had a closet. C&H's plan seems to have been used at several of the mining sites at which it was acquiring a controlling interest. In 1907 alone, companies built twenty-five houses to these plans at Isle Royale No. 5, south of Houghton; twenty-eight at Ahmeek; and five even farther east in Keweenaw County, at Mandan. The plan was tweaked over the years and used again, ten years later, when twenty more houses were built at Isle Royale No. 5 and another thirty at Ahmeek. At Isle Royale, the later plan included a stairway to the third floor so that full use could be made of that space. C&H's 1900 drawings note that the design was "Built at Champion Mine," so C&H may have borrowed the plan from Copper Range, which also built houses to a similar though slightly smaller plan, 20 by 24 feet.[14]

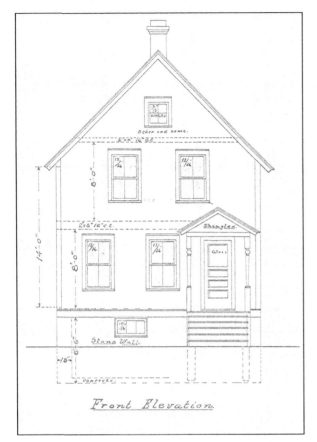

Front Elevation.

Construction of most company houses was a standard balloon frame. Usually, horizontal planks were placed on the outside of the frame, but in at least one instance they were placed only on the inside. In the 1860s houses at Central, the inside of the frame was planked, then lathed and plastered; the outside of the studs had only horizontal clapboards. In another house, probably built by the Huron Mining Company in the 1880s, the modest, three-room structure had planks both inside and outside of the studs, with lath and plaster on the interior and clapboards on the exterior. Insulation was almost unheard of, but more sophisticated dwellings would be "backplastered"—plastered on the inside of the exterior planking.

While it is tempting to see a progression through time of simple two-room plans evolving into intricate seven-room plans with closets, pantries, and porches, there are enough exceptions to this rule to call it into question. Simple plans continued to be built, even into the last building period. In 1917 Copper Range built basic four-room houses in the part of Painesdale called Seeberville. Log houses, too, continued to be built into the twentieth century. In 1913 U.S. Bureau of Labor Statistics investigator Walter B. Palmer surveyed company housing in the Copper Country and found 296 "log cabins" ranging in size from two to ten rooms, in addition to the 3,229 frame houses. He noted that "most of these cabins were built in the early days of mining in the district, but a few have been built within recent years." They might also have been built in the initial years of late-starting mines from the 1890s or 1900s, such as Victoria in Ontonagon County. Although not within the boundaries of Palmer's study, Victoria offers an example: the company built twenty hewn-log houses there in 1899, before it established a sawmill. Palmer assessed the quality of log houses throughout the district: "The spaces between the logs are well chinked up and these cabins are about as warm in winter as are the frame houses. However, they have comparatively few windows and the windows are small." He also noted their appeal: "The rent of these cabins is less even than the rent of the frame houses, and for that reason they are in demand by mine workers who wish to economize as closely as possible."[15] Modest houses with modest rents always filled a need.

Not only did minimal houses continue to be built, complex plans appeared early in the Copper Country's history, illustrating that the attainment of middle-class amenities was not strictly a function of time. At Central, where the 1860s saltboxes included small halls on the second floor so that both bedrooms were private, the other house form from the 1860s also offered an unusual degree of privacy. The 18-by-38-foot front-gable houses had front halls that gave access to the front room, to the second room, and to the straight-run stairway to the second floor. The front room could be used as a parlor or closed off and used as a bedroom. Traffic passed through the second room, clearly intended as a living and dining space, to two more rooms behind, the larger one serving as a kitchen. The second floor, not as deep as the first floor, had two bedrooms reached from a hall.[16] That both of these complex early plans appeared at the same mine suggests that either management was more enlightened or the Cornish workforce was more demanding than at other mines.

As mentioned above, some plans had enduring appeal. In 1917, during what would be its last period of residential construction, Quincy returned to one of the older forms—the saltbox. At the stamp-mill community of Mason, where more than three dozen T-plan houses had been built in the 1890s, Quincy constructed six dwellings in 1917 in the saltbox form. It is not known why Quincy interrupted the architectural cohesion of the community with this form, given that the saltboxes had the same amount of space as the T-plans, but it may have to do with a preference for a more "modern" Colonial Revival design, in which the massing is centered, unlike the more sprawling, many-cornered T-plan.[17]

While single-family houses predominated among company-built dwellings, double houses, accommodating two families, also appeared in considerable numbers. With living units placed side-by-side, double houses had a shared party wall but a separate entrance for each unit. Companies saved on construction costs with this form, and each unit was generally smaller than a single freestanding house. Double houses came in every form familiar to single-family houses—side-gable, front-gable, saltbox—and in both log and frame.

Figure 1.12 Dally house in Painesdale, photographed 1913. Double houses were also common, especially in Copper Range communities. In this house a fatal shooting occurred during the 1913–14 strike. Courtesy of Michigan Technological University Archives and Copper Country Historical Collections.

Copper Range built two-and-a-half-story double houses with gable fronts (Figure 1.12). Measuring 26 by 44 feet, these houses had presence. But each unit was only 13 feet wide, with three rooms, linearly placed, on the first floor and just two each on the second and third floors. One of these houses gained notoriety because of a fatal shooting during the 1913–14 strike in the Copper Country. Thomas and Julia Dally ran a Cornish boardinghouse in their half of a double house on Baltic Street in Painesdale. During the strike, the Dallys housed thirteen strike-breakers, including brothers Harry and Arthur Jane. In the middle of the night on December 6, 1913, John Huhta and some fellow strikers fired into the house, killing the Jane brothers on the third floor and Thomas Dally in the first-floor front bedroom and wounding a girl who lived in the other half of the double house. All of the victims had been asleep in their beds.[18] John Huhta, convicted of first-degree murder, died in prison five years later.

Whether tenants preferred double houses is doubtful. When contemplating new construction of a mix of single and double houses in 1917, Charles Lawton, general manager of Quincy, considered the appeal of singles versus doubles: "Some families strenuously object to the double houses, while others much prefer them, as they are warmer and require less fuel to heat them." Preferring more single houses "to meet all conditions," he suggested building twelve double houses and thirteen singles. Quincy's president, William R. Todd, responded, "The only objections we have to building single houses is the additional cost. I should think that double houses from a point of economy would cost two hundred dollars less than two single houses." Nonetheless, the company then built forty singles and only five doubles.[19]

Companies also built houses for their managers, easily distinguished from workers' houses by their size and amenities. The largest and most ostentatious house, of course, belonged to the top company official at the mine (variously called the agent, general manager, or superintendent). An interesting illustration of this is the drawings for alterations to the general manager's house at C&H. Although the house is long gone, the drawings indicate the original house as well as the changes that the new official wished to make (Figures 1.13, 1.14). That new official was James MacNaughton, who was hired in 1901 and wielded a strong hand over the company for the next thirty-five years. To accommodate MacNaughton, the company expanded an L-plan house of about five rooms per floor into something much more elaborate. Additions included two bathrooms and a powder room, a vestibule, a telephone room, space for a refrigerator, two rooms off the service end, and other incidental spaces. The living room, more than thirty-six feet long, received bay windows—those markers of middle-class gentility—at both ends. The stairway was set off with an arch. The library gained a window seat, and the dining room, new china closets. The public spaces received new oak flooring. The service area included a china pantry, maid's sitting room (previously the kitchen), pantry, pot closet, kitchen, laundry, one stairway to the second floor and two to the basement. On the second floor, the master suite included a sitting room, dressing room, bedroom, walk-in closet, and bathroom. Two other bedrooms shared a bathroom. The servant's room on this floor included the linen closet. MacNaughton moved in with his wife, Mary, daughter Martha, and three servants.[20] After his second daughter, Mary, was born in 1904, he authorized more changes to the house.

Despite the internal amenities and size, MacNaughton's house was never very grand architecturally. It had a sprawling appearance, reflecting its additive history. The gable front was decorated with a porch featuring mill-sawn woodwork, and

Figure 1.13 C&H general manager's house, photographed ca. 1880, since demolished. The house for the highest-ranking locally based official at the mine was much larger than those of his employees but only slightly more architecturally sophisticated. Courtesy of Keweenaw National Historical Park.

the peak of the gable had some stick-style ornament, but the house's squat proportions were from an earlier era. MacNaughton himself was neither flamboyant nor publicity hungry; he kept a low profile, despite being the most powerful man in the Copper Country. His house evoked power through its size, expansive lawn, and location near the works, but it was not architecturally sophisticated.

Managers of lesser rank also received company housing. They too were enmeshed in the paternalistic system, receiving benefits that indebted them to the company, but the negotiation was more transparent than with the lower-level workers. Company housing and other amenities were part of their compensation package, distributed on the basis of merit. Further, the top official at the mine took a personal interest in the conditions of their employment. Quincy's superintendent, in consultation with the president in New York, spent far more time worrying over the fifteen or twenty managers' houses than all of the four hundred or so workers' houses. When the superintendent hired a new doctor, he had to accommodate him and his wife, as he informed the president: "They have looked over the Doctor's house, and say they prefer to have it fixed up and live there than have to live in a <u>double house</u>. They, of course, would like very much to have a nice, new, 'modern,'

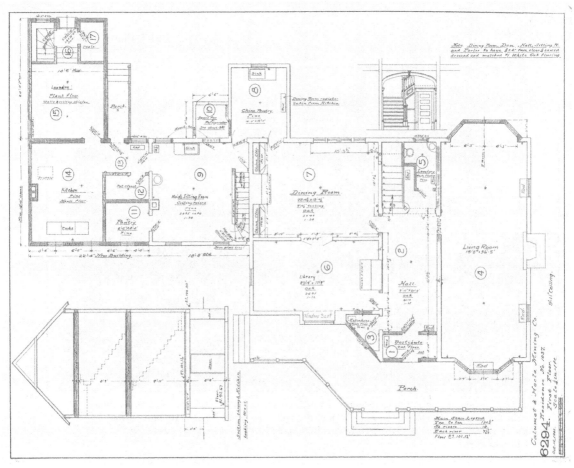

ABOVE AND FACING PAGE: Figure 1.14 C&H general manager's house, Calumet, 1901 plans of alteration. When James MacNaughton was hired as general manager, he ordered alterations and additions to the house, making it even more elaborate, as illustrated by the number and kinds of rooms shown on these drawings. Courtesy of Michigan Technological University Archives and Copper Country Historical Collections.

single house built for them, but I told them your idea was a double house."[21] The correspondence abounds with discussions of fixing up houses for specific tenants, turning single houses into doubles, and retrofitting furnaces and bathrooms.

At Quincy, initially the house was one of the perquisites received by salaried personnel. In 1900, with advice from auditors, Quincy's board of directors ordered that the system be changed, charging each man for rent but increasing his salary to cover it. As Samuel B. Harris, the superintendent, noted, "They do not take to the change at all kindly, and there may be a little squirming." Implementing this policy took some time; two years later, President Todd remarked on Chief Mining Captain Thomas Whittle's "turnout": "On passing his residence last week, [I] saw his horses, carriage, and coachman (a man working for the Company) standing in front." John L. Harris, Samuel's son who was then acting superintendent, agreed that Whittle's coachman's wages should be paid by Whittle, not the company, but the real problem

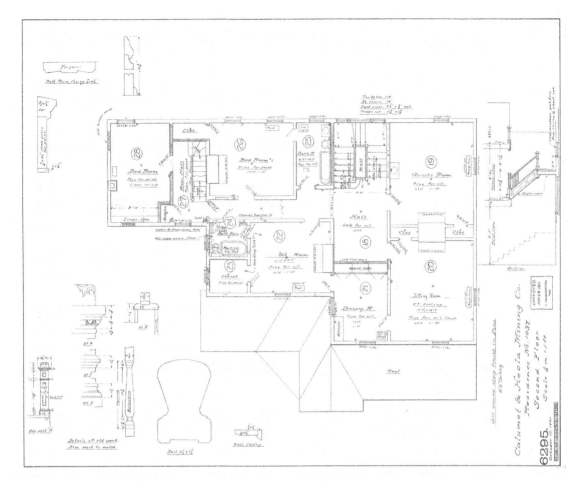

was that Whittle did not know his place: "Any subordinate officer employed by any Company should have tact enough to conduct himself as befitting his position." Whittle, who received the second-highest salary at the mine, held the post of chief mining captain for twenty-two years, 1889–1911, despite Todd's allusion in 1905 to questions about "the permanency of Capt. Whittle's stay in office."[22]

Whittle occupied a house on Quincy Hill, near the works and the agent's house. The two-and-a-half-story house had a cross gable in the front and bay windows on each end. Quincy built this for him in 1899, although stylistically it could have been built any time in the previous fifty years. The first floor had a broad center hall and four rooms, plus a kitchen and another room in a rear ell. On the second floor there were four bedrooms and a servant's room. The plans included a bathroom on the second floor and a toilet in the basement, probably for servants' use.[23]

Once Quincy decided to charge its managers for their housing, figuring the rent was a bit tricky. Todd determined that it should be 5 percent of the construction cost of the specific house. He was adamant that house rent be detached from salary: "The house question is easily settled. This we want entirely eliminated from the amount of salary to be paid. Pay such wages as may be thought proper, and charge rent according to value of house wanted." But Todd's flat rules ignored the reality on the ground. Some houses cost more than others, and occupants ended up in them somewhat randomly; was it fair, then, to charge some occupants more? John L. Harris asked, "If we were to erect houses to rent as an investment only, the case would be an entirely different one; but in order to get the best results, we must look after the 'Heads of Departments'; and if some of the present officers' houses—such as Morrison's, Whittle's and the Clerk's—cost more than they should on account of being larger than necessary or otherwise, that is a mistake that cannot now be entirely overcome, and is no fault of theirs." Todd reiterated his policy, but Harris preferred to have flexible rents as a negotiating tool when hiring new managers.[24]

Until the turn of the twentieth century, Quincy expected all officers and heads of departments to live on the mine location, but this was a rule that was soon broken. Abandoning his almost-new company house, Captain Whittle moved into his own new house in East Hancock in 1905. The superintendent recommended reducing his salary by thirty dollars a month. Todd clarified his position: "The relation between an employee's income and his expenses is a private matter entirely, and one in which the Company is not concerned. . . . Our intent, when this salary adjustment was made, was to divorce social and domestic matters altogether from business duties, and to proceed hereafter on a strictly business basis. The perquisite feature was a relic of the ancient days in which pioneer conditions made it almost imperative for the Company to stand in almost a paternal relation to its employees, but those days passed away long ago."[25] Todd also pointed out that the new tenant, however meager his salary, should pay the same rent as Whittle had.

In 1912, although Quincy had abandoned its policy of keeping its managers close, it still saw value in having at least some of its officers at the mine location. General Manager Lawton recommended building a new house for the machine-shop foreman, Thomas J. Thomas, who "is a very good man and has a very nice family, who are inclined to want to go down town to live." In order to keep them on-site, the company was willing to rehabilitate their house; three months later Lawton reported that "we have been able to satisfy Mrs. Thomas by remodeling their present house and by adding another bed-room and a bath-room."[26]

Manager's housing tended to be located close to the mine for convenience, based on the nineteenth-century idea of managers living near the works. At C&H, managerial housing was located mostly between Calumet Avenue and Mine Street, with higher-ranking officials south of the central office building and lower-echelon managers north of it (Figure 1.15).[27] At Quincy, the managerial housing was also

Figure 1.15 Map of Calumet, 1915. Except for the villages of Red Jacket (center) and Laurium (bottom right) and Tamarack Mining Co. lands (on the left), all of the property in this image was owned by Calumet & Hecla Mining Co. Company-owned buildings are filled in, while ground-rent houses are in outline only. The company office building is one block northeast of the roundhouse. Courtesy of Keweenaw National Historical Park.

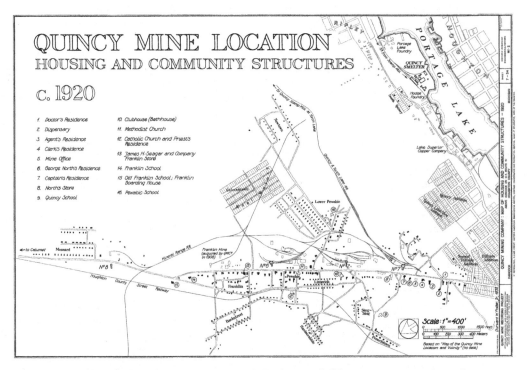

Figure 1.16 Map of Quincy Mine Location, ca. 1920. The steep hill between Portage Lake and Quincy's mine workings is not apparent on this map. Quincy held onto East Quincy but sold off the platted lands to the right, adjacent to Hancock. Company housing is clustered into small locations. Courtesy of Historic American Engineering Record.

clustered along the main road, near the agent's house, a towered mansion built in 1880 (Figure 1.16). At Copper Range, the last of the big mines to develop, management housing was accorded its own separate neighborhood in Painesdale (Figure 1.17). The superintendent's house, built in 1902, overlooked the mines but remained separate from the workers' housing. Nearby, on Algomah Street, Copper Range built six managers' houses on spacious lots. These were all proximate to the company office building, a modest wood-frame structure down the hill, close to E Shaft. The first house of the superintendent, constructed in 1899 in E Location, had been right across the street from the office building, but this clustering of management houses on top of a hill, separated from the mines and other housing by various ravines, signified a more detached relationship. Even the company doctor lived on Algomah Street, although his hospital was a mile or two away in Trimountain. The managers' houses had broad fronts, spacious porches, wide center halls, bathrooms, and accommodations for live-in servants. Most had clapboards on the first floors and shingles on the second. They formed a cohesive and exclusive neighborhood.

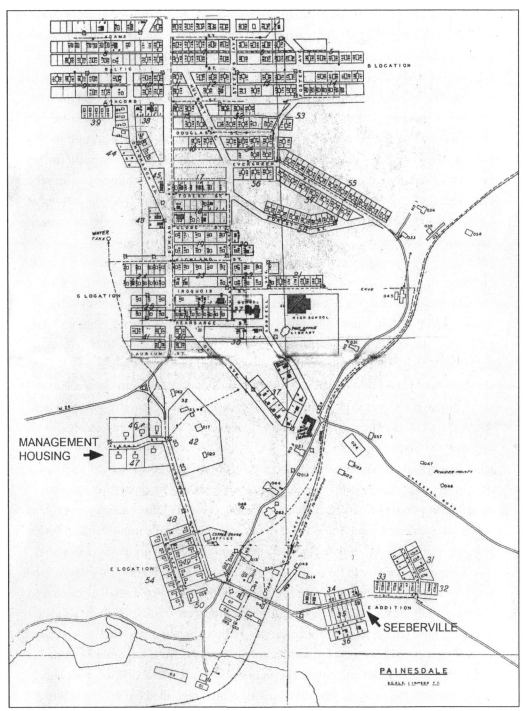

Figure 1.17 Map of Painesdale, probably 1940s. The railroad tracks run along the low, flat land, while the housing is laid out on the hills. In the center of this image, the schools and library form a community core. From Monette, Painesdale, *22–23, Michigan Tech Archives, with additions by the author.*

The layout of company residential areas—called "locations" in the Copper Country—did not receive much attention. The proximity of the industrial workplace would have been the overriding impression. Mid-nineteenth-century housing seems to have been scattered around the mine workings. The placement of housing among railroad tracks, rockhouses, steam hoists, and all sorts of industrial endeavors appears to us today to be dangerous and dirty as well as deafening, but there were few complaints at the time. By the time of the Civil War, companies built workers' houses more deliberately, separating them slightly from the works and arranging them in neighborhoods, facing each other across one or two streets, as at Quincy's Limerick and Hardscrabble locations, built in 1864. Locations at C&H were similarly arranged, seemingly expeditiously laid out, often interwoven with mine shafts. Streets were straight and buildings were aligned, but the grid plan was easily interrupted for railroad tracks or other higher priorities. In the 1890s, Quincy placed its stamp-mill housing at Mason parallel to the Torch Lake shoreline in four rows. Three railroad lines also ran along the shoreline close to the houses, and less than half a mile away, the stamp mill pounded rock night and day. In Painesdale, Copper Range employed a rough grid plan over a hilly landscape and named the streets in alphabetical order, north to south. Generally, though, the locations' attempts at order were overwhelmed by the imperatives of the mine.

The Copper Country residential landscape was architecturally messy. There was little aesthetic unity due to the lack of allegiance to a particular design, with companies building in several campaigns and in a variety of forms. Idiosyncratically designed noncompany dwellings (a subject that will be addressed in chapter 3) were interspersed among company houses. Furthermore, companies grew over time and acquired preexisting company houses, as when Quincy acquired Franklin and Pewabic mining companies. Proponents of architecturally unified model towns would have objected to the unplanned appearance of company-house locations.

The residents, though, readily identified with their neighborhoods or subneighborhoods. Because most neighborhoods were set apart spatially, relating to the mine shaft they served or the era in which they were constructed, they formed distinct units, easily claimed by residents as their neighborhoods. Workers perceived managerial housing as separate and different, as the companies intended it to be. Painesdale residents called the managers' houses "Snob Hill," a sobriquet that persists to the present. C&H's Calumet Avenue was called "Aristocracy Street" by a strike publication.[28] This did not mean that managerial neighborhoods were off-limits to workers; rather, hundreds of workers would have had to cross Calumet Avenue and pass by managers' houses on their way to work.

Building and Renting

Company houses were the products of many individuals' involvement. The people who authorized, funded, produced, assigned, and occupied these houses each played a different role in the worker–management relationship. The first four functions were associated with company management, and an examination of these interrelated actions demonstrates how managers delegated these tasks and how little direct involvement they had. Rather, senior management's main role was in authorizing construction of houses whose rents reflected their construction cost. Clarification of these various roles leads to an understanding of managers' and workers' points of view in the provision and acceptance of company houses.

The top manager at each of the major companies, while rightfully deserving credit and blame for most mine operations, rarely involved himself in the design of workers' houses.[29] Similarly, the presidents in the East to whom the managers reported were not interested in these details either. The manager would give an estimate and argue for the need for, say, twenty six-room houses, the president would authorize it, and the manager would pass it on to his construction staff. No discussion of what these dwellings would look like seems to have taken place. The important aspects were how many rooms, whether single or double and, of course, cost.

Once they had achieved a degree of stability and prosperity, the companies turned to architects and contractors for their more significant buildings, including management housing. Milwaukee architect Alexander C. Eschweiler, whose first cousin was married to Frederick Denton, general manager of Copper Range, designed most of Copper Range's important buildings, including houses for Denton and his top managers, but there is no evidence that he was consulted on worker housing. Similarly, Quincy hired a New Jersey architect—a neighbor of the company's secretary/treasurer—to design its new office building in 1895. The company occasionally engaged local architects for managers' housing, as when it hired Hans T. Liebert to provide plans for converting a manager's house into two units in 1902, but seems never to have consulted an architect on regular workers' housing.[30]

Calumet & Hecla, unlike most other companies, did bring in architects to design workers' housing. In 1897 the company engaged the prominent Upper Peninsula architectural firm of Charlton, Gilbert & Demar to design plans for "miner's cottages." The plans, for six-room and nine-room houses with decorative barge boards, were probably a little too expensive for C&H's needs. There is no record that any houses were built from these plans. But ten years later the company turned to Maass Bros. Architects to prepare drawings and specifications for twenty-five miners' houses, twelve two-compartment barns, one half barn, and twenty-five privies for Allouez Location; August Johnson of Laurium got the contract to build them. Charles Maass had been a draftsman in C&H's engineering department for nine years before hanging out his shingle as an architect.[31]

One known instance of a company resorting to outside design was when Quincy turned to Sears, Roebuck & Company in 1917. By then Sears was well known as a supplier of mail-order houses. The buyer would select a plan, pay a thousand to twenty-five hundred dollars, and Sears would ship all of the pieces for the homeowner to assemble on-site. Quincy contracted with Sears for what it originally planned to be mine captains' houses. Misunderstanding the simplicity inherent in off-the-shelf designs, Quincy sent a plan to the company, then insisted on tweaking the designs. Once satisfied, Quincy received specifications to bid out to a contractor, who then bought the materials from Sears and built the houses. The final design resembled the large front-gable company house but was quite a bit larger (see Figures 4.9 and 4.10).[32]

For ordinary workers' housing, though, the boss carpenter or his staff probably did the actual design work. Each mining company had carpentry staffs: in 1910, C&H had 63 carpenters and 23 painters out of a total workforce of 5,081, and Champion Copper Company had a comparable 9 carpenters out of a total workforce of 1,190. The carpenters' usual tasks involved the construction and maintenance of most of the wooden industrial buildings. In the winter, the slow season, Quincy's carpentry shop made ladders for use underground, ladder staves, sheave blocks, brake shoes, and other mine equipment.[33]

The carpentry force was also involved in building workers' houses until the companies reluctantly turned to outside contractors at the very end of the nineteenth century, when the mining business was booming and their need for housing overwhelming. One example of this was at Quincy's new stamp mill on Torch Lake, where construction began in 1888. Quincy built a few houses per year over the next twelve years—six managers' houses in 1889, nine workers' houses in 1890, five in 1892, three in 1893, and so on. In 1890 Superintendent Samuel B. Harris deplored his construction workers: "Labor of the kind required is so scarce that it is a sort of 'go as you please' with them." "The new dwellings at the mill . . . would have been ready for occupancy long ago if the kind of skilled labor required had not been so difficult to get here this season." Still, he kept the work in-house until 1899, when he wanted to build twelve houses at the mill. The Copper Country was booming; as Harris noted, "There is a great scramble for lime, cement, lumber, and all building materials, for there is so much new work going on and projected in this District that almost everybody is short of requirements." Harris decided to build the houses in May but did not act on them until late July, when he intended to "rush the work as fast as possible." He received bids on the construction contract and awarded it on August 4 to Erick Anderson, who offered to build twelve houses at a cost of $693 each, putting a force of eight carpenters, five lathers, and three masons on the job.[34]

Similarly, Bajari & Ulseth, Calumet builders, received a contract to build thirty houses for C&H in 1897; they claimed to have built a large percentage of C&H's houses between 1896 and 1902. Edward Ulseth expanded the firm after A. A. Bajari's death in 1902 and continued to build for C&H. At the southern end of the district, the Copper Range mines were just beginning construction in 1899. Champion initially brought in lumber from Houghton, but in late 1899, the company acquired a sixty-inch circular saw to produce its own lumber from the trees on site. Trimountain contracted the construction of ten new dwellings in late 1899, and Parker & Hamill built forty houses for Champion in Painesdale in 1901. But once these mines became operational, they also used their own laborers. In 1906 Baltic built sixteen new houses "with our own carpenter force," and in 1913 Champion used its own workforce. Although in September 1915 General Manager Denton asked for approval of new construction, arguing "our own regular force can put a good deal of time on the work, and I think those that we have built in this manner before have been the most satisfactory and the cheapest," the next summer Rashleigh Brothers of Houghton received several contracts, charging $247.75 each for "carpenter labor" only on fifteen five-room houses.[35]

Maintenance of houses also added to the carpentry staffs' workload; repairs alone could keep these staffs busy. In March 1916 J. S. Cocking, the head carpenter at C&H, reported on the work scheduled in 1914 that he could not accomplish until 1915: "35 houses shingled or roofs repaired, outside repairs made on 47 houses, 2 new rooms built, floors laid in 24 houses—total of 48 rooms, stone walls built under 4 double houses and 1 single house." Some work assigned in 1915—475 days' worth—then carried over into 1916, and 100 days of new work had already been approved in 1916.[36]

The in-house carpenters could also fabricate parts of buildings, especially in the off-season. In 1913 Quincy bought a flooring machine at a bargain: "Our thousand dollar hard wood flooring machine which we got for the carpenter shop and paid $150 for it, is an A. No. 1 machine. . . . This will enable us to get the best, first-class maple flooring and at a price less than the soft, cheap flooring; and, naturally, the hard-wood flooring will last much longer in our Company houses."

Similarly, C&H staff built the windows for the Calumet high school. MacNaughton wrote to his architects in January 1906, asking for working drawings of the windows. He noted that the price of glass was very low just then and it was a good time to buy; it was also a good time of year for his staff to undertake manufacture of sash and frames. Yet at other times the companies bought prefabricated pieces, as when C&H ordered window sash, doors, storm sash, wainscoting caps, and pilasters, all made to C&H specifications for the library, from a firm in Marinette, Wisconsin.[37]

Once a company had constructed houses, it had to assign workers to them. The lack of written records as to how this process worked indicates that this privilege was probably retained by lower-echelon managers—mine captains and shop foremen. A captain had the authority to hire and fire; it makes sense that once he hired he also found accommodations for the workers he most favored in the housing clustered close to their workplace. In 1891, however, C&H appointed Henry Brett as land agent, "whose principal business it is to take charge of the leasing of houses and lots." By 1893 C&H owned 698 company houses, 941 lots leased to homeowners, 20 lots leased to churches, 6 lots leased to schools, and a hotel.[38] Brett worked closely with the captains and foremen, who referred tenants to him. Long service and loyalty to the company were apparently the criteria.

When prospective tenants felt that they were not being treated fairly by Brett, they wrote to MacNaughton, the general manager. MacNaughton stated flatly that he did not assign houses, but the letters came in anyway. Judging from the surviving correspondence, company houses were hotly desired. Writers mentioned how long they had been waiting for a company house—ten years was not uncommon—and how long they had been working for the company. Prospective tenants first of all valued the low rents of company houses, as widow Rosa Dell'Acqua wrote in her request for a company house, specifying a log house, as that was cheapest. She was paying eight dollars a month rent and receiving ten dollars a month assistance from the county. Her husband had worked for C&H for more than twenty-five years. The petitioners also desired proximity to the workplace: Thomas F. Cocking wrote in November 1914, "I am living considerably over a mile from my work and I find it quite a hard walk in weather like today." Frank Olson desired a house in a quieter location: "My family and I have endured the noise from the engine at No. 17 Shaft for a number of years but now it seems as though we can not stand it any longer. Especially in the day time the noise seems to be more annoying and as you know I am night shift all the time so I have practically no sound sleep at all."[39]

Prospective tenants also wrote to MacNaughton to complain about Henry Brett's favoritism. Eighteen-year employee Stephen Vertin wrote to MacNaughton "directly so as to find out whether or not there is any favoritism in giving out these houses, or whether the company first investigates the employee's standing and the time that he has been employed by the company." MacNaughton assured him there was no favoritism and advised patience. Thomas Cocking was less complimentary about Brett, reporting to MacNaughton that he "said that the men in this mine including myself were the most ungrateful he knew of." MacNaughton demanded an explanation from Brett. But even more alarming was an anonymous letter to C&H President Agassiz which charged, first, that Brett took bribes ("A person who will pay him a reward can have a company house, and a good one right away, and persons in the employ of the C&H Co. for years cannot get one") and, secondly, that he demanded favors from the women ("He goes from house to house, insulting women especially among the foreigners[,] promising them better homes, hardwood floors and any improvement that they wish, this is done for a scandalous purpose").[40]

It was not until fifteen years later that MacNaughton changed the system. In 1917 C&H experienced a severe labor shortage, especially among unskilled trammers. The company acquired four hundred houses when it bought its neighbor, the Tamarack Mining Company. The complexity of "housing as many trammers as possible, rearranging the present housing situation, arranging for the occupancy of the Tamarack houses when repaired, etc." caused him to establish a committee that devised a new system. The application form developed by the committee asked for the prospective tenant's basic information, the names and ages of the members of his household, and what house he wanted and why. The form then circulated to the applicant's department head to provide a recommendation, then to the central employment office, which provided his work history, then to the "House Committee."[41] This formalization of Henry Brett's job, undermining his authority, must have rankled the land agent.

The most important part of the decision-making process, though, was the tenant. In most cases, there were other options to company housing—owning a house, either on company land or on one's own land, or renting an apartment or a house in a nearby village. All of these options cost more, however; Quincy's general manager estimated that housing in Hancock cost two or three times what it did at Quincy. Company housing was closer to the worksite, but leased company land would be just as close. Choosing a living arrangement is not always a simple matter of economics, especially when a family is involved—and company houses were rented only to families. Single men boarded with families, or in large boardinghouses, but only in rare circumstances did they get company houses.

The Champion Copper Company in 1905 kept statistics of the occupations and ethnicities of all its employees and how many of which type were married. Tracking marital status was clearly designed to determine how many houses were needed, and subsequent statistic sheets in a similar vein record how many of these couples rented company houses. In 1907, 481 of Champion's 1,136 employees were married, but only 220 of them (19 percent) were tenants of company houses. In 1910 the situation was similar, with 339 housing units, including both company-owned and those privately owned on company land. Tenants boarded about 500 fellow employees, and those with ground rents boarded another 200 men, so company lands accommodated more than three-quarters of Champion's workforce. Quincy also had many fewer houses than workers. In 1890 Quincy had 484 employees but only 182 of them rented company houses (37.6 percent). In 1902, after considerable growth, Quincy's employees numbered 1,636 and its renters, 394 (24 percent).[42] The relative scarcity of company houses increased their desirability and their usefulness as a perquisite to favored workers, but it also meant that employees were free to choose other arrangements.

The Copper Country's workforce was largely immigrant. In 1910, 80 percent of the county's population was foreign-born or born to foreign-born. A male immigrant arriving in the Copper Country would initially board with compatriots. After a few years, he might send for his wife, and they would set up housekeeping. He might ask his boss if there were any company houses available; he might promise to take in boarders to accommodate more workers or, later, he might argue he had a large family. His boss, or his boss's boss, would assess the employee's desirability—was he a good worker, did he have particular skills, was he English-speaking?—and recommend him for a company house. If he were fortunate enough to receive one, the rent would be deducted from his paycheck. Rents were usually pegged at about one dollar per room per month—so, generally five or six dollars a month, at a time when his wages were usually more than fifty dollars a month. Running water might be provided—all of C&H's and Copper Range's houses were so equipped, but not many of the others—but indoor toilets were far less likely. Most companies provided the water free of charge, although some charged fifty cents. Some companies provided electricity but charged for it. Garbage was removed weekly by C&H, biweekly by Copper Range, and annually in some places.[43]

Workers had to decide if low cost, convenience to workplace, and minimal amenities were a good deal. There were disadvantages: in a company-owned house, tenants relinquished certain freedoms and their housing was tied to their work; if they wished to change employers, they lost their housing. Standard leases prohibited tenants from selling liquor or transferring the lease. Control also could extend to minor intrusions, such as the case of the general manager of Copper Range who threatened to cancel the leases of five merchants on company property if they did not stop selling cigarettes to children.[44]

Linkage to employment was a tricky issue. The threat of losing one's house if one went on strike was a powerful tool and will be discussed in the next chapter. Losing one's house when one changed jobs voluntarily, though, was another issue, because it also reveals a certain flexibility. Rather than have his capital tied up in a house, a tenant was free to leave. Reformers in this period sometimes recognized the liability of capital investment, especially in resource-dependent mining communities. As reformer Graham Taylor noted, "Mobility of labor is one of its greatest safeguards against exploitation." Without an investment in housing, the worker had flexibility in his choice of employer; he could leave abruptly and without doubt many employees did. For example, Frieda Durocher Guilbault, born in 1908, recalled that she lived in ten houses, mostly company-owned ones, during the first eighteen years of her life as her father changed jobs and employers in the Copper Country.[45]

The relationship of the house to the job also meant that the house was dependent on one person in the family—the employee. If he died, the family could lose its house. Company managers often tried to soften this blow by giving the widow a set time to vacate, finding a cheaper house for her, or offering to employ one of her sons. For example, after Julia Dally's husband was killed in strike-related shootings in Painesdale, General Manager Denton noted that she had been "very self-helpful and proposes to keep boarders," so he moved her to another company house where she could support herself and at the same time help the company by providing housing for strikebreakers.[46]

The tenuousness of women's homes was also illustrated by the Martins at Quincy. On November 5, 1913, Joseph and Elizabeth Martin moved into a saltbox house near Quincy's No. 2 Shaft. The house had been built, probably in the early 1860s, by the Pewabic Mining Company, whose lands were acquired by its neighbor, Quincy, in 1891. Joseph Martin, born in England in 1860, had worked for Quincy since 1886. The Martins were given this house located so close to the works in the midst of the strike because Joseph, loyal to the company, was sworn in as a deputy. In 1916, after he had worked at Quincy for thirty years, he was given time off "for good time"—apparently a vacation as a reward for his service. Two years later he was out of work for three months due to a fractured skull. On August 11, 1921, Joseph was killed in an air blast, or mine collapse, in the No. 6 shaft. Joseph and Elizabeth had had eight children, but only one was still living at home—their youngest son, Russell, born in 1899. Fortunately Russell also worked for Quincy, so Elizabeth was allowed to remain in her house. In May 1925, though, Russell moved to Detroit, and soon after, Elizabeth moved out of the house.[47]

One sign of workers' contentment with company housing is lack of turnover. Calumet & Hecla had famously low rates of turnover among employees. In 1914, out of a workforce of just under 5,000, the company claimed that 1,660 men had worked for them fifteen years or longer. Similarly, there was little turnover among company houses. But C&H, the most profitable mine in the Copper Country, was known for its long-term employees and worker loyalty; as the Michigan Commissioner of Mineral Statistics noted, "Like Ohio office-holders, 'few die and none resign,' among C&H employees, and jobs are handed down from father to son." They were also paid better than at other mines. C&H miners were paid about seventy-five cents more per day, and its trammers received fifty to sixty cents more per day.[48]

Quincy's extant records provide an opportunity to examine the turnover issue further. In one ten-year period, 1890–1900, Quincy lost nearly two-thirds of its tenants; only 36 percent of the 182 renters remained. In one five-year period, 1897–1902, it lost a little more than half. And in one year, 1902, 13.5 percent of the tenants left (one because he had been killed in a mine accident). Similarly, in Quincy's stamp-mill community of Mason, the company built forty-two houses, fourteen of which were occupied by the same families in 1910 as they had been in 1900. In 1918 Quincy tracked the assignment of forty-five newly built houses. They were large and well equipped—all of them had furnaces and running water; some had indoor toilets and electricity. Thirty-eight of the houses were assigned to tenants, but within three years seventeen of them—nearly half—had changed tenants. Granted, these were years in which the price of copper dropped precipitously (twenty-five cents per pound in 1918, thirteen cents in 1921) and Quincy began to reduce its workforce.[49] Still, to have the best-equipped houses subject to such turnover confounded the expectations of management.

Yet these numbers compare favorably with other studies. Historian Eric Monkkonen, examining American cities, concluded that "every city lost about half of its inhabitants every decade." And Howard Chudacoff, looking at young men in Omaha, found that only 4.3 percent stayed in the same place between 1880 and 1900; 17.4 percent stayed in the same place between 1900 and 1908. He also found little difference between men with families and those without, and homeowners were only slightly less likely to move than renters. Working-class residents were most likely to move.[50] Given that mobility among Americans was much higher than conventional wisdom has it, Quincy was able to retain its company-house tenants at a respectable rate, with about 10 to 15 percent turnover every year.

A series of fires that occurred in Quincy's company housing indicated that the dwellings were not always treasured by employees, though. On at least three occasions, tenants apparently insured their furnishings at an inflated value, then burned the houses down to collect the insurance. General Manager Lawton noted that one tenant had insured his furniture for fifteen hundred dollars, which was four or five times its actual value. Another fire, started in a woodshed, was even more suspicious: "This same house caught fire recently in the bedroom, when the neighbors who extinguished the fire reported a strong smell of kerosene about the place." The tenant had insured his furniture for eight hundred dollars. Suspicion abounded in another fire, a year later: "It was occupied by an Italian whose wife is a sister of the wife of the Italian who lived in the last house that was burned. They kept a number of boarders but they were let out about a week ago: the children of the household were visiting at the home of the sister who had the previous fire, and again there was a large insurance upon the furniture—we understand $700."[51]

Company houses also had liabilities from management's point of view, the primary one being cost. Company housing was usually needed in conjunction with other capital improvements and constituted an additional expense. For instance, Quincy's new stamp mill on Torch Lake cost close to half a million dollars in 1890, but the company also had to build a ten-mile railroad to transport the rock and build bridges for the railroad. Needing workers to construct the mill, the company first built a boardinghouse for the construction phase, after which it planned to convert the boardinghouse to shops. Needing workers to run the mill, the company also built forty-two single-family houses. Ten years after the first mill came on line, Quincy opened a second one at a cost of half a million dollars, and additions during World War I meant the construction of six more houses.[52] Houses were a minor expense in the face of major capital improvements, but an expense nonetheless, and they brought in little income.

Rather than producing profits, company houses were break-even propositions in the Copper Country. Leifur Magnusson, a U.S. Bureau of Labor Statistics (BLS) investigator, examined two unnamed Copper Country companies over five years, 1911–15. One took in $15,623.11 in rent and spent $4,096.53 on maintenance (labor and repairs only), while the other took in $71,674.70 in rent and spent $88,810.32 on maintenance (labor and material, water, garbage, and sanitary collection). Walter Palmer, another BLS investigator, found that rentals equaled about 6 percent of construction costs, "but little, if any, more than the amount necessary to pay for taxes, insurance, and repairs, and to provide for depreciation." Similarly, MacNaughton testified before a congressional committee that over a ten-year period up to 1913, C&H collected annually, on average, rents of $61,863 and spent $61,229 on repairs. Even in private, managers thought they were spending too much on company housing. In a letter to Quincy President Todd, Lawton noted that for years, "in some instances . . . we actually spend more money upon repairs than we receive for rent . . . and in some instances we have actually paid out for repairs more than twice the amount we have received in rents." Three years later, the problem persisted: "I note by the last cost sheet that the amount of expenses that are being put into the 'Repairs and Renewals' of our dwelling houses is practically equal to the rentals receipt." Yet company housing was a cost that the companies were willing to endure, and its advantages did not always show up on the balance sheet. As Lawton argued, "I strongly approve and advise not only building a house for the Clerk, but also for the better class of laborers at the Smelter; and although we may not make money by renting the houses, we will be far ahead in the end, by being able to procure the very best of labor for the Smelter."[53]

Another aspect of company houses that must have aggravated the managers was the annoyance factor. While trying to run a large company, the general managers were forced to deal with hundreds of written requests from tenants for toilets and electricity (in MacNaughton's case), or reports of scandalous behavior (in Harris's case), or the selling of alcohol out of a home (in Denton's case).[54] The triviality of these situations in contrast to the main work of the managers—decisions on whether to spend hundreds of thousands of dollars on a new smelter, for instance—is striking. The flexibility inherent in paternalism—that managers did not set hard and fast rules—meant that small problems would be passed up the administrative hierarchy for resolution by the general manager. Yet the managers remained convinced that this system in general, and company housing in particular, were worth the cost and aggravation.

As Bureau of Labor Statistics investigator Leifur Magnusson found in his 1916 nationwide study of 213 companies that operated company housing, most companies cited the housing's ability to attract and retain better and more loyal workers as its primary benefit. In addition, 97.5 percent of the employers found company housing satisfactory to both employee and company. Nearly all of the Copper Country companies built housing to attract workers; in an undeveloped wilderness, the promise of housing was necessary to bring workers in. Company housing was also thought to retain workers. Copper Range's general manager justified the construction of houses to his president, "Men are beginning to leave as they do every Spring, and I think the starting or announcement of building a lot of such houses quickly will cause a good many of them to stick out longer."[55] Whether company houses succeeded in retaining workers is debatable, but the companies had the perception that it succeeded.

More importantly, the companies used houses to reward the particular workers they wanted to retain, treating company housing as a privilege to bestow. Because there were never enough of these adequate, cheap houses, the companies could be selective about who received houses, allowing them to cultivate a certain type of worker. Copper Range came closest to articulating this strategy in the charts it devised, analyzing the marital status (and hence the need for houses), ethnicity, occupation, and housing of its employees at its Champion mine. The company clearly preferred married, English-speaking, skilled workers as tenants.

In the act of building single-family houses, rather than extensive boarding-houses, companies were declaring their preference for families. After a mine proved successful and it appeared there would be several decades of work, companies wanted married men with responsibilities, men who would be most likely to stay and least likely to make trouble. As Walter Palmer explained, the companies "consider married men more reliable than single men, more apt to work regularly, and not so apt to leave the employment of the company."[56]

Secondly, they wanted to cultivate certain ethnic groups. Although English speakers might have been ensconced in company houses by the time the new wave of Finns, Austrians, and Italians arrived in the early twentieth century, even Copper Range, which was a relatively new mine, housed a disproportionate number of English speakers in company dwellings. For instance, in Painesdale, 29 percent of the English-born employees received company houses, although they represented only 18 percent of the workforce; at the same time Croatians received only 14 percent of the housing, although they formed a quarter of the workforce.[57]

Third, companies favored skilled workers. Underground workers fell primarily into two categories: miners were skilled workers who drilled and blasted, while trammers, considered unskilled, had the job of loading the cars with ore-bearing rock and pushing them, on tracks, to the shaft. In Painesdale, 119 of the 399 miners received company housing and only 9 of the 458 underground laborers did. Trammers' lowly status was upended, though, in 1917, when the Copper Country experienced a serious shortage of unskilled laborers. C&H suddenly prioritized trammers to receive company houses.[58]

The final advantage of company housing to the companies was that it provided an element of control. First, the companies wanted to control the land. As a land-based industry, the companies were reluctant to cede lands that they might need later for mining functions. Moving buildings around the location was common, as the company's needs changed. The companies also wanted to control their workers, and part of this control involved the granting of a favor such as housing, cultivating loyalty among the workers it wanted most. The effectiveness of this strategy, and the role of housing during the strike, will be discussed in the next chapter. The companies also used their low rents to keep the wage scale low. Private-market rents were much higher, reinforcing the advantage that company houses offered. It was a benefit distributed unfairly, though: "Single men claim that married men are to some extent compensated for low wages by the low rent, but that low rents are of no benefit to the single men and really is one cause of keeping wages low."[59]

The companies did not always have the advantage, even in regard to the rent charged for housing. In July 1901 Quincy Superintendent S. B. Harris raised rents, to the consternation of his workers. C&H general manager MacNaughton, viewing the action from afar, commented, "The trouble at Quincy is because of the fact that without in any way notifying the men, the Company raised the price of house rent an average of $2 a month." In early September the men threatened to strike and, although that was averted, they still demanded that the rents be decreased. Harris wrote to Todd: "The 'strikers' committee' will call on me tomorrow . . . for answer as to 'house rents,' and as these will be restored to the old rates I do not think there will be any further trouble."[60] Management backed down in the face of its tenants' strong objections, and rents remained stable into the 1970s.

Because management used company housing as a perquisite for good workers, generally the quality of the architecture was high. Quality is relative, however; today, few people would covet houses without central heat, insulation, indoor toilets, and private bedrooms, but in the early twentieth century there were few objections to the lack of such amenities. Outside observers familiar with company houses were uniformly impressed: Bureau of Labor Statistics investigator Walter Palmer described them as "substantially built," while Commission on Industrial Relations investigator Luke Grant called them "substantial and comfortable" and said, "The houses are plain from an architectural standpoint, but they are on wide lots and substantially built, most of them on stone foundations." Another industry observer, T. A. Rickard, wrote in 1905, "The companies build substantial dwellings, usually with stone foundations, arranged in orderly rows, whose neatness and regularity have not much of the picturesque, but bespeak far healthier conditions than that mingling of the squalid and romantic which characterizes other mining camps." Tenants tended not to rave about their dwellings, but it is worth noting that during the congressional investigation prompted by the 1913 strike, during a month of testimony that consumed more than two thousand pages of text, not one person complained about the quality of company houses. Pay, work conditions, supervision, unionization, and a host of other issues were raised, but housing was not among them.[61]

Living in the Company House

Another way of exploring what tenants thought about their company houses is to look at how they used them. A fatal shooting that occurred in a company house in the Seeberville neighborhood of Painesdale in 1913 offers an opportunity to do that. The parameters of the case are not important here and will be explained in the next chapter. But the documentation and testimony that survive tell us more about this house—the one that opened this chapter—than any other. The minimal appointments of the Putriches' house reinforce the nature of the nineteenth-century workers' house, as characterized by Hubka and Kenny: architecturally undifferentiated rooms with lots of people and little privacy.

The front-gable house, located at 17 Second Street in Seeberville, had two rooms and a kitchen, measuring 16 by 34 feet, for 544 square feet on the first floor (Figure 1.18). The two rooms on the second floor, under the steep gable roof, offered another 384 square feet of space. There were no halls, porches, or closets. Set on wood posts, the frame house, built as a temporary structure in 1902, had planks both inside and outside of the studs. On the outside, these boards had never been clad or painted. The kitchen in the rear was tar-papered (Figure 1.19). Inside, wallpaper covered walls and ceilings, except in the kitchen, where the boards

Figure 1.18 Putrich house in Seeberville, 1913 postcard view, since demolished. On this postcard, kept by the Putrich family, "Dad," "Mom," and "Aunt" are designated, indicating Joseph and Antonia Putrich and her sister, Josephine Grubesich. Courtesy of Michigan Technological University Archives and Copper Country Historical Collections.

were left bare. The flooring appears to have been tongue-and-groove on the first floor, with planks on the second; the kitchen floor was covered with linoleum. There was a storm shed protecting the rear entrance, adjacent to a woodshed (Figure 1.20).

The rooms were crowded and the furnishings were Spartan. Despite the front door opening into it, the front room was used as a bedroom, and the front door was seldom used.[62] Joseph and Antonia Putrich slept in this room with their four children and possibly the hired girl; there were two iron bedsteads, a flowered carpet, and a trunk (Figure 1.21). Framed religious pictures and a collection of family photographs decorated the wallpapered walls. The dining room served as the main gathering space and passageway. A simple wooden chair and a bench are visible in photographs but not the table that we know was there (Figure 1.22). There was also a sewing machine, probably Antonia's prize possession. Coats and hats were hung on hooks. There was a chimney between the front room and dining room, but no stove appears in the photographs. The stovepipe hole is visible in the dining room but had been covered.

Figure 1.19 Putrich house, side and rear, 1913. The kitchen was in the tar-papered section; the plank walls were neither clad nor painted. Courtesy of Archives of Michigan.

Figure 1.20 Putrich house, conjectural plans from contemporary descriptions and photographs. The small house had two rooms and a kitchen on the first floor and two rooms on the second, without closets or halls. Seventeen people lived in this house.

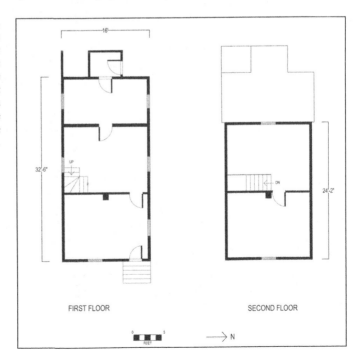

FIRST FLOOR

SECOND FLOOR

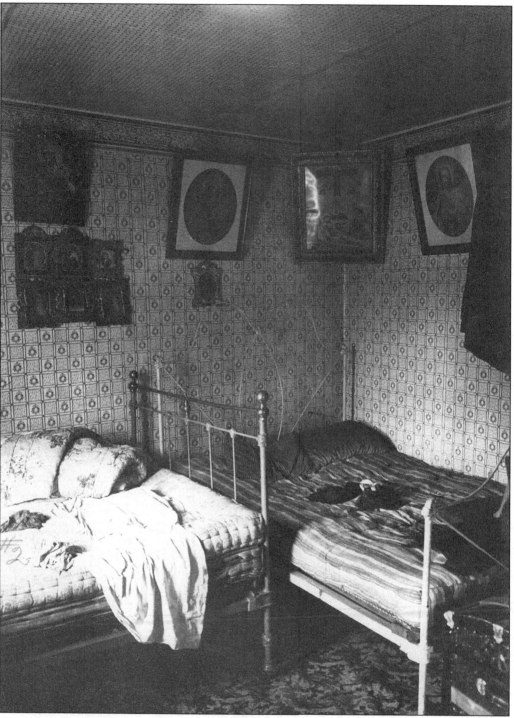

Figure 1.21 Putrich house, front bedroom, 1913. Furnishings in this wallpapered room include two iron bedsteads and a trunk. Courtesy of Michigan Technological University Archives and Copper Country Historical Collections.

Figure 1.22 Putrich house, looking from kitchen into dining room, 1913. Under the enclosed stairs to the second floor is a sewing machine. The walls and ceiling are papered and the floor is bare. Courtesy of Michigan Technological University Archives and Copper Country Historical Collections.

Figure 1.23 Putrich house, kitchen, 1913. The stove occupies a prominent place in this photograph. The sink has cold running water; above it hang miners' lunch pails. Pots, pans, and implements hang on the walls. Courtesy of Michigan Technological University Archives and Copper Country Historical Collections.

Everyone who entered the house would have passed through the kitchen, but it was so small that boarders would have probably gone through to the dining room before removing coats or stopping to chat. The kitchen had a sink with cold running water and a stove (Figure 1.23). An assortment of pots, pans, and other containers hung on the walls and sat on the stove. Ladles, spoons, and lids also hung on the wall. Miners' lunch pails were lined up over the sink. A barrel of flour is also apparent.

The ten boarders slept upstairs in two rooms, passing through one to get to the other (Figure 1.24). They may have shared beds, day-shift men sleeping in the beds of night-shift men, and vice-versa, in a system called "hot beds." Nonetheless, it must have been crowded. In the photograph an iron bedstead was located

Figure 1.24 Putrich house, second floor looking downstairs, 1913. The boarders slept upstairs. A bedstead is very close to the stairway; trunks and hanging clothes are also visible. Courtesy of Michigan Technological University Archives and Copper Country Historical Collections.

perilously close to the open stairway, and a couple of boarders' trunks were visible. Jackets hung on the wall.

More evidence of the material dimensions of the Putriches' lives can be gleaned from other sources. One inventory, of a house at Quincy suddenly abandoned by its occupant, offers an articulation of the objects that can be viewed in the photographs of the Putrich house. William Endain began occupying the six-room saltbox in May 1908 but seems to have disappeared during the 1913–14 strike. On April 6, 1914, Quincy inventoried his belongings before renting his house to a new tenant. Endain had seven beds, with springs, mattresses, sheets, blankets, quilts, and fifteen pillows; tables with oil cloths in the dining room and kitchen, and six chairs at each; a stove in the kitchen and a heater somewhere else; and four oil lamps. There were no furnishings for a living room—no sofa, no easy chair, no rocking chair, no upholstery. The kitchen appears to have been well equipped, with pots, pans, crocks, a wooden cuspidor, a rolling pin, potato masher, an egg turner, and more, and he even left some food behind: thirty-five pounds of flour, fifteen pounds of sugar, salt, pepper, horseradish, tapioca, a pound and a half of cocoa, and two pounds of baking powder.[63] Endain apparently had a wife—he left a pair of ladies' shoes behind, along with two pairs of men's shoes and two pairs of mining boots—and he may have been the William Endain that appeared in the 1910 census with his wife, Elizabeth, and two children. If so, the Endains must have had several boarders.

Boarders had much sparer material lives. All of their possessions were stored in trunks, which served as the only furniture other than beds in their rooms. A few inventories of trunks at Copper Range survive; after their owners' deaths, the general manager detailed their contents before sending them to their families. Italian Ernesto Specciana owned a modicum of clothing—one overcoat, one suit, two trousers, two pairs of shoes, six overshirts, two underpants, etc.—but had more than six hundred dollars in the South Range Bank. George Gasparac, from Croatia, had a similar assortment of clothing but also two pairs of white society gloves, a lodge cap and badge, three photographs and old letters, and thirty-two dollars. Elizabeth Bartle's brother, from Cornwall, along with fifty dollars in the bank had a derby hat and a "cigarette mouth piece." Each of these men owned a watch, clearly their most valuable possession, which the company sent home with special arrangements.[64]

In measuring how a family like the Putriches lived, it is also useful to think about how they did *not* live, how they were *not* middle-class Americans. If, culling from reformist literature, we would expect middle-class Americans to own their own homes, to live with a nuclear family and not strangers, to have one breadwinner (the father), and to speak English, we can define the Putriches as *not* middle-class Americans. But each of these issues is shaded with different meanings.

The American ideal of homeownership has existed since the nation's early days and, as historians have noted, reflects ideas about social order. Homeownership's ability to foster political stability and family life has been frequently heralded. By the mid-nineteenth century, middle-class Americans aspired to homeownership and continue to do so today. Some middle-class reformers promoted homeownership to the working class, while others preferred the flexibility inherent in not owning a house. Especially for miners, dependent on a natural resource that might become depleted and living in remote areas where a house's resale value was dependent on the success of one industry, homeownership may not have been a wise choice. Regardless of the debate among middle-class reformers, the working class *did* aspire to own their own homes. As John Mitchell, former president of the United Mine Workers of America, testified before a congressional committee investigating the copper strike, "Working men prefer to own their own homes. . . . There is in every man a desire to own his own home, and if it is not in the man it is in his wife."[65] Company housing, though, was antithetical to homeownership. It was not only rental but excessively so; companies deducted rent from paychecks of their workers and placed constraints on their behavior. Furthermore, the whole town, or "location" as it was called in the Copper Country, was owned by the company. Yet, as will be seen, it could be used as a step toward homeownership, as a first home that enables the renters to build capital.

A second American ideal that immigrants confronted was the sanctity of the home, with emphasis on the nuclear family, which boardinghouses seemed to undermine. Boardinghouses like the Putriches' were particularly hazardous in the eyes of reformers because in these facilities boarders mingled with the family. Purpose-built boardinghouses, which tended to be much larger and were leased by the company to an operator, will be discussed in the next chapter. Reformers objected to family boardinghouses because of the loss of privacy to the family, exposure of children to potentially sinister men, overworked mothers' potentially neglecting their children, and overcrowded conditions, especially among immigrants. Ethnic groups took in boarders disproportionately across the Copper Country, with Magyars, English, Slovenians, and Croatians far more likely to have boarders than Irish, Finnish, Polish, and Italians, probably reflecting different strategies among immigrants. In the Copper Country, Croatians took in boarders at twice the rate of most foreign-born households.[66]

Rather than a place of moral decay, the Putriches' boardinghouse constituted a Croatian mini-community where recent immigrants could adapt to American life and work. The boardinghouse was also a family, in more than a figurative sense. Joseph Putrich immigrated in 1905 and Antonia Grubesich two years later; they married shortly after she arrived in the Copper Country. They rented this house in Seeberville and began taking in boarders; in 1910 they had seven boarders, only one of whom was among the ten boarders they had in 1913. They also began having children, but that was not their only family. Josephine Grubesich, the hired girl, was Antonia Putrich's sister. Joseph's brother, Steve, who was killed in the shootings, had a wife and children in the old country. His last words to Antonia were a request that his money be sent to his children back in Croatia. Joseph's two nephews, Albert and Alois Tijan, also lived there with their uncle, Jacob Tijan. Alois was killed in the shootings, but Albert subsequently married Josephine Grubesich. John Kalan, the striker whom the deputies attempted to arrest, lived in the house with his eighteen-year-old son, Slave. John's wife, Slave's mother, was still in Croatia. So of the seventeen people who lived in this house, eleven of them were Putriches, or related to them, and two other men were related to each other.[67] Rather than a threatening crowd of strange men, the boardinghouse was an extended family, providing familiarity to immigrants in a strange land.

Furthermore, the nature of the boardinghouse undermined the company's control. The boarders' arrangement with their "boarding boss" was private; board was not deducted from their paychecks. The company did not even know who boarded with whom, as became evident when General Manager Denton wanted to rid the companies of some activist strikers; he did not know where they lived. Management also seemed to exhibit no control over or interest in how many boarders a tenant took in.[68] In effect, the Putriches re-created the precise situation that management, by building houses, wished to avoid: a large number of single men living together.

The third American ideal was the standard of living, a relatively new concept at the turn of the last century. The standard of living was based on the theory that there would be one breadwinner for the family and that he (always a man) should be able to earn enough to support his family. Wives of any class were not traditionally employed outside the home, but the immigrant worker's tendency to put his children to work to supplement the household income dismayed reformers. Reformers argued that industrialists should pay a wage that enabled a man to support his family—the standard of living. But this emphasis on the male breadwinner's wages overlooks the contribution made by the wife through the keeping of boarders. The husband's income became the definition of a family's status and also tied his job to his perception of his manhood. The implication that paternalism encouraged an "unmanly dependency"—by making him beg for favors distributed unequally rather than as a right—found particular resonance in the early twentieth century when masculinity was being redefined for an industrial world.[69] For the working class, though, reliance on just one wage earner was not always possible. Women in the Copper Country had few options for working outside the home, even if a lack of childcare obligations had made it possible. But they did take in boarders.

The decision to keep boarders was the Putriches' alone. Only about half of the households in Painesdale took in boarders, so keeping boarders was clearly not a requirement for obtaining a company house. The particulars of the relationships between the Putriches and their boarders are not known, such as how much the boarders paid, or if they paid directly to Antonia. But some estimates are possible. In another Croatian boardinghouse in Painesdale, Starko Iskra charged $20.45 a month, which compares to rates in more formal, purpose-built boardinghouses, which ranged from about $18 to $22 a month. So if Antonia charged $20 a month, her ten boarders would have paid $200. There were costs involved, of course. One was the hired girl, her sister Josephine, although, as Josephine boarded with the family, her cash wages would not have been high, probably $3 a week. Antonia would also have had to feed all these boarders. Copper Range estimated the monthly food bill of a miner to be $10.81. Rounding that up to $11, feeding her boarders would have cost her $110. In a month, the boarders might have paid $200, but Antonia's costs would have been, say, $133 ($110 for food plus $12 for Josephine's wages and $11 for her food). Therefore Antonia contributed about $67—as much or more than her husband—to the monthly family income. She worked hard to do it—preparing meals for her family and ten men, cleaning, and washing, while caring for four young children—but she contributed a substantial amount to the family savings.[70]

Eastern European immigrants rarely qualified as "Americans" in the public imagination. The concentration of Croatians in this boardinghouse raises the specter of immigrants crowding together, refusing to become Americanized. Most of them needed interpreters when they were called upon to testify in court; a native English speaker who encountered them described them as speaking a "broken English," adequate for the mines. Croatian was undoubtedly the language used in the boardinghouse. The adults in the house were newly arrived in the country, none of them having been in the United States as long as ten years. There is no doubt that these immigrants gained support from each other in a strange land. Moreover, their next-door neighbors, George and Kristina Rusich, were also Croatian, and Kristina served as godmother to the Putriches' daughter Mary.[71]

But they lived in a mixed neighborhood. Located on a low, sloping site, Seeberville consisted of ten company houses facing each other across a rutted muddy street; six ground-rent houses were located at either end of the row. Next door to the Putriches, to the west, was the boardinghouse of Emilio Vittori, who had six Italian boarders. Nearby were more Italians, Vincent Ricci and Emilio Guidi, and across the street were the Mutkas, who were Finnish, and the Sabanskis, who were Polish. They were friendly enough and recognized each other, but there were clearly barriers. Emilio Vittori described bowling as "some pins that the Austrian people [i.e., Croatians] use to play games," implying that the Italians did not play with them.[72]

Rather than being ethnically segregated, the Copper Country appears to have been ethnically clustered, often haphazardly. The Seeberville neighborhood, the least desirable housing in Painesdale, was occupied by the most recent, and therefore the most disdained, immigrants, but it was a mix of ethnic groups. Similarly, a study of C&H lease records found some ethnic clustering but not segregation. The "Swedetown" neighborhood in Quincy was built for Swedes recruited during the Civil War, but they left soon after arriving, and the houses were abandoned. Calumet's "Swedetown" was dominated by Finns, but a full range of other ethnic groups also lived there. Quincy's "Limerick" never had a majority of Irish households, despite its name. In 1870 only a third of the houses were rented by Irish, while the English (probably Cornish) occupied nearly a half. Irish numbers declined from there.[73] There are other ethnic names for neighborhoods, but if they ever had an ethnic concentration it was soon lost in the turnover in company housing.

Copper Country immigrants faced ethnic discrimination. Although Finns constituted the biggest immigrant group, forming 13 percent of the county's population in 1910, they were also the most discriminated against, due to their reputation for socialist politics. C&H undertook a policy of getting rid of Finnish workers. In 1912 General Manager MacNaughton requested four hundred to five hundred laborers from the commissioner of immigration, but he refused to hire southern Italians or Finlanders. Northern Italians and Austrians were acceptable. In 1908 Finns constituted just under 15 percent of C&H's workforce; their percentage then declined. By contrast, at Champion Copper Company in 1910 the Finns comprised 31 percent of the workforce.[74] The greatest number of immigrants employed at C&H in 1910 were Austrian, mostly Croatian and Slovenian, constituting 17 percent. They amounted to 26.5 percent of Copper Range's workforce. These recent immigrants were least likely to receive company houses.

Among ethnic groups, houses were not only allocated by number unevenly, they were allocated by quality unevenly. Thus Copper Range's general manager, Frederick Denton, wrote to the president, "While we are constructing a bunch of houses, they are of the standard design and construction which is adapted to our best families, and these will not . . . accommodate the Croatians, Italians, Finns and Armenians that we want to accommodate. The only way out that I can see is to rush the construction of about twenty-five or thirty four-room houses built like those in Seeberville."[75] Croatians and other less-favored workers were offered smaller and cheaper houses.

It is likely that Denton, when claiming that good houses "will not . . . accommodate" Croatians and others, was assuming that these immigrants deserved less, that they did not want good housing. But it may also be that they just did not want to pay for it, that they were using their houses to make money, to move up and move on. The Putriches' house was cramped and dilapidated, but it cost only two dollars and twenty-five cents a month, much cheaper than the better sort of Painesdale housing, which cost five or six dollars. Private housing in nearby towns cost two or three times the amount of company housing, so many workers preferred the loss of freedom attached to company houses to the independent but more expensive private stock. Joseph Putrich earned two dollars and sixty-one cents per day. In the ten months preceding the strike, he averaged a little more than sixty dollars a month in take-home pay; deductions from his paycheck included two dollars and twenty-five cents for rent, a dollar for the services of a doctor for him and his family, and fifty cents toward the aid fund, which was a type of life insurance.

Joseph and Antonia lived modestly in a cheap, overcrowded house, but this arrangement enabled them to save money. Joseph's income may have been exceeded by Antonia's. They stayed in this company house for ten years, then moved to Illinois, where they bought a house, free and clear. The uses of their Copper Country dwelling were not all revealed in the building.[76] How the Putriches lived in it (in crowded, frugal conditions) and what they used it for (a strategy for future homeownership) were significant.

The "negotiation" that the Putriches undertook with Champion Copper Company management was unspoken, but it went something like this: the company will provide barely adequate but cheap housing, and the Putriches will use it to further their own ends. They will use it as a site of production and source of income. They will also use it as a strategy toward achievement, toward the attainment of private property and a house. It will also foster a community of family members and a shared ethnic identity, a common transition to life in America. It will also be a home—maybe not a well appointed symbol of middle-class status, but a young couple's first home in a new country. How it functioned during labor conflict is the subject of the next chapter.

2 The Spaces of a Strike
Company Buildings and Landscapes in a Time of Conflict

On August 14, 1913, three weeks into a strike that crippled the Copper Country, eight men from the Putriches' boardinghouse walked three miles to South Range to collect their strike benefits at an office of the Western Federation of Miners. They drank some beer and headed home. John Kalan and John Stimac, lagging behind the others, cut across company property that had recently been declared off-limits. A company watchman confronted them, but after an altercation they continued on. They reached the Putrich house and had their supper. John Kalan went outside, joining the other boarders who were bowling ninepins in the yard. At that point, deputies employed by the mining company came into the yard and attempted to detain Kalan, who resisted and retreated with his fellow boarders into the house. As the deputies were leaving, one of the strikers threw a ninepin at them, hitting one in the head. That deputy drew his revolver and fired, and other deputies joined in, shooting through open windows. In the hail of bullets, boarders Steve Putrich and Alois Tijan were killed and Stanko Stepic and John Stimac wounded. The men in the house were unarmed. As one witness said, "They didn't have anything to shoot with except the spoons they had in their hands while they were eating."[1]

This event was the first galvanizing incident of what would be a long strike. The strike had begun on July 23, the result of several years of organizing by the Western Federation of Miners. The companies played it tough, refusing to meet with the union or listen to its demands. At issue were pay, hours, introduction of the one-man drill, grievance procedures, and recognition of the union. More broadly examined, though, the key issue was recognition of a workforce for whom paternalistic care was not effective in securing its loyalty. By and large excluded by company management from substantial company houses and other benefits of paternalism, the more recently immigrated workers organized in an effort to receive guaranteed improvements in their working and living situations, not benefits distributed unequally.

The companies, led by Calumet & Hecla, were well positioned to withstand a strike, having experienced a decade of high profits. The strike lasted for eight-and-a-half months across a divided landscape in which the companies' traditional paternalism played a significant but unspoken role. The harsh glare of publicity, including a congressional investigation that involved four weeks of testimony in public hearings in the Copper Country, exposed many aspects of the worker–management relationship, including how public space and private homes were defined when the companies owned nearly all the land.

Contested Space

The conflict that played out on a daily basis in the Copper Country landscape involved the use of public space more visibly than of houses. Initially, strikers gathered in non-company buildings such as Laurium's Palestra, an ice rink, and marched en masse to the mines to shut them down through attacks on nonunion workers. Once the strikers had succeeded in closing down operations of seventeen mines in the Copper Country, idling nearly fifteen thousand workers, the challenge was to keep them closed. Public intimidation was necessary to discourage company loyalists from returning to work. Beatings, fights, and tossed rocks attempted to persuade.

The strikers' rallies were essential to maintain unity and discourage defectors. Much of the strikers' rallying took place in platted villages and on public highways; company land, after all, could not be used for this purpose (Figure 2.1). Where there was no noncompany land nearby, as at Winona in the south end of the district, union members were reduced to meeting in the cemetery. Generally, though, there was ample public space for union events. The union held a series of Sunday meetings at the Palestra in Laurium and the Amphidrome in Houghton. One Sunday, three thousand unionists paraded from union headquarters in Red Jacket, past the National Guard troops encamped on company land, to the Palestra. Other parades occurred in the surrounding villages of Ahmeek, Mohawk,

Figure 2.1 Strikers' parade in Calumet, 1913. On the far right is the Union Building and next to it, the YMCA; on the far left is St. Anne's Church. These three buildings were on company land; beyond them lay Red Jacket Village. Courtesy of Michigan Technological University Archives and Copper Country Historical Collections.

and South Range. Women participated actively in these public displays, shocking observers with their unladylike behavior. Children were also called upon to parade. With a solid population of Socialist Finns, Hancock witnessed frequent parades on its main street. Kansankoti Hall at Franklin and Tezcuco streets not only provided a gathering place but also housed the radical Finnish printing press, which produced the newspaper *Tyomies*. At the parade on August 9, strikers

Figure 2.2 Citizens Alliance parade in Houghton, December 1913. Procompany forces also paraded on public property, here on Shelden Avenue. Douglass House, a prominent hotel, is in the background. Courtesy of Michigan Technological University Archives and Copper Country Historical Collections.

assembled at Kansankoti Hall, marched down Hancock Street and across the bridge to the Amphidrome in Houghton. There, famed labor leader Mother Jones addressed the crowd. Speeches in Finnish, Italian, and Croatian rounded out the program.[2]

The unionists also employed a strategy of preventing strikebreakers from getting to work. As Oreste Monticelli described the situation on Quincy Hill to the congressional investigators, in October three hundred to four hundred strikers would line the county road every morning between six and seven, when strikebreakers living in company boardinghouses would have to cross the highway to get to the dryhouse to change for work. As many as five hundred guards would be required to protect the strikebreakers. In late October, Quincy built barbed-wire fences across the road to protect its workers, impeding traffic. Similarly, on

Copper Range's property, paraders were so effective that the company built fences.[3] Company lawyers also obtained an injunction against violent intimidation. When Circuit Court Judge Patrick O'Brien dismissed it, company lawyers obtained a writ of mandamus from the Michigan Supreme Court, forcing O'Brien to reinstate the injunction. Strikers were still permitted to parade but not to use violence. O'Brien enforced the injunction halfheartedly, granting suspended sentences to hundreds of convicted strikers.[4]

The companies responded with violence and public displays of force. Loyal workers took up the fight. On the eve of the strike, the union claimed more than seven thousand members out of a workforce of nearly fifteen thousand, but gradually many of these men surrendered their union cards and returned to work. Strikers were found overwhelmingly among the ranks of underground workers; few surface workers joined the union. Quincy claimed that none of its shop or surface men at the mine, nor any of its mill or smelter employees, went on strike. The mines began to reopen on a reduced basis three weeks into the strike. A month later, the *Boston Daily Globe* estimated that 20 percent of Quincy workers, 60 percent of C&H, and 75 percent of Trimountain workers had returned to work. When the companies began to supplement their own workforces with imported workers, the unionists did not let these scabs pass unnoticed. Beatings and other violence were common, along with ugly confrontations and profane insults. By one count, at least 168 people were beaten or injured during the strike. Nine men were shot to death and 26 others injured by gunfire.[5]

The companies held procompany demonstrations in some of the same public spaces used by the strikers (Figure 2.2). On December 10 rallies in Houghton and Calumet drew an alleged fifty thousand people, some of whom arrived on special trains from outlying areas. C&H's lawyers, Rees, Robinson & Petermann, arranged the parade in the north end, which culminated at Calumet's Armory and Colosseum. Quincy's lawyer, Swaby Lawton, brother of General Manager Charles Lawton, arranged the southern one: "I got out the notice yesterday for the citizens to turn out at the depot, and had bills and dodgers passed all over town. We had quite a respectable parade, about five hundred turned out in Hancock and marched

Figure 2.3 Quincy No. 2 Shaft-Rockhouse, built 1908. During the strike, Quincy built a watchman's platform on top of its shafthouse, the tallest structure around. Courtesy of Michigan Technological University Archives and Copper Country Historical Collections.

with Citizens Alliance buttons to the Amphidrome in Houghton. I did not get an opportunity to make a speech, but there were some very warm expressions of indignation."[6]

The companies used the prominence of their industrial buildings to their advantage, with searchlights in particular emphasizing their omnipotence. C&H installed a searchlight atop a water tower that was powerful enough "to show to the watchmen at the tower anything that goes on at any point in the Calumet community" and that supposedly shed light as far as the villages of Mohawk to the north and Atlantic to the south strongly enough at night "to make it possible to read a newspaper." Quincy installed a watchman's platform and searchlight on top of its No. 2 Shaft-Rockhouse (Figure 2.3).[7] The union used humor to disarm this invasion, titling a gossipy column in its local paper "Seen by the Search-Light."

Perhaps the greatest public display that the companies arranged was the National Guard. As soon as the strike was called, company managers pressured the county sheriff to request troops from the governor. Responding to his urgent and perhaps overblown appeal, Governor Woodbridge Ferris sent the state's entire National Guard—2,817 men. The National Guard had been increasingly used for strike duty at the end of the nineteenth century, intervening on the side of industry despite a rhetoric of peacekeeping and nonpartisanship.[8] In the Copper Country, the mines had initially ceased operations in an effort to avoid violence; the troops secured the peace and permitted the mines to reopen. Generally, the troops' duties were to monitor the unionists' pickets and rallies and prevent violence between strikers and strikebreakers in a nonpartisan way.

The National Guard's alliance with the company, though, was unmistakable. The companies gladly allocated space for the troops to set up their tents, so 525 soldiers camped on Quincy Hill, and in Calumet the troops set up their tents between C&H's library and bathhouse (Figure 2.4). Furthermore, C&H extended to the troops the very amenities that made them such a benevolent company. The company piped water and strung electric lights through the campsite. Troops were permitted to use the bathhouse and pool at no charge; nearly nine thousand National Guard trips were counted. C&H also provided trucks and automobiles, apparently being better equipped than the Guard.[9]

Beyond an indebtedness to the company for material things, the National Guard also incurred a social debt. Governor Ferris received an anonymous letter about the commanding officer of the troops: "It looks to me as if General Abbey was a guest of the mining co. instead of protecting the inhabitants of Red Jacket. He was spending too much of his time in the Calumet & Hecla Club house drinking champagne and smoking cigars on their expense." Two weeks earlier Ferris had expressed concern that his officers were "hobnobbing" with company officials; he cautioned both the adjutant general, Roy Vandercook, and the medical officer, Dr. W. T. Dodge, to appear neutral. Dodge defended his actions, noting that the companies' "office men" "collectively form the life of the place. They are courteous and extend social favors." He also noted that the enlisted men fraternized with strikebreakers: "Likewise the workmen who appeal for assistance and protection are friendly with the soldiers."[10]

OVERLEAF: *Figure 2.4 National Guard in Calumet, 1913. Michigan's governor sent in the National Guard, which camped on company property. C&H's bathhouse is in the background; electric lights and piping for water are visible on the left. Courtesy of Michigan Technological University Archives and Copper Country Historical Collections.*

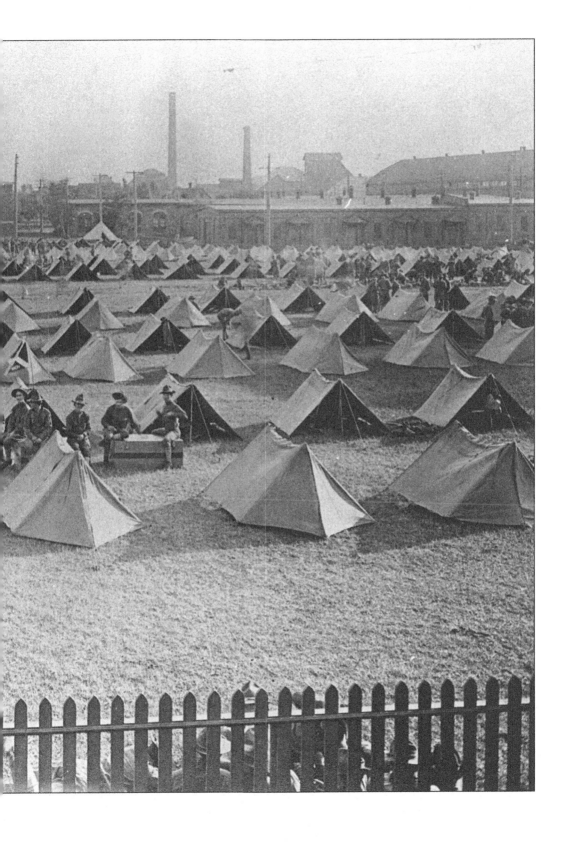

Figure 2.5 National Guard Armory in Calumet, built 1903, postcard view. Calumet's local unit of the National Guard occupied an armory on company land; C&H's library is to the left. Courtesy of Keweenaw National Historical Park.

Deploying the National Guard to the Copper Country was an expensive undertaking for the state, costing nearly four hundred thousand dollars. Ferris ordered about half of the troops out of the Copper Country on August 14 and continued to cut troop strength until January 12, 1914, when the last eighty-nine men were withdrawn. With the first withdrawal of the troops, the companies took over policing their own property, as the mines gradually began to reopen. They also hired policemen, predominantly from a company called Waddell-Mahon. The remaining National Guard soldiers patrolled villages and rushed to the scene of any outbreak of violence.[11]

Not all National Guard troops were outsiders, though; the Calumet Light Guard and the Houghton Light Infantry were also called up. The Calumet organization had been deployed during strikes in Ironwood in 1894 and Marquette in 1895 as well as in the intervention in Cuba in 1898. Its ranks included a large portion of C&H employees, and the other members were of course known in the community. These soldiers were placed in an uncomfortable position; at least two were threatened with reprisals from strikers. The newspaper reported that "one received an anonymous letter, and the widowed mother of the other was called upon by several men who told her that she might expect trouble for her son unless he deserted the company."[12]

The local National Guard had its own armories. Calumet's first armory was located on company land between the company's main works and the village. In 1903, with the Guard's popularity riding high due to its success in Cuba, the Guard received a new armory (Figure 2.5). Built by C&H and located between the library and the railroad roundhouse, the armory had a two-story, 81-by-42-foot headhouse with a low, hipped roof and two-story bay windows on the ends. The round-arched entrance of rough-faced sandstone gave the appropriate feeling of fortresslike solidity common in the castellated style so popular with armories. The armory was not very substantial, though; the rest of the building was a wood frame covered with corrugated iron for fire protection. Behind the headhouse extended the drill shed, whose arched roof indicated the iron trusses that spanned the 64-by-130-foot space. The headhouse furnished space for a gun room and locker room on the first floor, dining room and kitchen in the basement, and billiard room, reading room, and reception room on the second floor. The armory served as lodge rooms for the guardsmen, for whom service in the guard was a social, as much as military, undertaking. The presence of a large ladies toilet and wardrobe indicated the building's use for community functions, including balls and galas as well as high school graduations.[13]

There was also a National Guard company in Houghton, organized in 1885. In 1888 Quincy Mine Agent S. B. Harris was approached for a donation to the Houghton Light Infantry, which had been offered the former courthouse for use as its armory, but which would have to be moved. Harris donated two hundred dollars to the cause, arguing that "we, foreseeing possible labor, or other troubles, believ[e] that such an organization should be encouraged."[14] Like the Calumet outfit, Houghton's National Guard contingent served in Cuba. By the time of the strike, Houghton's National Guard headquarters were in the Amphidrome, the same public building used by strikers and procompany forces for rallies. The Amphidrome doubled as an ice rink, but its imposing façade had towers and crenellations that gave it a military appearance.

The unionists resented the Guard. Rather than the Guard preserving the peace so that less-committed strikers would see the folly of their ways and return to work, as the companies hoped, the Guard had the effect of further alienating the less-committed, thus solidifying strikers. This resentment may have been exacerbated by the Guard's use of company amenities. The strikers' publication, in an article titled "So Good to Soldiers," quoted a Guardsman extolling the gifts from C&H—bathhouse, electricity, trucks. The article called these "cheap bribes"—"Thousands of men can testify how susceptible the soldiers have been to these bribes and the return they may have made to the C&H by pick-handle excursions, and otherwise."[15] The "cheap bribes," unionists feared, further allied the troops with the companies.

The mine companies were well funded; the Western Federation of Miners was not. Propaganda efforts by the companies, including a pamphlet produced by the Copper Country Commercial Club and the formation of an antiunion Citizens Alliance, rallied public opinion to their cause. The shooting of three strikebreakers asleep in their beds in the Dally house in Painesdale on December 7 further alienated the public from the union. Yet just three weeks later, the greatest tragedy of the strike occurred, briefly bringing sympathy to the strikers. A stampede caused by someone apparently yelling "Fire!" during unionist Christmas Eve festivities at the Italian Hall in Calumet took the lives of seventy-three people, fifty-eight of them children. The loss of life shocked everyone. Some tried to use it to political advantage, charging the companies with provoking the stampede by the cry of "Fire!" But the union president's rejection of the twenty-five thousand dollars that was raised in a public out-pouring of sympathy, saying that the union would bury its own, discouraged public support.[16]

The strike dragged on until April. The congressional investigation that occurred in February and March received publicity but was inconclusive. Finally, the union ran out of money. After the national union announced a cut in benefits to its Copper Country strikers, the locals voted on April 12 to terminate the strike. Little had been gained. The companies had "voluntarily" instituted an eight-hour day, but they had also changed the calculation of shifts. The one-man drill was introduced, along with a state law that mandated that someone else be working within 150 feet of a driller; small comfort, perhaps.[17] Grievance procedures were formalized. But the companies never recognized the union.

The Seeberville shootings that began this chapter crystallized some of the issues of the perception of public space. On August 14, Champion Copper Company sent trammer boss Humphrey Quick, a Cornishman, to guard the E Shaft boiler house, which powered the pumps in E Shaft, keeping it from filling with water (Figure 2.6). Quick was instructed to prevent people from taking a path past the boiler house into Seeberville; as he testified later, he was defend-ing an unmarked "dead line." John Kalan and John Stimac used the "boiler house trail" daily and had even used it that morning. Stimac called it "the short cut we always take." While they might have been deliberately provocative once told not to take that trail, it is also clear that they assumed this was their right; it was a commonly used passage. All other routes through Painesdale were on company property as well, and the company did not try to prevent the strikers from walking through town. Despite the judge's finding that "none of these various roads or paths were public highways and it was within the rights of the mining company to close any or all of them temporarily or permanent

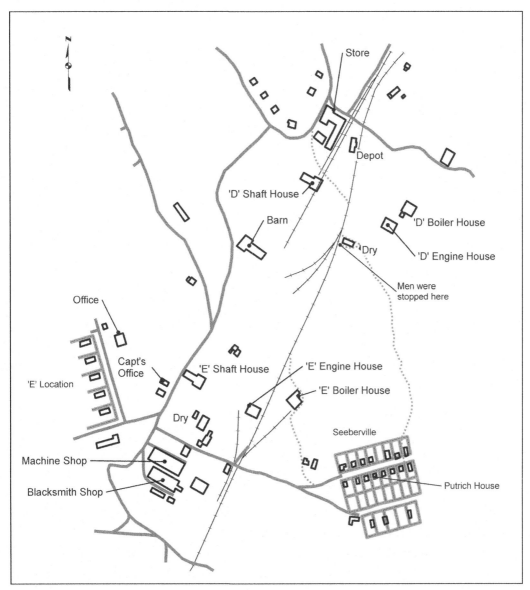

Figure 2.6 Painesdale, route of Kalan and Stimac, 1913. Based on a map created as an exhibit for the trial of the deputies, this map shows the trail past the E boilerhouse that Kalan and Stimac took, as well as the route on the east that they were directed to take, to their lodgings at the Putrich house. Map by Timothy A. Goddard, 2009.

whenever it saw fit to do so," the strikers clearly felt they had a right to traverse company property.[18]

After the altercation, Kalan and Stimac proceeded on to their boardinghouse. Humphrey Quick told Thomas Raleigh, a hired deputy in charge of the day-shift guards, of the incident when he came by; Raleigh took Quick to the mine office to

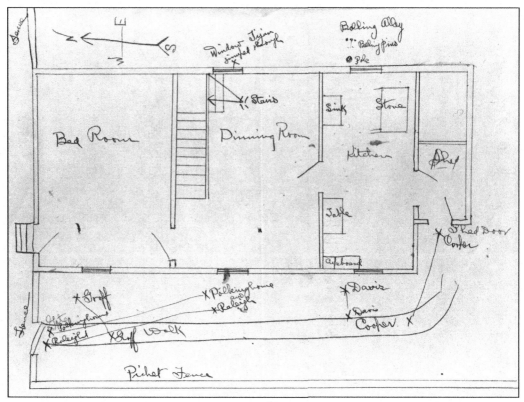

Figure 2.7 Putrich house, plan indicating where deputies stood. Attorney Swaby Lawton, hired to appeal the manslaughter convictions of company deputies, apparently drew this plan to understand his defendants' actions. He notes their locations outside the windows as they shot into the house. Lawton then sent the plan, along with other material, with a request to the governor for a pardon. Courtesy of Archives of Michigan.

repeat his story. Raleigh rounded up some deputies and hastened over to the Putrich house. The deputies jumped the fence into the Putriches' yard in their attempt to detain Kalan, but when he retreated into the house, they did not follow. Quick testified that one of the strikers said, "You can't get me now, I am in the house." At that point, according to their testimony, the deputies said, "Let's get a search warrant," and turned to leave, not shooting until a striker had hit a deputy with an object.[19] Thus the deputies saw the inside of the house as having a special protection, a privacy, which the outside did not (although their lawyer later disputed their need for a search warrant).

The shootings occurred in chaos and confusion, and subsequent eyewitness accounts differed. The court concluded, though, that five deputies stood at the three open windows on one side of the house and fired in (Figure 2.7). The deputies charged that the occupants of the house fired back, but no guns or bullets were found to substantiate this claim. Antonia Putrich testified that the dining room was so filled with smoke from the pistols that it was difficult to see through it. She ran out the back door, baby in arms, so close to the deputies that her child received powder burns on his face. When the smoke cleared, two men were dead or dying and two were wounded.[20]

When the deputies returned twenty to thirty minutes later to search the house for weapons, no search warrant was mentioned, presumably because the deputies were, by then, investigating murders. The deputies demanded the keys to the boarders' trunks and searched them thoroughly. The strikers were granted private property within company domain but only up to a point.

The shootings outraged the community, shifting public sentiment to the side of the strikers. Six deputies were charged with the murders. Judge Richard Flannigan was brought in from Norway, Michigan, to adjudicate the case when the local county judge, Patrick O'Brien, recused himself because he was a cousin of one of the defendants. The case went to trial the following February. Thomas Raleigh skipped out on bail, probably with the encouragement of the company; one man was acquitted; and the other four were convicted of manslaughter and sent to prison in Marquette.[21]

More so than the trial, the funerals provided an occasion for public display. When Steve Putrich and Alois Tijan, victims of the shootings in Seeberville, were buried in Calumet, more than thirty-five hundred people attended their funeral, lining Calumet's streets for the funeral procession (Figure 2.8).[22] Union leaders spoke at length, in several languages, at the gravesite. Similarly, when the Italian Hall victims were buried, twenty thousand people lined the route to the cemetery outside of Calumet. Public procession and display were very much a part of the strikers' strategy.

The violence and social divisions that marked the Copper Country strike were not unusual; a number of highly violent strikes occurred in late-nineteenth- and early-twentieth-century America. Labor violence reflected new conflicts in industry, as management attempted to consolidate control over an increasingly hierarchical workplace and an increasingly immigrant workforce responded by organized confrontations. Some of the most violent conflicts in the early twentieth century occurred in the mining industry. In 1912 coal companies in Kanawha County, West Virginia, evicted striking miners from their company houses. The strikers, organized by the union, set up tent colonies nearby. On February 7, 1913, less than six months before the Copper Country strike, company deputies on an armored train approached one colony in the dead of night and fired repeatedly into it, killing one and wounding a woman in her bed.[23]

Figure 2.8 Funeral of Steve Putrich and Alois Tijan, Calumet, 1913. Funeral processions were an occasion for public display; more than thirty-five hundred people attended the funeral of these men killed by company deputies. Courtesy of Michigan Technological University Archives and Copper Country Historical Collections.

At the same time as the Copper Country strike, Colorado coal miners, organized by the United Mine Workers of America, were on strike in Ludlow. When the Colorado Fuel & Iron Company evicted them from company housing, the strikers set up fourteen tent colonies on land that had been leased by the union. On April 20, 1914, the National Guard fired machine guns and rifles into one of the colonies during a daylong assault, then set fire to the tents in the evening. The bodies of eleven children and two women were found the next day in a pit beneath one of the tents. These victims were among the estimated ninety people who died in strike-related violence in Colorado alone.[24]

Tent colonies were, on the surface, a visible symbol of the strikers' homelessness. They also reflected the companies' near-total control of the landscape; strikers had no noncompany housing alternatives. But in the Copper Country, most companies did not evict their tenants, and the only tent colonies established during the strike housed National Guard soldiers and imported strikebreakers.

The Threat of Eviction

Eviction was the primary company tool by which control over worker tenants could be imposed. The companies' leases provided for it; C&H's, Quincy's, and Copper Range's leases contained identical language forbidding tenancy beyond fifteen days after the tenant ceased to be an employee of the company, whether because he was fired or because he voluntarily terminated his employment. Similarly, a tenant who leased ground from the companies and built his own house was bound to vacate it within ninety days of terminating employment. [25]

The companies usually exercised this control judiciously. In 1892 Quincy Agent S. B. Harris informed Mr. W. B. Bailey that, because his son, who presumably lived with him, no longer worked for Quincy, he would have to vacate his house. Harris gave him until three weeks after the last day his son worked. The companies also used the company house privilege to control behavior. One particularly egregious case was that of the Lynches; Harris wrote them (it is unclear if he was addressing Mr. or Mrs. Eugene Lynch): "Whereas serious complaints have been made to me by many of your neighbors that you are annoying and abusing them by your scandalous language and behaviour, now, therefore, this is to notify you that if any further complaints of a like nature are made to me, you, and your family, will at once be ordered from your house, and from the Quincy Mine Location. Take due notice, now." Similarly, at Copper Range, General Manager Denton threatened to evict Frank Santoni for selling beer out of his company house.[26]

But the real power of a company house was to discourage men from striking. Once they ceased working for the company, they lost their right to their house. It is remarkable that there were only a handful of evictions during the Copper Country's most turbulent strike, and those on the far south end of the district. Why didn't the companies use such a potentially devastating weapon? The answers are two-pronged: on the one hand, they tried to evict their striking tenants but were prevented by legal maneuvers and, on the other, few of the "troublemakers" lived in company housing.

Copper Range was the most forthright about trying to evict its striking tenants. About six weeks into the strike, on September 3, 1913, the company sent eviction notices to a number of strikers, giving some just three days to vacate, others six days. The language was terse: "This Company asks that [you] either go to work in its mine or vacate its house. You will be given until Saturday, September 6th, to comply with this request. Dated at Trimountain, Michigan, this 3rd day of September, 1913." Walter Dokmonovich, the lead plaintiff in the effort to obtain an injunction, had built a three-room house on Trimountain Company land. After the strike began, he asked for a lease but was denied unless he went to work. When he refused, the company told him to move his "shack" off company land or he would be forcibly evicted. The union's lawyers, Angus W. Kerr and Edward F. LeGendre, immediately obtained an injunction to prevent any evictions. Judge Patrick O'Brien accepted their argument that the eviction notices were illegal and that the companies were likely to carry out evictions in a violent and disorderly manner.[27]

Undeterred, Copper Range continued to issue eviction notices. On October 14, the company served notice on Joseph Putrich, along with many of his neighbors, this time citing nonpayment of rent. Apparently on advice of the union, Putrich and his neighbors paid their rent on December 1. Generally, the evicted strikers appealed their cases to Circuit Court Commissioner Herman A. Wieder, who heard landlord–tenant cases. When Wieder ruled against the tenants, they appealed to the circuit court. Thirty-seven Copper Range cases made their way to the courts. Joseph Putrich and his neighbors did not go before the commissioner until March 17, 1914, at which time Putrich was ordered to pay four dollars and fifty cents in back rent.[28] Copper Range General Manager Frederick Denton pursued eviction steadfastly and without reservation, but he was slowed down by the courts.

By contrast, Calumet & Hecla took a more paternalistic attitude. On August 11 the newspaper quoted General Manager James MacNaughton as saying, "We will not even evict a single tenant, striker or otherwise, for nonpayment of rent. . . . We do this because we know that our men have been misled." But there were two other reasons C&H did not evict. For one, there were not many strikers among its tenants. When the congressional investigating committee asked him about it in February, MacNaughton estimated that there were nine C&H houses and thirty-eight ground-rent lots occupied by strikers, out of more than eighteen hundred rented properties.[29] This is how quality company housing proved its worth: the company used the houses and lots as rewards to favored workers; in return, those workers were the least likely to strike against the company.

But, it turns out, MacNaughton was being somewhat disingenuous in his response. Under further questioning by the congressmen, MacNaughton admitted that C&H had served eviction notices to tenants of its company houses, but they were tied up in the courts. He made a point of noting that no one had been evicted. Quincy's lawyer asserted that C&H had "many times more eviction cases than we have," although C&H kept a lower profile.[30] So perhaps MacNaughton's reluctance to evict tenants was neither his paternalistic concern for his misled workers nor the loyalty of his tenants but rather that he was unable to. MacNaughton carefully maintained an above-the-fray, no-eviction posture, while his lawyers quietly proceeded with evictions.

The Quincy Mining Company offers a more shaded understanding of the eviction issue. William Todd, the president in New Jersey, was adamant that strikers be evicted, while the general manager at the mine, Charles Lawton, wanted to take a much softer approach. On September 6, Lawton attempted to collect rent from strikers, telling them that "their alternative is a workman for each house or the house." Even then, though, he expressed reservations about Copper Range's plan to evict its tenants. Pushed by Todd, Lawton pursued the eviction process, but he recognized that it would be counterproductive to evict all strikers, most of whom he would want to rehire. Recognizing the bitterness that the evicted strikers might feel, Lawton recommended that the company obtain fire insurance for all of the rental houses. He thought that the strikers might decide to "vacate by selling out their furniture to the Fire Insurance Companies, namely, incendiary fires." He was right; less than a month later, a double house burned to the ground. Lawton alleged arson. In late September he learned from Copper Range's lawyers that it would take twelve months to evict a tenant, "to go through all the various legal steps that the Federation can put up." He noted that "our men practically do not have any lease, but that is immaterial." Copper Range had what it thought was an "iron-clad contract," but still the union managed to get around it.[31]

On October 20, Todd ordered evictions. Lawton cautioned, "I would be a little doubtful of the results, fearing that we might stir up the strikers too much just at this time when they are becoming desperate before the general disintegration of their federation sets in." Nonetheless, he pledged to do as he was told. Todd reduced his demand, suggesting that they evict just the "worst element" among the strikers, and Lawton agreed. Lawton estimated that there were 23 men living in company houses whom he did not want to rehire, and he tried to oust the worst 12 of them. In addition, there were another 127 who were not paying rent, but whom he expected to rehire. One week later, Lawton added another 31 men to the list of those "whom we expect to carry eviction proceedings to a termination." Lawton cautioned Todd, "Conditions in the country are such that we cannot, as you know, at this time drive too hard, or be too arbitrary." A week later, Lawton reported that ten "very objectionable tenants" had moved out voluntarily, noting that it took some time for them to make new arrangements.[32]

Lawton recognized that persuading undesirable tenants to move out voluntarily was far preferable to eviction. One strategy of persuasion was harassment, such as obtaining search warrants for firearms in the houses of strikers. During one such raid in December 1913, in fifteen or twenty houses, the sheriff, aided by Quincy's deputies, found thirty rifles and shotguns, eight or ten revolvers, "quite a number" of billy clubs, and ammunition. Another strategy to coerce strikers to vacate company houses was to raise the rent to twenty-five dollars a month for those not working for the company. The raised rent had another purpose. When the court stayed evictions, tenants had to post bond equivalent to two years' rent; so by raising rent (which Quincy never really expected to collect), Quincy was also trying to increase the amount of the bond that would be required. At six hundred dollars per tenant, the cost to the union of covering the bonds would be considerable. In mid-November Quincy began proceedings against sixty-seven tenants, receiving favorable rulings from the circuit court commissioner. The union appealed sixty of these eviction cases to the circuit court (seven tenants had voluntarily vacated). On November 29, Judge O'Brien dealt Quincy a blow when he ordered that bonds be calculated on the basis of the rent last paid, not to exceed two hundred dollars. He also gave the defendants a ten-day extension, which allowed time for money to be transferred from WFM headquarters in Denver to cover the bonds.[33]

In December Todd was shocked to read that Quincy's lawyer, Swaby Lawton, had told the circuit court commissioner in discussions about the sixty-seven eviction cases that Quincy would rehire all of these men, if they so desired, and drop the eviction cases. Todd was adamant: "We should make every effort to get these families out of the houses as promptly as possible and not allow any of them to return to work under any consideration." Lawton countered that he had not promised that they would be rehired, only that they might ask. He noted that the commissioner identified them as Italians who wanted their jobs back and that "these particular men were mighty fine looking men and had money in the savings bank."[34] Once again, Todd's distance from the situation permitted him to be the hardliner, while the managers closer to the action expressed more ambiguity.

In November the WFM had approached company lawyers about a consent decree, in which the companies' right to evict strikers would be stipulated, but the companies would not evict until a certain date. The date was a sticking point. The union argued for April 15, insisting that it just wanted its families to make it safely through the winter. The companies urged a date in January, fearing that if the strikers made it until spring, they would prolong the strike through the summer. After the companies' request for a writ of mandamus from the Supreme Court was denied in early January, and it looked as though the union could delay evictions endlessly in the courts, the companies were finally ready to sign. The eviction date of April 1 was informally agreed upon. Announcement on January 27 of a congressional investigation, however, gave hope to the union, which then refused to enter into the agreement. During the monthlong investigation there was little movement on the evictions, but in late March, with Quincy still desiring to evict forty-five tenants, the consent decree was resurrected, with evictions holding off until May 1. C&H, Quincy, Copper Range, and a few smaller companies apparently agreed to this, but it was soon moot because the strike ended.[35]

After the strike, the union's lawyers, Kerr and LeGendre, claimed that they had successfully defended between five hundred and six hundred eviction cases, that although bonds were required "no man was held on a single bond," and that "under these eviction cases no strikers were thrown out of their houses." Yet there were a few evictions—perhaps fewer than half a dozen—that apparently escaped their notice. In Winona, in the far south end of the copper-mining district, about twenty miles south of Painesdale, the company evicted several striking tenants, apparently legally.[36] It is unclear why the union did not contest these cases.

Louis Zargnl, who was born in Croatia, immigrated in 1891 and came to the Copper Country soon thereafter. He became a U.S. citizen and had worked at Winona for eight years before striking in July 1913. He and his wife and baby rented a small house, four rooms and a kitchen, for four dollars and fifty cents a month. At the end of November, the company shut off the electricity. That did not faze Zargnl: "They say they turn off electric light. I say that is nothing. Lots of kerosene. Burn lamp with kerosene." The company then shut off his water supply, forcing him to go one-quarter mile for water. In December the company raised the rent to twenty-five dollars per month. On January 5, it evicted Zargnl and his family for nonpayment, removing their furniture from the house and dumping it in the snow. When asked how long he expected to use the company's property without paying for it, Zargnl responded, "I told him, 'when I work I pay you.' I never say I don't pay. I say when I work I pay everything fair." Zargnl's equation of rent and work is significant. His company house was so tied to work that he did not see rent-paying as separate from going to work; if he was not doing one, he was not doing the other. Zargnl also noted that three-quarters of the houses at Winona were vacant.[37]

The men threatened with eviction represented, to some extent, the ethnicities most active with the union. At Copper Range, General Manager Denton estimated that 142 houses in Baltic, Trimountain, and Painesdale were occupied by strikers. They were heavily Finnish (62) and Croatian (56); the others were Italians (10) and Poles (14). The Finns and Croatians were by far the biggest groups employed by Copper Range, comprising 31 and 24 percent of the workforce, respectively, at Champion six months before the strike.[38] For replacement workers, Denton recruited Bohemians and Armenians—ethnic groups not previously in his workforce, so that they would be unlikely to bond with the strikers.

At Quincy, Lawton also recruited ethnic groups—Germans, Russians, and Russian Poles—different from those on strike, which he identified as Finns, Italians, and Austrians. The Finns were also the largest ethnic group in the Quincy workforce, constituting more than half. After the strike, General Manager Lawton noted that the Finns were "the nationality above all others that gave me the greatest trouble during the strike." But he also noted that "some of the very best miners and trammers, as well as other workers in our employ, were Finns." During the strike, William Todd repeatedly cautioned Lawton not to rehire too many Finns, suggesting in November no more than 350, and revising that downward to 200 or 150 in January. Six months after the strike, Quincy employed 272 Finns. Five years later, Quincy employed 641 Finns, who constituted more than a third of the workforce.[39]

Unionist Land

In Copper Country the striking tenants who were evicted or who left their company housing voluntarily did not end up in tent colonies, as they did in other mining communities. Instead, there was enough noncompany land among the company-owned tracts to provide housing and, in fact, these communities served as core union strongholds. Many of the mines in the Copper Country had platted land for sale to private owners, usually at the very beginning of their mining ventures. In Hancock, near Quincy, Red Jacket, near C&H, and South Range, near Copper Range, the Western Federation of Miners set up local offices.

There were other noncompany villages as well. While Red Jacket Village was crowded and expensive, the nearby community of Laurium provided ample space for miners' houses and a more receptive atmosphere to strike activity. Near the company town of Ahmeek, known as Ahmeek Location, private interests platted Ahmeek Village and Copper City. Patrick Dunnigan, Ahmeek's marshal, deplored the militarization of his village during the strike: "I had the best little village in the country, and a man never got a slap in the face, either, until . . . they brought in the mounted police to ride over people and children in the street."[40]

Quincy Mining Company was also plagued by strikers on private land. Hancock was a stronghold, with an activist Finnish population. Up on the hill there were two other communities over which Quincy could exert little control. Near Quincy's Shaft No. 6, the five-acre village of Pewabic had been platted in 1859. Quincy had acquired the surrounding land when it bought up the Pewabic Mining Company's lands, but the village stood. Next to it, in 1896 Quincy platted 118 lots called East Quincy, which it leased. Together, these communities were known as Coburntown, but they also acquired the sobriquet "Hell Town," a reference to saloons there. Before the strike began, on July 10, General Manager Lawton learned of a meeting in Coburntown of underground men plotting strike action. During the strike, Lawton wrote, "we had a man and his wife arrested in Coburntown for intimidation. They frightened out three or four miners that had started to work. There are now two more that we are trying to locate over in that section."[41]

Farther northeast, near Quincy's Shaft Nos. 8 and 9, the village of Concord City was platted in 1895. Renamed Paavola in 1909, after its first postmaster and major original landholder, the community took on a distinctly Finnish cast. At first, Lawton encouraged settlement there, noting that his miners were buying houses from the defunct Arcadian mine, which Quincy bought out in 1908, and moving them to Concord City for occupation. "It expresses the returning confidence the miners have in the mine and their contentment to cast their lot with the future of the mine. In fact, I am very much encouraged to see it. I am encouraging the building all I can." But Concord City, too, became a thorn in his side. As the strike drew to a close, Lawton feared losing political control: "In checking up the voters of Franklin Township, we find that a great many of the Federation men who have left company houses, have gone over to Concord City to live, and still remain in Franklin Township. Therefore, the outlook for eliminating the Socialists and Federation men in the election of Monday next is not over bright. The idle labor vote seems to be very strong."[42] The political independence that homeownership brought—lauded by reformers—proved to be a problem for company managers who wanted to maintain political control.

Company Houses as Propaganda

Although the mining companies could not exert as much control over strikers through their company houses as they might have wished, the houses did serve another important function for them: propaganda. The generally high quality of the architecture and the low rents garnered favorable attention from most onlookers, and the homes' potential as propaganda did not go unnoticed. The Copper Country Commercial Club, a Chamber of Commerce type of organization, involved itself in the strike in mid-September, when it appointed a committee to mediate the strike. The club described itself as "an organization of 500 business men and others of Houghton and Keweenaw counties" that "should rise up and demand that violence, rioting and bloodshed must cease in this community." Quincy General Manager Lawton described the club to his president: "It consists of about twelve hundred members of the business men: the merchants of Houghton County. It was organized a little over a year ago. I think I am a member." He went on to describe the committee: "Mr. Edward Ulseth is a contractor and director in the First National Bank of Calumet. A man of considerable means. Mr. Henry Baer is a nephew of Baer Bros. and Mr. [John W.] Black is manager of the Van Orden Company dock in Houghton." He was certain they would support the mining companies.[43]

The committee apparently made little headway in mediation, with the union declining to participate, but three weeks later it issued an eighty-five-page booklet purporting to be an objective investigation into the situation, addressed to Governor Woodbridge Ferris. The complete text of the report was published in the *Daily Mining Gazette* on October 14. The committee had dutifully visited the mining companies, examined the documents provided, held hearings in Calumet that union officials declined to attend, and gone underground to inspect the mines. Their report is in many places a factual recounting of numbers of workers, amount of copper produced, dividends paid, and so on. Most of the report, though, deals in glowing terms with the "welfare work" of the company—the benefits given to the worker—and the bulk of that is the housing. The report lists, company by company, the kinds of houses and rents charged (using the same statistics collected and later published by Bureau of Labor Statistics investigator Walter B. Palmer) and includes nineteen photographs of company houses, as well as seven photographs of schools, libraries, and bathhouses (see Figures 1.2, 1.3, 1.10, 5.17). The photographs are impressive; usually oblique views down streets, they show a row or two of identical houses, with wide clean streets, fences and trees, and a notable absence of people. Most of the scenes are of C&H properties, or their subsidiaries', and three depict Copper Range houses, while Quincy declined to participate. Three of the photographs show log houses, which is surprising because log was generally thought an inferior material. But they are outweighed by neat clapboard-covered frame houses, freshly painted and seemingly well maintained.[44]

The Commercial Club's report also considered wage rates. Yes, wages were low, the reasoning went, but so was the cost of living. Company-house rents were demonstrably low. So was food. The report compared rents, grocery costs, and fuel costs in the Copper Country to those in Butte, Montana, a copper-mining town where the Western Federation of Miners had successfully organized workers. Their conclusion was, unsurprisingly, that the Copper Country's lower wages were offset by lower living costs, and that a miner was much better off in the Copper Country.[45]

The Commercial Club committee, in its role as volunteer mediator, also proposed a solution to the strike. Disregarding three of the strikers' demands—recognition of the union, abolition of the one-man drill, and a minimum wage—the committee met with the mining company managers and urged them to consider two other demands—the eight-hour day and grievance procedures. Surprisingly, the companies agreed, although they claimed that the eight-hour day had been in the planning stages before the strike.[46]

The Commercial Club's report was more effective as a propaganda tool. Lawton described an encounter with the wife of a striker, "one of our old time trust-worthy Germans," who had turned in his union card and gone back to work for Quincy. His wife, who was "very bitter" against the strike, told Lawton that she would take in more boarders if he would put an addition on her house, which he agreed to do. Lawton gave her a copy of the Commercial Club's report, which she had not seen. He thought it would have "a good effect" and wanted to distribute it to all of "his" miners. Quincy President Todd agreed, saying that "at least [it] will present facts that have not had their attention." Twenty-five thousand copies were printed.[47]

The Commercial Club's report also had some effect outside of the Copper Country. The support of other locals of the Western Federation of Miners (WFM) was critical to the success of the strike in the Copper Country, because they were funding it. Butte's WFM locals assumed a two-dollar monthly assessment of their workers to support the Copper Country strike, which they initially supported wholeheartedly. Their support gradually dissipated, though, as the Butte miners heard favorable reports of the conditions in Michigan and as they began to doubt that the WFM could win there. Photographs of neat, cheap houses undoubtedly helped to undermine their support. Angry at assessments that continued after the Michigan strike had ended, most members of the Butte local withdrew from the WFM in June. The strike took a heavy toll on the WFM as well, bankrupting it and forcing its reorganization in 1916. The WFM's Copper Country lawyers, Kerr and LeGendre, received only a fraction of what they were owed. In 1926

Edward LeGendre was still begging for payment, unable to meet his expenses in a copper-bust economy. WFM president Charles Moyer responded combatively, professing "little sympathy for the workers in the Copper Country" because they had left the WFM so heavily in debt.[48]

Company Boardinghouses

Housing was an issue during the strike, not because company houses were inferior and emblematic of poor working conditions, nor because strikers were evicted from them, but because the companies effectively used the housing to undermine support for the strikers. There was, in addition, a housing type that reappeared during the strike in a somewhat sinister way—the company boardinghouse. Companies built boardinghouses only when they were forced to supplement their workforce with single men, their less desired worker. The need arose in the beginning of mine operations, at times of labor shortage, and during strikes.

When the congressional investigators toured a Quincy boardinghouse that the company had built to house strikebreakers, company officials explained that "the Quincy Mining Company had never before engaged in boarding any of its men and had never operated a company boarding house." This was not true. In its infancy, Quincy had to board its workers because there was simply no alternative. In the early 1850s, Quincy deducted thirty-three and a half cents per day as a board charge from about two-thirds of its employees. In 1862 Quincy ran a boardinghouse that accommodated forty to fifty men. Two years later, the company converted an old hospital into a second boardinghouse, at a cost of almost four thousand dollars, and paid Bradford Grimes eight hundred dollars a year to operate it.[49]

The custom of building boardinghouses early in mines' histories continued to the very end of the nineteenth century. Champion Mining Company, which started operations in 1899, built a boardinghouse there by May, added another one over the summer, a third one the next year, and six more in 1902. Julia Hubbard Adams, daughter of the general manager, Lucius L. Hubbard, stayed in the first boardinghouse in Painesdale for a few days in 1899 while their house at E Location was being completed. She described it as a "camp":

The camp was one enormous room with double bunks around the sides where the men slept. Down the middle ran a long table with benches where they ate

Figure 2.9 Ahmeek bunkhouses, 1913. Companies housed imported strikebreakers in hastily built bunkhouses. The two-story streetcar station stands behind them. Courtesy of Michigan Technological University Archives and Copper Country Historical Collections.

and, after supper, played dominoes and checkers or struggled with pencil-smudged letters to the folks at home. At the right of the entrance were two huge wood stoves and a storeroom filled with barrels of apples, potatoes, and flour, and sacks of beans and what not. The cook, the biggest man I had ever seen, greeted mother at the door wiping his hands on the dirtiest apron I had ever seen. His feelings were obviously divided between pride and apprehension over this responsibility for the boss's wife. . . . He led us to our bunks which had been roughly boarded off for all of us. . . . Let me tell you about our first meal! In the first place there was no crockery. Our plates were the tops of lard tins, we used tin cups, and the salt, sugar and spoons were kept in empty tomatoe [sic] cans arranged along the centre of the table.[50]

Young Miss Hubbard's shock at the rough conditions of this boardinghouse stayed with her well into adulthood.

Fifteen years later, though, Copper Range's boardinghouse was displayed as a model of gentility to congressmen conducting the investigation of the strike. Quincy's lawyer, Swaby Lawton, who accompanied the congressmen, described it as "a very nice up-to-date boardinghouse which boards about seventy-five men; all the dishes were china and the kitchen was filled with pies." The congressmen also toured company boardinghouses in Ahmeek, where the wood-frame buildings were covered with tarpaper (Figure 2.9). Like other C&H bunkhouses, these probably had unfinished interiors with studs and rafters exposed (Figure 2.10). Swaby Lawton described them as "very fine bunk-houses, all built brand new, and apparently permanent. One I went in, Ping Foster was cook, and he is a good cook and I think they pay him $100.00 a month. All the dishes on the table were china, and they had a very swell supper."[51] The companies were obviously anxious to display boardinghouses with the best conditions to the congressmen. Swaby Lawton, for one, equated these conditions with china dishes and good food.

Company managers chafed at having to run boardinghouses, though. Frederick Denton, Lucius Hubbard's successor as general manager of Champion, complained: "We have built several large boarding houses for the accommodation of single men, costing about $10,000.00 each, but they have been failures as far as serving the purpose intended. . . . They were simply well arranged, with electric lights, individual rooms, a sitting room, lavatories, etc. The trouble was that the men preferred to board with families and we could not operate the boarding houses at the regular prices for board without loss, nor could we get boarding house keepers to run them satisfactorily even with no rent. We therefore shall not build any more." Quincy too struggled with boardinghouse management. Its solution was to support good boardinghouse keepers, as in this 1906 letter from General Manager Charles Lawton: "I have this day agreed to let an Italian build a large Boarding-House out at No. 8, upon the foundation of one building that was burned. . . . I have looked the matter up and find that the man is able to put up a good building; that he controls quite a number of Italians; and that he is a quiet and peaceful man."[52] This arrangement, though, was not considered a company boardinghouse, and Quincy did not directly run boardinghouses in its mature period, until the strike.

One of the effects of not evicting strikers from company housing was that there was no place to put the strikebreakers that the companies imported. In late September, Quincy began importing workers, and the other companies soon followed suit. These imports were often surprised to find themselves in the midst of a strike.

Figure 2.10 Bunkhouse interior, 1913. The caption, "C&H scabs at feast," on this union-produced postcard refers to the imported strikebreakers. Courtesy of Michigan Technological University Archives and Copper Country Historical Collections.

The commanding officer of the National Guard observed that of the first group of thirty-one men that Quincy brought in, seventeen joined the union. The safety of the imported workers who stayed with the company was of concern, because they were particularly reviled by unionists. It is unlikely they would have fared well dispersed in the community in company houses. Just as the strikebreakers were

brought into the Copper Country in heavily guarded trains, they were also kept in secured group housing. C&H set up boardinghouses accommodating forty to fifty men each, near the shafts. Photographs show large open rooms with exposed framing. The aforementioned Ahmeek boardinghouses had "a big barrier put up there to protect the federation men from Copper City, which lies over to the east, from shooting into the bunkhouses—this barrier is made of two thicknesses of two inch hardwood."[53]

Quincy's general manager, in making plans to bring in trammers by recruiting Italians in New York City, had to find accommodations for them. "We can arrange to board them," he promised, "or, if they could bring their own cook, we can house them in a colony—get a man and his wife to be in the crowd we could put them in one of our larger houses, or in No. 7 Dry which we have equipped." A few weeks later, he complained to Todd about the influx of strikebreakers: "Ordinarily, the men that you are sending in could be very easily cared for by the many families about the location; but when we have to provide cooks and camps, we are not in a very good position to care for them." Then he described the housing situation, which was complicated by having to accommodate National Guard troops and private policemen from the Waddell-Mahon Company: "We have the militia quartered in Quincy Hall; the Waddell men are in the Kitt house just this side, and are using the old No. 4 compressor-house as a bunk-house. The soldiers are quartered in the South Quincy Captain's office, and we have had to move out the four families in the big boarding-house by the South Quincy Captain's office, so as to quarter the cavalrymen. We have rigged up the south end of the old Quincy dry, where we can care for upwards of one hundred men or better." But Lawton was reluctant to put inexperienced workers to work all in the same shaft, and he could not transport them aboveground to another shaft because of the violence. As he said, "We cannot put all those green men at work just in No. 2 shaft, and in these chaotic times it is pretty hard to get them to and from No. 6 shaft—they have to be sent down into No. 2 and underground across into No. 6 shaft."[54]

The threat of violence also compelled Lawton to insure the boardinghouses "for every dollar's worth of insurance that it is possible to get," certain as he was that strikers would set them on fire. Operations were difficult; Lawton noted, "We are having boarding-house troubles galore, and have had from the start." Quincy turned to a professional to run its boardinghouses, hiring John C. Mann, proprietor of the Douglass House in Houghton, to operate four boardinghouses. Lawton continued to be plagued with cook troubles, and Mann lasted only about two months.[55]

Similarly, at Copper Range, General Manager Denton attempted to arrange boardinghouses for the imported strikebreakers without increasing the company's burden. "We have started up two new boarding houses, one to be kept by a Bohemian who has sent for his wife, and the other by the Armenians who will batch [i.e., live together as bachelors]. In this way we have made more room for about 30 more men. We shall expect soon to get still others out of the Company boarding house, who are as well able to board themselves."[56] The companies not only saw boardinghouses as temporary solutions for extraordinary circumstances, they also saw the boarders as temporary, so that the company boardinghouses would serve an intake function. Once the new arrivals got their bearings they would "board themselves," or find their own housing, making space for new arrivals. The boarders undoubtedly saw their situations the same way and may also have viewed their tenure with the company as even shorter than management did.

Several financial arrangements could be involved in boardinghouses. Ideally, from the company's point of view, a responsible couple, in which the wife ran the boardinghouse and the husband worked in the mine, would rent a building from the company and take in boarders. This was a similar arrangement to a house, just on a larger scale. The wife would have hired a servant girl or two to assist her. A second option, "batching" it, was for a group of single men to form a household and hire a cook. The company would not be directly involved in either of these arrangements. In a company boardinghouse, however, the company would hire the "keeper" and collect the rent and board. But even for the first option, the company had to equip the boardinghouses, at a cost of four hundred to five hundred dollars each.[57]

Lawton, the general manager at Quincy, also found boardinghouse preparations onerous. When the company president forbade the construction of new buildings, Lawton complained about the conversion of old boardinghouses. First, he had to gain possession, apparently by displacing whoever was in them. Then, "one of the buildings had to be renovated and changes made, so as to adapt it for use as a boarding-house; supplies had to be shipped in, some from Duluth, and some from Chicago—consisting of heating stoves and big ranges, or cook stoves, all of the kitchen utensils and dining-room utensils, and the beds and bedding," all of which took time. Furthermore, "long ditches had to be dug, and pipes laid to furnish the water; ditches had to be dug and tiling laid for sewer connections; the building had to be wired for electricity, as we could not trust to oil lamps; and barbed wire fences had to be built about the building to protect it against the invasion of strikers; extra lights also had to be placed outside as a still further protection," all of which took even more time.[58]

After the strike, the copper industry hit its most volatile period. Prices plunged in the summer of 1914, forcing companies to cut back production and reduce wages. But once the United States entered the First World War, prices soared and production rose. The Copper Country faced a severe labor shortage, having lost a considerable portion of its workforce due to the unsettled conditions and low pay. Detroit, meanwhile, was thriving, and when Henry Ford introduced his five-dollar day, thousands of Copper Country workers took heed. Congressman William J. Macdonald told the congressional investigators that the automobile factories in Detroit were full of young men from the Copper Country.[59]

Once again, in an effort to accommodate new workers, the copper mines built boardinghouses. In 1916 Quincy built a boardinghouse between the Pewabic and Mesnard shafts to accommodate forty to fifty men. The next year, the company enlarged or remodeled three more boardinghouses. Drawings exist for one of these; the April 1917 drawings reflect the enlargement of the boardinghouse near Shaft No. 8. (Figures 2.11, 2.12) The core of the building is a two-story, gable-fronted house, domestic in appearance but much larger than most houses. Accommodating a hundred men, the boardinghouse consisted of a living room, hall with stairway, and keeper's apartment in a linear arrangement in the central core. Perpendicular to one side was a dining room that seated a hundred. Perpendicular to the other side was a wing with some bedrooms and a bathroom with toilets and trough sinks; perpendicular to that was another wing with more bedrooms. The second floor, which was over the central linear portion only, contained more bedrooms. The rooms slept two or four men or, in one case, eight.[60]

General Manager Lawton registered his disapproval of the plan to enlarge this boardinghouse: "To have so many men congregated in one place would necessitate deputy sheriffs in control all the time, 24 hours of the day and would add to the expense of maintaining the boarding house, as there are apt to be more quarrels

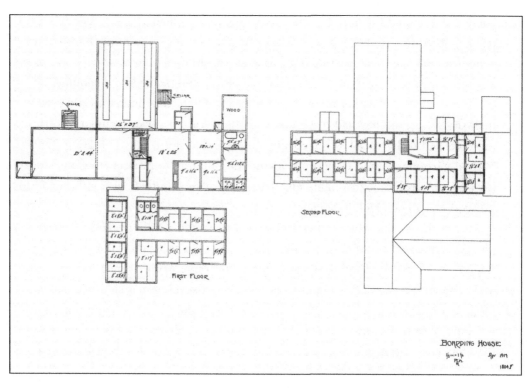

SECOND FLOOR

FIRST FLOOR

BOARDING HOUSE

Apr 1917

1804 F

and gambling occurring among such a large body of men together; and yet, as a temporary institution, it may be best." A few months later, Quincy President Todd noted, "While we do not want to get into the boarding house business, it is necessary for us to see that the boarding house is properly run and the men have proper food and attention." Three years later, the boomlet over, Quincy closed its remaining two boardinghouses, which were not financially viable.[61]

In the World War I period, Copper Range and Quincy rushed construction of new houses to accommodate an expanded workforce. Copper Range noted that its workforce was aging and therefore more likely to be married and needing a house.[62] By far the most common boarding arrangement was in houses, similar to the Putriches' arrangement. It was only in times of stress that mining companies resorted to undertaking the housing of single men, and then reluctantly. As a result, these boardinghouses' ephemeral appearance on the landscape indicates extraordinary circumstances.

Public spaces and private homes framed the conflict that tore through the Copper Country in 1913–14. The mining companies may have regretted the many platted towns and public spaces that were out of their control and that provided the arenas for displays of union solidarity and harassment of strikebreakers. At the other extreme were the company-run boardinghouses expressly built for strike-breakers, surrounded by barbed wire, searchlights, and guards. A more complex role was played by the company houses. In other mining districts, company houses during strikes meant mass evictions, with tenants retreating to tent colonies. In the Copper Country there were few evictions. Instead, the companies used their houses to favor certain workers, to engender company loyalty, to keep wages down, and as a propaganda tool in the battle for public opinion.

FACING PAGE, TOP: Figure 2.11 Quincy boardinghouse, plans, 1917. During a labor shortage, Quincy expanded a boardinghouse as shown in this drawing by "P.C.A.," or Peter C. Audette, the company's chief carpenter. Courtesy of Historic American Engineering Record.

FACING PAGE, BOTTOM: Figure 2.12 Quincy boardinghouse at Shaft No. 8, since demolished. The two-story core of the boardinghouse is obvious in this photograph. The dining-room wing depicted in the drawings is on the left. Courtesy of Historic American Engineering Record.

3 | "Home for the Working Man"
Strategies for Homeownership

After the strike, Joseph and Antonia Putrich stayed in their house in Seeberville, and Joseph went back to work for the company. In 1917, though, they moved to St. David, Illinois, where Joseph's brother John and father, Matthew, had immigrated to work in the coal mines. In St. David, Joseph and Antonia paid $1,025 in cash for three lots and a house (Figure 3.1). The one-and-a-half-story frame house, on a stone foundation, had four bedrooms. Joseph and Antonia lived there with their seven children. They cultivated extensive gardens on their large property, with vegetables, fruit trees, berry patches, a chicken coop, and a smoke house. For a few years, they took in a couple of boarders, but most importantly, they owned their house free and clear. Joseph and Antonia lived there for the rest of their lives, dying in 1949 and 1950.[1]

Homeownership—the very opposite of company housing—was perceived as an American ideal. As historian Olivier Zunz has shown, it was more often an immigrant ideal, with homeownership rates for that group outpacing native-born Americans during this period. Reformers promoted homeownership as a way to make good citizens. Company management promoted homeownership as a way to make loyal workers, through their implicit need for a steady income. Paradoxically, activist workers saw it as a way to gain independence from the company, which the promanagement newspapers noted in the waning days of the 1913–14 strike: "Not a few of the men that remained with the Federation since the strike was called last July own their homes, so the hardships inflicted on this element have not been so severe as others."[2]

In a paternalistic setting, though, where mining companies owned much of the land, homeownership became one more negotiation with the company. The management–worker relationship, so obvious in company housing, where the rent is deducted from the paycheck, was also a factor when the worker bought land or a house from the company.

Figure 3.1 Putrich house in St. David, Illinois, photographed 2006. After leaving their company house in Seeberville in 1917, the Putriches bought their own house in St. David, where Joseph worked as a coal miner.

The option that afforded the greatest independence from the company was to own land outside the company's influence. Many immigrants, especially the Finns, used mining as a stopgap job on the way to acquiring farms, where they could be self-sufficient. In 1926 one geographer estimated that more than 80 percent of the farmers in Houghton County began as miners. With the wages earned in mining they could buy some unimproved land. Wives and children would begin clearing the land and cultivating a few crops. The husband would continue to work at the mine, then shift to seasonal employment as the farm became more established, and finally become a full-time farmer.[3]

Most mine employees, though, lived closer to the mines and negotiated their housing arrangements in a variety of ways. Early in the development of the

Copper Country, the companies platted land for sale to private individuals. The villages that resulted provided a full range of commercial activities as well as accommodations for workers. The companies retained some control over the situation by charging low rents for their own housing on their own land, thus trying to keep the private rental market in check. At times the companies operated their own stores in an effort to keep costs of food and merchandise down.

As sites for privately owned workers' homes, though, these villages were not fully satisfactory because the demand was so great. As early as 1890 the Calumet newspaper declared that "houses in the village are at a premium." In 1900 the newspaper deplored the housing situation for workers: "Rents are far too high within a reasonable walking radius of either of the big mines and only the successful business or professional man can afford to pay the high rentals demanded for flats and dwellings in either Laurium or Red Jacket." In 1910 in the village of Red Jacket, 41 percent of households were owner occupied, higher than the nationwide nonfarm rate of 38.4 percent. But none of them were owned by miners or underground workers, and only twelve (3 percent) by men employed at the mines. The availability of Red Jacket's real estate for lower-income homeowners might have been limited because Red Jacket was an older village with intense commercial development. But even at South Range, platted in 1903 and touted as the "Home for the Working Man" in advertisements that advised "A Home of your own in a town surrounded by mines is a good thing to own," fewer than two dozen workers owned their own homes in 1910. Homeownership rates were lower than at Red Jacket—about 25 percent of the 396 households were owner occupied. Still, fewer than 6 percent of owner-occupied dwellings were owned by mine workers. In Hancock, Quincy's lawyer estimated in a statement before the congressional investigation in 1914 that "at least" three hundred Quincy workers lived "downtown" in their own homes on their own land, but it is unlikely that this figure was more than a wild guess on his part.[4]

In addition, in the Copper Country workers could own a house without owning the land underneath it. That several thousand residents opted to do this—build a house on land leased from the company—suggests that the home itself might have been more important than the land. Land was available, but the cost was prohibitive for many. One solution was to own more than one house and rent out the surplus, although the rental market was dependent, like everything else, on the company. Another solution was to buy land from the company in installments or, in rare circumstances, to buy a house and land from the company in installments. Quincy's offer of houses and land for sale in the early twentieth century was unusual. Because the circumstances surrounding it are enlightening and the ways that workers managed to become homeowners so creative, they bear examination here. After consideration of homeownership through purchase of land and sometimes house from the company, the strategies of ground rents and rental houses will be explored. Finally, long-term tenants' acquisition of company houses in the 1930s provides an opportunity to examine the ways that the new home-owners made their houses middle class.

Buying Land and House from the Company

In 1891 Quincy platted additional land next to the village of Hancock, a neighborhood that would become known as East Hancock. After extensive grading of the hilly terrain and laying of a water pipe, the lots sold well. Quincy stipulated in each bill of sale that the house to be built on the lot had to be at least two thousand dollars in value, thus ensuring that the neighborhood would be an exclusive one.[5] Copper Country businessmen and Quincy management found homes there, including the chief mining captain, Thomas Whittle, and Samuel Harris, the former superintendent, who shared a house with his son who succeeded him in that job, John Harris. The houses were, by and large, ornate declarations of status and prestige.

Thus, when Quincy started eyeing another piece of land that it owned adjacent to the village of Hancock for possible platting, there was precedent. Here, however, its motives were slightly different. The land concerned was just north of the village, on a steep hill occupied by a shantytown—an area in which residents had built houses without title to the land, paying a ground rent to Quincy. The houses might have been built by the occupants themselves; they probably were not elaborate, not on masonry foundations, no taller than a story and a half.[6] This neighborhood outside the city limits received no services in the way of water or sewer. There were few roads but probably many foot trails. To make its new neighborhood feasible, profitable, and respectable, Quincy aimed to eliminate the existing shantytown.

Quincy's motivations were threefold. First, profit: as in East Hancock, Quincy was willing to sell off surplus property at a profit, retaining the mineral rights just in case things changed. Second, civic-mindedness: Quincy had received some pressure about the hillside from Hancock village officials, who wanted to "clean up that part of the town." Quincy Treasurer William R. Todd claimed that the company's "chief object" was "to improve the general appearance of the property north of Hancock and in that way also add value and beauty to the village itself." If Quincy platted it, the village could annex it, control nuisances, and begin to provide it with services. But, third, Quincy's greatest motivation in sub-dividing this land was to provide housing to its workers. Quincy's employment had nearly tripled in a decade, burgeoning from fewer than five hundred employees in 1890 to close to fourteen hundred in 1900. The expansion of other mines meant a competitive atmosphere for new workers; if they could not find a place to live near Quincy's mines, they would find jobs elsewhere. Quincy built nearly fifty new houses to rent to workers in 1899 and 1900; it also platted more land to lease to workers, where they could build their own houses.[7]

None of those options were enough to satisfy demand, however, and Quincy was drawn to the idea of letting the private marketplace fill the void. Accordingly, the company platted the Quincy Hillside Addition to the village of Hancock, offering lots for sale in 1900 (Figure 3.2). Stipulations in the sales contract prevented the perpetuation of a shantytown on the site. The contract required that the purchaser build only one house on a lot, costing at least $750, with a stone or brick foundation. These requirements made building by the owner difficult. Other requirements were geared toward creating a presentable neighborhood: houses had to be set back fifteen feet from the front lot line, nuisances such as smith shops and livery stables were prohibited, and the sale of "any spirituous or intoxicating liquors, either distilled or fermented" was likewise banned.[8] Pre-existing houses were expected to conform to these strictures. Quincy also retained the mineral rights.

The company made an effort to retain the current occupants of the shanty-town. When possible, it drew lot lines to accommodate existing houses and offered those lots to their present occupants at a hundred dollars less than what it was charging the public. If occupants did not want to buy, they would receive that hundred dollars but be placed on a thirty-day lease. Still, as Quincy's real estate lawyer, Charles Hanchette, noted, "There are quite a number of people who have houses on this property, who are unable to buy the lots or to remove their houses."[9]

The solution that Hanchette proposed was that the company build some houses for sale or lease to these unfortunate homeowners. They would be cheap— eight hundred dollars or less. If these homeowners did not want them, they could

Figure 3.2 Map of Hancock, 1945. Quincy Mining Co. platted the blocks for the village of Hancock in 1859, the Quincy Hillside Addition (blocks denoted with letters) in 1900, and the Quincy Second Hillside Addition (blocks denoted with numbers) in 1903, in an effort to let its employees provide their own housing. Courtesy of Michigan Technological University Archives and Copper Country Historical Collections.

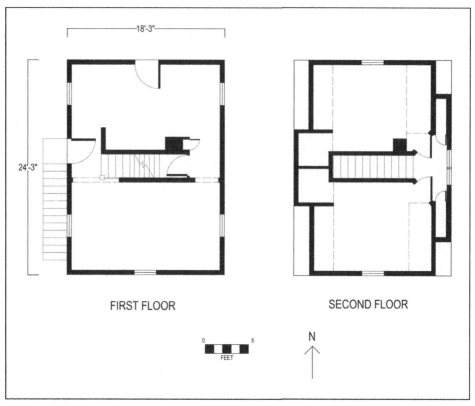

FIRST FLOOR

SECOND FLOOR

Figure 3.3 House at 327 Wright Street, built 1900, plans. Quincy built ten houses for sale in Quincy Hillside Addition to Hancock; this is the smallest version.

be sold or leased to company employees or to the public at large. As Hanchette wrote, "The only solution I can think of for getting these people out of the way is either to go to them and buy their houses from them, and then remove it or tear it down, or let the Quincy Mining Company erect eight or ten houses on say [$]400 lots, costing not to exceed [$]800.00 and sell them or lease them to these parties on such terms and conditions as might be applicable in each case. In case the houses were not needed to take care of these occupants, they could be used by the Quincy Mining Company for their men, or rented or sold to others." The company agreed, although in the process the "sale or lease" turned into sales, and there is no record that existing homeowners were given preference. By October 1900, ten houses were under construction. Quincy's one qualification was that sales be handled by the law firm, because "we want to draw a line here between this and the regular mine business." Todd must still have been thinking that the Quincy-built houses were to be rented, not sold, because he added that "in renting Quincy employes [sic] to be given preference."[10]

Figure 3.4 Houses at 331 and 327 Wright Street, photographed 2007. Quincy's houses occupied steep lots in its Hillside Addition, requiring high stone foundations.

There were three versions of the houses designed by architect C. Archibald Pearce and built by contractors Parker and Hamill: six basic four-room houses, which sold, with lot, for a thousand to twelve hundred dollars (Figures 3.3, 3.4); two five-room houses, with the fifth room forming a T-plan, which sold for fourteen hundred; and two six-room T-plan houses, which sold for sixteen hundred.[11] All located on one street, they had gable fronts with pent eaves, drop siding, and high stone basements. The smaller version measured 18 by 24 feet, with four rooms, the ones downstairs fairly large. A straight-run stairway divided the two rooms on each floor. Upstairs, the sloping ceiling reduced the space in the two bedrooms, but small closets were provided. The purchasers were mostly Quincy employees and mostly miners—skilled workers earning higher salaries.

Figure 3.5 Arvola House, 444 White Street, built 1900, photographed 2005. Christian and Anna Kreeta Arvola took out a three-hundred-dollar mortgage to build this small house in the Quincy Hillside Addition to Hancock and then added to it a few years later; the addition is not visible in this photograph.

The other lots in Quincy Hillside Addition sold well too, with prices in the $300 to $400 range. In 1900 Finnish immigrants Christian and Anna Kreeta Arvola bought one lot and paid $400, plus interest, over two years, in installments. They took out a $300 mortgage from the local building and loan association and built a small one-and-a-half-story house, measuring just 12 by 24 feet (Figure 3.5). Because of the steep hillside and provisions of the sale, it needed extensive stone foundations. The house was smaller than those built by Quincy for its workers, or for sale in the Hillside Addition, but it had possibilities. Just a few years later the Arvolas added a 12-by-12-foot wing, one room on each floor, set on wood posts. They sold the house for $1,250 in 1906.[12]

Of the ninety-three lots that were laid out in the Hillside Addition, Quincy sold eighty-six, mostly within three years. The new lot owners became homeowners; more than 80 percent of the houses were owner occupied. And of those, more than three-quarters were blue-collar workers. Seven of the fifty-nine owner–occupants were women, mostly widows.[13] As a working-class neighborhood that encouraged homeownership, Quincy Hillside Addition was a success.

Such a success, in fact, that Quincy immediately began plans for an adjacent neighborhood established along the same lines. Again, Quincy tried to accommodate extant houses. John L. Harris noted that he drew the lots to include, "as near as may be, the present dwellings; thereby giving the individual owners an opportunity of purchasing the lots on which their houses are located." Quincy Second Hillside Addition, platted in 1903, did not sell as well, though; only 64 of the 150 available lots sold, and only 54 houses were built. By 1903, other additions to Hancock had been platted, so there were more neighborhoods for workers to choose from. Reflecting this increase, Hancock incorporated as a city in 1903, with a population of a little more than six thousand. After two years of slow sales in Quincy Second Hillside, the company decided to set an example by building six houses for sale. This time, though, it pursued a slightly different strategy. As the newspaper noted, "These houses are to be an improvement over those formerly built by the company."[14]

Rather than lining the Quincy-built houses along one street in a pattern reminiscent of company housing, in 1905 Quincy sprinkled the houses around the neighborhood. Again, the company offered two types, but this time retained a new architect, Hans T. Liebert. Gauthier Brothers undertook construction of the six houses for $7,730. At an average cost of nearly $1,300 each, the houses were quite a bit more elaborate than the previous ones, and they were also in a different style. Abandoning the hall-less and T-shaped plans reminiscent of the nineteenth century, these new ones were similar to bungalows in their square shape and compact plan, thus tapping into national popular taste rather than generic company-housing strategies. The smaller version measured about 22 by 24½ feet, with a large entrance hall and two rooms on the first floor, and two bedrooms and a hall on the second floor under a sloping roof (Figures 3.6, 3.7). Quincy built three of these smaller versions, selling them for between $1,700 and $2,000. The larger version measured 25 by 29½ feet, with a foyer, hall closet, entrance hall, parlor, dining room, and kitchen on the first floor (Figure 3.8).[15] As a two-story building, the house had three spacious bedrooms with closets on the second floor, as well as a bathroom, and a large attic.

FIRST FLOOR

SECOND FLOOR

TOP: *Figure 3.6 House at 42931 Roosevelt Street, built 1905, plans. Quincy built six more houses, in two styles, for sale in the Quincy Second Hillside Addition. This is the smaller version. Measured by Pat Baird and Erin Timms in 2004, drawn by author.*

ABOVE: *Figure 3.7 House at 42931 Roosevelt Street, built 1905, photographed 2008. The small, shingled house, designed by architect Hans T. Liebert, offered a more "cottage" feel than contemporary company houses.*

Figure 3.8 Houses at 317 and 315 White Street, built 1905, photographed 2008. Quincy's larger houses in the Quincy Second Hillside Addition to Hancock had a plan similar to a four-square, with a three-fixture bathroom, closets, and porches.

There was one other effort at encouraging development of this neighborhood. Charles Hanchette, Quincy's real estate lawyer and brother-in-law of Quincy's superintendent, bought six lots himself and built speculative houses for sale in 1905. These houses were also of the compact, bungalow-type plan (Figure 3.9). Measuring about 24 by 26 feet, the house had a similar plan to the larger Quincy houses, but on a reduced scale. Three bedrooms and a bathroom on the second floor crowded under the gable roof. A dormer window was located in the south front. Hanchette paid $225 for the lot and sold it, with new house, for $2,250. In a house of this type, Ernest Spear, a brakeman for the railroad, lived with his wife, Margaret, and baby daughter. In another of these houses, Ole Peterson, a copper

Figure 3.9 House at 19547 McKinley Street, built 1905, photographed 2008. Quincy's real estate lawyer, Charles D. Hanchette, also built six houses for sale in the Quincy Second Hillside Addition, with a plan similar to Quincy's larger houses in the neighborhood. Two of the second-floor rooms were illuminated by a large dormer window on the south side, not visible in this photograph.

miner, lived with his wife, Hanna, their baby daughter, a niece, a sister-in-law, brother-in-law, and five male boarders.[16]

To market these houses, Hanchette suggested advertising by putting notices in Quincy employees' pay envelopes. Quincy still had two of its larger houses for sale, and Hanchette wanted to dispose of all six of his. As he put it to Quincy, "These buildings were erected particularly for the benefit of the Quincy in connection with its real estate, and also in connection with the supplying of houses for men at the mines." In his ad, Hanchette noted that the houses were "wired for electric light, and have bath room and water closet, with hot and cold water."[17]

With the two Quincy Hillside Additions, Quincy engineered an upgrading of the former shantytown to a level that it achieved middle-class status in some respects. It did not have sewers throughout, and paved roads were still years away, but the neighborhood had clearly defined streets, an abundance of houses owned by their occupants, land that was traded on the open market, and a smattering of small but fashionable dwellings. With upgrading, though, came the risk that the target audience would be priced out, although that did not happen here. Working-class homeowners undertook a number of different strategies to enable them to buy lots and build houses.

One strategy, common in company houses as has been noted, was to take in boarders. Homeowners pursued this at different rates and at different times in their life cycles.[18] The strategy was to use the house to produce more income, offsetting the increased house expenses. It also shifted the burden for funding the home more onto the wife, whose responsibility the boarders became. And it undermined the single-family ideal that homeownership, in reformers' views, was supposed to cultivate. Although these houses seemed to represent middle-class ideals, they were not necessarily inhabited in a single-family, middle-class way.

Another strategy, one frequently pursued today, was to spread out the cost of the house over several years. Generally, this meant taking out a mortgage, which is a means of yielding ownership to a funder until the house is fully paid for. In the early twentieth century, the most common way of doing this was through a building and loan association. The first of these in Michigan was founded in the Copper Country in 1889. Northern Michigan Building & Loan Association was established, perhaps not coincidentally, by Charles Hanchette, Quincy's lawyer and erstwhile real-estate developer. The Northern Michigan Building & Loan "encouraged and aided workingmen to build homes for themselves," as the newspaper noted in 1894. By 1905, the building and loan association was advertising in Finnish and clearly courting the immigrant worker. For as little as twenty-five cents a week, a member bought shares in the association. The money raised through these sales was lent out to members at a rate of 7 percent interest. Members used their shares as collateral for their loans.[19]

Many homeowners found this attractive. In Quincy Hillside, three-quarters of the properties had a mortgage put on them. For example, in one year, beginning in April 1904, Sebastian Salfenauer, a contract miner earning about $60 a month, made a series of $5 payments to buy a $350 lot from Quincy. He and his wife, Rosalia, then took out a $900 mortgage from Northern Michigan Building & Loan, as well as a $300 mortgage from Charles Hanchette. They built a house, paying off both mortgages in 1913. But they used another strategy to pay them off: taking in boarders. Two Finnish families lived with the German-born Salfenauers and their three grown daughters. The use of mortgages appeared to reflect the value of a house as a commodity—using it to leverage cash—as much as using mortgages to build houses. For example, Mary Toomey mortgaged her house to Charles A. Wright, president of Superior Savings Bank, from which she also had a mortgage. With her mortgage to Wright, though, she guaranteed the appearance of Michael J. Toomey, probably her husband or son, at the U.S. Circuit Court in Marquette. If he had not shown up, she would have lost her house. Fortunately, he appeared at his court date.[20]

The other method of delaying payment, used by a majority of property owners, was installment purchasing offered by Quincy. Quincy allowed buyers to spread their payments out over time, gathering 6 percent interest. If the purchaser were a Quincy employee, the company would deduct it from his paycheck. This was particularly beneficial to those who bought houses, not just lots, from Quincy. Louis Brisson, a Quincy fireman, had eighteen dollars per month deducted from his pay for thirteen years to acquire his house, one of the larger Quincy-built ones, where he lived with his wife, Mary, and their ten children.[21]

One homeowner who used several of these strategies was Christian Arvola. Just six years after buying a four-hundred-dollar lot in Quincy Hillside, the Arvolas bought the largest of the houses Quincy constructed in the Second Hillside Addition. The new, two-story house, across the street and a block or two down, cost twenty-five hundred dollars (Figure 3.10). This large house offered one strategy to pay for it not available to him in his previous, small house. He lived there not only with his wife, two daughters, and two female cousins but also ten male boarders, most of whom worked at the copper mine. He also had another means of paying for the house. Because the seller was Christian Arvola's new employer, the Quincy Mining Company, Arvola had the company take money out of his paycheck. He paid twenty-five dollars a month for ten years, out of his earnings of about sixty-five dollars a month as a contract miner. This financial arrangement did not, apparently, make him any more loyal a worker. His payments stopped abruptly in July 1913 when he went on strike. He returned to work three months after the strike ended and resumed payments in June 1915. He finally acquired the deed a year later.[22]

There were failures, though, too. Gabriel and Jennie Moreau had been living with their family in the shantytown that predated the Quincy Hillside Addition, probably in one of the substandard or inconveniently placed houses that Quincy wanted moved. In 1901 the Moreaus bought one of the ten houses that Quincy built to house displaced residents. The sale price was twelve hundred dollars and

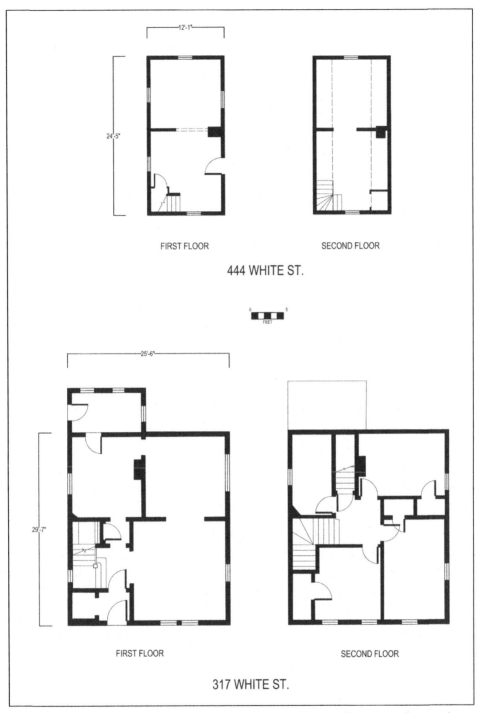

FIRST FLOOR   SECOND FLOOR

444 WHITE ST.

0   5
FEET

FIRST FLOOR   SECOND FLOOR

317 WHITE ST.

Figure 3.10 Houses at 444 and 317 White Street, built 1900 and 1905, plans. These plans, to the same scale, show the size difference in the houses owned by the Arvolas. Quincy built the house at 317 White, and the Arvolas purchased it in installments, taking in ten boarders so that the house paid for itself.

after sixty-two payments over eight years, the Moreaus were only halfway toward paying off their house. Gabriel Moreau worked a variety of unskilled jobs, listed variously as a teamster, a wagon driver for a lumber company, a laborer, and a shipping clerk for a meatpacking company. When he and Jennie moved into their house, they had six children under the age of ten. The Moreaus stopped making house payments in 1909 and in 1912 were evicted from their house. Peter Orella then bought the house for eight hundred dollars, having Quincy deduct ten dollars a month from his paycheck. After Orella died in 1918, however, Quincy President Todd forgave the rest of the payments, "in consideration of decreased value and hard luck of widow Orella." Benefiting from Quincy's paternalism, Josephine Orella managed to hold onto the house into the 1930s.[23]

Working-class homeowners operated on the edge of affordability. Skilled workers were obviously more able to buy houses, even though taking in boarders was often necessary to make the economics work. Unskilled workers had a tougher time. Miners earned $60 to $65 per month, while unskilled trammers earned $50 to $55. The requirement that lot purchasers build a house costing at least $750 and the company's initial desire to build houses in the Hillside Addition to sell for $800 indicated what the company thought its workers could afford. Several years earlier, Quincy's superintendent had insisted that "few employes are likely to erect a building costing more than eight hundred, or one thousand dollars."[24] But in 1900 when Quincy priced its four-room houses at $1,000 or more, including the lot, it priced the shantytown's existing residents out of the market. Five years later, in Quincy Second Hillside Addition, the company's smaller houses went for $1,700 and up, putting them out of reach of unskilled workers; the addition of electricity and bathrooms made these houses even more unaffordable.

Yet, another question has to be asked about working-class homeownership, and that is if it is a good idea at all. Did homeownership free a worker from his dependence on the company, by not renting from it, or did it further tie him to the company, by reinforcing the need for a steady income? Detractors pointed out that precious capital was tied up in a way that further obligated the worker to his employer. The procompany *Daily Mining Gazette* suggested that home-owning strikers felt this pressure. In March 1914, just weeks before the end of the strike, the *Gazette* thought it noticed a wavering of resolve among homeowners: "These men feared the mining companies would soon refuse them work whether they quit the union or not. . . . All their savings were represented in the houses they had built and the improvements that had been made to the property. It is this class of men, the element that have more than a livelihood at stake, that met Sunday and decided to seek their former positions." The *Gazette* was not a reliable observer of strikers' actions, but it identified here the bonds that homeownership created—the necessity for a job. On the other hand, advocates of homeownership cited the solid achievement that it represented.[25] Regardless of the wisdom of such a purchase, in the Quincy Hillside Additions, workers wanted to own their own homes and sacrificed to do so, even at the risk of further indebting themselves to their employer. The strategies were impressive: getting a mortgage from a building and loan association, paying for land and house in installments, or having the employer deduct payments from wages.

The long-term view was not so rosy, though. As long as the Quincy Mining Company was thriving, Hancock's neighborhoods thrived. Quincy reached its peak of production in 1910, and the Copper Country reached its peak of population soon after. But after World War I, Quincy went into a permanent decline. In 1921, for the first time in fifty-five years, the company paid no dividends. Similarly, property values in the county dropped by nearly a third in one year—1920—and continued to decline. In 1920, just four years after paying off his house, Christian Arvola quit working for Quincy. He and his family left the area in a decade when a quarter of the county's population also departed. He sold the house for which he had paid more than three thousand dollars (principal and interest) to Eric and Hilma Seppala. The sale price was not recorded, but the Seppalas immediately mortgaged the house for five hundred dollars.[26]

Renting Land, Building a House

Another solution to the problem of the cost of houses was to lease company land and build a house, so that land acquisition costs would not be part of the expenditure. Ground rents were common in England, where they derived from feudal law, and Cornish miners would have been familiar with the system. Another possible antecedent might have been the concept of mineral rights, in which a landowner could sell the surface rights of land, down to fifteen feet or another specified depth, while retaining mineral rights below that point. Mine companies saw land in three dimensions, and what was on top and what was below the surface could be legally and conceptually separated. In 1862 the Pewabic Mining Company rented half-acre lots to employees, who immediately constructed twenty houses. Five years later, Pewabic issued a twenty-five-year ground rent to Henry Benson. He subsequently assigned it to Maggie Haggerty; Pewabic was acquired by

Quincy. In 1892 Quincy notified Haggerty that her lease was up and the company wanted to occupy the site. Quincy demanded that she remove her buildings and belongings, although Haggerty was then living in Hurontown.[27]

The ground-rent system was an easy way for companies to house their workers because the companies did not have to fund construction. Workers liked it because they could own their own homes and pay just five dollars a year for the lot. As Pewabic's annual report noted, it was "to the great advantage of the Company, as well as of their employees." *The Engineering and Mining Journal* heralded the merits of the system, giving a common argument for homeownership, which was that it created good capitalists, when it discussed C&H's plan to lease land in 1885:

> The company has lately adopted a policy with its employes [sic] that will place labor demagogues and socialists at a disadvantage that will be hard to overcome. During the past year, about thirty lots have been leased to employes. . . . This new departure makes the employes of the company citizens in something more than name, as the holding of property means taxation and consequent interest in the selection of the best men possible for officers to expend public funds; or in other words, seldom is a property owner found participating in the gatherings of socialists or so-called labor reformers.

The neighborhood where C&H started this system of ground rents was Blue Jacket, just east of the village of Red Jacket. Rather than extend the plat of Red Jacket, C&H adhered to a policy of retaining ownership of all lands it owned. By 1893 the ground-rent neighborhood of Blue Jacket had been almost completely built up with privately owned dwellings. Meanwhile, though, C&H had platted other lands to rent, including Swedetown, west of the village, where individual owners constructed fifty houses in 1890 alone.[28]

Something of the managers' states of mind about ground rents was revealed by Quincy Agent S. B. Harris in 1896 when he was platting 118 lots in a community called East Quincy, next to Coburntown. He first intended to sell the lots, then changed his mind. As Harris noted, leasing the lots "will pay us better than selling the lots for $50.00 or $75.00 each (as we talked about) and will give us the practical control all the time." Harris's change of mind was due to the copy of the ground lease that he acquired from C&H, calling it "the best thing of the kind that I have seen."[29]

The terms of these leases are critical because they delineate the riskiness or security of the venture. Leases usually ran for five years. Tenants were subject to restrictions: they had to be employees of the company; they could not sell liquor on the premises; they had to maintain good morals; and they could not transfer the lease without permission of the company. C&H even required that tenants get the company's permission before installing toilets or electricity in their ground-rent houses.[30]

In the nearly thousand ground rents that C&H issued in 1890 and 1891, the company included repurchase provisions. If the tenant lost his job or wished to leave and was unable to sell his house to someone else, the company promised to buy the house through a negotiated appraisal. An addendum to the lease, printed in the margin, qualified this offer by terminating it in 1911 and refusing to pay for buildings that were older than twenty years. Nonetheless, C&H seemed to regret the buy-back provision after purchasing more than fifty houses from ground-rent tenants. Trying to forestall these purchases, the company offered advertising space in the newspaper, hoping that tenants could find their own buyers. In C&H's subsequent leases, the company dropped the repurchase agreement; if a tenant left his job for any reason, he could take his house with him or sell it to an approved buyer. Otherwise, it would become property of the company.[31]

The strictness of other companies' leases fell somewhere between C&H's two variants. Before Quincy issued ground leases in East Quincy, Harris obtained a copy of C&H's older ground lease and adapted it, adding a provision that the valuation of an employee's dwelling that Quincy was obligated to purchase not exceed a thousand dollars. As Harris said, "Few employees are likely to erect a building costing more than eight hundred or one thousand dollars." Copper Range included repurchase as an option but not a requirement for the company and also asserted that the company could buy the house at any time, whether or not the ground-rent tenant was willing to sell. A Department of Labor investigator concluded that the terms of these ground rents were "drastic."[32]

The reasons for sale included wishing to move on or financial difficulties. Some of the ground-rent holders who sold their houses to C&H were located in places such as Buffalo, Minnesota, Chicago, Illinois, San Bernardino, California, or King County, Washington. Mortgages were frequently mentioned. George Fuller owed Roehm and Douglas, a real estate and construction firm, $1,000 on his house at 505 Blue Jacket in 1894. The house at the corner of Fourth and Elm streets was larger than most—two stories with a two-story bay window. It was also fancier than most; C&H land agent Henry Brett described it: "There are 8 rooms, a bath room and closets. The house is backplastered throughout, cellar under the whole and is wired and equipped for light even to lamps." Apparently unable to pay his debt and wishing to relocate, Fuller sold the house to Roehm and Douglas, along with one upright Kimball piano and a cabinet containing five hundred geological specimens for $2,900. A little over a year later, Roehm and Douglas sold the house back to C&H for $2,761 (probably not including the piano or the specimens). From Ohio, Fuller expressed relief that C&H bought it back at a price that covered his note, "even though I am out all that I borrowed on the house through your kindly aid."[33]

But usually, the records do not indicate a motive. In April 1903, the house at 720 Pine, also in C&H's Blue Jacket neighborhood, was advertised for sale in the newspaper. The two-story frame house with one-story wing stood on a stone foundation, although the newspaper ad did not describe it. Apparently there were no takers, because a year later Jacob and Ida Pesonen sold it to C&H. The odd sale price, $1,133, suggests that the price had been arbitrated.[34]

The houses that resulted from the ground-rent arrangement, like those built on private land, are difficult to characterize. A prospective homeowner could build a house himself, hire a builder, or buy one that someone else had built. Self-building usually leaves little record, except in items such as this one, where the newspaper commented on building activity in Florida Location, near Laurium, in 1897: "Nearly a dozen new houses are now on their way toward completion. Most of the residences are being erected by Finnish people and a great many are building their own houses."[35] Architecturally, houses on leased land took a wide variety of forms and sizes. Sometimes they were almost perversely different from company houses, like the one front-gable house in a row of side gables on Kearsarge Street in Painesdale. Some ground-rent houses appear to be identical to company housing, but some were undoubtedly smaller than company houses and either grew over time or do not survive.

Other ground-rent houses were decidedly larger than those the company provided. These larger houses caused some consternation; whether out of a concern that home builders were indebting themselves unwisely or because they were aspiring beyond their class is not clear. In 1890 the Calumet newspaper noted somewhat snidely, "From the class of buildings being erected on the company's property near the Red Jacket and at Swedetown, by the employes, it would look as if the company paid their men well, or they could neither build such fine houses nor furnish them when built, nor keep them running after they were built." Fifteen years later the newspaper quoted a local builder as saying, "There is going to be a lot of building this summer for men who are working on moderate salaries. . . . The desire to own a home is a laudable one, but the apparent ease with which one can

Figure 3.11 House at 25980 Cedar Street, Blue Jacket, Calumet, probably built 1887, photographed 2006, since demolished. Although this appears to be a single-family house, it always accommodated multiple families in varying spatial arrangements. The house occupied Calumet & Hecla land; its owners paid a ground rent of five dollars per year. Photograph by James A. Rudkin.

be secured under the present competition among contractors and builders should not influence the man of small means into building better than he can afford." Calumet & Hecla, though, was not so resentful. The company's 1894–95 annual report noted that ground-rent holders paid in taxes and interest about twice what company-house tenants paid in rent, but by taking in boarders the ground-rent holders "reduce their own rent to that of employees living in Company houses, and as a general rule are better housed."[36]

The spacious houses built on leased lots, then, could be deceptive. While appearing to be large, single-family houses with middle-class inhabitants, they were often packed with boarders. A house on Cedar Street in Blue Jacket illustrates this (Figure 3.11). Probably built in 1887, the 28-by-22-foot single-family house had two stories with a side-gable roof. A lunette in the gable end and narrow glass in the front door added some touches of gentility, but inside the plan had few frills. The center door entered into a small hall leading to the stairway, which divided the plan into two rooms on each side. The original owners were two men, Erik Kantor and Sacris Silvola, about whom little is known. They may have shared the house or used it strictly as an investment.[37]

By 1900 Louis Basso and his wife, Jennie, owned the house. Louis Basso, twenty-eight years old, had immigrated just seven years earlier, but he could speak English and owned the house free and clear. He and Jennie had three young children. Louis was a trammer, one of the lowest-paid jobs in the mine, but he could use the house to help pay for it. Living in the house were two other families: John and Johanna Gendroni and their two young children, and John and Theresa Tiorina and their baby. All the adults were Italian.[38] Like Louis, the men worked as trammers in the mine. By 1900 the house had gained a one-story addition on the west side.

Ten years later, all of these residents had left, but the house was still owned and occupied by Italians. Peter Baudino, a blacksmith, and his wife, Mary, owned the house and occupied the west side with their three daughters as well as another family: Mary Mileo and her three daughters. Although Mileo had been married for eighteen years, her husband was not living with them; she worked as a laundress. Also living in the house, in a separate unit on the east side, were George Ponsetti, a timberman in the mine, his wife, Jennie, and her sister, Kate Postello. Around this time, the house gained another one-story addition, on the east side of the rear, and another room on the back of the west addition. The house would have accommodated these multiple families fairly easily. At some point, a door between the two rear rooms was closed up, so that the four basic rooms could have been divided into two units of two and one of them might have had access to the second floor.[39]

By 1920 the Ponsettis had acquired the house. They rented the other unit to a Finn: Margaret Simonen and her five children. Margaret was married, but her husband was not present. Her youngest child was less than a year old. The Ponsettis continued to own the house into the 1930s. One-story additions continued to be made to the house, including one on the northwest corner before 1942 and one on the west side of the front of the house that contained a three-fixture bath, probably in 1951. A porch stretched across the front. There was also a toilet in a water closet off the second-floor landing and a sink in one of the second-floor rooms. At some point, as indicated by numbers on the doors, the house served as a rooming house. It was demolished in 2006.[40]

The house's descent into rooming-house use was paralleled by its lack of maintenance and patchwork of additions. But the house seems to have always accommodated multiple families. With the appearance of a genteel single-family home, the house might have expressed its first owners' ideal, but the reality of affording such a home on working-class wages meant that it saw a steady stream of boarders. Its location on company ground also helped the original owners build such a house by relieving them of land-purchase costs.

An examination of the larger Blue Jacket neighborhood finds that most of the homeowners attracted to the ground-rent situation worked in the mines. In 1900 seventy-one of the ninety-seven homeowners had occupations noted in the *Polk Directory*. Of these, only five were white-collar or commercial: a clerk at the mine, two shop owners, an insurance agent, and a clerk in a store. Seven were higher-ranking mine-company workers: trammer foreman, carpenter foreman, three timber bosses, an engineer, and a yardmaster. Twenty-eight were skilled workers, including twenty miners, while thirty-one were unskilled.[41] Similar to the Quincy Hillside Additions, blue-collar homeowners tended to be at the upper end of their pay scale and unskilled workers, such as Louis Basso, took in renters and boarders.

The neighborhood as described in the 1900 census—which coincided only partially with the tax-book definition of the neighborhood—contained ninety-two households in seventy-eight houses. The forty-five owner–occupants listed there appeared to use three strategies for homeownership: ground rent, which they all had; taking in boarders, which fifteen of them did; and taking in families, which thirteen of them did, sometimes renting separate units to them. The Bassos were the only ones to take in more than one family. The neighborhood was occupationally consistent but ethnically diverse: aside from the five women who headed households, nearly all heads of households worked at the mine. Of the ninety-two household heads, twenty-five were Finnish, twelve Italian, and ten Austrian—the more recent immigrant groups. The rest included fifteen Americans, eight English, six Norwegians, six Swedes, and a few Germans, Scotch, Canadian, Irish, and one Frenchman. Different strategies among ethnic groups are apparent in this small sample. The three Italian-run boardinghouses had most of the boarders, with fourteen, thirteen, and seven, while Austrians operated two boardinghouses, accommodating eight and six boarders, but none of the rest had more than four boarders.

The Italian and Austrian boardinghouses were operated by homeowners in buildings that were not noticeably different from buildings that housed nuclear families.[42]

This cloaking of multifamily residences in single-family exteriors was also found in Swedetown, where a few of the houses had two units, arranged on different floors. Rather than two front doors, though, as many two-flat buildings elsewhere had, these had a front door in the center. The stairway to the second floor, rather than running from the front of the house up toward the rear, began in the back of the house, close to a back door, and ran up toward the front. This design allowed easy conversion to single-family usage, once the homeowner was financially secure.[43]

Another ground-rent house on company land illustrates the use of the house as a survival strategy. Edgar Richards immigrated from Canada as a child and went to work for C&H in 1890. Over a thirty-five-year career with the company, he worked as a laborer and teamster; his last job, as a carpenter's helper, paid $3.40 a day. He and his wife, Minnie, and their four children lived in a company house on Rockland Street. On November 4, 1925, Edgar fell from a thirty-foot trestle at work and died from his injuries five days later. According to family legend, the company gave Minnie $50 and one month to vacate her house. She bought a double house on company land and used it to support herself (Figure 3.12). Research shows, however, that the story was not so simple. According to company records, Minnie received $3,672 plus $200 in funeral expenses from the company, in addition to $1,500 in insurance money. The 1930 directory shows her living in another company house, on Church Street. On May 4, 1929, she married John Urbon, a miner who was eleven years her junior. Five weeks later, Urbon was in jail for assault and battery, and he seems to have faded quickly from Minnie's life.[44] Perhaps because she married a man who was not a company employee and thereby lost her company house, she soon moved to the double house on Hecla Street.

The house had been moved from a couple of blocks away on Rockland Street, quite close to Shaft No. 15, around 1910 for George Kotze. The dwelling, a small side-gable double house, had received a one-story addition that boasted two hallmarks of middle-class status: a bay window and a porch. George and his wife, Mary, both Slovenians, lived there with their three children, seven boarders, a man and his daughter, and a widow and her son. In the late 1910s, George got a job at a stamp mill and moved his family to Osceola Township, so he rented this house out.[45] Perhaps bankrupted by her shady second husband and needing to provide for herself and four children, Minnie Richards began renting this house in the 1930s and taking in boarders. She and her family occupied the first floor of one

Figure 3.12 House at 56755 Hecla Street, Hecla, Calumet, built late nineteenth century, photographed 2008. This double house, privately owned on company land, served for a time as a boardinghouse with one operator, then again as a double house.

side of the house, while boarders occupied the rest. The family remembers the boarders using "hot beds," day-shift workers using the beds of the boarders on the night shift; every other Sunday, when the shifts changed, some boarders would have to sleep on the floor. The two-and-a-half-story house appeared to be a double house but was in fact used quite differently. Measuring about 30 by 42 feet, it was three rooms deep on each side, with an additional first-floor room added on one side, creating a 15-by-12-foot parlor with bay window, bull's-eye corner blocks, and fancier molding than the rest of the house. Interior doors connected the two halves of the house. The dwelling had running water but only a toilet in the basement; chamber pots were used upstairs.

Richards succeeded in eking out a living and raising her children. Kotze sold the house to another landlord in 1934, but in the 1940s Minnie Richards was finally able to buy the house. Because this house was on company land, the price was low enough that a widow who supported her family by taking in boarders was able to afford it. When her oldest son, Harold Edgar, returned to the area with his family after World War II, he occupied one half of the house, and Minnie the other half. Harold modernized his half, installing a bathroom on the first floor where there had been a dining room and adding picture windows to the front of the house. Minnie died in the mid-1960s. In 1980, when the neighborhood was platted, Harold bought the land under his house for $2,850 and continued to live in the house until his death in 2003.[46]

Department of Labor investigators were appalled at the ground-rent arrangement. Walter Palmer called it "strange that any person would build a house on land leased on such conditions" and "astonishing that 1,000 houses have been built on land so leased from the Calumet & Hecla Mining Co." He also mentioned that companies were refusing to buy the houses of strikers who wanted to move out of the area. He quoted the newspaper: "Some others of the strikers who own houses located on company land are finding out that they have a difficulty to which they gave little consideration. These men, realizing that in the past the company always stood ready to take their houses off their hands at a fair appraised valuation, presumed that unwritten law would always continue. Now they want to move to other camps, being unable to get their jobs back. They want the company to buy their houses. The company is not in the house-buying business right at this moment." Or as Graham Taylor wrote, "To an outsider one of the most inexplicable facts in the whole situation is the mental comfort of the people who thus build their homes on ground from which the company has absolute power to force their removal at almost any time."[47] It was clearly the arrangement that was most beneficial to the companies: they did not bear the expense of housing their workers, they retained control over the land, and, through that, they could exercise some degree of control over their workers.

Nonetheless, workers found this an advantageous arrangement, because it enabled them to build their own homes at less cost. And, not foreseeing the kind of conflict that would arise with management, they believed they had a certain buyer if they chose to leave. As one of the congressmen investigating the strike observed of the ground-rent system, "Miners have placed implicit confidence in the honor and justice of their employers in such cases."[48]

The major companies undertook the ground-rent system with different levels of enthusiasm, with C&H leading the way. C&H issued more ground rents (1,000 in 1913) than leases to company houses (804). Quincy had about half the number of ground rents (202) as company houses (468), and Copper Range about a quarter (144 versus 607).[49] The ratios reflect employee confidence in the respective companies as much as they do company policy. C&H, which paid well, was on sound financial footing, and had long-term employees, found ground rents to be popular among its loyal workforce, whereas Copper Range employees, looking at a young company, expressed less confidence in its future. The disparity among the companies may also reflect the relative wealth of the employees. C&H had older employees who had been in the Copper Country for decades, whereas Copper Range, as a new company, attracted recent immigrants with little savings. It is fair to assume that ground rents reflect employee demand as much as company design.

Renting a House

Rental houses were another strategy for homeowners. While owners of houses on company land often rented them out, houses on noncompany land were even more likely to be rented out—probably 60 to 75 percent of them. Just as with ground-rent houses, rental houses differed little architecturally from owner-occupied houses. There were few apartment buildings in the Copper Country. In denser villages and cities, tenants as well as owners lived on upper stories, above first-floor commercial spaces. Mostly, though, tenants occupied houses that at one time were, or some time could be, owner occupied.

An enterprising homeowner could build a house for himself and one to rent. Just as some homeowners lived with their boarders, others lived next to their renters. These rental houses were generally not architecturally different from their owner-occupied mates. One example of a rental house offers an illustration of this while also being distinctly different. A rental complex on 7th Street in Red Jacket Village housed the owner as well as several renters. But its layout was in a court arrangement uncommon in the Copper Country, and the construction was log, unusual in a time and place of sawn lumber.

Daniel Ryan, about whom little is known, acquired two 50-by-120-foot lots in 1879 and built two double log houses by 1881 and two more by 1884. Located on mid-block lots, these houses faced each other, creating a court. Each of these houses measured about 30 by 20 feet and was one-and-a-half stories high with a side-gable roof. The two units had separate entrances but shared a central chimney. One room occupied the first floor while upstairs each unit had two rooms under the sloping roof. The substantial log buildings were set on stone foundations.[50]

In 1889 Oliver and Stephanie Labine bought the property and added two more single houses adjacent to the rear alley, so that these two lots held six houses with ten units (Figures 3.13, 3.14). Oliver Labine, a barber, lived in one of the units with his family. In 1897 the Labines sold the two lots to Homer Forest, a single man with his "own income," as the census noted.[51]

In 1910 Forest boarded with one of the families, the widow Leona Lamarche and her three grown children, in one of the houses in his complex. Like Labine, both Forest and Lamarche were French Canadians. In 1908 Forest removed one of the log houses on Seventh Street and moved the former rectory for St. Anne's Church onto its site. This wood-frame building had a strikingly different appearance—vertical rather than horizontal and low, ornamented rather than plain, and irregular with bay windows and cross-gables rather than centrally massed. John and Josephine Luka, Polish immigrants, lived here with their four children. John was a laborer for the village, his older son was a salesman in a department store, and his younger son, age seventeen, worked as a drill boy in the mine.[52]

The double houses were converted to single houses by 1910. A French Canadian family headed by a shoemaker, a Slovenian family headed by a tailor, an Austrian family headed by a miner, and another Slovenian family headed by a mason for the mining company occupied the other units, illustrating the mix of artisan and industrial worker that characterized the population of the village.[53]

Just as the density on these lots reflected the density of the village during the boom times of Calumet & Hecla, the removal of these houses reflects hard times in Calumet. Between 1917 and 1928 two of the houses on the interior of the court were demolished. In 1929 Homer Forest sold off all but the log house he was living in. In about 2000, the other remaining log house was dismantled, allegedly to be reerected in Montana.[54] It is striking that the element of these buildings most valued, in the end, was the logs, which is also one of the most puzzling aspects. Why build in log when sawn lumber was cheaper, easier, and readily

FACING PAGE, TOP: Figure 3.13 Site plan of Labine Court, Calumet. The dense arrangement of dwellings on these two lots in Red Jacket Village reflects the scarcity of privately owned land close to the mines. Four log double houses faced each other across a court; then two more houses were built on the alley. The dotted lines indicate a frame house that replaced one of the log buildings. Map by Timothy A. Goddard, 2008, based on 1884 and 1917 Sanborn maps.

FACING PAGE, BOTTOM: Figure 3.14 Labine Court, built 1880s, photographed 1998. The house on the far left and the second one from the right are the original log houses. The house on the far right was moved there in about 1908, replacing another one of the log houses. The house on the left has since been demolished.

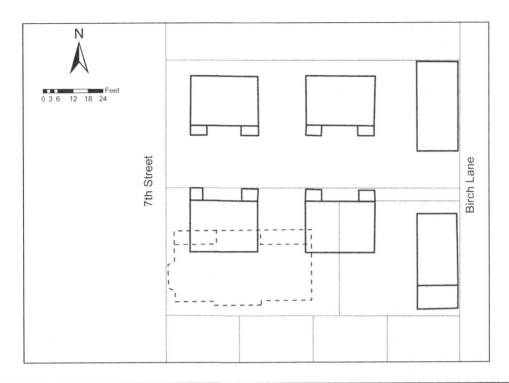

available? Log would also have been seen as less prestigious; the wood-frame building that replaced one of them would have had much greater appeal.

But what is more significant for historians is the layout of this complex in a court arrangement, reflecting the intense use of the limited space in the village. Surrounded by company land, Red Jacket Village could not expand, despite the great demand for noncompany housing. Yet, six separate buildings were not the *most* intense use; that would have been an apartment building. While such tenements were common in major cities in the 1880s, in the Copper Country single or at most double rental houses were the norm. Individual buildings also allowed the owner to spread out construction over several years, in contrast to multifamily buildings, which would have required greater capital.[55] Further, the occupation of these houses by their owners, along with numerous tenants, also indicates that rental housing was a strategy for homeownership as well as a temporary accommodation for aspiring homeowners and a permanent solution for those uninterested in owning a home. Homer Forest, with his "own income" and living on his own land, may have been independent of C&H and other mining companies, but to produce or augment that income, he rented to company employees.

Buying a Company House

Some residents achieved homeownership status by buying the houses they had leased from the companies. As the companies curtailed operations, or as successor companies reevaluated their holdings, they sold houses to the tenants for nominal amounts. C&H began selling its houses to their occupants in the late 1930s, while Copper Range started in the 1960s and 1970s. Just about every company house in the Copper Country is now in noncompany hands. One of the interesting effects of this move to homeownership is the alterations that the new owners make to their houses. There were several reasons for extensive alterations: the houses were old by the time of acquisition and needed refurbishing; rising expectations meant that occupants wanted more space, central heat, three-fixture bathrooms, and more; and the houses when built were inadequate, revealed by the changes required later.

Broadly speaking, the new homeowners upgraded their houses with middle-class amenities. A cursory examination of the former company houses reveals the kinds of changes that were made: new siding, new windows, reroofing, porches added or enclosed, garages placed close to the street. The houses that once shared a color and a texture—either clapboard siding or shingles—now sprouted a variety of finishes in a mix of colors. Double houses might be finished in completely different materials, split down the middle; if not, often they have been combined into one unit. Most strikingly, the uniformity that once characterized these streetscapes has been lost in a profusion of individualistic statements.

In 1938, with copper selling at only ten cents per pound, C&H put its workforce on half-time and began selling off its company houses.[56] Significantly, it did not sell the land; instead, it converted hundreds of houses to the ground-rent system. Rather than an act of empowerment to its workers, it seems a desperate attempt to shed responsibility for maintenance. All of the houses were at least twenty years old, most of them thirty or forty. The Copper Country had experienced severe outmigration during the 1920s, losing 27 percent of its population, as the copper industry began to falter. The outmigration rate slowed in the 1930s, though, when Houghton County lost only 10 percent of its population; it is thought that many of those who sought work in the automobile industry in Detroit in the 1920s came back to the Copper Country, where it was easier to eke out a subsistence life, during hard times in the 1930s.

In 1946, during a nationwide coal strike that shut down operations at C&H for five weeks, the company newsletter sketched some of the improvements that its employees were making to their homes in their new free time. In happy, human-interest photographs and captions, the newsletter showed some three dozen acts of home improvement, including Jimmy Adams hanging wallpaper, Jack Wilson adding an enclosed porch, and Art Marcotte putting up new siding. It was an optimistic, postwar period, copper was up to sixteen cents a pound, and Calumet seemed to be a worthwhile place to invest in one's home.[57] But rather than prosperity alone fueling home improvement, it is also intimately connected with homeownership. People tend not to invest in home improvements unless they own their own homes.

The photographs of home improvement are in some ways universal, delineating the kinds of changes that would be made for the next sixty years. In a country with long winters and average snowfalls of more than two hundred inches, one important impetus was warmth, so re-siding is common. In 1946 Charles Koupus put asphalt siding on his house, Art Kauppila did the same the next year, and in 1948 John Tolonen put wood shingles over clapboards (Figure 3.15).[58] Those sidings persist in the Copper Country, joined by cement asbestos shingle,

Figure 3.15 Art Kauppila painting trim after putting up new asphalt siding. From C&H News *and Views, August 1947, courtesy of Michigan Technological University Archives and Copper Country Historical Collections.*

aluminum, and vinyl. Insulation inserted between studs has also added to the warmth of these houses. New windows are also a commonly seen alteration today. The original windows and heavy wood-framed storm windows have been replaced with vinyl windows with built-in storm windows and screens. The new windows tend to be smaller and fewer than the originals.

Another common alteration was adding space, an implicit critique of the company house's small size. In the 1940s this was accomplished by enclosing a porch, as did Francis Hall and Pete Bracco, or adding an enclosed porch, as did Charles Larson and Joe Notario (Figure 3.16).[59] Another method is to turn a double house into a single. More recently, additions are less modest, and usually involve an attached garage.

Other alterations addressed serious shortcomings of the original houses, such as putting foundations and basements under buildings that had been on wood posts, as did Arne Karna and Oliver Michaud. More motivations for alterations include changing uses and new demands. While interior realignments were not

Figure 3.16 Francis Hall enclosing a porch on his gambrel-roofed house. From C&H News and Views, September 1947, Courtesy of Michigan Technological University Archives and Copper Country Historical Collections.

covered in the newsletter photographs and are not visible to the casual viewer today, items such as garages reflect new needs. George Geshel built a freestanding garage, and Herman Anderson built one adjacent to the house, projecting a few feet in front of it. More recent garages, despite the common use of snowblowers, tend to be built next to and slightly in front of the house, minimizing the length of driveway that needs to be plowed or blown. As historian Donna Zimmerman pointed out, this is a fundamental change to the use of the yard. Earlier, barns at the back lot line were converted into garages, so the first garages would be in the backyard. Cars would be decommissioned during the winter.[60] But placement toward the front means that people enter houses through side entrances or covered entrances accessed through the garage. Finally, and perhaps most importantly, comfort and convenience are strong motivations for home improvement, and these will be considered at length in the next chapter. Indoor bathrooms were certainly a priority for many but, again, not usually visible on the exterior.

The modernization of one company house will show the kinds of alterations that homeowners made. Isle Royale Mining Company built six-room, front-gable houses at its No. 2 Location in 1899–1900 (Figure 3.17). In 1948 the company sold one house to Peter and Alina Manninen. In 1975 their grandson and his wife moved in. The house had been little altered at that time. In 1980, though, the location received water and sewer systems, replacing the need for the hand pump at the kitchen sink and the privy in the yard. The occupants placed a new bathroom in

ABOVE: *Figure 3.17 Isle Royale No. 2 Location, built 1899–1900, photographed August 24, 1913. Company houses face each other across a muddy street. Courtesy of Archives of Michigan.*

RIGHT: *Figure 3.18 House at 47596 Second Street, Isle Royale No. 2 Location, plan of first floor. Home-owners altered company houses to suit their needs, as seen in this plan, in which hatch marks indicate walls that have been added and dashed lines indicate walls that have been removed. Measured by Larry Mishkar, Alicia Valentino, and author in 2002, drawn by author.*

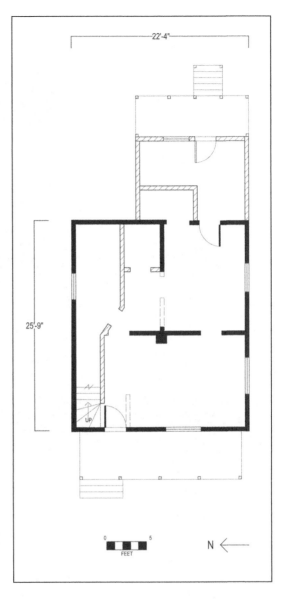

part of the room that had served as a first-floor bedroom (Figure 3.18). The Jungers two-burner oil heater in the living room was replaced with an oil furnace in the basement. Reacting to the warmth brought by central heating, the occupants removed the wall between the living room and the stairs to the second story, opening up the first floor. They covered the walls with paneling and drywall and the floors with carpeting and linoleum.

In 1984 they undertook changes to the exterior, replacing all of the windows and adding pressboard siding (Figure 3.19). In the front wall of the first floor they

Figure 3.19 House at 47596 Second Street, Isle Royale No. 2 Location, photographed 2002. Homeowners also alter the exterior, as seen here in the new porch, new siding, and different window sizes. Photograph copyright 2002 Larry Mishkar.

added a large, square fixed-pane window, but most of the other windows are smaller than the original, horizontal rather than vertical, with horizontal sliding sash. In 1998 they removed the barn, privy, and shed to accommodate a new two-car garage.[61]

The occupants have changed their company house in many ways, from altering room sizes to replacing windows. The alterations were driven by conveniences, such as water and sewer; warmth, such as the siding, the furnace, and the windows; and new needs, such as a garage rather than a barn. These residents did not gain official ownership of the property until 1997, but the house belonged to family members, and they never would have undertaken this kind of renovation of a house if it had still been owned by the company.

Workers in the Copper Country went to extraordinary lengths to own their own homes. A house was almost within the grasp of many workers, but it took some ingenuity and oftentimes hard work to make it happen. Creative financing was one solution, as workers explored building and loan associations, mortgages, installment purchasing, and ground rents. Creative use of the house was another means of making it affordable, as homeowners packed their houses with boarders or built neighboring houses to rent. Improving a house, either to sell for an increased price or to make it livable, was another strategy that reflected home-owners' uses of their houses. Yet homeownership, ostensibly offering freedom from company influence, was intimately connected with the company, whether the homeowner bought his house from the company on installment, built his house on company land, boarded or rented to other company employees, or bought an old house from the company and rehabilitated it.

4 | Acquiring Conveniences
Water, Heat, and Light

The house that Joseph and Antonia Putrich rented from the Champion Copper Company came equipped with cold running water, but that was its only convenience. The kitchen was located in a shed-roofed, tar-papered addition on the rear of the house, where water would have been heated on the cooking stove. Another stove, probably located in the dining room, heated the rest of the house, fueled by wood likely cut by Joseph Putrich on company lands. Out back were a number of outbuildings, including a privy and a chicken coop. Furnishing each company house with a bathtub was deemed unnecessary because public baths were located in the basement of Painesdale's library. Nor was the house equipped with electricity; the Putriches used oil lamps and candles.[1]

Conveniences such as running water, indoor toilets, central heat, and electric lights make an enormous difference in how people live in a house. People use rooms differently, depending on the light and heat sources. The convenience of having water, toilets, and heating fuel indoors, rather than out in the yard, affected circulation routes through the space. They also affected domestic labor—usually the work of women, who bore the burden of carrying water, emptying chamber pots, tending stoves and heaters, fueling and cleaning lamps. Ruth Schwartz Cowan's groundbreaking work on domestic technology pointed out that the acquisition of new technologies did not always mean less work for the women of the house; it just changed the nature of that work.[2] But what bears examination is how and why these new technologies were acquired and, particularly in the case of the indoor toilet, where it was located.

To some extent, the story of adopting domestic technologies is the story of bringing yard functions indoors. Rather than water reaching a pump in the yard, or a hydrant down the street, it was now available from a faucet at the kitchen sink. Rather than going outside to the woodpile, residents fed furnaces with coal that had been dumped into cellars. Rather than a privy in the backyard, an indoor

Figure 4.1 Putrich house, Seeberville, photographed 1913. The tall pole in the Putriches' yard supported a suspended ball used to play a type of bowling. The privy and sheds are visible in the backyard. Courtesy of Archives of Michigan.

toilet saved that trip. Even later technologies, beyond the scope of this book, maintained the same pattern: laundry is no longer scrubbed in washtubs outside, or in the wash house in the backyard, but is now done in a machine indoors. And only occasionally is laundry dried outside on a line any more; it is dried in a machine indoors. This shift of functions not only changed how the house was used but also how the yard was used. Yards were able to be devoted to lawns and gardens, both floral and vegetable.

Work and Play in the Yard

This discussion of conveniences begins, then, with the yard, and for this we return to the Putriches', which is well documented (Figure 4.1). The Putriches' yard was

Figure 4.2 Unidentified yard, probably Painesdale, photographed early twentieth century. Back-yard sheds appear to have been made of scavenged materials and might have housed a cow, chickens, and ducks. Courtesy of Michigan Technological University Archives and Copper Country Historical Collections.

hard-packed earth. No plants were visible, even in mid-August photographs, except for some flowerpots on a window sill. Measuring about 40 by 60 feet, the Putriches' was on the small side of yards in the Copper Country; Bureau of Labor Statistics investigator Walter Palmer found that yards were generally 50 by 100 feet. Just one mine offered yards as narrow as 25 feet, and several were much larger. Like most yards, the Putriches' was enclosed by a variety of fencing—vertical sticks, horizontal planks, and a few pickets. Copper Range apparently did not build fences for its tenants. Neither did Quincy until 1918, when General Manager Lawton argued that it was to help the workers care for their "war gardens." Calumet & Hecla provided fences; horizontal board fences appear in many photographs of C&H houses, in contrast to the picket fences that surround schools and managers' houses. Beginning in 1927, at the urging of landscape architect Warren Manning, C&H removed domestic fences and replaced them with barberry bushes to lower maintenance costs and improve the appearance of the locations.[3] The fence removal program also indicates that by that time animals were not a consideration.

The yard was an important place for food production. The lot behind the Putriches' was vacant until, it appears, they planted a large vegetable garden. Throughout the Copper Country, workers cultivated extensive gardens. They often grew potatoes, which were well suited to the climate, in community plots, while they grew other vegetables and fruits in the yard. During both world wars companies assisted tenants with their gardens, such as Quincy providing fences in World War I and C&H sponsoring Victory Garden contests during World War II.[4]

Mine families often kept cows, goats, pigs, and fowl for food. Chickens wandered around the Putriches' yard, and sheds along the back lot line included a chicken coop. Photographs of another yard, which is unidentified but appears to be in the north end of Painesdale, also show ducks and poultry sheds (Figure 4.2). In addition, this yard contains a larger

Figure 4.3 Putrich house, back, photographed 1913. A woman does laundry outside the kitchen door. A storm shed, which provided a sheltered entrance, and a woodshed are attached to the kitchen. Courtesy of Michigan Technological University Archives and Copper Country Historical Collections.

shed with a ramp to its door; it may have accommodated a cow. Some companies provided barns, particularly in the nineteenth century, and encouraged the keeping of cows by offering grazing lands for free for one cow per family. Children collected the family's respective cow at the end of the day and brought it home for milking, then took it to pasture again the next morning. C&H built single, double, and even quadruple barns for their tenants. The double barn measured 12½ by 20 feet and was centered on the lot line. The interior had two compartments, not connected, each with a stall.[5] Quadruple barns were placed at the conjunction of four lots. In Painesdale, though, the outbuildings appear to have been built by the tenants of scavenged materials. In the unidentified yard, the chicken coops are built of rough materials, the barn is board and batten with torn-away tarpaper, and attached to it is an addition built of log slabs. The Putriches' outbuildings have a similarly varied appearance, with a mix of roofing materials.

The one exception is the privy, which is a gable-roofed board-and-batten structure. Although some shingles are missing, it appears to have been built by the company in a uniform way. In 1913 none of Copper Range's houses were equipped with indoor toilets, and only half of C&H's. The companies commonly provided outdoor privies and cleaned them once a year. Like those in Painesdale, these were simple frame structures with gable roofs, set on wood posts. A C&H drawing depicts a privy that measured 5 by 4½ feet with a plank-lined vault and shiplap siding.[6]

Other domestic functions that occurred in the yard included laundry. In one of the Putrich photographs, someone, probably Josephine, is doing laundry in washtubs perched on wooden crates outside the kitchen door (Figure 4.3). She would have gotten water from the faucet, heated it on the stove, and then lugged it no farther than she had to. In other photographs, laundry is hung to dry in the yard.

Residents needed fuel to burn to heat water as well as the house. The Putriches had a woodshed attached to the back of the house, but open to the yard. It would have been possible to obtain firewood freely on company land. Companies provided coal upon request, charging about five dollars a ton for soft coal and eight for hard coal. Both wood and coal fueled stoves; furnaces were not introduced into workers' houses until after World War I. Many workers' houses had a chimney that began about 5 feet above floor level on the first story, then extended upwards. This "hung chimney" or "shelf chimney"—so named because it was partially supported by a wooden cabinet—was frowned upon by experts. In the prescriptive *Houses for Mining Towns* issued by the Bureau of Mines in 1914, Joseph White called this kind of chimney "hazardous" and recommended that chimneys be built "from the ground up." He also noted that few miners' houses had central heat due to the expense of building a cellar.[7]

Chopping wood and doing laundry were hard work, but at least one domestic chore was eliminated when water was piped indoors. Photographs of the Putriches' kitchen show the lone faucet (see Figure 1.23). In this, Copper Range and C&H were ahead of their competitors: by 1913 all of their houses were equipped with running water. Smaller companies such as Tamarack and Winona provided running water to more than half of their houses, while Quincy, Ahmeek, Allouez, and Mohawk had no houses with running water.[8]

Beyond being a place of work, the yard was also a place for play. Although most companies did not provide porches for their tenants, perhaps reasoning that it was an unnecessary expense for their workers, who did not need a space identified with leisure time, photographs show a number of recreational pursuits. A hammock adorns the front of one such porchless house in Trimountain (see Figure 1.8), while a swing set occupies the yard next to a log house in Ahmeek (see Figure 1.2). In their 13½-foot-wide side yard, the Putriches had created a level playing space by filling the otherwise steeply sloping yard. The play space was not for children but for the men's game of bowling, which involved a ball suspended from a tall pole and nine or ten pins on the ground. The boarders were engaged in this activity when John Kalan was approached by deputies, starting the incident that resulted in the fatal shootings. Joseph Putrich was sitting on a bench next to the house with his two-year-old son, Paul, watching the game. Bowling was popular throughout the Copper Country; there was an indoor bowling alley not far from the Putriches' house, in E Location.

Small houses meant that as much activity as possible, both work and play, took place in the yard. The Putriches were not alone in this; their neighbors would have used their yards as extensively as the Putriches did. In some cases neighbors would be quite close, as the Putriches were with their fellow Croatians, the Rusiches. For women, especially, the yard provided a place to socialize with neighbors. Where language barriers impeded friendships, neighbors were nodding acquaintances. Neighbors were bound by their employment with the same company and, at times, united in their opposition to it.

Yards underwent shifts in usage. Some buildings changed their functions, such as barns being converted to garages. In 1915, when John Caron's son won an automobile in a voting contest, he asked C&H if the company would change the doors on his barn to accommodate the car. By that time, the company had received so many requests for similar alterations that the general manager refused. The next year, Elbert Boyd asked that his barn be extended in length by four feet and that the floor be lowered to accommodate his automobile, but he too was denied.[9] Nonetheless, the conversion of barns to garages proceeded without company help.

While many of the yards' domestic functions moved indoors, food production in the form of vegetable and fruit cultivation continued to be important, at least for the Putriches. When they moved to Illinois in 1917 their new house was on a double lot where they planted extensive gardens. They made their own wine, sauerkraut, sausage, and other food items.[10] Bringing other functions indoors involved an architectural realignment and, of course, a negotiation with the company.

Conveniences in C&H Company Houses

On May 5, 1914, laborer Philip Miller wrote a letter to the general manager of the Calumet & Hecla Mining Company.

Dear Sir: While living in house No. 2628 Liberty St., Raymbaultown, and a very comfortable home indeed, I would like to ask the General Manager if he would kindly grant us a little favor, providing it would not make any trouble or extra expenses for the company. I would like to know if we could have a toilet put into our basement. As the old one which we have now is about 12 to 13 ft. away from the kitchen, which makes a very bad smell in the summer time and brings many flies. Hoping you will do this for us, and thanking you in advance, I remain Yours Truly, Philip Miller.[11]

In the 1910s C&H General Manager James MacNaughton demanded that his employees write him letters if they wanted to have utilities installed in their houses on company land. About four hundred of these letters survive, describing householders' desires for the new (to them) technologies of flush toilets, electric lights, and telephones. This collection of requests for basic services offers an opportunity to find out what his employees thought, in small measure, about their domestic arrangements. They also reveal the provision of conveniences to be another negotiation between management and worker. The introduction of utilities into company houses involved the convergence of desire and opportunity, reflecting the householders' aspirations (did they want them), the company's capabilities (could it provide them), and management's attitudes (should it provide them).

The householders usually wrote their own letters; at least, their signatures match the texts. Nearly all are handwritten, most of them in admirable penmanship. Occasionally a wife would write to MacNaughton, but the general manager replied to her husband; after all, it was the husband who had the official relationship with the company, not the wife. Only a few letters were signed with an "x," indicating a literate workforce.[12]

More than three hundred letters requested toilets. Although MacNaughton did not ask for a reason why a householder wanted a toilet, many of them felt compelled to give one. Because they could not argue that they *needed* a toilet—after all, they had managed for years without one—the householders tended to cite "convenience." They did not call them "necessary" or even "useful"; instead, repeatedly, they described utilities as a "convenience." Engineer John Hicks explained, "It being very inconvenient for grown people (especially women folks) and almost impossible for small children (especially in the winter time), to use the old fashioned toilets now in the back yard." Miner Thomas Ellis wrote, "It would be more convenient for my family because I have three children." William Becker said, "My wife is in poor health and it would be more convenient for her." Only one used the word "necessity": "Will you please investigate and consider the absolute necessity of a toilet. . . . The one now in use is so near the back entrance so that in the summer months it is very disagreeable." Several commented on the inadequacy of the existing privy: "because the one we got now is all rotten"; "the out side toilet makes an awful odor at this time of the year"; "because the out house, cause such an awful smell in the warm weather on account of the box leaking." Blacksmith William Taylor said both: he wrote in August, "As it is now [the privy] is right at the back door and is decidedly obnoxious and very inconvenient in the winter time."[13]

Some of the petitioners cited illness of someone in the family or the presence of children. Mrs. George Gipp wrote, "My mother is with me and she is blind and it is pretty hard to lead her when you got your work to do." Brakeman Daniel MacDonald wrote, "My wife is troubled with rheumatism and being out in the cold bothers her." As patternmaker Thomas Cocking said, "I have four small children and it is very inconvenient for my wife to be running out side so many times a day." Some cited sick children: "My child has turberculoses of the bone. . . . Now she has a Plaster Paris on the foot. And soon she will have to walk with crutches. . . . We must be careful in every way. She must not take any fresh air with her bowels. Mr MacNaughton please would you put the water closet in the house. That will help me very much for her care."[14]

Other householders felt it wise to state their qualifications. Four petitioners mentioned their loyalty to the company through the 1913–14 strike. In her request, Mrs. John Brown wrote, "My husband is working for the Company and he worked all through the strike." Others mentioned their long service to the company. Louis Nadeau wrote, "I have been working in the blacksmith shop for the last twenty-five years and think I ought to be able to have this done [have a toilet installed]." Still others pointed out that the sewer had been laid in the street so it would not be difficult to hook the house up to it. The sewer is here, it is no trouble to the company (the implication was), so give me my toilet. But others were more subservient; John Bracco phrased his request to install a toilet in his own house: "asking your permission, to have the privilege of placing a toilet in our basement."[15]

Similarly, householders requesting electricity gave reasons. Some mentioned convenience, but safety was a more common angle. Steven Kestner said, "Toilet is located in basement and is very dark, continually lighting matches makes it very dangerous, for this reason and the added convenience would like your approval for electric lights." Mrs. James Moyle noted that lamps were "inconvenient as well as dangerous." Mason Henry Peck, trading on the company's workplace safety program, said, "It will mean 'Safety First' for my family in every way." John Vertin reasoned, "because it is very dangerous with lamps where there are children always fiddling with them." One woman, who taught at Calumet High School, lived with her aged mother, and when a lamp exploded and caused a small fire, her mother did not notice. John German expressed some urgency: "I would want them in this week if you please for the lamps are very poor they smoke awful so I would like them right away." Mrs. Charles Nelson cited incapacitation; she was wheelchair-bound "and in the evenings it is so hard for me as I cannot carry lamps with me." Miner Oscar Larson wanted to give electricity as a gift: "Could you possibly put the lights in the house before Christmas as because I would like to have them as a present and surprise the boys for it will be their Christmas present."[16]

As with toilets, petitioners for electricity mentioned their loyalty to the company. Alex Kerr, a night watchman, stated, "I think my record as an employe of the C&H Company for the last 23 years justifies me in asking this favor of you." W. A. Sullivan, a clerk, lived with his father, who had been "an employe in the Underground Department of the Calumet & Hecla Mining Company for the last thirty years." Mrs. James Moyle, in her request written while the strike was on, said that she had recently taken eight men, presumably strikebreakers, to board.[17]

Occasionally, a superintendent would vouch for his employee, as when Foundry Superintendent McIntosh Morrison wrote on behalf of molder Charles Fien: "I think it may be good policy to give to such desirable men as Mr. Fien such inexpensive inducements as may be permissible to settle down and regard this place as their home and I hope you may be able to give his request favorable consideration."[18] Morrison understood the role that company housing, and even electricity, played in retaining good workers.

Because they would be paying for it, the petitioners believed that they had a right to electricity. In their requests, nine of them said that their neighbors had it and eleven said that poles were in their streets or alleys, implying that the service was close by and it would not take much effort on the part of the company to bring it to their house. "This is a double house and the family on the other side of the house have had their part wired for some time."[19]

Before workers could receive these technologies, the company had to be able to provide them. Mining towns are remote but dense, thus requiring city services on a small scale, and it fell to the companies to equip these settlements with utilities. The domestic water and electricity systems were supplemental to the industrial workings. C&H drew nonpotable water from Calumet Pond, an artificial lake it had created for industrial use. And it built a powerhouse to provide electricity to its machinery; after initially providing electricity to some houses, C&H let the local electric company take over the supply for domestic use. The only utility that served both industrial and domestic purposes was steam heat. Five boilers generated steam for the mines; C&H also piped steam to its offices, the school, the library, and the houses of a few managers. When Samuel Jess, a mining captain, asked that his house be connected to a nearby steam pipe, MacNaughton referred the letter to T. H. Soddy, the superintendent of motive power, to see if it were possible, then approved the request. But four years later, in 1917, MacNaughton ruled that "we will not permit of any more of our houses being connected with mine steam." The company would, however, install furnaces if the householders paid for them.[20]

In 1889 C&H undertook construction of a waterworks on Lake Superior in order to provide drinking water to all of its property; a second system for fire suppression used Calumet Pond water. For drinking water, an intake pipe extended twelve hundred feet into the lake, bringing water into the waterworks by a steam-powered suction pump. The pump then sent the water four and a half miles to a water tank on a small hill at Swedetown, where it was distributed by gravity to all of C&H's property as well as the villages of Red Jacket and, later, Laurium. By 1913 every one of C&H's houses had running water free of charge. Ground-rent tenants did not pay for their water service either.[21]

The village of Red Jacket provided the water free to public hydrants but charged people who piped their water directly to their houses. The village charged a dollar per month for the service. In August 1890, when the population of the village exceeded three thousand, the *Calumet and Red Jacket News* lamented that only 240 households had signed up for this service; if another 135 did, the cost would be lessened to all. The sale of water to Red Jacket and Laurium became hugely profitable to C&H; in 1906 MacNaughton calculated that Red Jacket, Laurium, and the Hecla & Torch Lake Railroad consumed less than 10 percent of the water but paid more than half (54 percent) of the operating cost of the water-works. For this reason, C&H actively discouraged the villages from going elsewhere for their water. In 1898, when Red Jacket Village considered getting its drinking water from the Tamarack Mining Company, Agassiz said, "I want the Red Jacket village notified that we shall shut out our [nonpotable] dam water [for fire suppression], and that we do not propose to supply them with one if we do not supply them with the other." In 1908 C&H lowered the rate from twenty-five cents per thousand gallons to eighteen cents. C&H's cost was less than ten cents.[22]

Along with a water system, C&H developed a dual sewer system, a sanitary sewer for household waste and a storm sewer for runoff. In 1893 C&H boasted that it had "complete drainage and sewage systems" in place, which it updated in 1901. Most of the sewage ended up in the aptly named Sewer Creek, which, as an investigating doctor put it, "loses itself in a swamp." In 1911, 263 of C&H's houses had "inside [water] closets," increasing to 325 two years later. The village of Red Jacket elected to build its own sewer system concurrently with C&H, tying into C&H's at the village line.[23]

But sewers were not always a foregone conclusion. In 1897 Laurium, then a young village, voted down the installation of sewers. One advocate of rejection argued that for a village with a lot of houses not yet paid for, carrying a debt of

$35,000 or $40,000 against the village was too much. Secondly, because Laurium residents received piped water and did not use wells in their yards, the use of privies was less of a health concern. Finally, he pointed out that few residents could afford to have fixtures installed to take advantage of the sewer system; he put the cost at $100 to $150 per house. Laurium soon reversed itself, however, and sewers were under construction a few months later.[24]

A typhoid epidemic in 1907 prompted a serious examination of C&H's water and sewer systems. MacNaughton brought in V. C. Vaughan Jr., dean of the University of Michigan's Medical School and a noted authority on typhoid, who provided a thorough report. The doctor pointed out that Calumet experienced a few cases of typhoid every year, usually no more than fifteen, in the fall and winter months. But this May–June outbreak of forty-eight cases was cause for alarm. Vaughan inspected Calumet's water and sewer system and found them satisfactory; he sampled water at several sites and could find no typhoid bacteria; he considered and dismissed milk, beer, and ice as causes. He noted that the cases concentrated in "congested and unsanitary" districts. He singled out Blue Jacket, where the greatest number of cases—seven—occurred. The one part of Blue Jacket where no cases occurred was Elm Street, "which is well drained, clean and free from cow dung." That also happened to be the one street where C&H owned the houses. In the village of Red Jacket, six of the ten cases occurred in three boarding-houses where men on night and day shifts shared beds.[25]

Vaughan's report made some mild recommendations, such as more frequent cleaning of privy vaults, particularly at boardinghouses, and the installation of screens on windows. MacNaughton's interpretation of the report was that "the water is held practically blameless," meaning that C&H's water and sewer systems did not appear to be the cause. Nonetheless, both he and Agassiz took the recommendations seriously. Despite the appearance of typhoid predominantly in noncompany houses, both Agassiz and MacNaughton perceived the epidemic as their responsibility, and their desire to prevent further outbreaks seems to have been sincere.[26]

By 1912, when the series of letters to MacNaughton requesting toilets began, nearly half of C&H's company houses had toilets. Generally, C&H's policy on toilet installation was that, if the sanitary sewer had reached the street where the house was located, the company would provide and install a toilet at no charge to the tenant. For ground-rent houses, the company would either install a fixture that the homeowner had purchased and take the plumbing expense out of his paycheck or encourage the homeowner to hire someone else. The company would also install toilets for charity cases at no charge. MacNaughton wrote, "You may install a water closet in house No. 3102, owned by Mrs. Mary Muretic, a widow, and charge expense of doing same to Charity."[27]

But where would the company *put* a toilet? Getting these utilities *to* the houses was only part of the problem; they then had to be accommodated *in* each house. They did not go into a bathroom. Most of these workers' houses were wood-framed, two-story dwellings of four or five rooms, generally lacking hallways, pantries, porches, and closets. By the early twentieth century, acquisition of a toilet was a task that required an architectural solution not a technological one. The sign of middle-class status, the three-fixture bathroom, was not easily won by the working class, and these Copper Country examples indicate why.

While the first element of the bathroom, a sink, was generally installed in company houses, albeit in the kitchen, the second element, a toilet, was more difficult. No room previously existed for it. Workers' houses were too small to sacrifice a bedroom to it. And the company was unwilling to build additions to houses to accommodate a toilet.

The most common solution was to put it in the basement. It is unclear if this is what the company limited its actions to, or this is what the householders perceived as the company's obligation, or this is where householders preferred that their new fixture go, but time after time householders requested that the toilet be installed in the basement. Miner Nels Olsen wrote, "I understand the Calumet and Hecla Mining Company is willing to install toilets in the basements of its houses." Similarly miner Michael Sullivan began his letter, "Hearing that the toilletts are being installed in the basements of the homes of those who wish them."[28]

Timberman John Messner requested that a toilet be put in his house "for the sake of Father." Messner lived at 151 Calumet Avenue, half of a small double house. The house had a 6-foot-10-inch high cellar, reached through a trapdoor in the kitchen. But there were few options for placement: the 550 square feet of the first floor of the house were occupied by a parlor, dining room, kitchen, and pantry; on the second floor, there were two bedrooms under the low gable roof.[29] MacNaughton granted Messner's request, and there is still a toilet in the basement today.

In 1914 nineteen residents of Laurium Street sent a request to MacNaughton. Because their gambrel-roofed houses were identical, it made sense for them to send in an identical request. They asked for an additional room on the first floor—volunteering to pay more rent "as compensation"—and to have toilets installed in the basements. The Laurium Street houses were exceptionally small, 18 by 25 feet, with only two rooms on the first floor (see Figure 1.9). MacNaughton refused to build the additions but did grant them their toilets.[30]

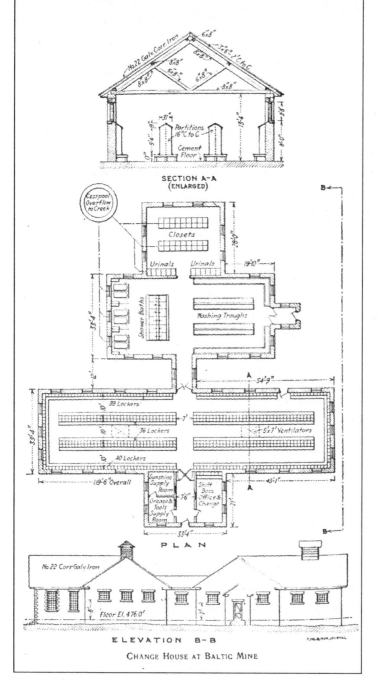

Figure 4.4 Change House at Baltic Mine, built 1907, published in 1912. The state-of-the-art change house at Baltic, featured in an industry journal, provided 462 metal lockers, wash basins, tubs and showers, and toilets and urinals. Although this facility was better equipped than most, mines commonly offered change houses in which miners could change their clothes and wash up. From Rice, "Labor Conditions," Engineering and Mining Journal, December 28, 1912.

Some houses, such as the Putriches', were built on wood posts without basements, although a trapdoor might give access to a root cellar. Stone foundations elevated houses off the ground and saved the sills from decay. C&H installed some stone foundations after construction, as a means of protecting its investment, but it drew the line at basement stairways. Access to the basement toilet was generally through a trapdoor, down steep stairs that resembled a ladder, and into a dimly lit space.

More rarely, the alternative to the basement was to give over preciously won closet space to the new utility. At the beginning of the twentieth century, C&H increasingly provided closets in new company houses. But in a house at C&H's stamp mill, the closet toward the front of the house was occupied by the toilet and the closet behind it by the bathtub. Each fixture filled up its allotted space, leaving no room for a sink; occupants used the kitchen sink for all sink functions. Even more rarely, houses were built with full bathrooms. C&H drawings from as early as 1898 labeled "miner's house," not a manager's house, were equipped with bathrooms, but it is not clear if they were actually built as such.[31]

The final ingredient for a three-fixture bathroom was a tub. Companies supplied tubs to workers' houses only in rare circumstances. Probably in an effort to forestall such requests, C&H provided public baths in the basement of the library that was constructed in 1898. These and other company baths will be discussed more fully in the next chapter. Company baths had two precedents. First, privately run public baths appeared in the Copper Country as early as 1862, evidenced by E. Romer's ad in the *Portage Lake Mining Gazette* headlined "Baths! Baths! Baths!" In 1910 Franz Isaacsen operated a bathhouse in Red Jacket, while John Johnson did the same in Laurium. Second, the companies furnished a change house or "dry house" near the entry to each mine shaft, which provided a place for each shift of men to change their clothes, leave their work clothes to dry, and wash hands and faces after work (Figure 4.4). Increasingly in the early twentieth century, these dry houses included showers. Having washing facilities at the shafts was a benefit to wives, who did not have to provide hot water to their husbands, as much as to the men themselves. A third alternative was the steam bath known as a sauna, preferred by Finns for bathing; a public sauna survived in Calumet into the 1990s.[32] Given these alternatives, the companies avoided installation of tubs in their houses.

Installation of a three-fixture bathroom in C&H houses usually did not occur until after the house had gone into private ownership. At 151 Calumet Avenue, Philip Messner got his toilet in the basement, as noted above. Much later, a subsequent owner built an addition on the rear to accommodate a full bathroom. Even later, an owner acquired both halves of the double house, converting it into a single house and putting a large bathroom in the room that had been one unit's dining room. Similarly, in the double house at 94–96 Pine Street, C&H installed toilets in the basements, reached through trapdoors in the kitchens. After the house went into private ownership, the two owners took different approaches to installing bathrooms. In the right half, space for the bathroom was carved

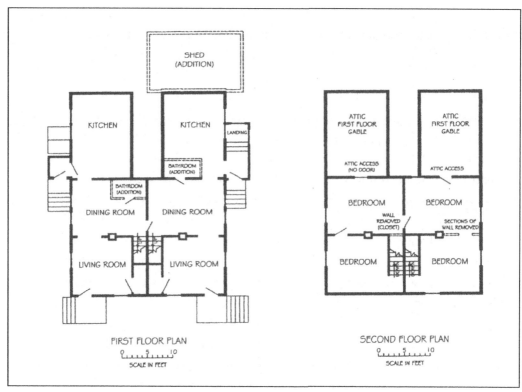

Figure 4.5 House at 94-96 Pine Street, Calumet, plans. Owners of the two halves of this former company house had different strategies for adding bathrooms. From Zimmerman, "From Paternalism to Privatization," 182.

out of the kitchen in the 1950s and in the left half, out of the dining room in the 1960s (Figure 4.5).

Electricity, another convenience desired by workers, was much easier to provide. In 1912 MacNaughton arranged with the Houghton County Electric Light Company that, in return for rights of way over company property, the utility would supply electricity to C&H houses—both company and ground-rent—at a bargain rate of eight cents per kilowatt hour; the regular rate was twelve cents. As MacNaughton explained it, his negotiation of this rate reduction with the electric company was at the request of his employees.[33]

As far as getting electricity *into* the house, MacNaughton's main concern was protecting his investment. As early as 1906, MacNaughton prohibited any tenants from receiving electricity from the local utility without his permission. In 1911 he outlined his revised policy for electrical installations in a memo to his electrical engineer, Frederick Bosson. MacNaughton declared that the company would not provide light fixtures, nor would it pay for wiring, but it would "undertake to see that the wiring is done according to its specification." Bosson argued that the company should do the work, "as the wiring contractors of the county are not careful in their work and do more or less injury to the buildings they work in, owing to the carelessness and hurry to finish the job. Should contractors do the work, then all work should be done . . . under the specifications of the National Code and inspected by the Calumet & Hecla." Bosson foresaw that "quite a few" employees would install electricity under these conditions and "the Calumet & Hecla would be a gainer by lessing their fire risk." MacNaughton accepted these conditions and added that if the householder left his house, he "will be entitled to take the fixtures with him but must leave the wiring undisturbed." Householders were to apply in writing to MacNaughton and then sign a form acknowledging the conditions.[34]

Two years later Bosson, his workforce inundated with wiring jobs, asked to subcontract the work and MacNaughton refused, seeing no rush: "It is not necessary that all the house wiring be done at once. Keep pushing it along as fast as you have opportunity and without increasing your force if possible." MacNaughton amended his policy in 1916, at least "in the numerous changes we are making at Lake Linden": "Where we move a man out of a house he has had wired at his own expense, we should wire the house into which he moves." For privately owned houses, the householder was encouraged to arrange for his own installation, although C&H would inspect the work. The cost for wiring depended on the house but averaged about twenty to twenty-five dollars, roughly one-third of a miner's monthly pay. Miner Richard John Nottle's request for electricity instructed simply, "Deduct 8$ a month from my pay until the same is paid for."[35]

Although MacNaughton required householders to send him a written request, he granted just about all requests received. He turned down one applicant because his house was slated to be moved and another because he had not paid his ground rent.[36] For each request, he asked his electrical engineer if poles were needed but then granted the request regardless of the answer.

The requests could be extensive. Blacksmith William Berryman rented an eight-room house on Elm Street in Blue Jacket to accommodate his wife Louise and their eight children (Figures 4.6, 6.8). He outlined his request: "Parlor, one chandelier, three lights; dining-room, one chandelier, two lights; five bed-rooms, one drop light in each; one drop-light in kitchen, one in both upstair and downstair halls, and one in basement." C&H's electrical engineer estimated the wiring cost, exclusive of fixtures, at thirty dollars.[37] Subsequently six of Berryman's neighbors in identical houses made the same request.

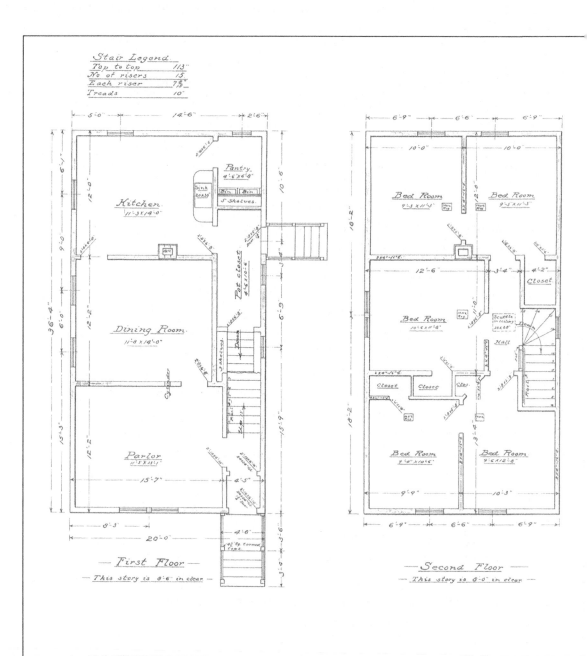

Figure 4.6 C&H eight-room house, 1900, plans. Blacksmith William Berryman paid thirty dollars to have lights installed in his company house on Elm Street, Blue Jacket, built to these plans. Courtesy of Michigan Technological University Archives and Copper Country Historical Collections.

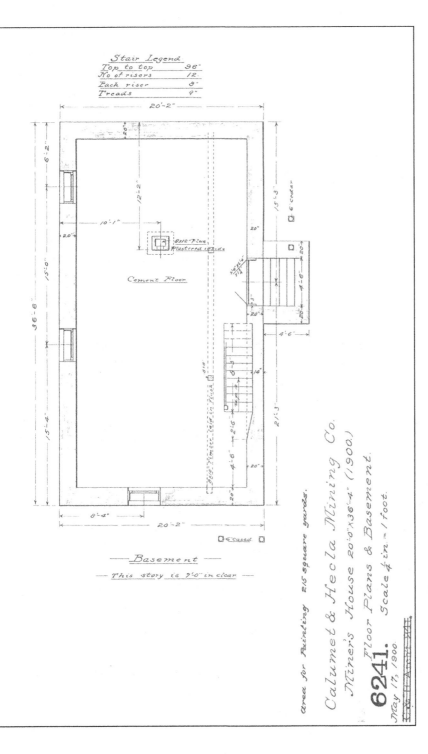

Stair Legend

Top to top	96"
No of risers	12
Each riser	8"
Treads	9"

8x12" Flue
Plastered inside

Cement Floor

6" cased

6" cased

8x10 Timber laid in Floor

Area for Painting 215 square yards.

Basement

— This story is 7'-0" in clear —

Calumet & Hecla Mining Co.

Miner's House 20'-0"x36'-4" (1900.)

6241.

Floor Plans & Basement.

Scale 4 in = 1 foot.

May 17, 1900.

Telephones were another convenience that C&H controlled. C&H managers received their home phones free of charge, placed on the Calumet & Hecla exchange. Other householders contracted with the Michigan State Telephone Company but needed MacNaughton's permission for installation. He invariably granted it, but the petitioners felt compelled to cite reasons. As William Moore, a stationary engineer at the Superior Engine House, phrased it, "We have a daughter who is a dress-maker, and a son employed as Agent of the Mineral Range Railroad. . . . On account of the nature of their work, they receive numerous telephone calls and we have to bother the neighbors to call us to their telephone very often." James Collie, superintendent of the stamp mills, requested telephones for Francis Gray, whose daughter was a professional nurse, and Michael Schenk, whose daughter was a dressmaker. James Berryman, a blacksmith, wanted a telephone because his wife had "spells" and she was alone all day. Thomas R. Eddy argued that "there is two in this house that belong to the C&H Band, and one that is a school teacher." Superintendent Morrison requested a phone on behalf of William Marcham, a core maker, who had moved to Calumet from Hancock, ten miles away, and "His wife being a stranger here, they would appreciate this privilege as she could communicate more frequently with acquaintances in Hancock."[38]

The question remains: why did MacNaughton insist on receiving written requests for the installation of utilities? There is no doubt that he micromanaged the process. Even though he was running a company that in 1915 produced seventy million pounds of copper and paid five million dollars in dividends, and even though he was introducing efficiency measures in accordance with management beliefs of the time, he did not proceed methodically with the installation of utilities. Hooking up all the houses in a street where a sewer had been laid would have been efficient and cost effective. Instead, MacNaughton waited until the residents asked for the utility. Having a lower-echelon employee track these requests might also have been more efficient, but MacNaughton insisted on signing off on hundreds of requests for toilets and lights. By contrast, the assignment of company houses, a much more contentious job, was handled by an employee; MacNaughton refused to involve himself in that.[39] Utilities were another matter.

This is more than a sign of an intense need to control. It also says something about MacNaughton's relationship to his workforce. The part of the workforce that rented company houses and lots was privileged. C&H's householders were not typical members of the working class, even in Michigan's Copper Country. They were skilled, relatively well paid, and mostly English-speaking—none of which was true for the rest of the copper-mine workers. They also had running water at twice the rate other copper miners in Michigan did, and they were three times as likely to have indoor toilets, so these householders were better off than most workers. Even so, or perhaps because of their exalted position, MacNaughton made them file a written request to have utilities installed in their houses. Despite the householders' perception of utilities as a convenience, not a necessity, and despite their sometimes obsequious language, they viewed these utilities as an amenity they deserved, or they would not have asked for it. Utilities involved a negotiation with the general manager, albeit one that was generally successful. By making his employees request something that they thought was their right, MacNaughton cast the new technology as a privilege and reminded his workers of their subordinate status.

Conveniences in Other Company Houses

Companies other than C&H were also faced with adding bathroom facilities. At Painesdale, Champion built a water tank of fifty thousand gallons and a pumping plant in 1899, just when the mine was being established, in order to supply both domestic and industrial uses. By 1907 all workers' houses were "supplied with water faucets in kitchen and cellar." After the first few years, Copper Range built managers' houses with fully equipped bathrooms, but bathrooms came much more slowly to workers' houses. Mary Grentz Butina remembered being the first tenant in Seeberville to get a toilet in the 1930s, which was installed in the basement. Her neighbor Joseph Sergey recalled the installation of his pull-chain basement toilet at the end of the 1940s. The company never installed a sewer system in its towns; Painesdale did not receive a sewer system until 2003.[40]

Quincy had a similarly reluctant approach to installing bathrooms. As at Copper Range, managers' houses were equipped with bathrooms early on. A clerk's house built in 1890, which apparently served as something of a boardinghouse for professionals, had ten bedrooms and two bathrooms. Wells or cisterns supplied the water. Quincy installed a "complete waterworks system" in 1916, drawing water from the No. 9 shaft and pumping it to a hundred thousand-gallon tank on a fifty-foot tower at the Limerick Location. The reliability of the water supply remained an issue, though, so that the company turned off the water at ten in the morning and turned it on again in the evening. Undeterred, tenants had "the habit of drawing water in the evening for morning use." By 1918 Quincy claimed to have fixed this problem by additional drilling in the No. 9 shaft, "so that at this time there is ample water for 24-hour service at all the mine locations."[41]

With the advent of running water, drainage became an issue due to the arrangement of having water from the kitchen sink run into the yard and under the house. In 1918, "Following out the plan of welfare work to improve the living conditions at the mine," Quincy began laying sewer lines. Building sewers for the Limerick Location cost four thousand dollars, and General Manager Lawton estimated a similar amount for No. 8 and Hardscrabble locations, but these sewers, which ran into ditches or streams, were for gray water only, not for indoor toilets. Once they were used as sanitary sewers, they would have to be piped down to Portage Lake, Lawton said, at an estimated cost of four thousand dollars.[42] Meanwhile, houses with indoor toilets used cesspools.

The complexity of adding a three-fixture bathroom to a house that already had too few rooms often meant an addition. After private owners bought a seven-room T-plan company house in Mesnard, they built an addition for a bathroom, apparently in the 1980s. Replacing a basement toilet, the 6-by-8-foot one-story addition was nestled in the corner of the T, off the dining room.[43] This was precisely the spot that earlier Quincy drawings had placed a pantry in some versions of the seven-room T-plan that it built.

At a saltbox on U.S. Highway 41, Quincy undertook a different kind of addition. The Pewabic Mining Company had built the saltbox about 1860, and Quincy acquired it, along with the rest of Pewabic's holdings, in 1891. It appears to have been a fairly standard 22-by-26-foot saltbox with six rooms. At some point, it gained a one-story kitchen in the rear, enabling the formerly rear rooms to be united into a dining room. In 1912 its tenant, machine-shop foreman Thomas J. Thomas, expressed dissatisfaction with his house and wanted to move into Hancock. Lawton valued his influence on local politics and did not want to lose him from the township, so he recommended building a new house for him. Three months later he reported that "we have been able to satisfy <u>Mrs.</u> Thomas by remodeling their present house and by adding another bed-room and a bath-room." The company raised the roof on the back slope about 5½ feet higher than its original ridge in order to create more space on the second floor, with an attic above (Figures 4.7, 4.8). In the new second-floor space, the company placed a three-fixture bathroom, a 10-by-7½-foot bedroom with large closet, a hallway, and the stairway, which it moved from the front section of the house. These changes fostered others: no longer were the original two upstairs rooms connected directly; a doorway was closed and both were reached from the new hallway. Downstairs, the doorway between the front room and the dining room was moved and made into an archway. The Thomases stayed for only a few months, however, and the next tenant, mining engineer Harry S. Chamberlin, had

Figure 4.7 *Pewabic Mining Co. house on Quincy Hill, built ca. 1860, photographed by Jet Lowe, 1978. Quincy raised the roof of this saltbox to accommodate a second-floor bathroom, which it installed in order to keep its tenant. The garage was built by 1920. Courtesy of Historic American Engineering Record.*

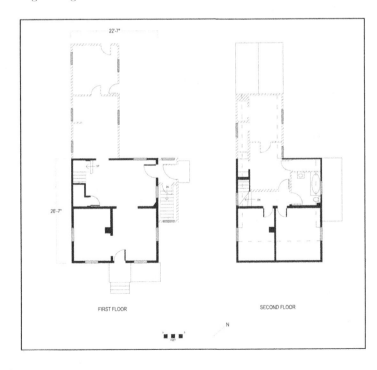

Figure 4.8 *Pewabic Mining Co. house on Quincy Hill, built ca. 1860, plans. The original building was a six-room salt-box but underwent the removal of a wall and the addition of a bathroom, several rooms in the rear, and an exterior stairway to the basement. Measured and drawn by Chris Merritt, 2005.*

more changes made, adding another room over the one-story rear addition and building a one-story addition onto the rear. By 1920 the house, valued at fifteen hundred dollars and renting for seventeen dollars a month, was equipped with electric lights, water, bath, toilet, sewer, garage, and a company telephone.[44]

Not all homeowners were anxious to get full bathrooms into houses. A house near Frog Pool Lane, on the west side of Houghton, was probably built by the Huron Mining Company in the 1880s, then acquired by the Isle Royale Mining Company. One of a row of six, it originally had a three-room footprint in an L-plan, with two rooms upstairs under a side-gable roof. When new owners acquired it in 1960, they converted it into a standard saltbox, stretching the kitchen across the rear so that there was room to eat in it. They shored up the wood-post foundation and installed hardwood flooring in the front rooms. They also arranged for running water in the kitchen and installed a toilet. The house had no basement, however, and with seven children the new owners did not want to sacrifice a room, so they installed the toilet in the downstairs bedroom, under the stairs. There was no sink or tub. The homeowner recalled bathing and doing laundry in nearby Huron Creek. This situation remained the same until 2000, when the homeowner moved out; the house was demolished a few years later.[45]

This homeowner did not have a sauna, but many Copper Country residents, especially Finnish-Americans, prefer saunas to bathtubs. One elderly resident, eligible for state housing assistance in the 1990s, nearly refused seven thousand to eight thousand dollars worth of assistance because the state insisted on putting a bathtub in his house. The resident was content with his sauna and saw no need for a bathtub.[46]

Hierarchy and Conveniences

Quincy's last housing construction program, in 1917–18, reflected the importance of conveniences to both occupants and management. It also reveals subtle distinctions in hierarchy expressed in the provision of amenities. In addition, the planning of the houses in 1917 reflects Quincy's prosperity; the company was clearly looking to the future as it planned modern, well-equipped houses. But the boom was short-lived and by the time the houses were completed in 1918 the company's decline had begun.

Quincy began by planning "fairly good substantial modern houses" for six shift captains and two engineers. General Manager Charles Lawton developed the plans in-house, first by sending "half a dozen blue prints of different plans of houses" to Quincy President William R. Todd "as a starter." It is not known where Lawton got those plans or what they looked like. By the end of May 1917, Lawton had decided on a design, which was drawn by Peter C. Audette, Quincy's chief carpenter. Audette provided only two plans, no elevations, although in his accompanying letter to Todd, Lawton contemplated various sidings of clapboard, clapboards on the second story and wood shingles on the first, brick veneer, and concrete block.[47]

Todd critiqued the proposed plans, arguing for a butler's pantry between the kitchen and dining room, sliding doors from the library and parlor into the hall instead of a "colonnade," a wider and centered front door, and closets in different locations. Lawton responded that the butler's pantry was obsolete and made "too many steps." He also thought that two closets in the master bedroom, "so that the two heads of the family could each have an individual closet," would better satisfy "our Cornish mining captains" because, as he said, "we know their habits and customs." Nonetheless, Lawton did as he was told and most of Todd's suggestions appeared on the next iteration, which was then sent to Sears, Roebuck. Audette's plans were for a 31-by-28-foot house with off-center hall, which had sliding doors into the parlor and library. The parlor had an arched opening into the dining room, which had a bowed window with a "flower shelf." The library in the front of the house had a rectilinear bay window with seat, a bookcase, and a china closet. On the second floor were four bedrooms and a full bathroom. Sears redrew the plans, labeling them B885, and also produced elevations that showed hip-roofed four-squares with hip-roofed dormers. But Todd was not yet finished. He recommended the installation of a servant's stair, leading from the kitchen to the landing of the main stairs, which Sears incorporated into Plan B900. With these changes, Lawton estimated the construction cost at six thousand dollars. The high cost apparently put an end to the consideration of this plan.[48]

At the same time, Lawton planned to build fifty miners' houses. The reasoning for so many was "Owing to the continually congested living conditions in Hancock, and to the growing desire of our employees to dwell at the mining locations and be nearer their work, it was decided to build fifty good substantial eight-room dwelling houses with full basements." Lawton articulated the under-lying purpose, in a time of labor shortage, clearly: "So that we can have a steadier crew about the mine; fewer transient single men and more of the better families." Because these houses were initially designed for miners, not captains, Lawton did not seek design approval from Todd. Carpenter Audette produced plans in

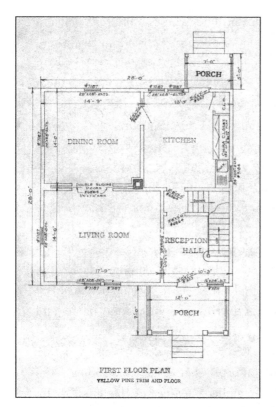
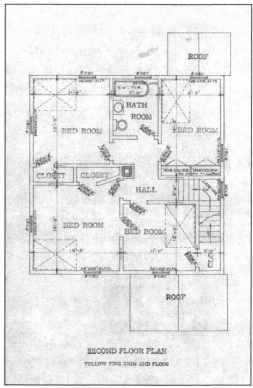

May 1917, and Lawton sent them directly to Sears. Lawton did consult Todd on how many doubles and singles to construct and, when the cost savings on doubles turned out not to be great, they decided to build only five of them. The designs were the same, though, with the double consisting of two abutting singles, in mirror image. The houses would be expensive, due to labor and materials costs, but Lawton pointed to the company's profitable position by saying, "now that we have the money."[49]

Sears Plan No. B879½ offered a gable-front house measuring 28 by 28 feet, with a plan of wide stairhall, living room, dining room, and kitchen in each quadrant (Figure 4.9). Upstairs were four bedrooms with a closet for each except for one that had two "wardrobes." A double bed was sketched in each bedroom. A three-fixture bathroom was located between the two bedrooms on the rear wall. A 7-by-12-foot gable-roofed porch was located at the front entrance and a smaller one at the rear. Paired windows adorned the first-floor front façade.

Once Lawton had received construction bids, he sent the contract, specifications, and drawings to Todd, who once again interfered. By this time, the plans for captains' houses had been scrapped, and it was clear that some of these houses would accommodate captains, so Todd must have felt the house designs were in

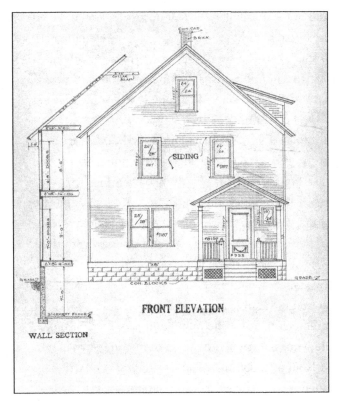

FRONT ELEVATION

WALL SECTION

FACING PAGE and LEFT: Figure 4.9 Sears Plan No. B8791/2, 1917, plans and elevation. Quincy commissioned this design, providing a suggested plan to Sears, Roebuck & Co. Sears developed the plans, elevations, and construction specifications, then provided the materials. Archie Verville built forty-five of these Sears houses, and five double houses, for Quincy in 1917–18. Courtesy of Michigan Technological University Archives and Copper Country Historical Collections.

his purview. He thought that maybe the stair tread was too narrow, that four- and five-panel doors were preferable to "the so-called 'new and very popular' five cross panel design," and that "the side window in the right front corner room be moved toward the front of the house about two feet so that the bed could stand to the rear of the room between the closet door and side wall without interfering with the window, as it would hardly seem probable that our men would place their bed between the two windows."[50]

Lawton let the contract to Archie Verville on July 24 before receiving Todd's comments, but even Lawton wanted to make changes. He changed the stairway by adding a servants' stair, which necessitated removing a window from the kitchen, he widened the treads on the stairs, he changed the dormer window from shed- to gable-roofed, and he added an exterior entrance to the cellar. These changes were all made between the time Verville bid on the contract and when he was awarded it, so the contract was adjusted. Privies and barns were also provided to each house, except for the eleven designated for mining captains and shift captains. Todd's suggestion of moving a bedroom window so as to place the bed differently was seemingly ignored.[51]

Lawton had not given up his plan for providing new houses for captains, and the way he distinguished them among these large dwellings for miners was to provide them with three-fixture bathrooms. The captains' houses received "bathtub, lavatory, closet, kitchen sink and hot water boiler with all necessary hot and cold water pipes and soil pipes to the outside of the walls." Here, one of the hallmarks of middle-class status, the three-fixture bathroom, was awarded to low-level managers. In the other houses, the plumbing was roughed in and bathrooms were planned for future installation. As Todd said, "We hope to use some method of sewerage or drainage within the near future."[52]

The next issue was what rent to charge. Verville had built the houses for about twenty-seven hundred dollars for the singles and forty-nine hundred for the doubles. Lawton planned to lease houses without plumbing or heating for twelve dollars per month, and those with those amenities for fifteen. He knew that he would not recoup the construction costs through rent: "The great benefits to accrue from the houses will be in the better class of high grade employes with their families who will be attracted." He also noted that similar houses in Hancock were renting for twenty or twenty-five dollars a month. Todd, though, wanted to figure the rents based on the construction cost, and suggested fourteen dollars, sixteen for those with hot-water heat, and eighteen for the fully equipped ones, or 6 percent of the construction cost. Lawton questioned if basing rents on construction costs was wise "when that cost is admittedly high, due to the present extremely high cost of the materials and high wages." He suggested charging part of the cost of the dwellings to general operating costs. Ultimately, only four of the houses rented for eighteen dollars, three for sixteen, and most of the rest for fourteen— even the fully equipped ones. But even fourteen dollars was more than twice the usual rate for company houses.[53]

Construction, begun in late July 1917, proceeded apace until October, when the New York office suggested cancelling the contract on some of the buildings. Lawton replied that the construction was too far along to cancel, but in December he instructed the contractor to slow down, because the weather was too cold for plastering. In June 1918 Lawton changed his mind about not installing furnaces and plumbing, apparently responding to the reactions of the would-be tenants. He discussed the reception of the houses: "Many of our best men:—viz., the shift bosses and hoisting engineers—want the houses fully equipped; and, although there is a general demur to the rentals, still they are being accepted fairly well, especially those to be fully equipped." The lower-ranking miners, though, were less willing to take on the higher rents; Lawton reported that they "are inclined to hang back and want their present homes fixed up." He did not think the houses would rent quickly or at least not to the right people. He refused to rent to tenants who could not afford them or who would not keep them in good repair.[54]

Three days later Lawton advised installing hot-air furnaces and full bathrooms in all of the houses. He noted that "nearly all our men say that they would rather pay the extra rent and have all the modern conveniences." Lawton's change of mind on this issue reflected the power that tenants had; the provision of new houses was a process of negotiation between worker and management. But with President W. R. Todd ailing and the United States involved in the war in Europe, his son, Parsons Todd, the vice president, replied that "because of present conditions, we are not anxious to spend any more money on new work than is absolutely necessary, but we must put the houses in condition to live in." Nonetheless, a month later he authorized the purchase of hot-air furnaces for the houses, acknowledging that eventually they would have to put steam heat in all the houses.[55] The houses were finished in July 1918, and Lawton immediately provided for the construction of a sewer to some of them, just for sink and basement drains (Figure 4.10). The forty single and five double houses were spread out among various locations, with the greatest concentration in Lower Pewabic.

As well equipped as the captains' houses were, it was still not enough. A few months after completion, Lawton informed his president, "Some of the Shift Captains and Hoist Engineers who are occupying new houses, are asking for storm sheds and storm windows." A chart of the new houses compiled in 1918 showed which had which of the following amenities: furnace, plumbing, electric lights, water, sewers, back storm shed, screens, storm doors and windows, and interior painting. The listing of these amenities shows that they were not distributed equally, continuing the paternalistic customs the company wanted to shed. The interest in storm windows appears to correlate with central heating. The type of central heating was significant as well. The captains' houses received hot-water heat, through radiators, while the others received hot-air furnaces, which involved unmechanized heat circulation through ducts and registers.[56]

Most of the new houses were equipped with electricity. In 1906 Lawton noted that most of the management had electricity in their homes through the commercial utility, Houghton County Electric Light Company, and suggested that Quincy provide them electricity at a lower rate. Apparently Todd did not agree, because eleven years later Lawton made the same suggestion. He estimated Quincy could provide the service at three cents per kilowatt hour as opposed to the twelve

OVERLEAF: *Figure 4.10 Sears houses in Lower Pewabic, built 1917–18. Quincy instructed Verville to paint the houses in alternating colors: straw yellow with dark buff trim, navy green with dark green trim, light drab brown with chestnut trim, oxide red with white trim, and blue gray with white trim. Courtesy of Historic American Engineering Record.*

cents its tenants were paying. At about this time, Quincy began wiring all of its houses, presumably letting its tenants arrange for their own service with Houghton County Electric Light Company.[57]

There was high turnover among tenants in these new houses but not among the eleven who got plumbing and heating. Granted, they were all well up in the company hierarchy, being captains and shift captains, but only one of them, Captain W. J. Sampson, left in the first three years. Among the houses with fewer conveniences, Lawton was correct when he said that they would not rent quickly; two of them were not occupied until 1924, and four were vacant until after 1926. Lawton also said, however, that he was being cautious about whom he was renting them to, and the list of first tenants shows a preponderance of English names and fewer than half a dozen that might be Finnish, Croatian, or Italian, even though, at this time, those three ethnic groups comprised half of Quincy's workforce. The turnover and vacancies also indicate that Quincy workers did not accept the new large houses because they did not have the amenities they expected. If a house did not have a three-fixture bathroom, tenants would just as soon stay in their cheaper, similarly ill-equipped housing. This picture is clouded somewhat by Quincy's financial situation, though. In 1920, for the first time in more than fifty-five years, the company did not make a profit. Reductions in wages and hours resulted in a depleted workforce. By 1921, 116 company houses—more than 20 percent of Quincy's housing stock—were vacant through the winter.[58]

Quincy's 1917–18 construction program illuminates several issues. It is especially well documented because these miners' houses were also serving managers, so upper-level management was involved, and the New York office tended to leave a paper trail. One aspect that makes this program unique is the involvement of Sears, Roebuck & Co., the only known occasion that one of the big three mining companies turned to a mail-order firm.[59] But Quincy did not buy off-the-shelf plans; the company provided its own plans and let Sears develop the elevations, details, and specifications. Quincy's production of the plans is critical because it reveals what was most important to Quincy: the number and arrangement of rooms and the provision and arrangement of conveniences.

Quincy's correspondence also reveals the presumption of upper management in claiming to know what its mining captains wanted in their bedrooms. Lawton's certainty that they would want two closets and Todd's that they would not place their bed between two windows reveals an extremely proprietary attitude, as upper management speculated on how their tenants lived in their houses. But it is their captains they were most concerned with, not their miners. Upper management never involved itself in such details of its housing for rank-and-file employees.

The fifty housing units built in 1917–18 are also an interesting study of hierarchy. The houses are all the same size, with the same number of rooms, so that was not how class was differentiated. Instead, it was through the provision of amenities, especially the three-fixture bathroom, but also the kind of furnace and the existence of storm windows. By 1918, though, with a robust market for copper and a shortage of labor, Quincy's workers were in a strong position and did not accept this differentiation. Rising expectations meant that mine workers wanted these conveniences too, and if they were not forthcoming, workers were unwilling to pay more for a house without them.

5 Churches, Schools, Bathhouses

Building Community on Company Land

Aside from the community they fostered in their boardinghouse and imme-diate neighborhood, Joseph and Antonia Putrich also engaged with the larger community of Painesdale and even the Copper Country. These connections are highlighted by the number of institutions that came into play on the day of the shootings. A group of eight men from the boarding-house walked to South Range to collect their strike benefits and also to have a few beers, first in a saloon, then in a park. On their way home, John Kalan and John Stimac stopped in a candy store on the north side of Painesdale to get some tobacco and a pop. After the shooting, Joseph Putrich went to another store to use the telephone to summon the doctor.[1] Stanko Stepich, wounded in the shootings, was treated in the hospital in Trimountain. Steve Putrich and Alois Tijan, killed in the shootings, were buried in Lakeview Cemetery after a service at the Croatian Church in Calumet, twenty miles north. (Although there was a Catholic church in Painesdale, there was only one Croatian Catholic church in the Copper Country.) And the trial of the perpetrators of the shootings took place in the Houghton County Courthouse in Houghton. So this one incident brought the Putriches into contact with a number of businesses and services: saloon, store, hospital, church, court-house. In addition, their children, once old enough, attended the public school in Painesdale and may have used the library nearby. Most of these community services and businesses were housed in their own buildings.

Company management was involved, at least to some extent, in all of these community facilities. Companies had to do more than build housing if they were to attract and retain workers; they also had to provide or encourage all of the institutions that made life in the Copper Country possible and enjoyable. The companies forcefully took initiative in implementing some of these institutions, others they let the free market supply; some of the institutions were embodied in architectural landmarks, others were not architectural at all; some of them were natural developments in communities, others were considered "welfare work" of the company.

In his report for the Bureau of Labor Statistics during the 1913–14 strike, Walter Palmer enumerated Calumet & Hecla's extensive welfare work: public library, bathhouse, hospital, free fuel distribution to widows and special cases, broom factory to give employment to blind miners, pasturage for cows, garbage removal, electricity at a reduced rate, churches, and schools. In addition, C&H established a number of funds: an aid fund for sickness or accidents, pension fund for select older employees, aid outside of regular aid fund, voluntary relief fund for widows and orphans, and insurance (death benefits not covered by aid fund). The aid fund was particularly noteworthy, involving a regular contribution from employees of fifty cents a month, matched by the company. The fund was invested in C&H stock, and at a time of great profits, 1898–1901, the company suspended its workers' payments into the fund for three years, in effect giving its employees a raise.[2]

C&H, as the largest and most profitable company in the Copper Country, led the way on the provision of benefits. Of the other companies, only Copper Range had a company-administered aid fund, and the company did not match employees' contributions.[3] C&H's involvement in the provision of schools, churches, hospitals, pasturage for cows, garbage removal, and the like meant that these services became an expectation of employees of other large companies as well. At times, C&H built large, architect-designed buildings to display its concern for its employees in a conspicuous manner. Its followers, Quincy and Copper Range, tried to keep pace.

The larger companies established a core area, separate from a commercial core or "Main Street" area. At Calumet, where development occurred without a coherent plan, the school was adjacent to the boiler house, the bathhouse next to the railroad roundhouse (Figure 5.1). About a quarter of a mile away, the platted village of Red Jacket provided the commercial needs. Similarly, at Quincy, the schools and churches were within a block of the mine buildings. Painesdale, one of the few planned communities, clustered its schools, library, and church in the residential area, but the store and post office were down by the railroad tracks and probably served as more of a hub.[4] The platted communities, not owned by the companies, accommodated stores, bars, hotels, theaters, and other entertainments—community aspects that the companies were just as glad not to have to manage.

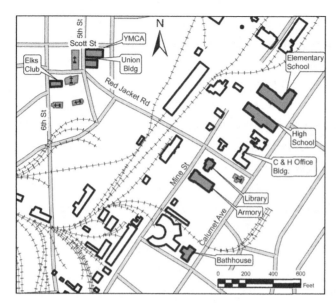

Figure 5.1 Map of C&H core area. C&H's mine buildings are outlined; community institutions are shaded and labeled; churches are marked with a cross. C&H owned all the land on this map, except for the blocks north of Scott Street and west of Fourth Street, which were in the village. Map by Timothy A. Goddard, 2008.

Stores may be a surprising addition to this list, but in the Copper Country the companies got into the store-operating business only reluctantly and got out as soon as they could. Quincy established a store in 1863 only in an effort to keep prices down by undercutting merchants in Hancock; when prices had stabilized, the company turned the store over to a private business. By 1913 only Copper Range operated company stores, but there were other options, both on and off company property, for employees. Several tenants increased their income by running stores out of their houses. At least five tenants in Painesdale did this and one in Mason. At the larger end of the scale, Tamarack Cooperative store, a thriving member-owned food-and-merchandise venture in Calumet, kept prices down in that area. A government investigator during the strike found that prices, in general, "were not considered dear by the people in the district."[5] Company stores were much less of an issue in labor–management relations in the Copper Country than in other company-dominated mining towns.

Six institutions built on company lands made major architectural statements on the landscape: churches, libraries, bathhouses, schools, hospitals, and office buildings. Each of the three largest companies involved itself in the construction and operation of these institutions, all in the interest of fostering community. The extent to which these were amenities and not necessities, though, is illustrated by their absence in outlying communities. While Lake Linden, C&H's stamp-mill community, had a branch library and a small hospital in addition to schools and churches, most of the companies' subsidiary communities had only a school and a church. Libraries, bathhouses, and hospitals were associated with the main office, the heart of the company.

Churches

Churches were built both in platted towns and on company property. Company management encouraged the establishment of churches as a sign of civilization, symbolizing that a settlement was ready for the moral influence of women as well as the church, and as an alternative to the evil influences of the saloon. Congregations did not need any help to form but, surprisingly often, they turned to the company for a site on which to build or for a donation towards construction. Churches thus became tangled in the web of management–worker relations.

In the United States, churches signify the relative strength of various ethnic groups, and thus serve as a guide to the ethnic composition of a place. The first church established by the New England management of Calumet & Hecla was a Congregational Church, located on company property next to the office building.[6] Later, Scottish-born managers founded a Presbyterian church, located beside an Episcopal church. But the predominantly Cornish workforce, at C&H as well as at other nineteenth-century mines, worshipped at a Methodist church. Generally, the companies supported the churches demanded by their workforce without discriminating among them.

The earliest Methodist church still standing in the Copper Country is located in Central, a mining town that peaked in the 1860s and was out of business by 1900 (Figure 5.2). Founded in 1854, Central had a population of nearly 845 by 1868, when construction on this church began. The Central Mining Company furnished materials and the congregation provided the labor; the total expenditure was about two thousand dollars. [7] The church stood on company land.

The church is a simple rectangle, about 26½ by 45½ feet, with a 10½-by-10½-foot bell tower centered on the gable front. The frame church is set on a stone foundation; clapboards cover the walls. The doorway has modest Classical detailing, and the cornice continues across the gable front of the church, forming a pediment. The bell tower is topped by crenellations, perhaps an allusion to the castellated stone Methodist churches of Cornwall. Three tall windows with six-over-six lights are on each side of the church. Inside, the church is extremely

Figure 5.2 Methodist Church, Central, built 1868, photographed ca. 1930. Cornish immigrants at Central Mine built this Methodist church, a simple frame building with a crenellated tower. Courtesy of Michigan Technological University Archives and Copper Country Historical Collections.

plain. Across the far end of the church, an elevated platform, separated from the rest of the church by a balustrade, accommodated an organ and seating for a choir. The walls are plain, with a horizontal-plank wainscot and plastered walls.[8]

With the town's loss of population, the church closed in 1903 but almost immediately became a focal point of nostalgia. The arrival of the Keweenaw Central Railroad, which was built past the community of Central in 1907, enabled a "homecoming" of former residents. This reunion of Cornish descendants has become an annual event, continuing to the present. On the last weekend in July, two services are held in the church to accommodate the reunion-goers.

Most of Quincy Mining Company's workers' churches were located in Hancock on sites that the company had given or sold to the congregations. When donating land, though, Quincy added a clause in the deed providing that if the church should cease operations, the land would revert to Quincy. Up on Quincy Hill, in 1893 the Methodists of Quincy and Pewabic abandoned their existing church, having outgrown it, and requested a lot for a new church. Quincy sold them a new lot, and the congregation built a handsome frame church in a cruciform plan, with a bell tower in the reentrant angle. Thomas F. Mason, Quincy's president, donated a bell to the new church. Although the congregation considered selling the old church to the Sons of St. George, a Cornish organization, Quincy bought it for $850 and rehabilitated it to be used as a hall by several organizations. The rents would "pay good interest on the purchase price," Agent S. B. Harris argued, "besides being a credit to the location and a moral and social elevator to the people."[9]

Calumet & Hecla preferred to lease land, not give it away. In 1913, when the Reverend P. W. Pederson wanted a deed for the lot under his Norwegian–Danish Methodist Episcopal church, MacNaughton replied huffily that "you are the very first to ask the Company to give a church congregation a deed gratis." The churches received five-year leases "with the promise of renewal," according to General Manager MacNaughton. By 1893 C&H had twenty churches on company property, "the greater number of which have been materially assisted by the Company at some time in their history," according to the company's annual report. By 1913 the company had provided sites to more than thirty churches as well as contributed nearly thirty-six thousand dollars. The ethnic diversity of the workforce, especially after 1893, meant that the number of churches in Calumet mushroomed. When a Finnish Methodist church requested a site in 1910, MacNaughton pointed out that he had already given sites to three Finnish churches, three Finnish parsonages, and one Finnish Sunday school.[10]

After the Holy Rosary Church in Lake Linden, C&H's stamp-mill town, burned down in 1905, MacNaughton and Agassiz saw the wisdom of merging that congregation with St. Joseph's, another Catholic church in Lake Linden. But Holy Rosary's congregation was German and Irish and St. Joseph's was French Canadian—an insurmountable hurdle. MacNaughton and Agassiz mused privately that they would like to merge three-fifths of the churches, deploring the waste of money that these separate churches represented. They noted that churches tended to expand beyond their means; in fact, St. Joseph's was heavily in debt, owing sixteen thousand dollars on its partly constructed church, and anticipating a further

expenditure of eighty-five thousand dollars. Nonetheless, for all the complaining, Agassiz agreed to donate another thousand dollars, in addition to the two thousand dollars he had already donated, to enable Holy Rosary's reconstruction.[11]

A vivid example of churches' competitive development occurred in Calumet, where there were six Catholic churches. One of these belonged to the French Canadian congregation, which formed in 1884 and bought the former St. Patrick's Hall at Fifth and Scott streets for thirty-five hundred dollars, on land belonging to C&H. After renovations, the church was consecrated and named in honor of St. Louis in 1886. In 1899, with the congregation numbering about two thousand, it undertook to build a new church, moving the old one aside. The new church, to be named for St. Anne, would be grand: measuring 52 by 140 feet, it was constructed of rough-faced Portage Entry sandstone ashlar, laid in a random pattern (Figure 5.3). The steeple on the corner rose 140 feet.[12] Three Gothic-arched entrances stood at the top of a broad flight of stairs. Buttresses along the sides framed the Gothic-arched windows. The first floor was elevated 7 feet above grade, creating a large basement that held a chapel, classrooms, and toilet.

The congregation contracted Marquette architects Charlton, Gilbert & Demar for this design. Prendergast & Clarkson, of Chicago, received the construction contract for twenty-eight thousand dollars in the spring of 1900; interior furnishings brought the complete cost to forty-three thousand dollars. Prendergast & Clarkson's steam hoisting derrick aroused some interest, identified as "an innovation in the copper country." It lifted three or four "huge" building blocks at a time and eliminated the need for hods and hod carriers. Inside, the nave rose forty-five feet (Figure 5.4). The main altar was thirty feet high, while the side altars were twenty-one-feet high. The altars were fashioned by Joseph Svoboda of Kewaunee, Wisconsin; the main altar, which cost more than a thousand dollars, was "finished with a metallic background magnificently ornamented in colors and surmounted with handsome electric light brackets." No artist was identified for the stained-glass windows, although they were one of the most remarkable features. "On entering, one is struck by the beauty of the mild and mellow light occasioned by the artistic tinting of these handsome windows. . . . The apex of each window is in dark purplish blue with tiny circular stars of contrasting colors. The body and sides are . . . in tasty designs and the coloring here is especially marked, the

FACING PAGE: Figure 5.3 St. Anne's Roman Catholic Church, Calumet, built 1900, photographed 2003. The French Canadian congregation funded construction of this substantial Gothic Revival church, built of Jacobsville sandstone.

Figure 5.4 St. Anne's Roman Catholic Church, interior. The elaborate paint scheme and intricately carved altars contributed to the opulent feel of this church. Courtesy of Michigan Technological University Archives and Copper Country Historical Collections.

predominating shades being russet, golden brown and green in the most delicate tints of autumnal beauty." Associated Artists of Milwaukee, headed by Conrad Schmidt, did the interior decorating, which included "fresco painting, the ceilings being cream color into which pictures of the saints and apostles are arranged, while the walls are of a greenish tint," for two thousand dollars. In the sanctuary, "The decorations there represent the firmament with the holy ghost in plastic relief. The dome of the sanctuary is blended in an azure atmosphere effect with golden stars radiated by relief ribs. The surroundings of the altar is in a French tapestry." There were also two large historical paintings undertaken by "the celebrated ecclesiastical artist" Joseph Vittur, of Austin, Illinois. Dark oak pews were provided by the Phoenix Chair Company of Eau Claire, Wisconsin, for fifteen hundred dollars. The 104 pews seated five hundred, with room in the balcony for two hundred or three hundred more.[13] St. Anne's Church was dedicated on June 16, 1901.

The impressive stone exterior and lavish interior decorations were intended to make a statement, not only about the strength of this Catholic congregation but also about the spending power of French Canadians. Craftsmen throughout the upper Midwest were called upon for various elements of this church. Allegedly, Father Achilles Poulin, priest at St. Louis from 1895 to 1897 when planning was underway for the new church, threatened to resign if the congregation decided to repair the old church rather than build a new one. The newspaper goaded the congregation, "Hurry up, Canadians, and put yourselves on the same level as the others." But it was not an unreasonable expenditure, given the strength of the congregation, which delayed construction until it could afford the building that it desired. The congregation borrowed only ten thousand dollars for the new church and paid it off within three years. As the Copper Country's fortunes shrank, however, so did size of the congregation. By the 1920s, St. Anne's congregation consisted of only "a handful" of families. Finally, in 1966 several dwindling Catholic congregations consolidated into one, and St. Anne's was deconsecrated. After sale to a private individual in 1971, the church was stripped of its pews and main altar.[14] Calumet Township acquired the church in 1994; restoration and renovation for use as a museum have been ongoing.

St. Anne's also has to be seen in two contexts: Catholic churches in Calumet and churches in its immediate neighborhood. Within a few years of St. Anne's completion, there were five other Catholic churches in Calumet; several of them had been built or rebuilt in the previous decade. Sacred Heart, the first Catholic church in the area, serving an Irish and German population, was founded in 1869;

a new sandstone structure was built in 1897–98. Although the church's founder, the Reverend Edward Jacker, was offered a lot in Red Jacket, to which he could have obtained full title, he elected to lease a lot more than half a mile way from Red Jacket from Hecla Mining Company, setting the pattern for the others. A Polish congregation built St. Anthony's in 1882, but it closed in the 1920s, the congregation's numbers having dwindled. Slovenians built St. Joseph's in 1889–90; it burned in 1902, and when rebuilding was complete in 1908, the magnificent twin-towered Jacobsville sandstone Gothic church had cost a hundred thousand dollars. The Italians, who had been worshiping at St. Joseph's, desired to break away in 1893, but because they participated in a walk-out against C&H that year, the company refused to lease them land. Several years later, the company relented, giving them "the usual support" of two thousand dollars and leasing them two lots in the slightly remote location of Yellow Jacket. The congregation built a handsome sandstone church, St. Mary's, in 1896–97. The Croatians also broke away from the Slovenians and built their own church, dedicated in 1903 to St. John the Baptist. After it burned in 1925, its new brick building was not completed until 1941.[15]

Most of these breakaway congregations located their churches on company-owned lots within the village of Red Jacket, but St. Anne's sat on company property just outside the village. Near St. Anne's, at the edge of the village, was a cluster of other churches. Just south of St. Anne's, the First Presbyterian Church was established in 1894 to serve a largely Scottish congregation. Just south of that, Christ Episcopal Church was built in 1893. The modest shingled church had no tower, in contrast to the bulky tower of the Presbyterian church next door. West of the Presbyterian church, facing onto Sixth Street, Carmel Lutheran Church was built in 1896 for its Swedish congregation. The sandstone church with a tower in the center of its front façade cost a little under ten thousand dollars to build and is the most modest of the sandstone churches in Calumet.

Other institutions occupied this borderland. Just north of the Swedish church, west of the Presbyterian church, and completing the quadrangle known as "Temple Square," stood the Young Men's Christian Association building, constructed of Jacobsville sandstone in 1897. After the YMCA moved to a new building in 1908 at the corner of Fifth and Scott, the old YMCA housed the Benevolent Protective Order of Elks. Next to the new YMCA was the oldest of these institutional buildings, the Union Building, which represented a coalition of two primary fraternal organizations—the Masons and the Independent Order of Odd Fellows. Together they leased land from C&H and erected a large three-story brick building in 1889. There was always a close relationship between fraternal organizations and churches in the companies' minds, if not in their members'. Both were for the betterment of the worker and therefore deserved company support. This collection of churches and societies at the entrance to the village huddles together on company land, straddling the company and noncompany worlds.

The location on company property might have been advantageous when constructing a new church—removing the burden of land costs—but was a constraint on the independence of the congregation. During the strike, none of the clergy of the main congregations spoke out in support of the strikers. The clergy tended to join the Citizens Alliance, the promanagement group, not parade on behalf of strikers. MacNaughton related an instance in which a Catholic priest, who heard "murmurings among his people and knew of the preaching of the agitators and was afraid of its result," arranged for them to meet with MacNaughton. At C&H, one observer wrote, "The strikers inferred from the very beginning that the churches would be on the side of the companies."[16]

Libraries and Bathhouses

"A Boon to the Community!" the newspaper crowed. "The Big Corporations Are Certainly Not All Soulless," was the sub-headline. "C.&H. Co. Once More Show Their Interest."[17] One of the great symbols of a company's largesse and paternalism is the library. Not classified as a necessity, it is an amenity—a gift to the workers. A library signifies a cultured, literate workforce with enough leisure time to use it. Andrew Carnegie, the steel baron famous for funding the construction of more than sixteen hundred libraries in the United States and more abroad, also saw them as places for self-betterment; there, a dedicated workingman could educate himself and improve his lot. Others saw libraries as part of a broader Americanization movement, helping to educate the foreign-born working class in the English language and in American ways.

Calumet & Hecla heralded its library as one of its finest achievements, proclaiming its concern for and generosity toward its workers (Figure 5.5). Designed by Boston architects Shaw & Hunnewell, the library was built in 1897–98 at a cost of forty thousand dollars. Located diagonally across from C&H's general office building, it had the same "mosaic" stone walls trimmed with brick. The front entrance, directly across from President Alexander Agassiz's house, led into a large

Figure 5.5 C&H Public Library, built 1897–98, photographed 1898. The construction crew poses in front of the library, presumably soon after completion. A corner of the seasonal home of C&H President Alexander Agassiz is visible on the far left. Courtesy of Michigan Technological University Archives and Copper Country Historical Collections.

reception room, an open area where librarians charged books to readers. This imposing room was decorated with fluted pilasters and a coffered ceiling. Behind were two floors of open stacks. To the right were the stairs up to the reading room, a large, 42-by-38-foot space, which rose 24 feet to the coffered and trussed ceiling (Figure 5.6). Mahogany tables and Windsor chairs encouraged reading, while

Figure 5.6 C&H Public Library, interior. On the second floor, the grand reading room included a large fireplace. The library had open stacks and offered free access to Calumet residents. Courtesy of Michigan Technological University Archives and Copper Country Historical Collections.

a large fireplace against the southeast wall attempted to give the room a homey feel. Also on the second floor, above the stacks, was a men's smoking room with oak tables.[18]

The basement housed baths for men and women, perhaps an odd pairing with a library but consistent with the company's view that both books and baths were amenities for personal betterment (Figure 5.7). A few months after the building opened, Alexander Agassiz sent plans for a secondary entrance to the library located on the west side that provided patrons of the baths their own separate entrance, so that they did not have to enter through the library's reception room.[19] They were further sorted; halfway down, at a landing, the stairway divided, sending women in one direction and men in the other. Once they reached the basement, an ornamental screen reinforced the separation, as each gender went into its own bath room.

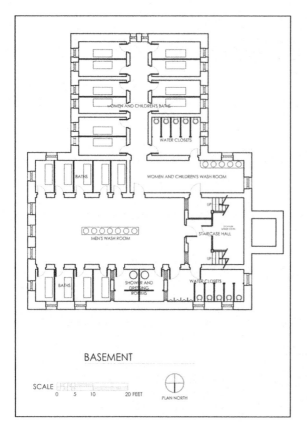

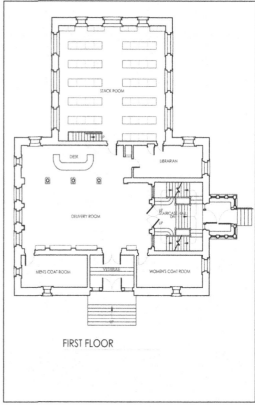

ABOVE and FACING PAGE: Figure 5.7 C&H Public Library, plans. The library included baths in the basement as an additional amenity. Drawn by Quentin Peterson, Keweenaw National Historical Park, 2004.

In 1904, a year after the men's reading and smoking room was lauded as "a sort of clubroom to some young men" and a healthful alternative to the bars, this room was remodeled into a children's room capable of accommodating more than a hundred children at a time. The new room promised to keep children off the streets and give them the means of educating themselves, according to the newspaper. It also reflected progressive reformers' ideas about the importance of childhood, resulting in the establishment of playgrounds, kindergartens, and children's reading rooms nationwide. By this time, other changes had occurred as well: the men's coatroom, left of the front door, had been replaced by a "repair room," while the women's coatroom, right of the front door, had become a "picture room" for the storage and display of graphic material, necessitating enlargement of the first-floor windows. Finally, after the baths were removed to a new building in 1911, the basement was remodeled to accommodate additional stacks as well as a book-repair room and an unpacking room.[20]

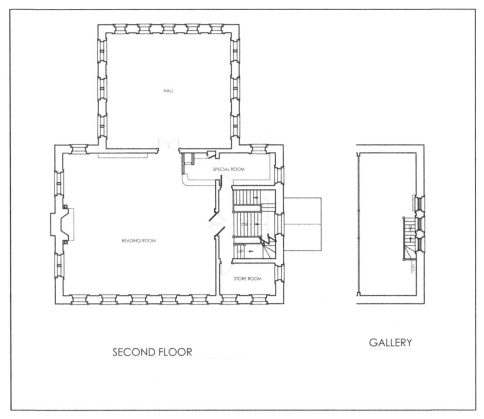

From the beginning, some doubted whether the workers would actually use the library. When the library opened, the newspaper noted that it "is not for the use of a favored few, but for the laborer and his family, who, as long as they behave themselves, will be just as welcome within its walls as the biggest 'boss' in the community." The newspaper alluded to a previous attempt to open a public library in the school, but workers did not feel welcome and so stayed away and the library closed. Nonetheless, the company recognized that its very support could be perceived as a drawback, so it set up an agreement with the Calumet School Board to run the library jointly. C&H provided the building and apparently did not consult the school board until construction was completed. C&H appointed and paid the principal librarian and a boy assistant, while the school board appointed and paid an assistant librarian and a boy assistant. C&H paid for the lighting, heating, and cleaning of the building and took full charge of the baths in the basement. Labels were applied to the books to indicate which institution had donated them, and C&H supplied a "trained librarian" for the start-up. A Library Committee, composed of two members appointed by C&H and three by the school board, administered the library. C&H also pledged to appropriate money annually for subscriptions and new books. C&H described this arrangement in its annual report as the library being "under the control of the Library Board of the Calumet Township School Board," although the library's official name was the Public Library of the Calumet & Hecla Mining Company.[21]

In accepting C&H's offer of joint administration, the secretary of the school board, Charles Briggs, noted, "It was the opinion of the Board that many people would use the Library more freely under this arrangement than they would if the Company ran it." C&H put a notice in every employee's pay envelope that the library was open to them and all residents of the school district. To run the library, C&H selected Marie F. Grierson, whose husband, Edward, was the company's chief mining engineer. Thirty-seven years old and childless, Marie Grierson served as head librarian from the building's opening in 1898 until 1930. She had no training as a librarian, but in an attempt to educate herself she attended meetings of the American Library Association, becoming an officer of the Michigan chapter. To equip the library, C&H hired Bertha H. Merrill, a librarian from Boston, who bought three thousand books for the collection to be added to the school's thirty-eight hundred.[22] Grierson's first assistant was a man, but he was soon replaced by Miss Anna J. Fiske, who boarded with the Griersons.

The library appears to have been well used. Four thousand people attended opening-day festivities. In 1902 the library circulated more than 100,000 volumes, giving it the third-highest usage among libraries in Michigan. Attendance in the main reading room in 1910 was 22,818, when Calumet's population was less than 40,000. By 1915 the library boasted 8,800 registered users, and another 750 registered patrons at the branch library in Lake Linden. The library contained 32,606 volumes in 1910 and 42,120, of which 5,600 were in nine foreign languages, in 1915. The impressive foreign-language collection was apparently intended to instruct foreigners in American ways; the foreign-language book collection focused on "the Bible, dictionaries, translations of good English and American fiction, translations or original works on American history and biography . . . in fact, any good books describing America, its institutions, and its great men and women, [and] books on citizenship." Besides books, the library also offered mineral specimens, Underwood and Keystone photographic travel tours, pamphlets on needlework, 14,000 pictures, public documents, maps, magazines, and newspapers.[23]

One attempt to make the library more appealing to patrons was apparent architecturally. Shaw & Hunnewell's original drawings provided for closed stacks, common at the time. Patrons would enter the "delivery room," put in their request, and an attendant would retrieve the book from the stacks. The original drawings show a desk and barrier across one end of the delivery room, impeding access to the stacks by patrons. When C&H produced the working drawings, however, the barrier had shrunk to a simple desk and the stacks were open. The delivery room was renamed the reception room. Although reformers were urging open stacks at this time, in the early twentieth century only about a quarter of American libraries had them, so the Calumet library was modern in this respect. In addition, no fee was required to use the library.[24]

The librarian also identified the "homelike atmosphere" of the building as part of its welcoming nature. Comfortable furniture, plants and flowers, open shelves, and "the absolute freedom with which everybody uses every department" were on Mrs. Grierson's list of attributes. Creating a "homelike atmosphere" was consistent with women's work in the public sector in the early twentieth century, in which their influence in "municipal housekeeping"—a natural extension of the woman's role—was viewed as beneficial. But Anna Fiske, in an address to the state association of libraries, further explained that the library offered an opportunity to instruct recent immigrants on "what a home should be, judged by American standards." Part of this was achieved by aesthetics: "by having a building in itself beautiful, and adorning it with plants and flowers, but also by the placing of good pictures on its walls, and in providing plaster casts of at least a few of the great pieces of sculpture." Fiske also said that there were no signs in the library, in another effort to model domesticity. She emphasized courteous and respectful treatment of library patrons and gentle reminders about personal cleanliness and use of handkerchiefs. She articulated a philosophy of openness, not only in open shelves, which she termed "almost indispensable," but also in foreign-language books, sympathizing with the difficulties adult immigrants had in learning a new language.[25]

Grierson and Fiske apparently succeeded in creating as welcoming a library as they intended, judging from attendance figures. Many Copper Country residents today have fond memories of using the library as children. Still, some stayed away. As the 1913 strikers' publication said, the workers "would rather read one book at their own fireside, paid for by themselves, than to take a hundred from the boss's library." C&H's perception of the library as a paternalistic gift to the workers was also revealed in its closing. In July 1943 the workers of C&H finally unionized, affiliating with the International Union of Mine, Mill, & Smelter Workers of the CIO. Later that year, C&H disbanded the library, sending the books to the public school.[26] The company moved some of its offices into the library building.

Figure 5.8 C&H Bathhouse, built 1910–11, photographed probably 1913. Girls appear to be chatting with a National Guard soldier outside the bathhouse. On the right was the women's tub room, with the men's shower room in the corresponding space on the left. Courtesy of Michigan Technological University Archives and Copper Country Historical Collections.

The baths in the basement were another sort of paternalistic benefit that C&H provided its workers. The six tubs and two showers for men and six tubs for women were immediately popular; six months after opening, they had "barely been equal to the demands made upon them by both men and women." C&H soon added eight bathtubs for men. The original plans had allowed for expansion; apparently, C&H wanted to see how popular they were. The librarian reported that in 1906 24,675 men and 7,951 women used the facilities, even though the water supply was inadequate, particularly on Fridays and Saturdays. But Marie Grierson saw a better use of the space. She called the baths "a nuisance, though they have proved to be both useful and necessary" and argued that "they occupy space that is sorely needed for library purposes." She even spoke optimistically of a large addition to the library building.[27]

MacNaughton began planning a purpose-built bathhouse in 1907, seeking advice from Mrs. Grierson, who recommended doubling the number of showers and baths and providing "comfortable waiting rooms," and passing the advice on to his architect, D. Fred Charlton. But the project languished until 1909 when

Figure 5.9 C&H Bathhouse, men's shower room. Below the shower room was the men's locker room, adjacent to the men's tub room. Courtesy of Michigan Technological University Archives and Copper Country Historical Collections.

MacNaughton asked Mrs. Grierson for an update on her advice and again engaged Charlton, who was then in partnership with Edwin Kuenzli. With President Quincy Shaw's approval of the design, construction started in the summer of 1910 and the bathhouse opened in December 1911 (Figure 5.8). Located about a block away from the library, the bathhouse cost an estimated forty-five thousand dollars.[28]

The two-story, Italian Renaissance brick building had a low profile with a flat roof and broad eaves. Inside, the bathhouse offered not only tubs for men and women and showers for men but also a swimming pool. Two stairways led into separate waiting rooms for men and women. Men were routed downstairs; they could not go directly to the pool. Once downstairs, men could go either to the tub room, where there were fourteen tubs, or to the locker room, where there were eighty-one lockers. They then went back upstairs for a shower, before going to the pool (Figure 5.9). Women went from their waiting room into their tub room. The women's facility had only fourteen bathtubs—no lockers and no showers—despite Mrs. Grierson's recommendation that a couple of showers in the women's department might be welcome.[29] After a bath, the women could enter the pool room.

Figure 5.10 C&H Bathhouse, swimming pool. The 26-by-40-foot pool was lit on three sides by windows and overhead by a skylight. Men and women swam at separate times. Courtesy of Michigan Technological University Archives and Copper Country Historical Collections.

This fifteen-foot-high space, lit by a skylight as well as other windows, contained the 26-by-40-foot pool, which sloped from 3 to 8 feet in depth (Figure 5.10). The building also contained laundry facilities in the basement. D. Fred Charlton, the architect, advised MacNaughton that a pool and public laundry were "now usually considered in connection with a Modern Bath House, both here and abroad." But C&H did not intend for this to be a public laundry; rather, this is where towels from the bathing facilities and laundry from the hospital—another company facility—were cleaned.[30] The interaction of C&H facilities continued underground as well; C&H steam heated the bathhouse.

As with the library, the real test of a fancy bathhouse was if the intended patrons actually used it. As Mrs. Grierson cautioned, "The use of such a bath house will depend so much upon its location and its management." Its location was convenient, in the heart of the industrial district next to the railroad roundhouse, near the library. To run the bathhouse, C&H selected Mr. Evelyn Carter, who had been in charge of the baths in the library. The bathhouse was open to all, not just C&H employees and their families. Charging three cents for men, two-and-a-half cents for boys, and nothing for women and children, and offering coupon books to

Figure 5.11 Sarah Sargent Paine Memorial Library, Painesdale, built 1903, since demolished. Copper Range President William Paine donated funds for the library and named it after his mother. The Tudor Revival building was constructed of Portage Entry sandstone. Courtesy of Michigan Technological University Archives and Copper Country Historical Collections.

further reduce the rates, the bathhouse saw 40,413 bathers in 1912 and 62,286 in 1915. C&H was willing to adjust schedules and prices. Initially, the company charged five cents to users between 10 a.m. and 2 p.m., but the baths received little patronage then, so it dropped the charge. The company also instituted free times for boys "on account of the questionable ways some boys obtain money and coupons for towels." Users of the pool were required to bathe first, and an attendant checked them for skin rashes before they were allowed in the pool. Use of the pool was strictly segregated by gender, and men and boys swam naked. C&H underwrote the cost of the bathhouse operations at more than seven thousand dollars a year.[31]

C&H's role as the leader in paternalistic ventures that other companies aspired to is evident in Copper Range's own library, which also contained baths. Copper Range was a new company, founded in 1899, and its Champion mine attracted the company's largest settlement, in Painesdale. There, in 1902–3, the company's president, William A. Paine, financed construction of a forty-thousand-dollar public library, dedicated to his mother, Sarah Sargent Paine (Figure 5.11). Designed by Milwaukee architect Alexander C. Eschweiler, the two-story building introduced the Jacobean Revival style to the Copper Country. Tudor arches, parapeted gable ends, small-paned windows, and bay windows lent an air of Old World erudition to the building. Its Portage Entry sandstone walls were laid in a rough-faced random pattern, accented with smooth-faced stone. Measuring about 86 by 37 feet, it was a little smaller than C&H's library, but it served about a quarter of the population.[32]

Also like C&H's, the Painesdale library served several functions. The library occupied the first floor, with a wide hall and delivery room in the center, in front of the closed stacks. To the right, the adult reading room extended the full length of the building, with a portrait of Sarah Sargent Paine prominently displayed. On the left were two rooms, in the front a smoking room, which hosted checkers tournaments among other activities, and a children's room in back. Both the adult and children's reading rooms had fireplaces. The library's collection, which by 1912 consisted of six thousand volumes, included subscriptions to six foreign-language newspapers. Books in Finnish and Croatian languages were acquired through donations from immigrant residents. A large hall that seated four hundred people, with stage, occupied the second floor. In 1905 the hall accommodated 110 church services, 20 lectures and concerts, 22 dances and socials, and 3 "miscellaneous entertainments," bringing in nearly four hundred dollars in rent. In the basement the bath room, containing four tubs, served 3,715 bathers.[33]

At the library's dedication on November 14, 1903, William A. Paine gave the deed of the library to a board of trustees composed of himself, the general manager of the Trimountain Mining Company, and the general manager of the Champion Copper Company, Lucius L. Hubbard, who chaired the board. The library served a shifting number of communities as Copper Range expanded. The companies underwrote the operational expenses of the library at a cost of about twenty-five hundred dollars a year, plus heating and lighting. A board of managers, chaired by Charlotte Hubbard Goodell (daughter of Lucius Hubbard) and probably composed of women, ran the library, reporting annually to the male board of trustees. In one year, Mrs. Goodell acknowledged the contributions of fourteen volunteers, all women.[34]

In 1911, after construction of the township high school next door, the library also took on the duties of a township library, circulating books to every school in the township. In the late 1920s, a tunnel joined the library to the high school, facilitating the students' use of the library. But when an addition was built onto the high school in 1934, it included a library, thus ending the school's partnership with the Paine Library. With the closure of Trimountain and Baltic mines in the early 1930s, and the outmigration of people from the township in the 1920s and 1930s, revenues and circulation dropped sharply. The baths were discontinued in 1946. In 1962 the building was declared structurally unsound, and the library moved into a new building, part of which it leases to the post office. The old library was demolished in 1964.[35]

Quincy chose not to compete with these two grand libraries. Instead, in 1915, the company contemplated a "possible bath house, or clubhouse," estimated to cost about ten thousand dollars "as an initiatory step in welfare work." Initial plans included a gymnasium, two bowling alleys, and a billiard room, all of which were dropped as the plans evolved into a bathhouse. Quincy President Todd said that his idea "would be to take the Calumet as a model, but without a tank or swimming pool," after Lawton advised him that pools "cost like the mischief if they are kept supplied with water so as to be sanitary."[36]

Quincy hired local architect Charles W. Maass, who designed a two-story, Classical Revival brick building with flat roof and modillioned cornice (Figure 5.12). The ground floor of the 92-by-30-foot building had a women's bath room with three tubs and three showers, a men's bath room with three tubs and six showers, and living quarters for the attendant. The second floor underwent a slight shift in uses. The 1916 drawings show a 35-by-30-foot "lecture room" and a large "men's room" leading to a screened porch. President Todd thought that the second floor should have separate rooms for working men and bosses, who would head in different directions halfway up the stairs. The 1917 furnishings plan reflects this hierarchy, calling the men's room a "foremen's room" and the lecture room a "lecture room and men's room." Between these two rooms, toward the front of the building, was a 21-by-17½-foot reading room, equipped with one large table surrounded by ten chairs, two newspaper racks, and one range of shelving for books and magazines.[37]

Todd's strategy for the library was to use it to attract more men to the building so that they would then use the baths. Todd noted that there were many men and families using the bathhouse, "but I think we should arrange to try to make it of even greater benefit to our employees by encouraging the men to use it more freely." The library, which had previously been housed in the basement of Quincy's office building, was moved into this central space in 1918. Todd thought the addition of current magazines and newspapers would "induce the men to use the second story rooms" so that "it will tend to bring their attention more forcibly [to] the bathing privileges on the first floor." Accordingly, the annual report that year touted that "an attractive reading room, with a librarian in charge, together with

Figure 5.12 Quincy Mining Co. Bathhouse, built 1916–17. The basement contained men's and women's baths, while upstairs were a foremen's room, a lecture hall/men's room, and a library. The screened porch on the right was off the foremen's room. Courtesy of Historic American Engineering Record.

a considerable number of new books and a liberal supply of newspapers and periodicals, have popularized the library and rendered it more useful to the employees and their families." The company retained a librarian until 1930, paying her thirty-five to forty-five dollars a month.[38]

Libraries and bathhouses are clearly two of the more altruistic endeavors undertaken by the companies. They could have considered their educational responsibilities fulfilled with the provision of schools. Bathhouses might have been a way to avoid installing bathrooms in company houses, but C&H's construction of a swimming pool in its bathhouse went beyond duty. Pools were seen as a means of luring people, especially boys, into the baths. While C&H's reasons may have been less calculated, and the company may have built the pool simply because that is what modern bathhouses provided, nonetheless C&H as well as other companies seemed concerned that its facilities get as much use as possible. The openness of C&H's library, the pool in C&H's bathhouse, and Quincy's provision of a library to attract users to the baths were all attempts to have their gifts to the community used and not stand as empty showpieces.

Schools

On the evening of August 31, 1905, an explosion in the chemistry lab set off a fire that destroyed Calumet's Manual Training School and High School and heavily damaged the Miscowaubik Club next door.[39] No one was injured and the cause was never determined. Calumet & Hecla, which owned the school building and leased it to the school district, set out immediately to rebuild.

C&H had a long-standing interest in the schools. In 1875 the company built a state-of-the-art facility, the Central School, later called Washington School, at a cost of more than eighty thousand dollars (Figure 5.13). The school was located near the company's offices, next to Shaft No. 2, the Superior Engine House, and the boiler house. The flamboyant stick-style building had a broad hip roof with cupolas, dormers, and a center tower. The four cupolas sheltered ventilation shafts, part of a complex heating and ventilation system that included steam heat provided by C&H. Above a stone foundation and first floor, the second floor was clad with clapboards, and the third with board-and-batten siding. The 192-by-100-foot building accommodated twelve hundred students in twelve grades and, besides classrooms, included an assembly room, a lecture hall with Steinway grand piano, a laboratory, and a museum of stuffed birds and animals and mineral specimens. The school was reputed to be among the largest in the country when it was built. The school district paid fifteen hundred dollars annual rent to the company.[40]

C&H continued to build grade schools on company property, although the school board also built some of its own schools. Of the thirty schools built in Calumet by 1930, thirteen had been built by the school district, the rest by mining companies. After 1895 the schools were given American patriotic or literary names, such as Jefferson and Garfield, Longfellow and Whittier, not missing an opportunity to instruct. C&H General Manager MacNaughton reported that the company received eleven thousand dollars in rent, or 3 percent of the cost of construction, for the twelve schools that it had built by 1913. MacNaughton also pointed out that the company paid 85 to 90 percent of the taxes in the district, implying that the company provided most of the funding for the schools, one way or another. The company's influence was evident in other ways, too: the school board, which met in the company offices, was composed of three officials of C&H, one resident of Red Jacket Village, and one from Laurium.[41]

In 1897–98 C&H built a Manual Training School at a cost of a little more than forty-seven thousand dollars, including two thousand dollars worth of chemicals

Figure 5.13 Central School, Calumet, built 1875, burned down 1929. Calumet & Hecla built this well-equipped school and leased it to the school district. Courtesy of Keweenaw National Historical Park.

and "apparatus." The school included a drafting room, carpenter shop, pattern shop, blacksmith shop, machine shop, chemical laboratory, and biology room. The domestic science department, added later, included sewing and cooking facilities. Three years later the company built at a cost of thirty-three thousand dollars an adjacent high school with a large assembly hall and more than a dozen classrooms. The appearance of these buildings, which were connected at the second and third levels, was undistinguished: three-story, wood-frame, flat-roofed buildings covered with corrugated sheet iron. A cupola and round-arched doorway marked one building. In 1904 the editor of the Boston-based *Journal of Education* described them: "Such schoolhouses! They look like temporary sheet-iron-cased car sheds after a conflagration. There is not a line of grace or a bit of ornamentation anywhere without, but within! Here there is everything a teacher's heart can desire."[42] When these buildings burned less than eight years after construction, C&H unhesitatingly took on the burden of reconstruction.

D. Fred Charlton of the Marquette-based architectural firm of Charlton & Kuenzli sent a letter to MacNaughton two days after the fire, offering his firm's services and pointing out that his firm had designed more than fifty schools in the Upper Peninsula. Charlton got the job. First, though, MacNaughton and Agassiz had to decide what and where to build. As soon as he heard of the fire, Agassiz suggested maintaining the separation of functions in different, and more widely spaced, buildings, making them fireproof to some degree, and providing sprinklers. After studying the uses of the school buildings, though, MacNaughton concluded that they needed to be near each other because high school and grade school students also used the manual training facilities. The solution he offered was to construct an "absolutely fire-proof" training school and a "practically fire-proof" high school. He noted that high school attendance was growing faster than the grade school, "denoting a more prosperous condition of the community," and that the new school should be planned to accommodate 500 or even 600 students, in contrast to the 325 of its predecessor.[43]

By the end of September MacNaughton sent Charlton & Kuenzli's sketches to Agassiz. By then he and the architects had decided to combine the two schools into one; MacNaughton's rough estimate of the cost was eighty-five thousand. From Boston, Agassiz responded with a four-page handwritten letter, including a sketch of the façade as he would prefer it. Agassiz argued for a flat roof, not gable, and certainly no tower. He thought the windows were too numerous and too large. He thought assembly rooms in high schools were "useless" and favored more section rooms, "but that is a matter I have argued over and over with Supt. and they are all hidebound to what I consider our antiquated method of handling children." He was equally suspicious of architects: "Give up all cornice work and don't let us spend any money on looks. We want first of all a serviceable Bldg, and architecture has no claim whatever on us." And his concluding advice in the letter was "don't let the architect run away with you."[44]

Once MacNaughton had passed Agassiz's suggestions on to him, Charlton agreed that a flat roof would be preferable, but he objected to reducing the size of the windows. He suggested storm windows. Neither MacNaughton nor Agassiz favored including a gymnasium. MacNaughton did not like assembly rooms, either, but thought that they were so accepted that C&H could not avoid providing one. As he said, with some exasperation, "This has been my first experience with a high school and I trust it may be my last." Finally, on October 10, Agassiz declared that "the plan, the position, the distribution of space is most satisfactory" and gave his go-ahead for construction.[45]

*Figure 5.14 Calumet Manual Training School and High School, built 1905–7, photographed 1958.
Calumet & Hecla built this large building, which combined the high school and manual training
school, at a cost of two hundred thousand dollars. The assembly hall is on the second floor of
the center section. Courtesy of Michigan Technological University Archives and Copper Country
Historical Collections.*

MacNaughton and Agassiz continued to express concerns over details. One discussion dwelt on the architect's plan to have the roof slope toward the center and have the water carried down through a downspout in an interior wall in order to avoid ice jams; MacNaughton found several other examples in the Copper Country and concluded that it would work. In January MacNaughton asked for window details from the architects because the price of glass was low and he wanted to buy it then. C&H's carpenter shop could fabricate the windows in the slow winter months. In February Charlton & Kuenzli sent most of the drawings and in April billed C&H thirty-five hundred dollars for professional services rendered. This price was computed as 3.5 percent of the total construction cost, then estimated to be a hundred thousand dollars, which would be covered by insurance. Despite the rush to have drawings by the time ground could be broken in the spring, construction, supervised and undertaken by C&H employees, took more than a year, and the school was not occupied until fall 1907. Finishing, furnishing, and equipping the school were expensive; the total cost of the new school was two hundred thousand dollars.[46]

The building that resulted was large—272 feet long—and quite plain but more architecturally sophisticated than the corrugated-iron buildings that preceded it (Figure 5.14). The company's concern that it be fireproof was reflected in the stone

foundation, brick walls, and concrete floors. The center section of the building was a little taller and wider;
tall round-arched windows on the second floor illuminated the assembly room. The 88-by-84-foot assembly
hall had a 23-foot-high ceiling, and the blank wall on
the façade above the windows concealed the steel
trusses necessary to span that space. Flanking the
center section were three-story, ten-bay-long wings,
58 feet wide, with large segmental-arched windows.
A flat roof with modillioned cornice crowned the
structure. Although the cornice was quite plain, the
upper part of the wall was finished in Jacobsville
sandstone, which was also used for keystones, string-
courses, and the foundation. On the north front,
facing Washington School, two pedimented entrances
flanked the center section.

In the architects' drawings, the Manual Training
School occupied the basement (blacksmith shop and
machine shop), first floor (woodworking room, laboratories, and sewing and cooking rooms), and second
floor (drafting room), while the high school also
claimed space on these floors: recitation rooms and
laboratories on the first floor, assembly hall and recitation rooms on the second floor, and more recitation
rooms on the third floor. In the first year, woodworking
was shifted to the basement, and soon blacksmith and
machine shops were moved to the first floor, but the
basic dual use of the building remained (Figure 5.15).[47]

Almost immediately, the school was too small.
Within a year of opening, the school population exceeded the capacity of the assembly hall; fortunately,
the plans had allowed some space for expansion, which
was immediately occupied. Unassigned space on the

east end of the third floor became a freshman study hall known as "the nursery."[48]
By the 1910–11 school year, 775 students enrolled in the high school.

C&H considered the Manual Training School its particular domain. Some of
the manual training teachers were paid directly by the company, not the school

Figure 5.15 Calumet Manual Training School, blacksmith shop. Calumet & Hecla was interested
in training future employees. As students, they made items to C&H specifications for the
company's use. Courtesy of Michigan Technological University Archives and Copper Country
Historical Collections.

board, and the head of the manual training department was paid more than the principal of the high school. There were other links to the company; as one historian wrote, "When machine shop and forge shop instruction were added, every effort was made to have the boys turn out articles for the use of the mining company, in accordance with specifications the Company set." Clearly, the manual training school was designed to train future employees of C&H. The students also saw the benefits of this arrangement; as MacNaughton wrote, "Students have taken more interest in school work in general and have a greater desire to keep in school on account of the training work than formerly."[49]

But what of the girls, almost none of whom would find employment with C&H? Home economics classes began at the end of the nineteenth century, about the time that manual training for boys did, but C&H viewed them quite differently. In 1901 Agassiz refused to supply equipment for a cooking school and "did not care to have it located in either the High School or Training School buildings."[50] The sewing and cooking rooms appeared, nonetheless, in both old and new buildings, but MacNaughton and Agassiz's main concern with them was that the cooking room posed a fire hazard, second only to the chemistry lab, which also had gas piped in. Clearly the home economics program was not as integral to C&H's interests.

As important as manual training was to C&H, it was also in the company's interest to have a complete high school with college preparatory courses. C&H's amenities were intended to attract and retain not only workers but also managers, whose children needed a full range of educational opportunities. By the 1920s, the high school offered three tracks of college preparatory courses: Latin, engineering, and academic. Physics was required of all boys, but girls could choose among physics, chemistry, or biology. The school also offered three tracks of vocational courses: commercial (for boys and girls), home economics (girls), and industrial (boys). The high school reached its peak enrollment of 1,417 in grades nine through twelve in 1932.[51]

C&H's unwillingness to provide a gymnasium in the school building while another was available nearby reflected the company's holistic view of the amenities it underwrote. In 1897 a YMCA formed and built a handsome sandstone building on company property at the edge of the village. Within a year, the organization had nearly 400 members to take advantage of the building's gymnasium, bowling alley, and swimming pool. Calumet High School's boys' basketball team, begun in 1903, used that facility. Even the girls' basketball team, founded two years later, used the YMCA. Given that arrangement, MacNaughton saw no need to put a gymnasium in the new high school. Just after the high school was constructed, in

Figure 5.16 YMCA, Calumet, built 1908, photographed 1910s, since demolished. The YMCA building on company land included a swimming pool, gymnasium, bowling alley, billiard room, and dormitory. Courtesy of Keweenaw National Historical Park.

1908 the same architects, Charlton & Kuenzli, designed a new, expanded facility for the YMCA, a three-story, Classical Revival brick building at the corner of Fifth and Scott streets (Figure 5.16). First, the YMCA reorganized, forming a board of trustees, whose function was to manage YMCA property, distinct from the board of directors, whose concern was the work of the YMCA. Both were closely tied to the company: MacNaughton chaired the board of trustees, and Edward S. Grierson, C&H's chief mining engineer, presided over the board of directors. C&H donated money toward construction of the building and also donated the land on which it stood. The facility included not only a gymnasium and track but also a swimming pool, bowling alley, billiard room, meeting rooms, and a dormitory. Although the YMCA had a membership of 2,013 men and 6,384 boys in 1920, within a few years the high school had taken over the YMCA as its athletic facility.[52] After construction of the new Washington School, which included a gym, in 1930, the high school abandoned the YMCA, which was demolished a few years later.

C&H did make one more effort for athletics, and that was the construction of a skating rink. With trusses fabricated by Worden–Allen Company of Chicago, Milwaukee, and Houghton, the building was a large, 130-by-259-foot round-arched structure. MacNaughton signed off on the drawings just a few days before the 1913 strike began, but construction continued through the strike.[53] Procompany rallies occurred at this "Colosseum."

C&H may have claimed to have no interest in architecture, but Copper Range did, evidenced by the high school in Painesdale. Designed in a Jacobean Revival style and executed in Jacobsville sandstone, the school exhibits the most sophisticated architecture of any school in the Copper Country (Figure 5.17). Located adjacent to the Sarah Sargent Paine Memorial Library and across the street from the elementary school, the high school was located in the central civic core of the town. Since the removal of the elementary school in the late 1950s, the block in front of the high school has been vacant, showing it off to great advantage.

The township funded construction of the high school, beginning in 1908, but the company's influence is evident in the choice of the architect: Alexander C. Eschweiler of Milwaukee, who had designed the library and general manager's house, among other buildings for the company. The company donated the land and arranged for the school to be heated by the C Shaft boiler house, for which it charged the school. Built at a cost of $125,000, the school accommodated four hundred students.[54] It drew not only from Painesdale, Trimountain, Baltic, and South Range but also from the mill towns of Freda and Beacon Hill. The school was located just up the hill from the railroad, by which these outlying students commuted to school.

The building, which opened in the fall of 1909, was arranged in a rigidly symmetrical form, with the end and center bays projecting. Groups of five windows characterized each bay, except for the center, which was only three windows wide. Rough-faced sandstone was trimmed with smooth, and the parapeted roofline gave the building a distinctive profile. The 140-foot-long building contained an assembly hall in the center of the second floor, illuminated by skylights, with a

Figure 5.17 Painesdale High School, built 1908–9, photographed 1913. Painesdale's large high school, constructed of Jacobsville sandstone in the Jacobean Revival style, like the library next door, included some manual training rooms and bathing facilities. Courtesy of Michigan Technological University Archives and Copper Country Historical Collections.

stage and dressing rooms. The first floor had recitation rooms, a chemical and physical laboratory, and a science lecture room. Like C&H's high school, vocational schooling was evident in the provision of a sewing room and kitchen for the girls and a manual training room for the boys in the basement. Also in the basement was a gymnasium with boys' and girls' locker rooms with showers.[55]

The provision of school, gymnasium, and bathing was maintained as at C&H, but Copper Range placed them all in one building. Students were required to take a shower every Monday, under supervision.[56] They were also required to take physical training, which, for the girls, included "Swedish exercises for the strengthening of their bodies." Cora Jeffers, principal of the high school from its opening until her death in 1949, was an enthusiastic proponent of physical education, leading the exercises herself.

In 1933–34 the school was expanded through a two-hundred-thousand-dollar Civil Works Administration project. Architect John D. Chubb, with offices in Marquette and Chicago, designed the addition even before the CWA construction program was announced in November 1933. The addition on the rear, which more than doubled the size of the school, was constructed of the same Jacobsville sandstone as the original building, in the same style. Three-story wings projecting to the rear contained a study room and library on the second floor, four classrooms on the first floor, and locker rooms and showers in the basement. Between them were a new gymnasium and swimming pool. The old gymnasium space was converted to bleacher seating for the new gym. The swimming pool—the first to be built in a high school in the Copper Country—featured Art Deco-style tiles. Principal Cora Jeffers, aged sixty-four when the addition was completed, had never swum before. But she took up the sport and soon was teaching the students.[57]

In contrast to its competitors, C&H and Copper Range, Quincy did not build a high school, sending its older students to school in Hancock. Quincy was content to provide less schooling, keeping expenses and taxes down. Its main elementary school was a large frame structure built in 1867. Its clapboard siding, shutters, and side-gable roof gave it the appearance of an elongated house, but the bell tower centered on the roof indicated that it was a school. Quincy expanded it in 1875–77 to 96 by 26 feet, accommodating three hundred students. In 1891, Quincy added a hot-water furnace and a cellar in which to put it. S. B. Harris commented to Mason, "I told the School Board (!) that I decidedly disapproved of doing the work this year, so it will be put off until next summer," his exclamation point indicating his dislike of being accountable to a "lesser" organization such as a school board. In 1895, a 26-by-46-foot addition provided two new rooms and a wing for indoor privies. Quincy also acquired the Pewabic and Franklin schools when it bought those companies.[58]

As in Calumet, Quincy owned the schools and leased them to the school board, which it controlled. The company's managers and foremen served as officers of the school district. General Manager Lawton's interest in keeping costs low, rather

Figure 5.18 School at Mason, built 1892, since demolished. Companies also built small one-room schoolhouses, such as this one at Quincy's stamp mill. Courtesy of Historic American Engineering Record.

than providing a quality education, was revealed in a letter to President Todd when he proposed building a new house for the machine shop foreman. Lawton wanted to keep Thomas J. Thomas in a company house because "I find him of great assistance in matters pertaining to the Franklin Township politics, and especially on the school board where he is helping hold down the expenses—thereby helping out our school taxes."[59] Quincy was of course the largest taxpayer in Quincy and Franklin townships.

At the stamp-mill community of Mason, the company considered establishing its own school district but then decided to work with Osceola Township. Quincy built the schoolhouse, a small frame building, 26 by 38 feet, with a small belfry, accommodating thirty students (Figure 5.18). The Township School District paid rent to Quincy and paid the salary of the teacher. Harris initially said that he had no preference as to the selection of the teacher, "except to insist on having a Protestant. Must draw the line somewhere." A few days later, Harris agreed to hire the teacher and purchase coal, while the school district provided the desks and the stove.[60]

Schools posed something of a quandary to companies that seemed at times to view them as money pits, organizations that would consume any funding that came their way. Schools, though, were necessary to the civilized society that the companies were attempting to foster and, like churches, they were essential to attract families. Thus every company-run community had elementary schools, invariably wood-frame, ranging from one room to eight or more. High schools were rarer, accommodating only a select number of students who proceeded to the upper grades. Both Copper Range and C&H built showpiece high schools, but even here C&H tried to temper its investment, as when Agassiz cautioned, "Don't let us spend any money on looks." C&H's approach to providing and equipping schools was summed up by W. E. Trebilcock, longtime superintendent, who wrote that "the attitude of the Company has always been one of sincere interest in and benevolent feeling towards the schools . . . and liberality without extravagance is the way that attitude may be characterized plus emphasis on the practical in the work of the schools."[61]

Hospitals

Copper Country mining companies were quite advanced in their health-care system, yet not innovative in their hospitals. Early mining companies, following Cornish precedent, kept a doctor on staff. Employees paid a monthly fee, usually fifty cents for single men and one dollar for families, that guaranteed them access to this doctor and medical care—in effect, a form of health insurance. The companies also offered a place for treatment, either a doctor's office, a dispensary, or a hospital.

Copper Range's hospital was typical, in that it was not purpose-built but, rather, was an adaptation of an existing house. Trimountain Mining Company built a house for its superintendent probably around 1900, but when that company merged into Copper Range a few years later, the new company converted the house into its hospital. Trimountain was located centrally, between Painesdale and Baltic. The company doctor lived in Painesdale, where there was also a dispensary. The company built accommodations for nurses next to the hospital.

The 1906 rehabilitation of the superintendent's house for use as a hospital is revealing in just how minimal it was. The house was a two-and-a-half story, gable-roofed, wood-frame structure, with porches, bay windows, and a hip-roofed dormer. The first floor accommodated waiting and consulting rooms as well as the doctor's office. The operating room on the second floor received a white enamel finish, extensive lighting, and hot and cold running water, operated by foot pedals. The men's ward was on the second floor and the women's on the third. The greatest changes seem to have occurred in internal transport and communications, with an internal bell and telephone system as well as an elevator and dumbwaiter. The oak woodwork, though, "could not be changed without going to a large amount of trouble so it was left in the present state."[62]

Calumet & Hecla had also converted a preexisting superintendent's house. A house was under construction for the superintendent of the Calumet Mining Company when Calumet & Hecla was formed in 1871. The superintendent of the combined company preferred to live elsewhere, so the house was converted to a hospital.[63] Located on Calumet Avenue next to Shaft No. 16, it was a simple two-story, side-gable house, three bays wide. Additions over the years created a rambling structure.

In 1897 C&H decided that a new hospital was necessary, but instead of building a new, completely modern building, the company elected to heavily renovate the one it had (Figure 5.19). The company hired the Marquette architectural firm of Charlton, Gilbert & Demar to devise the plans. The poor-rock foundation, framing, and roofline survived from the original house, although additions to the rear were all made uniform at two stories. Windows were added, so that single windows became double, and two spaced windows were made triples. The footprint was a general "I" shape, with waiting room in the front section, a double-loaded corridor flanked by consultation rooms along the stem of the "I," and minor surgery and library in the rear. On the second floor, the men's ward occupied most of the stem of the "I"; the women's ward was in the back, along with the operating room (Figure 5.20). Private rooms and offices occupied much of the rest of the space. When this "new" hospital opened at the end of 1897, C&H claimed that it was "fitted with the best laboratory and surgical apparatus procurable in Europe and America." By this time, the company had eight physicians, two interns, three pharmacists, and four nurses.[64]

In June the architects advised on paint colors, with the understanding that General Manager S. B. Whiting preferred red. "It might be best to tint the roofs a light tint of red and the walls a deeper tint of the same color, taking care not to let the painters pick out particular parts in different shades or colors. Nothing in our opinion gives such a cheap effect as this 'picking out.'"[65] Inside, the hospital

Figure 5.19 C&H Hospital, built ca. 1871, remodeled 1897, since demolished. Calumet & Hecla boasted about the modernity of this revamped hospital, which had twenty-four beds. Courtesy of Michigan Technological University Archives and Copper Country Historical Collections.

appears to have been well appointed, yet still domestic in scale, with low ceilings. The facility offered about twenty-four beds.

It was not enough. Ten years later, the company began to consider expansion. In the late nineteenth and early twentieth centuries, hospital use increased nationwide, reflecting a shift in public perception. The limitations of home care became obvious in the face of the hospital's antiseptic environment and technologies such as the X-ray. Increased hospital use in the Copper Country also coincided with sharp growth in the number of C&H employees. Dr. A. B. Simonson replied to a query from MacNaughton that "the time is rapidly approaching when something must be done—either enlarging our hospital, or some decision as to the care of women and children which require hospital treatment." Simonson suggested offloading the women and children patients onto the Calumet Public Hospital, with C&H picking up part of their costs, but instead MacNaughton considered constructing a new hospital. While it might have been comforting to

Figure 5.20 C&H Hospital, operating room. When it opened, the hospital had eight doctors, two interns, three pharmacists, and four nurses on staff. Courtesy of Keweenaw National Historical Park.

patients, the house form of hospital was outmoded. The modern hospital demanded an antiseptic, easily cleaned environment in which ventilation was key.[66]

MacNaughton began discussions with Charlton & Kuenzli (the then-current form of Charlton, Gilbert & Demar) in 1910, going through three iterations of drawings. The new hospital would be generally I-shaped but with the long side facing the street; the new location, across Calumet Avenue from the old one, was a more expansive site. The brick building would stretch 160 feet across the front. There were multiple wards totaling ninety-five beds, many specialized rooms, and an "aid fund room" for settling the bills. The drawings never got to the elevation stage, though.

MacNaughton sent the floor plans to C&H President Quincy A. Shaw, who took them to Boston architects "who have a great deal of experience in the building of hospitals." A few weeks later, MacNaughton begged off the project, turning it over to Shaw. As a result, MacNaughton dismissed Charlton & Kuenzli, and Shaw hired

Haven & Hoyt, the Boston architects he had consulted. Charlton protested, offering to work with the Boston architects, but MacNaughton paid him off in full and that was the end of Charlton's involvement.[67]

From then on, MacNaughton dealt with Shaw, not the architects. Shaw relayed the architects' questions, such as the prevailing wind in winter (answer: west and northwest), the lowest temperature in the last eleven years (–22 degrees), and the coldest two weeks in the past eleven years (January 4–17, 1912, when the mean temperature was –5 degrees). Shaw considered designing the new two-hundred-thousand-dollar hospital with the capability of having a third story added later but assessed the situation this way: "There are likely to come so many changes in the concentration of labor, for instance, at Ahmeek and Allouez, and the general independence of the public, that an addition is more likely to be taken care of by some separate building rather than an increase in this one."[68]

C&H broke ground in May 1913, but labor became a problem. The company elected to build the hospital with its own force, not contract it out, but MacNaughton noted a "scarcity of labor of all kinds." He was also overseeing construction of an electrolytic plant at the stamp mill, where he could find only five bricklayers to do the job.[69] The company got the foundations poured, but an even larger labor problem occurred at the end of July: a district-wide strike. Work on the hospital ceased and never resumed.

It is not clear why C&H did not continue construction of the hospital after the strike. It is possible that Shaw or MacNaughton felt so embittered by the strike that such a gift to C&H workers was no longer merited, although construction of the skating rink continued, suggesting a lack of hard feelings. Perhaps Shaw's observation on "the general independence of the public" was realized. Perhaps C&H's financial situation did not permit it; copper prices fell to a new low in November 1914, and the company instituted cutbacks.[70] Or perhaps the Calumet Public Hospital had begun to take up the slack.

The Laurium hospital opened in 1903 as Northern Michigan Hospital, but after the death of Dr. Charles Sorsen, its driving force, in 1907, it reorganized as Calumet Public Hospital. Like other hospitals, its original building was a wood-frame, house-like structure. It was not until 1923 that it built a brick, three-story modern hospital—apparently much like the one that C&H had been planning.[71] C&H's hospital operated until 1953, and the Calumet Public Hospital continues today as Aspirus Keweenaw Hospital.

The first modern hospital in the region was St. Joseph's in Hancock, which built a new five-story brick-and-stone building in 1904. The hospital had been founded as St. Mary's in 1896, occupying a domestic structure—in fact, one that was formerly the bishop's house. The presence of this hospital allowed Quincy Mining Company to provide only a dispensary at the mine site and not to build a hospital of its own. When the Sisters of St. Joseph's asked for five or six acres of land for a hospital, Quincy gave it to them on the condition that they allocate two beds in the hospital to the company for free.[72]

C&H's decision not to proceed with construction of its modern masonry hospital in 1914 marked a turning point in the company's largesse. The new hospital would have been a handsome, modern, and efficient landmark of benevolence—all qualities that C&H valued in its "welfare work." Instead, C&H, like Copper Range, was content to make do with its outmoded houselike hospital. The extravagance of new construction during unsettled times in the Copper Country and abroad was finally too much for the company; its prewar and prestrike generosity would not return.

Office Buildings

While Quincy may not have expended much architectural energy on its community institutions, the company did produce a showpiece office building. Although the offices were meant to accommodate the managers and clerks based in Michigan, the East Coast managers had as much, if not more, say in the design of this building than most. Treasurer Todd commented with false modesty, when sending the drawings to Agent S. B. Harris, that "it will certainly make a handsome, and commodious office, and when finished, imposing enough to make us all take off our hats, and be on our best behavior, when we come to see you."[73] Todd usually did not hesitate to remind Harris of his—Todd's—superior status.

The venture began in the summer of 1895, when Harris sent internally produced drawings to the New York office for approval. Todd urged some grandeur on Harris: "Hope you will get up a nice building that will be ornamental, with enough ground in front to set it off nicely, and a place in rear to drive into, so that fellows won't hitch their horses at the front door." But two days later, after conferring with President Mason, Todd referred the issue to his friend and neighbor in Morristown, New Jersey, architect Robert C. Walsh, effectively taking the design out of the hands of the Michigan office. When sending the new drawings, Mason downplayed his involvement, offering the new design "only . . . that you may get some new ideas from which to obtain what you want," but Harris knew his place;

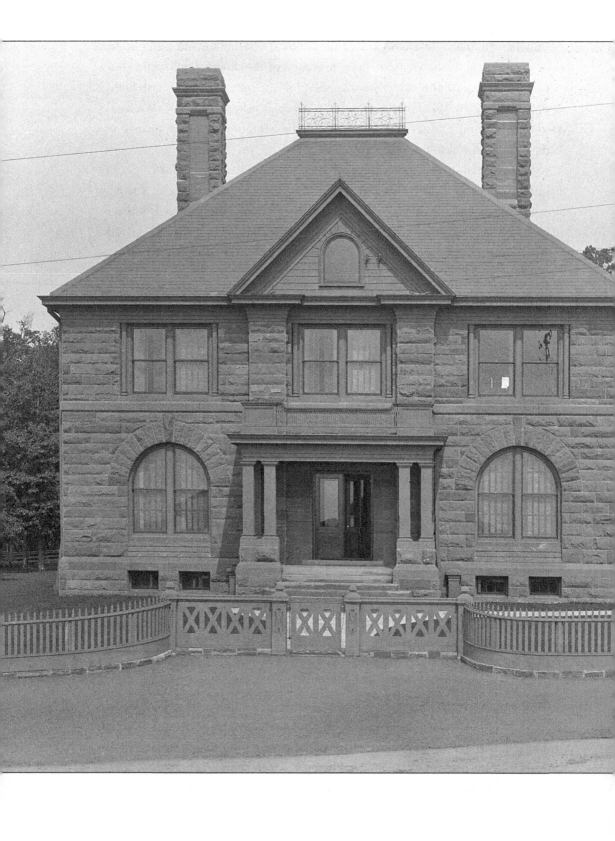

he pronounced "the whole design to be very fine indeed." He did offer "certain trifling suggestions," such as moving an interior door, rearranging the pay window to avoid crowding, and providing a sink on the second floor for the blueprint room.[74] Still, it was the architect in New Jersey who developed the specifications.

Walsh, whose practice in Morristown reflected his connections to high society, designed a 56-by-45-foot Colonial Revival building with a symmetrical façade (Figure 5.21).[75] The two-story office building had a high, hipped slate roof and prominent stone chimneys. The center bay was pulled forward slightly and surmounted by a pediment; there was a one-story portico with paired columns. Knowing that the building was to be constructed of stone, Walsh designed broad round-arched windows on the first floor, with paired windows above. But it was the stone that seemed a little out of place on the building. Harris argued for a rough-faced Jacobsville sandstone, giving the building a dark red color, while Walsh's Colonial Revival design would have been more appropriate with red brick or a smooth-faced, lighter colored stone.

Nonetheless, Quincy went with high-class local materials in selecting Jacobsville sandstone. The front and sides of the building were of the highest grade, a pure red. Mason suggested, and Harris concurred, that the rear could be of a cheaper, variegated stone, although this was not done. Harris ordered the stone in early October; the order was filled in about six weeks. The stone shipped from quarries at the south entry of the Portage by scow, then was dressed in Hancock before being hauled up to the site on Quincy Hill. The company broke ground in the spring. Over the winter, much of the woodwork had been fabricated by the company's carpenter shop, and the remainder was ordered from local producers. Construction proceeded over the summer and the offices were occupied December 30, 1896.[76]

Figure 5.21 Quincy Mining Co. office building, built 1895–96. Designed by an East Coast architect and built of local sandstone, Quincy's office building was intended to present a solid and respectable image to passersby. Courtesy of Michigan Technological University Archives and Copper Country Historical Collections.

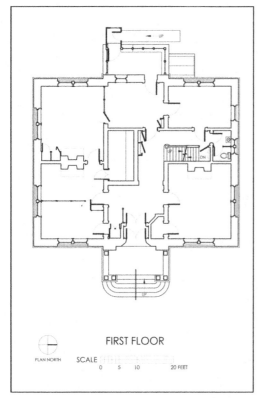
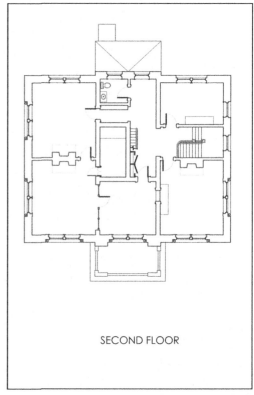

FIRST FLOOR

PLAN NORTH   SCALE

0   5   10   20 FEET

SECOND FLOOR

Figure 5.22 Quincy Mining Co. office building, plans. The agent occupied the prime right-front corner, with the chief clerk across the hall. The central two-story vault was an essential feature for keeping money, engineering drawings, and essential documents safe. Drawn by Quentin Peterson, Keweenaw National Historical Park, 2004.

The agent occupied the office in the right-front corner of the building on the first floor (Figures 5.22, 5.23). The chief clerk occupied the other front corner, with the assistant clerks in the adjacent office. The pay window in the assistant clerk's office opened into the rear hall; employees would enter through the back door to approach the pay window. The second floor accommodated the drafting and blueprint rooms. There was a two-story vault in the center of the building. With tall ceilings and rich woodwork, three of the four large rooms on each floor had fireplaces with elaborate overmantels, although Harris, foreseeing that central heating would be desired soon, asked that the cellar be built tall enough to accommodate a furnace. There was a toilet and sink on the first floor.[77]

Among other functions, the building originally served as a pay office. Underground captains kept track of the hours their employees worked. Each employee, who was assigned a number, drew his pay in cash, personally, at the mine office once a month. The first change to this system occurred in 1900, when Quincy

Figure 5.23 Quincy Mining Co. office building, chief clerk's office, photographed in 1902, according to the John A. Roebling's Sons Co. calendar on the mantelpiece. The building was constructed without central heating, but it did include ornamental woodwork. Courtesy of Michigan Technological University Archives and Copper Country Historical Collections.

began paying the men with checks, not cash. A greater change occurred as the result of the Michigan Workman's Compensation Act of 1912, which required that workers be paid twice a month. In enacting this change, Quincy also went to a time-card system and employed timekeepers—a specialization of one of the underground captains' tasks. The company also decided to pay the men at the shaft where they worked, not at the mine office. To accommodate this, the company built timekeeping and waiting rooms at each shaft. Quincy's workforce had doubled in size since the office building was first planned.[78]

But just as Quincy was decentralizing the payment system, the company was also centralizing and professionalizing tasks related to it. In 1900 Quincy's clerical staff consisted of eight people: six clerks and assistant clerks, one chief engineer, and one assayer. By 1916 the number was up to thirty-two: eight clerks, three time-keepers, ten general office workers, three telephone operators, and eight assayers or engineers. General Manager Lawton requested an addition to the building in 1913,

Figure 5.24 Calumet & Hecla office building, built 1886–87. C&H's office building, like the library constructed later, had stone walls in an unusual "mosaic" arrangement. The pay shed is on the left. The building was added onto several times as the company grew. Courtesy of Michigan Technological University Archives and Copper Country Historical Collections.

and again in 1915, but these were not granted. Drawings that survive may date from the 1913 request. A twenty-foot-deep addition across the rear accommodated a "safety and efficiency office" and a timekeeping office. The pay shed on the west side of the building had an efficient traffic flow to the pay and time windows. Other changes included a telephone board and rear door to the general manager's office. The drawing may represent Lawton's ideas for expansion; when Todd rejected the plan as too expensive, they decided to move payment functions to each shaft. Even though Quincy employees were no longer trooping into the back door to receive their pay envelopes, there was still a lot of traffic. As Lawton complained, "The

settlement and employment room, because of the talking with the men in different languages, attracts a great deal of attention, and, therefore, should also be in an enclosed room by itself," along with the noisy addressograph.[79]

Quincy's office building was designed for the impact it would make on the businessman approaching it or the casual visitor passing by. The front façade was sturdy, upright, impressive. The company used expensive building materials and hired an East Coast architect. The building was set back from the road to increase the effect. Horses were not parked out front, and mine workers did not approach the front door, even though the front door was closer to their workplaces than the rear.

As impressive as Quincy's office building was, once again it was following C&H's lead. C&H hired Boston architects Shaw & Hunnewell to design an office building, constructed in 1886–87 (Figure 5.24). Although it was located on Calumet Avenue, it faced the other way, toward the mines. In a modest Classical

Revival design, the building's most distinctive feature was its stonework, a mixture of different stones laid in a random, uncoursed manner, trimmed with red brick. The newspaper was unimpressed; a reporter wrote that the building "may not possess much architectural beauty, but the interior is very conveniently arranged." But the permanence of the masonry building made an impact: "Judging from the ponderous appearance of the building, the company intend[s] it to last as long as the mine, and that, by nursing its resources, will, no doubt, be very many years."[80] This implication of permanence was a major purpose of a costly masonry office building.

Inside, the building accommodated the company's white-collar workers. The 70-by-46-foot building placed the "superintendent's private office" in the right-front corner, the "superintendent's room" in the right-rear corner, adjacent to the "head clerk's private office," which led to his other office in an alcove off of the "office," a 20-foot-wide space stretching the full depth of the building, on the north side. Beyond the office was the pay shed, accessible through two windows. The second floor had a large drafting room above the office, as well as two chambers and a sitting room to house single clerks.[81]

The company expanded the building as the company grew. In 1899 it added a one-story section on the east and the next year a two-story section on the north, moving the pay shed to the north end of the addition.[82] In 1909 Charlton & Kuenzli designed a large two-story addition to the east, which accommodated a drafting room on the second floor and suite for the general manager on the first. Both additions were of the same distinctive stonework as the original building, giving the building an architectural coherence. Having been more than doubled in size, the office building had an increased presence at the corner of Calumet Avenue and Red Jacket Road, highly visible to passersby, patrons of the library, and students in the high school. It was also nestled between the Congregational Church, the denomination favored by the company's East Coast management, and the Miscowaubik Club, the club of the elites. Employees also knew the building well, receiving their pay there. But they did not enter the building, only the unheated metal shed at one end.

Copper Range took a different tack with its main office building. The company, along with its subsidiary Champion Copper Company, constructed an office building in 1899–1901, just as the company was getting underway. The two-and-a-half-story frame building, measuring about 48 by 36 feet, was located between E Shaft and E Location, across the street from the home of Champion's first general manager, Lucius Hubbard.[83] In the next few years the company built architect-designed houses for its managers up on the hill, but the office building kept its modest appearance in its unobtrusive location. The company also built dramatic masonry structures such as the library and high school but apparently did not see its office building as an advertisement for itself in the way that Quincy and C&H did.

The uses of the building were consistent with the other companies. The general manager and chief clerk had offices on the first floor, with a pay shed on the south side. A drafting room occupied the south side of the second floor, and a three-story vault in the center safeguarded drawings and money. The third floor initially housed single engineers. Small one- and two-story additions were made over the years, and with these changes the building served as the main local offices into the 1960s.

Office buildings housed the company's local managers and white-collar workers: clerks, draftsmen, engineers, timekeepers. But they also served two other important functions, external and internal. These buildings presented a face to the public by which the company's solidity and sophistication might be judged. Both Quincy and C&H were conscious of the appearance of these buildings, using fine stonework and situating them prominently. Internally, these office buildings were approached by every workman once a month. Although workers were routed to the side and rear and not even permitted entrance into the building when collecting their pay (except at Quincy), they were still reminded of the power of the company through the grandeur of its office building.

The Architecture of Paternalism

Because churches, libraries, bathhouses, schools, hospitals, and office buildings express the relationship between workers and management, it is worth exploring the impact of the architecture. Most of the grandeur of these buildings derived from their size and masonry construction, not from the sophistication of their designs. Agassiz's caution not to "let the architect run away with you" offers a clue as to management's desires. Company managers did not want to spend frivolously, especially on nonessential buildings. For the most part, they built the institutional buildings only as big or as elaborate as they needed to be. The institutional buildings were showpieces, mentioned in all the promotional literature, but as much for what they provided as for their architecture in itself.

It is tempting to see a building like the C&H library as a construction of control, occupying a prominent site with a prominent building, guiding the leisure reading of the working class. And there was undoubtedly an element of that, particularly among C&H's Boston management. President Alexander Agassiz, a zoologist by training, grew up around Harvard and probably felt comfortable with libraries; he hired a Boston architectural firm, whose principals were related to C&H board members, to design the library, and he probably enjoyed working with them. But generally, managers found the construction of these community buildings to be a distraction from the real business of the company. General Manager MacNaughton's hope that this be the last high school he ever designed reveals his frustration with the process. He was only too glad to turn over the design of the hospital to Agassiz and his Boston architects.

Company managers would have been happy if someone else had provided these institutions, but there was no solid middle class, apart from company employees, to fill the breach. Painesdale, newly built and isolated, provides the best illustration of this. Located ten miles south of Houghton, Painesdale had no merchant class to lead the effort to construct churches, schools, libraries, and hospitals. If the company and its managers had not undertaken to build these institutions, it is unlikely that many of them would have existed. In Calumet, there was a thriving merchant class in the village of Red Jacket, but it was more concerned with providing theaters and entertainment than high schools and libraries. At Quincy, the nearby city of Hancock provided most of the institutions but, as a result, the city lured company managers to reside there rather than in company housing closer to the works. Companies provided institutions in order to attract and retain workers and managers, but the corollary of this axiom is that the employees would go where the institutions were.

Company management's sense of responsibility to its communities was revealed in a letter Alexander Agassiz wrote to the general manager in 1895. He had begun planning the library and noted, "This with the YMCA building will then put the public buildings in fair shape except a Town Hall which Red Jacket supplies."[84] These were only a fraction of the public buildings that C&H would build, but it shows that Agassiz was thinking holistically about the community's needs. It was quite a system: the company built a high school, but the gymnasium was in the YMCA, the swimming pool was in the bathhouse, and the library and skating rink had buildings of their own. Baths were not in houses but first in the library and then in their own building, where the hospital's laundry was also washed. These institutions were part of C&H's efforts to create a modern community, which particularly explains the company's provision of a swimming pool in the bathhouse. The architect said that pools and laundries were now common in "Modern" bathhouses. The desire to be modern may have explained managers' *desires* to build these institutions, but their *ability* to create this web of interlocking services was due to a centralized planning effort possibly only in an autocratic society.

In contrast to the companies' reluctance to use architects to design workers' houses, they turned to architects for these large institutional buildings. Copper Range hired Milwaukee architect Alexander Eschweiler to design its large institutional buildings, C&H hired Boston architects Shaw & Hunnewell for two of its institutions, and Quincy hired New Jersey architect Robert Walsh for its office building. All of these architects had personal connections to company management. C&H also employed the Marquette firm Charlton, Gilbert & Demar and its successor firm on at least four buildings. MacNaughton kept close tabs on the architects and initially suggested that their draftsmen work in Calumet, although Charlton demurred.[85] MacNaughton did not use architects to supervise construction or to develop specifications, because these large projects were constructed by C&H's own workforce. As noted above, he did not use architects to design cutting-edge or even fashionable buildings that would uplift the viewer by their architectural polish. Instead, he seemed to approach them as professionals who could offer some expertise in building types with which he and his carpenter staff had little experience.

Nonetheless, these institutional buildings did have an impact. They were large—the Calumet high school stretched 270 feet; the Painesdale library was nearly 90 feet wide. In contrast to the housing, they were masonry, either brick or stone. They were centrally located, which added to their impact but also added to their identification with the company. As one observer said during the strike, "The soldiers brought into the district camped on a part of the same piece of ground on which one of the churches is located. Among the strikers this church [the Congregational], the Y.M.C.A., the armory, the schools and the public library were all classed as property of the Calumet and Hecla."[86]

The community institutions fostered by the companies were not one-way gifts but, rather, involved a negotiation with the workers. Although the companies designed and constructed these buildings without any apparent consultation with their users, managers seemed genuinely concerned that the institutions receive widespread use. Their reception in the community was undoubtedly mixed. Unionists spurned them, recognizing the deal that using company-provided facilities implied. Others, especially Finnish, Eastern European, and Italian immigrants, probably did not feel welcome in many of these places. Immigrant women, especially, were less likely to speak English and would have been less likely to circulate freely in the community.[87] Yet some institutions, such as schools, were universally used. Overall the numbers of library cards and bathhouse patrons show heavy usage, and it is fair to say that these community institutions were successful in helping to create a vibrant community that offered shared experiences to its residents.

6 Preservation and Loss

Remembering through Buildings

On August 17, 1913, Steve Putrich and Alois Tijan, the two unionists who were killed in Seeberville, were buried in Lakeview Cemetery at a funeral attended by thousands. Eight Croatian and American flags decorated the gravesite at the time, but there was no grave marker. When Joseph and Antonia Putrich moved to Illinois in 1917, that severed their connection with the Copper Country until their grandson, Joe C. Putrich, and his wife, Elaine, began researching their family's history. Their search brought them back to Painesdale, where their family had lived, and to Calumet, where family members were buried. On May 8, 2004, the family installed a tombstone for Steve Putrich and Alois Tijan. Erecting a grave marker was a way to acknowledge the past.[1]

Joe and Elaine Putrich's "memory" of the Copper Country was not literal, as neither had lived here. Their memory consisted of family photographs and stories told by Joe's grandparents, such as his father, as a baby in Antonia's arms, receiving powder burns on his face during the shootings. The house at which this occurred had burned down before Joe was born, so there was little direct material evidence in the Copper Country of his grandparents' lives here. But there is much to remind people of the copper-mining days in general: a few shaft houses and related mine buildings, rock piles and stamp sands, railroad beds converted to snowmobile trails, communities of company houses with an eerie similarity, multiple grand churches in a community that is now hardly large enough to support one.

The legacy of the Copper Country's past is as complex as paternalism itself. Companies fueled by Eastern capital built great mines and thriving communities. They attracted immigrants from all over Europe as well as Canada and the United States. They ran their societies in an autocratic and paternalistic manner but provided much more than they had to in the way of libraries and schools, swimming pools and skating rinks, hospitals and housing.

Workers did not accept this largesse passively. They tacitly bargained for better equipped or cheaper houses; they avoided the company-house arrangement with a range of alternatives; they congregated in their own churches, bars, and fraternal halls. They organized a massive strike, claiming public spaces as their own. The grand community institutions and substantial frame houses were tainted to greater or lesser extents by the involvement of the companies, but many employees were satisfied with the paternalistic system. Many others were not, evidenced by constant outmigration. The Copper Country developed according to its own unique social contract.

If, as this book has shown, buildings can reveal intricacies of management–worker relationships, then it should also be true that buildings can tell us about how people think about the past and their ambivalence toward a history of negotiated paternalism. Preservation projects indicate choices in terms of what kind of buildings merit the intense work of raising money and mobilizing community support necessary to preserve them. Certainly, some buildings are easier to preserve than others. Some are already in public hands and are perceived as a community asset, while others have private owners who quietly maintain and care for them. Other buildings, though, demand intervention and vision to be preserved, and here, where the work is the greatest, the choices are most revealing. Preserved buildings can tell us how a community values the symbols of its past. Buildings that are preserved and opened to the public can further help us understand what stories a community wants to communicate about its past.

To understand how Copper Country residents today view their past, this chapter examines three preservation stories. The first is a story of loss—how and why the community allowed the demolition of Italian Hall as a means of burying a controversial incident that occurred at a divisive time. The many other ways of remembering that tragedy, though, show that it still reverberates. The second story concerns the preservation of the Calumet Theatre, just a block away from Italian Hall, and why that was possible and desirable. Finally, a broad look at preservation and interpretation efforts in the Copper Country today suggests a more complicated narrative, one which is less a story than a collection of multivalent efforts. In them, though, lie the clues as to how people think about their past.

Remembering Italian Hall

Preservation failures are revealing. One of the most significant buildings in the Copper Country, and one strongly associated with workers, no longer stands. Italian Hall, site of a tragedy during the 1913 strike, resonates even today, representing the conflict in many people's minds (Figure 6.1). Concerned citizens attempted to

Figure 6.1 Italian Hall, Calumet, built 1908, photographed 1913, demolished 1984. The Italian Benevolent Society provided a large meeting hall on the second floor, reached through the arched doorway on the left, and two commercial spaces on the ground floor. Courtesy of Michigan Technological University Archives and Copper Country Historical Collections.

save this building, but it was demolished in 1984. The stories and controversies continue to swirl about this structure, even in its absence. How people remember this building, and through it, the tragedy, reveals an aspect of how people think about worker–management relations in the Copper Country.

Five months into the bitter strike, the Western Federation of Miners held a Christmas party for strikers' children. Anna Clemenc, a local organizer known as "Big Annie," arranged the event. About 500 children and 175 parents crowded into the second floor of Italian Hall in Calumet. The partygoers played games, sang songs, and, late in the afternoon, lined up to receive presents from Santa Claus. Then disaster struck. Someone apparently yelled "Fire!" and panic-stricken partygoers raced down a wide flight of stairs to reach the main exit. But someone tripped and fell and others on top of them, until dozens of bodies lay at the foot of the stairs, crushed. Of the 73 people who died that day, 58 were children. Tragically, there was no fire, and thus no need to rush. The official cause of death was suffocation.[2]

Given the intensity of feeling about the strike, it is no wonder that the Italian Hall tragedy was instantly politicized. Public sympathy immediately shifted to the strikers. Donations to a relief fund amounted to twenty-five thousand dollars within a day. Charles Moyer, president of the Western Federation of Miners, rejected this charity, however, maintaining that the "union will bury its own dead." Some observers saw this as a missed opportunity. Luke Grant, an investigator for the U.S. Commission on Industrial Relations, suggested that the union could have used public sympathy deriving from this tragedy to force the companies to negotiate.[3] But the opportunity was lost. Two days later, the county sheriff's men confronted Moyer and an assistant in their hotel room, shot Moyer during a struggle, and put them on a train out of town. Public support for the strike began to slip away, as did the support of the national union. Finally, in April, the locals voted to abandon the strike effort, with no tangible gains.

The Italian Hall tragedy remained the most prominent incident of the long and bitter strike. Its impact was compounded by the fact that, while there was a clear sense of a wrong having been committed, no one was ever charged with a crime. A few days after the tragedy, the coroner held an inquest, summoning seventy witnesses. His verdict, issued on December 31, was that the cause of death was "by suffocation, the same being caused by being jammed on the stairway leading to the entrance of the Italian Hall . . . and the stampede was caused by some person or persons within the hall, unknown to the jury at this time, raising an alarm of fire within the hall."[4] Two unresolved questions haunt the history of this event, affecting the way that the incident, strongly associated with a building, persists in public memory: who, if anyone, cried fire? and how and why were people trapped in a stairwell?

Witnesses differed widely on who had raised the alarm. At the coroner's inquest, twenty-six witnesses heard a man cry "fire." They described the perpetrator variously as dark, fair; mustached, clean-shaven; wearing a hat, wearing a cap. They also differed on where in the hall the perpetrator stood, some placing him by the door, others in the back of the hall. As the *Miner's Bulletin* reported, "A fiend in the shape of a man sneaked up the stairway leading to the hall, opened the door and waving his arm cried 'fire, fire!' then quickly making his way to the street where he disappeared in the gathering darkness." Seven witnesses said he was wearing a button; three identified it as a Citizens Alliance button. But fourteen did not see a button on the man at all.[5] These varied recollections are not surprising; eyewitnesses often contradict one another.

The unionists felt strongly that the Citizens Alliance or other procompany men precipitated the disaster. Much of the questioning at the inquest was designed to counteract this, pointing out that union representatives checked for union cards before allowing people to enter the party. And although others noted that identification was not checked later in the day, the coroner, anxious to absolve procompany forces of involvement, found "that no person or persons was allowed inside of the hall where the celebration was being held without producing a union card or having some member of the union vouch for them before they be allowed admittance."[6]

Other explanations surfaced. Perhaps someone cried for water, which in Croatian sounds very much like the word for fire. Another account emerged in 1982, when Leslie Chapman of Calumet related a story that he had heard decades earlier in Butte. In 1924 an unidentified dying man confessed that he and his partner "were both single men and drunk and thought we'd have some fun. As we walked by the hall we decided to holler fire and watch the people come down. We didn't know it would turn out bad. We both left town afterward."[7] Some witnesses never heard a cry of "fire."

The second unresolved question concerns the pileup in the stairway and its cause. Witnesses described a rush to the stairs, someone tripped and fell, causing others to fall, creating a pile of people that just got bigger. Eyewitness John Antila described it as "just a moving mass down the stair." Others, approaching from the outside, found a mass of bodies four or five feet high, packed so tightly that people could not be removed from the front; rather, rescuers went in the back of the building to the top of the stairs, and pulled people off the top. Eyewitness Charles Meyers described it as "a mass mostly all children mixed up and tangled in one mass in front of the door, that I don't believe any children got out. I tried to pull some of these children but I could not, they were so tight and tangled up I could not do anything." When asked how many people were in the stairway, he estimated 200 or more, and said, "It was just one scream, they were squeezed so tight they could not give a loud sound. It was just a scream, and death showed in almost all their faces especially the lower ones." The *Miner's Bulletin* described the tragedy: "The way was made for the children first and they filled the stairway so full and crowded from the rear so fast that some of the children were swept off their feet. These little bodies acted as stumbling blocks for those who followed and within a few seconds the stairway was a mass of bleeding, crushed, dead and dying humanity."[8]

In the midst of a bitter strike, a theory arose as to why so many died in the stairway. The union claimed that detectives in the employ of the companies held the door shut and prevented exit. This account showed up first in a special edition of *Tyomies,* a Finnish-language newspaper, on December 26; the next day sheriff's deputies raided the newspaper's offices and charged four employees with "publication of matter that might have the effect of inciting a riot." Perhaps because of this intimidation, neither the union local's newspaper, the *Miner's Bulletin,* nor the national union's publication, the *Miners Magazine,* charged that deputies had held the doors shut. At the inquest, only two witnesses reported that deputies blocked the doors, while sixteen testified that they had not.[9] Some witnesses pointed out that some officials at the scene prevented people from entering and compounding the mess.

In the 1950s, though, another explanation surfaced; Harry Benedict, in a Calumet & Hecla (C&H) company history, alleged that the doors opened inward, thus preventing exit under the circumstances. This explanation has gained wide acceptance, even appearing on a Michigan Historic Site marker. But this is clearly a latter-day explanation; not one witness at the coroner's inquest mentioned inward-opening doors. The procompany *Daily Mining Gazette* specifically said that the doors opened outward, and neither union publication, the *Miner's Bulletin* or the *Miners Magazine,* alleged inward-opening doors, an explanation that might, in fact, absolve deputies from holding doors shut.[10]

The Italian Hall had had previous experience with inward-opening doors as well as with disasters. The Societa Mutua Beneficenza Italiana was a benevolent society organized in 1875 along ethnic lines. In 1890 its nearly completed hall collapsed in heavy winds. The organization rebuilt the next year, producing a large wooden building on a stone foundation, divided into two stores on the first floor, with a second-floor hall. In 1904 this building was cited by the marshal for having inward-opening doors. On January 1, 1908, the hall burned to the ground, without fatalities or injuries. The Italian Hall in which the tragedy occurred was its replacement.[11]

The society's new brick building of 1908, designed by architect Paul H. Macneil, measured 58 by 100 feet. At ground level, the Great Atlantic & Pacific Tea Company and Vairo's saloon occupied two storefronts with recessed entries. In the southernmost bay of the front, double doors in a large round arch led to the stairway to the second floor. Seven round-arched windows on the second-floor façade illuminated the meeting hall. A handsome cornice, topped by the society's name, crowned the building. The second floor contained a well-equipped meeting hall, with a stage, balcony, ticket window, men's and women's toilets, barroom, and kitchen. At ground level, the doorway from the street opened into a foyer that measured 6 feet wide by 8 feet deep. To the right off the foyer a door led directly into the saloon. Two feet from the foot of the stairs, double doors separated the stairway from the foyer. The stairway was 5 feet 9 inches wide. A newspaper article at the time of its dedication mentioned safety features such as "the ample main stairway" and two fire escapes and noted, "All doors open outward."[12]

The belief that the doors opened inward may have derived from a misleading stereoview published soon after the tragedy (Figure 6.2). The foreshortened view shows two sets of doors, one opening outward and one inward, apparently from the same door jamb. But this is impossible, because the foyer between the two doorways was deep enough to contain a door off to the right to Vairo's saloon. In order to put a door at the bottom of the stairwell that did not interfere with the saloon door, a folding door seems to have been the solution. This door was hinged in the middle so that one leaf folded flat against the other and both lay flat against the wall on the left. Part of the popularity of the inward-opening-door theory is due to the fact that it explains logically how so many could have died in the stairway. It is possible, though, for too many people to simply jam into a space, with tragic results.[13]

The Italian Hall tragedy was commemorated in a variety of ways, tangible and ephemeral, interpretive and documentary, by outsiders and residents. An examination of these expressions of memory offers insight into how attitudes about the incident have changed over time. These varieties of commemoration also remind us that preservation of a building is only one means of remembering. Immediately

2   The disastrous stairway, Italian Hall, Calumet, Mich.
Tuhoisa porraskäytävä, Italialaisten Haali, Calumet. Mich.

Figure 6.2 Italian Hall, doorway. In this foreshortened photograph, both doors appear to open off the same jamb, and one set of doors opens inwards, which was not the case. The photo is part of a stereopair captioned in English and Finnish. Courtesy of Michigan Technological University Archives and Copper Country Historical Collections.

afterwards, the incident received nationwide attention, appearing in the *New York Times* and other newspapers. Photographer John W. Nara documented the hall right after the tragedy (Figure 6.3). Some of those images were distributed in a set of stereoviews along with other strike scenes, captioned in English and Finnish. Some were also made into postcards. The funerals of the victims, which attracted thousands of mourners who lined the route of the funeral processions, received extensive coverage. Newsreel footage of the funerals played in Chicago; the Western Federation of Miners used the showing as a fundraiser. Even the film was contested; the union alleged that someone attempted to steal the film footage in Calumet, but the photographer had put a dummy in its place. The union also charged that the companies had tried to buy the film to prevent its being shown.[14]

Inevitably, though, the furor died down. In April 1914 strikers surrendered their union cards and returned to work or left the area. There is no doubt that the tragedy cast a pall over the region. For people who lost family members and friends, it was a personal loss. For people who had been there it was a searing experience. Ted Taipalus, who survived the tragedy as a boy although two of his sisters died in it, never spoke to his surviving sister about these events and vowed never to enter the building again.[15]

For decades there was no physical memorialization of the tragedy. The most famous commemoration of the Italian Hall tragedy was offered by Woody Guthrie, who wrote a song about the incident in 1946. Guthrie never visited Calumet but became aware of the tragedy by reading the autobiography of a labor organizer, Ella Reeve Bloor, who had been present that day. Guthrie's song had an unequivocal take on the event, as reflected in its title, "1913 Massacre."

. . . The copper boss' thugs stuck their heads in the door,
One of them yelled and he screamed "There's a fire." . . .

A man grabbed his daughter and carried her down,
But the thugs held the door and he could not get out. . . .

The scabs outside still laughed at their spree,
And the children that died there were 73 . . .

The parents they cried and the miners they moaned,
"See what your greed for money has done."

Asch Records first released Guthrie's song on an album called "Struggle: Documentary #1." The other songs on the album related aspects of American history and workers' lives, including one called "Ludlow Massacre." Guthrie's song remains popular, giving the Italian Hall tragedy nationwide exposure, and guaranteeing Woody's son, Arlo, sold-out audiences when he plays Calumet.[16]

Figure 6.3 "The Italian Hall Disaster in Pictures," photographed by J. W. Nara, 1913. Photographs depict Italian Hall, the interior soon after the tragedy, the victims, and their funeral. Courtesy of Michigan Technological University Archives and Copper Country Historical Collections.

Although the Woody Guthrie song is by far the most enduring and far-reaching public commemoration of the Italian Hall tragedy, a number of other artistic renditions have attempted to tell the tale. One major, recent event was an opera, commissioned by a local music festival and funded by a Michigan bank and the National Endowment for the Arts. *The Children of the Keweenaw,* by composer Paul Seitz, opened in the Calumet Theatre in 2001. Librettist Kathleen Masterson noted that she wanted to honor different points of view. Recognizing the complexity of the Italian Hall incident, Seitz and Masterson commented on the "unresolved nature of the event." In the last scene, a funeral, members of the chorus sang the name and age of each of the dead. But the last lines are given to the narrator who repeats his first lines, which include a reference to Anna Clemenc:

> I do not claim
> That all I have told
> Of this, of her
> Is strictly true.
> What's true for me
> May not be true for you.[17]

The opera is one of the few interpretations that does not attempt to provide a definitive explanation.

Outsiders from beyond the Copper Country developed these recountings and observances. Locally, among those who had experienced Italian Hall and the strike firsthand, this history received very little public discussion. Residents recall that the tragedy was not taught in local schools or discussed in homes. One resident remarked that it was "too emotional" a subject to discuss casually and also pointed to a lingering fear of speaking out against the company, even though the company is long gone. Perhaps the very divisiveness of the subject made it unsuitable for a polite, civil society. One reporter called the strike and the Italian Hall tragedy "an open wound in the memory of the community."[18] The unresolved nature of the tragedy—the fact that no perpetrator could be identified or punished—contributes to the raw feelings. But also the fact that this was a strike-related incident, the epitome of a divisive event, prevented open commemoration for several decades. To those who were present in 1913, the strike tore apart the community like nothing had before or since. The strikers were a minority and a foreign-speaking one at that. Although the tragedy garnered the sympathy of the community, the strikers did not gain unanimous support from the public, contributing to the mixed emotions that resulted in the various interpretations of the incident. The residue of that divisiveness persists even today.

Renewed interest in the event derived from threats to Italian Hall and its ultimate demolition. In 1980 the village threatened to condemn the building as unsafe; its owner, Helen Smith, was unable to maintain the building. A Friends group formed to preserve the building, but when the cost of doing so was put at five hundred thousand dollars, even the Friends agreed that preservation was not possible. The negative feelings associated with Italian Hall—as a site of tragic deaths and community strife—also contributed to its demise. The Calumet Township supervisor recalled, years later, that "a lot of people did want it torn down, because they didn't want to look at it. They wanted it to go away."[19]

The Friends proposed that a memorial be made out of the doorway behind which so many died. Italian Hall was demolished in 1984 and the archway set aside. Nothing happened for several years, but the seventy-fifth anniversary of the tragedy in 1988 sparked some action, and the next year the Friends reerected the archway on the building's original site. Unionists, under the aegis of the Northwest Upper Peninsula Labor Council, provided volunteer labor. Further plans for buildings at the site to house a museum and theater to properly interpret the event have gone nowhere.[20]

Set in the middle of a lot on the edge of Calumet's commercial center, the memorial consists primarily of a stone and brick archway, adorned with brass plaques contributed by donors to the memorial effort (Figure 6.4). Brick paths, concrete benches, shrubbery, and a flagpole define the space, while several signs relate the story. One side of a large Michigan Historic Site marker describes the event; the other side gives the history of the building. A smaller stone marker displays a photograph of the Italian Hall. And in the rear of the lot, a "Historical Women of Michigan" sign relates the story of one activist present at the Italian Hall tragedy, Anna Clemenc. The arch stands disconnected, acting as sculpture as much as building fragment.

Locally, commemoration also appeared in the format of privately published books, such as Peggy Germain's *Tinsel and Tears,* and Wilbert B. Maki's poem, *Stairway to Tragedy,* around the time of the building's demolition. A video created in 2003 by a sixth-grade class at the Calumet school provided some sign that, after ninety years, this was finally a fully open and acceptable topic for discussion. In 2004 Larry Molloy produced a transcript of the coroner's inquest, with a close analysis of the text. In 2005 Peggy Germain reproduced every death certificate in another book. The next year Steve Lehto published *Death's Door: The Truth*

Figure 6.4 Keweenaw National Historical Park Ranger Dan Brown in front of the Italian Hall Memorial; park created 1989, photographed 2007. Concerned citizens saved the arch of the doorway, behind which seventy-three people died, and erected it in a park on the site of Italian Hall.

Behind Michigan's Largest Mass Murder, a somewhat partisan account, as its title would suggest.[21]

Historians have also related the story of the
Italian Hall tragedy. Angus Murdoch's popular 1943
history of the Copper Country painted a rosy
picture of management–labor relations and blamed
the union for making wild accusations about
the tragedy. In 1952 C. Harry Benedict, in the
company-authorized history of Calumet & Hecla,
called the incident an "inexplicable tragic panic"
and gave the management point of view. Benedict
was the first to mention inward-opening doors.
In 1984 Arthur Thurner, a Calumet native who
became a professor of history, published a history
of the strike called *Rebels on the Range.* In his
two chapters on the tragedy, Thurner recounted
the controversy and divisiveness but ultimately
supported the companies' claims of innocence. In
the most authoritative history of the region, historian Larry Lankton cast the tragedy in political
terms, characterizing the conflict as one that
both sides attempted to use to advantage. Even
the Historical Society of Michigan's magazine
entered into the controversy, publishing a photographic essay and the text of Woody Guthrie's
song shortly before the building's demolition. The

magazine then published an exchange of letters that demonstrated that the history
of this event was still controversial. Burton H. Boyum, an iron-mining company
executive, charged that Woody Guthrie, "in his haste to inflame hostilities,
abandoned all truth and common sense." In response, John P. Beck, a labor
historian, pointed out that the hostilities did not need inflaming; oppressive
paternalism in the Copper Country had produced a large number of dissatisfied
workers.[22]

Later, a piece of public art stirred up old animosities. In the summer of 2000,
the Copper Country Community Arts Council commissioned three works of art
that reflected aspects of local life or history. Ed Andrzejewski's 12-by-6-foot mural

Figure 6.5 Mural of Italian Hall tragedy, painted by Ed Andrzejewski, 2000. A local artist created controversy with this depiction of the Italian Hall tragedy, hung on the wall of a building in Calumet. The mural was moved to Hancock, where it was photographed.

depicting the screaming faces at the Italian Hall tragedy hung on St. Anne's Church in Calumet—but only for a few days (Figure 6.5). The board of the nonprofit organization administering the church building objected, ostensibly because of its size, perhaps because of its seemingly flippant attitude toward its subject matter— even the artist conceded that he had a "somewhat cartoonish style"—but even more likely because of the still-divisive nature of the event.[23] The mural was moved to Hancock where it was displayed for several months.

These various attempts at commemoration omit some of the more compelling aspects of the Italian Hall story. The Italian Hall tragedy was the most galvanizing incident of a bitter, nine-month-long strike, which is commemorated nowhere else. The strike is an important reminder that the Copper Country was not the harmonious work setting promoted by some observers. The memorial remains a unionist construction, the clearest rallying point for labor. Plaques on the arch, placed there by organizations that helped fund the reconstruction, include a bold statement by the Northwest Upper Peninsula Labor Council: "Mourn the Dead, Fight for the Living."[24] But after the collapse of the WFM local after the strike, the copper companies managed to keep unions out until the 1940s, when the copper industry was well into decline.

C&H's paternalism was evident even in the Italian Hall itself, a noncompany building on noncompany land. At the building's dedication on Columbus Day, 1908, James MacNaughton, the general manager of C&H, was invited to speak but was unable to do so due to a death in his family; in his absence his speech was read by someone else. He wrote, "The hall stands as a monument to the intelligence, the thrift, and the good citizenship of the Italian population of Calumet."[25] The Italians' desire for the imprimatur of the general manager and the condescending nature of his remarks indicates a complex relationship between working-class immigrants and company management.

One of the more poignant plaques on the memorial arch reads, "In Loving Memory of Mary"; Mary Krainatz was eleven years old when she died. A tragic aspect of this event was that so many children lost their lives. Sixty-nine of the victims were women and children. The fact that these were not striking men but, rather, women and children enabled the community at large to unite in sympathy for the victims. Often overlooked in the historical record, however, is the role that women and children played during the strike. Striking women paraded through the streets frequently, often led by the dynamic Croatian Anna Clemenc. There was also at least one children's parade; a stereoview of it was captioned in English and Finnish, "Parading children. (Several of these met their death in the disaster.)." Women rallied to the companies' side too; thousands of petitions from "mothers" of the Copper Country sought the release of deputies who had been convicted of killing unarmed strikers.[26] The commemoration of the strike, in the form of the Italian Hall tragedy, focuses attention on women and children not for their activism during the strike (aside from Anna Clemenc, whose popularization merits a study of its own) but for their passive deaths. Nonetheless, it reinforces the idea that the strike, working conditions, and management–worker relations had an impact not only on employees but also on their families and the community. The disproportionate suffering of women and children in this tragedy broadens the strike story to include everyone.

Another aspect of the resonance of this tragedy was that it was not confined to one ethnic group but, rather, like the strike itself stretched across ethnic lines. Forty-nine of the victims were Finnish, fourteen Croatian, six Slovenian, three Italian, and one Swedish. These numbers reflect the ethnic variety of the strikers; noticeably absent were Americans and English. Although immigrants socialized in their own churches and fraternal organizations, they engaged in some cross-cultural contact. Six or seven different organizations met regularly in the Italian Hall, and the Croatian Printing Company had occupied space in the previous building.[27] One triumph of the union was its ability to unite so many ethnic groups under one banner.

Italian Hall, then, stood for so much more than an ongoing debate about whether company sympathizers triggered the stampede and caused the deaths. It also represents the larger context of the strike and the ultimately futile attempt to unionize a large workforce. The paternalistic environment is reflected in the request to have C&H's general manager speak at the building's dedication. It is one concrete event where women and children were deeply affected by violence, whether intentional or not. Finally it represents the ethnic diversity of the strikers attending the party in the hall—a party planned by a Croatian woman, attended by a majority Finnish crowd, in an Italian hall. Still, the fascination with the potentially sinister cause of the tragedy—or the simple question "who did it?"—overrides all other concerns.

The sheer variety of commemorations—postcards and photographs, films and videos, songs and poems, plays and operas, murals and histories—indicates an enduring interest in the event, a repeated delving into the past to obtain greater meaning. Unfortunately there is no building to commemorate the tragedy—a building that would provide a tangible connection to an ephemeral event, that would show how substantial the Italian society's achievement was, that would give a sense of the size of the gathering, and that would show which way the doors opened. Instead, the doorway's arch stands, incapable of performing these functions, but acting in another way: as a blank slate on which viewers can write their own understanding of the event. The memorial and its site reflect the unresolved nature of the tragedy as well as the Copper Country's unresolved feelings about company management and workers.

Preserving the Calumet Theatre

One block from Italian Hall stands a preservation project that complicates the picture of public concern about the past. The Calumet Theatre, representing positive stories of community success, architectural accomplishment, and entertainment and good times, is a showcase of noncompany achievement (Figure 6.6). The village of Red Jacket funded and built it, private companies operated it, and the village still owns it. But like most things in the Copper Country, it was not free from the company's influence.

Incorporated in 1875, Red Jacket Village built a handsome new village hall at the corner of Sixth and Elm streets in 1886. Designed by architect J. B. Sweatt (whose Houghton County Courthouse was then under construction in Houghton), the fourteen-thousand-dollar village hall was constructed of Marquette brownstone, at a time when the competing Jacobsville quarries were just opening up. The second floor of the village hall contained an "opera house"—a large room with a stage and footlights—used for public performances and a host of other activities. The village hall also accommodated the council and clerk, fire station, police force, and jail. Twelve years later the village, enjoying sizable income, built a fire station across Sixth Street. Charles K. Shand designed the Jacobsville sandstone building in a Romanesque Revival style. The two-story building cost about twenty-thousand dollars to construct and measured 54 by 83 feet.[28]

While that was under construction, the village council decided to build an addition to its own facility. Desiring to convert the former fire department quarters into a large public dining hall and kitchen, the council also wanted a larger opera house. In 1898, facing an expenditure of more than twenty-five thousand dollars, the council decided to ask for the approval of the citizenry to borrow that amount. Although only 214 people voted, the addition was endorsed by almost a 3-to-1 margin. Eight months later, the council asked the public for approval to borrow another forty-five thousand dollars, which again was resoundingly approved. Although these referenda were phrased in terms of an addition to the village hall, it was clear that the new theater was a vital part of it. Veiled allusions to neighboring Laurium's plans to build a theater, as well as a desire to be modern, provided the impetus. The village council's resolution stated that it believed it "wise, expedient and necessary to make alterations and additions thereto commensurate with the present and future necessities and requirements" of the village. The council also argued that it had the responsibility for building an opera house, because the council could build on land leased from C&H, whereas a private developer would have the additional cost of the land.[29]

The funding of the theater, which reflects the village's independence from the company, has been the subject of differing accounts. In a story repeated by many, Angus Murdoch in 1943 asserted that the village had a surplus of fifty thousand dollars in its treasury, mostly due to twenty-seven thousand in taxes on saloons, and was looking for a way to spend it. In fact, the village had a surplus of only five thousand dollars in the spring of 1899. The village borrowed the funds it needed, paying off the loan at a rate of twelve thousand dollars per year. But Murdoch was right in that liquor taxes formed a significant part of the village's budget. In 1898 the liquor tax brought in more than twenty-five thousand dollars, about half of the village's income. By 1910, when the village issued more than seventy licenses, its income from liquor was more than forty-three thousand dollars.[30]

Five architectural firms entered the competition for the project and coincidentally the winner was Charles K. Shand, who was already designing the fire hall for the village. He proposed an addition on the south side of the village hall that would more than double its frontage on Sixth Street to 121 feet. The walls would be of Jacobsville sandstone and two towers would crown the façade. The opera house would have a triple entrance, a raked auditorium, and one balcony. As built, the village hall and theater had a frontage of 116 feet. The rough-faced sandstone of the walls encompasses only the first floor; the rest of the building is faced with a cream brick. The sole tower marks the division between the village hall and the theater. With light, arcaded windows on the second floor giving the building an air of the Italian Renaissance Revival, the theater portion is marked by a higher front wall, a pediment over the entrance, and a porte cochere extending over the sidewalk. The theater seated twelve hundred on the main floor and in two balconies. The stage measured 64 by 26 feet, being 32 feet wide at the proscenium arch. The newspaper claimed that "the new theatre will be the largest and finest north of the Straits of Mackinac . . . away ahead of anything in Northern Michigan, as far as the seating capacity is concerned and in beauty of architecture and finish it will be equal to anything in the State."[31] The exterior of the village hall on the corner

OVERLEAF: Figure 6.6 Calumet Theatre, built 1900. The two-story section on the corner houses the Village Hall, which included council chambers, clerk's office, and police station on the first floor and a large meeting room on the second floor. The theater, in the portion right of the clock tower, originally seated twelve hundred. Courtesy of Michigan Technological University Archives and Copper Country Historical Collections.

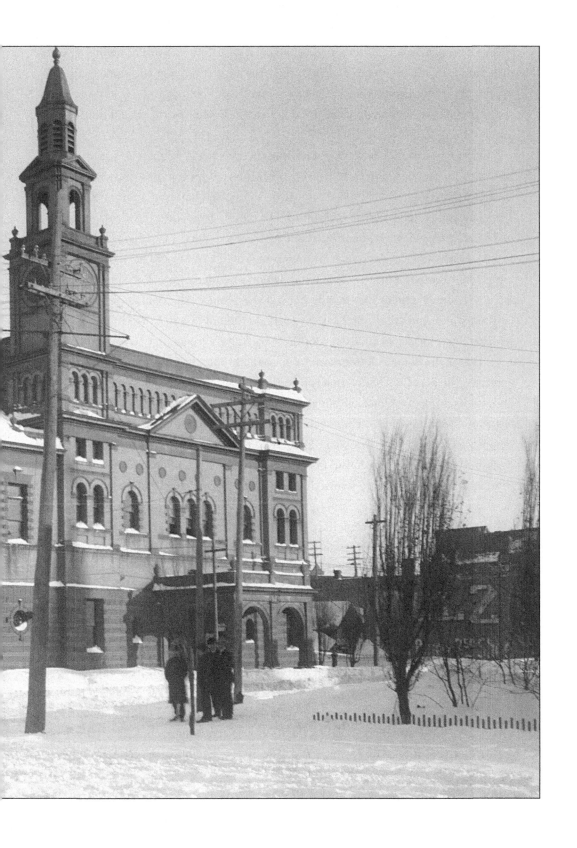

was redone to match the theater addition; even the front wall was brought forward to be in line with the theater. Inside, the uses stayed roughly the same, with an open hall on the second floor and clerk, council, and police on the first floor. The space previously occupied by the fire department was converted to a dining room and kitchen.

Contracts were let to Paul Roehm for the masonry ($19,538.68) and Bajari & Ulseth for the carpentry ($17,987). With interior furnishings, the cost of the theater approximated $65,000. Renovating the village hall cost another $23,000. The theater opened to great acclaim on March 20, 1900, offering a performance of *The Highwayman.* Dedicatory remarks were provided by William E. Parnall, superintendent of the Tamarack Mining Company.[32] C&H would have been absent entirely if it were not for the C&H Band, which provided musical accompaniment.

C&H's involvement was mostly behind the scenes. The company owned the land on which the village hall sat. As early as the fall of 1897 the village council realized that to lease an additional lot they would have to obtain C&H's permission. A year later the village clerk assured the council that C&H President Agassiz had approved the plan "but stated that the council must build the addition as a city hall and not as an opera house, although he had no objection to the extension of the latter at the same time." The clerk, or perhaps the newspaper, concluded that "there was therefore no trouble connected with getting the grant of the ground." Agassiz's approval, however, did necessitate phrasing the referendum as an addition, hardly the large opera house that dominates the original building today. The newspaper translated for the public: "Although on the ballot the vote was on the question of making improvements to the town hall it is generally understood that the principal part of the improvement will be in making a modern opera house out of the present building."[33] At that point the opera house was planned for the second floor of the expanded building, while the municipal offices would occupy the first. If Agassiz objected to the opera house that resulted, he gave no sign.

In 1910 C&H indicated that it would be willing to sell the three lots containing the village hall and theater to the village. As it turned out, the company gave the lots occupied by the village hall and theater to the village for free and charged four thousand dollars for the empty lot to the south, which was used as a public park. In addition the company charged the village thirty-five hundred dollars for the lot across the street occupied by the firehouse. The village considered the deal a great bargain, intending to cover the cost by the sale of its previous firehouse, constructed in the 1870s, on Fifth Street.[34]

The theater was a huge success, providing a focal point for entertainment in the Copper Country, even though Hancock built its own Kerredge Theater two years later. The Calumet Theatre chartered trains to bring patrons from Lake Linden and Hancock for special performances. In its first two decades the theater hosted performances by Sarah Bernhardt, Lillian Russell, and John Philip Sousa, lectures by Jane Addams, Jacob Riis, and Elbert Hubbard, and a boxing exhibition by John L. Sullivan, among many other entertainments. Film was introduced in 1913; D. W. Griffith's *Birth of a Nation* enjoyed a run in 1916. The theater converted to sound projection in 1929, and movies edged out live performances.[35]

By the 1960s, the theater was struggling to stay afloat. Even after the destruction by fire of the Kerredge Theater in 1959, leaving the Calumet Theatre as the only formal entertainment venue in the region, the theater's survival was in doubt. But the local pride invoked by the municipal theater, as well as its architectural presence, made it a likely project for preservation. Its abandonment or destruction would have symbolized the demise of the village. A variety of programs, including a professional summer-stock company called the Keweenaw Playhouse, offered performances in the late 1950s and early 1960s. In 1971 the village leased the building to the school district and a rehabilitation costing $118,000 took place, financed by a variety of agencies, including Michigan's Department of Natural Resources, the Michigan Historical Society, and the Upper Great Lakes Regional Commission.

The theater's historic character contributed to its value; the building was listed on the National Register of Historic Places in 1971, and the site received a Michigan Historic Site marker in 1973. Its significance, though, was based on a false claim, which was that it was "one of the first municipal theaters in America." This apparently derived from the promotion of the first theater manager, John D. Cuddihy, who called it the "only municipal theater in the United States," a boast that was taken up by the newspaper. In fact, there were dozens of municipally owned theaters that preceded it.[36] Despite hyperbolic claims, the theater is today valued as one of the grandest buildings in the village, or even the region, and it still serves its original function.

In 1983 the nonprofit Calumet Theatre Company was established to run the theater. Since then, the membership organization has scrambled for funds to keep the doors open, receiving just enough support in the community to remain viable. In 1988 another rehabilitation was funded by a Michigan Equity Program grant, Community Development Block Grant funds, and the village.[37] A mix of musical performances, community theater, and old movies keeps audiences coming. Volunteers give tours of the building in the summer, charging a small fee.

Preservation work on such a large building is expensive, far exceeding the resources of local donors, so theater supporters look to government funding. The theater has an advantage over some other historic sites, in that it provides entertainment to a broad swath of the public, so it has a base of support that extends beyond history lovers. In its tours and brochures, the theater promotes itself as a historic site by noting the famous people who have performed there, which sparks recognition in many visitors. Further, its past as a municipal construction, not as obviously a paternalistic creation as some other substantial buildings, enables it to appeal to public pride more than company buildings do. Although the theater's connection to liquor taxes is interesting in itself—the number of bars in a village of less than four thousand people clearly points to the village's role as noncompany oasis for a population of more than thirty thousand—the building is more often seen as tangible evidence of the wealth and sophistication the Copper Country once attained.

Interpreting Paternalism

The preservation activity that enabled the survival of the Calumet Theatre did not happen in a vacuum. The closure of Calumet & Hecla in 1968, and the subsequent sale of all its lands in the Copper Country to Universal Oil Products (UOP), was devastating to the community. Faced with an essentially useless industrial landscape, UOP soon began thinking in terms of developing Calumet's rich history. Although the term "heritage tourism" had not yet been popularized, UOP saw the tourist potential in Calumet's historic landscape as the seeds of a new economy. The company promoted a scheme called Coppertown USA to capitalize on the nation's bicentennial and the attendant interest in history (Figure 6.7). Coppertown was a theme park in a real landscape, focused on a "core area" of twenty-eight acres that stretched from the roundhouse and library on Mine Street to the edge of the village. Arrayed around a "Festival Plaza," the existing buildings of this "historic mining, ethnic and tourism complex" would be joined by new construction that included a multistory hotel on the site of the armory and an Ethnic and Cultural Center, all of it overlooked by a seventy- or eighty-foot-high statue of a copper miner. UOP's vision was that this would be a public–private partnership, directed by a local nonprofit development corporation, which would create

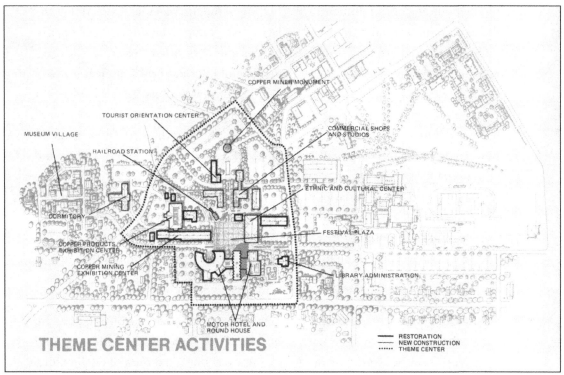

Figure 6.7 Coppertown U.S.A. plans, 1976. This plan to create a theme park in C&H's then-defunct industrial core included significant new construction. From Barton-Ashman Associates, Copper-town, U.S.A.: A Historic and Tourist Center Concept for the Keweenaw Peninsula, *1976, Michigan Tech Archives.*

270 jobs and have an annual payroll of $1.6 million. When federal funding was not forthcoming, though, the plan foundered.[38]

Deriving from its origin as a way of coping with UOP's newly acquired lands, the plan considered Calumet Village secondary. Nonetheless, the village's Calumet Theatre, having recently completed a costly rehabilitation, was featured in various accounts as symbolic of the rebirth that was possible. The only concrete remnant of Coppertown's ambitious goals is the museum in C&H's former pattern shop, also known as Coppertown. Here the broad outlines of Calumet's mining past are interpreted in a museum run by a struggling nonprofit organization.[39]

With the failure of Coppertown USA's grand plans, a more direct assault on federal funding was envisioned. In the 1980s interest grew in a national park. Various studies confirmed the historical significance of the Copper Country and the wealth of historic resources that remained. A National Historic Landmark nomination of Calumet mentioned the Calumet Theatre's success: "The magnificent Calumet Opera House has been restored and sees a full season of theatrical productions and entertainment." In 1992, when the fire marshal decreed that the theater required seventy thousand dollars worth of improvements to keep open—money that it did not have—the newspaper's editorial, titled "Save the Theatre," argued that the theater was "more than a community cultural center. It is also a cornerstone of the movement to establish Keweenaw National Historical Park. It would not be an exaggeration to say that the loss of the theatre could very well wield a killing blow to the park proposal." Finally, less than two months later, Keweenaw National Historical Park was established. Envisioned as a new kind of national park, it relies on a public–private partnership in which most of the buildings within the boundaries of the park remain in private hands. The boundaries encompass the industrial cores of C&H and Quincy as well as Quincy's waterfront smelter and most of the village of Calumet. The park's purpose is "to preserve and interpret the natural and cultural resources relating to the copper-mining industry." The park has acquired four historic buildings in the Calumet unit and one at Quincy.[40]

An examination of these five buildings indicates the park's involvement in the paternalistic landscape. The park owns the office buildings of both C&H and Quincy; its own headquarters are located in C&H's headquarters office building. The park also owns the C&H library, using it as a curatorial and archives facility, and a C&H warehouse, serving as curatorial storage. The only noncompany building in park ownership is the 1889 Union Building, which contained meeting halls for the Masons and Odd Fellows, built on company land. The buildings, four of them architectural landmarks in their own rights, are worthy of preservation and can reveal, by their presence and appearance, interesting aspects of the Copper Country's paternalistic past. The buildings' acquisition was also opportunistic; they were empty, available, and threatened due to lack of alternative purchasers. The park has not yet implemented a comprehensive interpretive program, so it remains to be seen how these buildings' history will be presented.[41]

One aspect of the public–private partnership outlined in the park's legislation and its subsequent General Management Plan is that local historic sites would carry much of the burden of interpreting the history of the area. Both the Calumet Theatre and Coppertown—along with seventeen other historic sites throughout the Copper Country—have been designated Keweenaw Heritage Sites by the park and its Advisory Commission, which aim to work with them to upgrade their facilities and interpretive programs to complement those of the park. These Heritage Sites, some of which have been in operation for decades, currently represent grassroots preservation and interpretation efforts.[42] An exploration into what has been preserved by these sites and what stories they choose to tell reveals, to some extent, how residents think about their region's past.

The nineteen Heritage Sites are operated by small organizations (sixteen non-profits and three for-profit), half of them without paid staff. These sites' very existence expresses what Copper Country residents found important to preserve in order to understand their past and present it to the public, both tourists and locals. The sites also reflect opportunity, in that they tended to be created at places that were no longer viable for their original uses, such as copper mines. And the park and its commission also selected them from a slightly larger field of applicants, so the group is not representative of all historic sites open to the public. Nonetheless, they are worth examining as a haphazard sample.

Not surprisingly, half of them are closely related to mining. Although all of C&H's shafthouses—the most visible identifier of a mine—have been taken down, along with most of the other mines', a few others remain. At the Quincy Mine, a shafthouse, hoist house with hoisting engine intact, and a number of other buildings remain. The Quincy Mine Hoist Association, established in 1958, offers underground tours and operates the site, which is within the boundaries of the park. Delaware and Adventure Mines, at the northern and southern ends of the Copper Country, also offer underground tours. Three other Heritage Sites offer surface remnants of mines. The Keweenaw County Historical Society displays the mine ruins at Central, and both Fort Wilkins and Porcupine Mountains State Parks interpret early mining sites with few surface remains. Other Heritage Sites occupy mine-related industrial buildings: Coppertown in C&H's pattern shop, Houghton County Historical Society in C&H's stamp mill office building, and A. E. Seaman Mineral Museum, which plans to build a new facility inside the walls of Quincy's machine and blacksmith shops. Generally, the mining past is interpreted as a technological and geological marvel, because it is the superlatives that impress: the depth of the mine, the height of the shafthouse, the quantity of the mine rock and copper extracted.

A number of the Heritage Sites occupy public buildings: a theater, two schools, a firehouse, a fort, and three lighthouses. The lighthouses, with little relation to mining except that they were occasioned by the immense increase in ship traffic as the mines were developed, have great romantic appeal. Having been decommissioned, they are operated by the Keweenaw County Historical Society, the Ontonagon County Historical Society, and Fort Wilkins Historic State Park.

The latter park is more focused on the mid-nineteenth-century fort at the northern end of the peninsula, also built in response to the 1840s mining rush. Two of the Heritage Sites display school buildings, both notable for their architectural integrity: Chassell Historical Society and Keweenaw County Historical Society. Calumet's sandstone firehouse, now the Upper Peninsula Firefighters Memorial Museum, and its theater are also valued for their architecture.

The noncompany and nonpublic buildings operated as Heritage Sites include a small bank, the home of the Copper Range Historical Society; a Finnish farm called the Hanka Homestead; and two churches: a wooden one at Phoenix maintained by the Keweenaw County Historical Society and the sandstone St. Anne's operated by the Keweenaw Heritage Center. The Laurium Manor Inn, a bed-and-breakfast facility in a grand house built for a mining company executive, is one of the great high-style houses in the Copper Country. In addition, three small communities of workers' houses are included as Heritage Sites. At the mining community of Central, operated by the Keweenaw County Historical Society, about ten houses out of several hundred survive. At Quincy Mine, a few houses close to the works have been preserved but are barely interpreted. And Old Victoria exhibits four log cabins, again, a fraction of the community at its height.

The stories told at these Heritage Sites are not limited by the buildings they occupy, and most of the sites interpret the copper-mining history in significant ways, but looking at these places as preservation choices is telling. The buildings or structures that house the museum or provide the focal point for the site possess qualities that attracted committed volunteers; in most cases the nonprofit group's acquisition of the building or site drove the subsequent interpretation or collection, not the other way around. The mining sites grapple with a complicated history that is largely invisible—the remains are either underground, in structures removed from the landscape, in waste rock that is being converted to gravel, or in stamp sands that are being sodded over to mitigate their possibly harmful effects. The other buildings that are preserved, meriting public expenditures and volunteer hours, are those that are found in any community—the best architecture and the fanciest buildings. As at most local museums, the past is celebrated uncritically, in an effort to appeal to a broad swath of supporters and visitors.[43] In the Copper Country in particular, this seems to be a remembrance of glory days, when copper was king, the region had money, and Red Jacket Village could afford to build a twelve-hundred-seat theater.

Few sites directly represent the mining company employees, though. The Copper Country's ethnic diversity is hardly represented, except in the Hanka Homestead, a farm built and operated by a Finnish family, and the Finnish-American Archives at Finlandia University. The Keweenaw Heritage Center operates St. Anne's, the French Canadian church in Calumet, with little interpretation. The divisive strike, which Italian Hall could have exemplified, is not represented in preserved buildings, nor is the labor movement. The grassroots Heritage Sites, wittingly or not, tend to present a consensus history, one that points to commonalities rather than divisions.

Further, the sites generally fail to interpret deindustrialization or the causes behind the closure of the mines and the related outmigration of the populace. The sites are available, by and large, because they are not being used for what they were intended. The copper was not exhausted, and the strike (which, after all, failed) did not cause the demise of the industry. Relating the larger forces of capital and competition to empty house lots is a bigger leap than most of the small Heritage Sites can undertake.

As is true anywhere, the houses that constitute most of the built landscape are preserved through private efforts (Figure 6.8). In the Copper Country much of the preservation has been by happenstance more than intention and could be characterized as mere survival. Without redevelopment pressures, buildings tend to endure. The Copper Country has experienced depopulation since 1911, the copper-mining industry went into decline in 1918, and no new industry has replaced copper since the last mines closed in 1968. The mining companies sold their houses to their occupants for minimal sums. Although not particularly valued for their history, the company houses continue to serve as single-family houses. There is little preservation awareness in terms of the value of the architecture, and vinyl siding, smaller windows, and attached garages tend to distort the original buildings, but their survival rate is high.

In addition to this passive preservation, there is an active preservation movement. Calumet Village is a Main Street community, part of a state program to encourage commercial development in historic buildings. In connection with the formation of the national park, Calumet Village has been surveyed and a local historic district ordinance enacted. Tax credits for approved rehabilitations are available through both state and federal governments, and some property owners have taken advantage of these. Without a strong local economy, though, these efforts will be limited in scope.

Figure 6.8 Elm Street, Blue Jacket, Calumet, photographed 2003. Company houses, now in private hands, have been altered in many ways, but their overall conformity is still apparent. Photograph copyright 2003 Larry Mishkar.

In thinking about how people remember the past, it is important to recognize which people. The Copper Country is now less than half the size it was at its peak; many people, like Joseph and Antonia Putrich, moved on. Those who remained tended to be satisfied with their lives here, and they maintained that attitude even after the closure of the mines. The rosy glow of the past also affects people's memories, especially their childhoods. So the remembrances that survive tend to be positive, viewing the company as an omnipresent but benign force. But it is tinged with awe at the extent of the company's control. While residents might fondly remember the days when the company took care of snowplowing and school-building, they also recognize that such company control was a tangled web.

The complexity of management–worker relations survives in the buildings. It is not always interpreted as such or consciously preserved, but it permeates the landscape. The hundreds of worker houses, whether built by the company or enabled by the company on its land, are the best evidence of how much the companies pervaded workers' lives beyond the workplace. The survival of buildings such as the Calumet Theatre or the loss of buildings such as Italian Hall indicates that Copper Country residents view their past with mixed feelings: pride at what copper allowed them to accomplish, regret at the divisions and tragedies it caused. As time passes and the copper era fades in public memory, new understandings will emerge. Perhaps company houses, as a symbol of reasonable choices and strategies in the face of extensive company control as much as a symbol of the long arm of the company, will evoke both pride and understanding.

Notes

Introduction

1   Lankton, *Cradle to Grave*, 5–10.

2   Ibid., 9–13.

3   "An Interior Ellis Island," Web exhibit, http://ethnicity.lib.mtu.edu/intro.html. Gates, *Michigan Copper*, 106–7. Thurner, *Calumet Copper*, 13.

4   Lankton, *Cradle to Grave*, 62–63. Palmer to Commissioner of Labor Statistics, August 13, 1913, RG 230, Box 89, File 41/7-Q, National Archives.

5   List of twenty mining companies, nine of which were controlled by C&H, in MacNaughton to Palmer, August 23, 1913, RG 280, Box 89, File 41/7-Q, National Archives. Lankton and Hyde, *Old Reliable*, 152. Between 1869 and 1946, C&H paid $200 million in dividends (although the company started only in 1869) out of a region-wide total of $350 million for the period 1845–1946. Gates, *Michigan Copper*, 215, 219.

6   U.S. Department of Labor, *Michigan Copper District Strike*, 113, 116–17.

7   Gates, *Michigan Copper*, 196–200, 205.

8   Lankton, *Cradle to Grave*, 72–73.

9   Gates, *Michigan Copper*, 208–9, 229. Lankton, *Cradle to Grave*, 22. Thurner, *Strangers and Sojourners*, 158.

10   Phoenix Copper Co., *Annual Report of 1860*, 10.

11   Harris to Mason, August 8, 1896, MS-001, Box 337, Folder 5, Michigan Technological University Archives and Copper Country Historical Collections (hereafter MTU). Ground rents and house sales are discussed more fully in chapter 3. McNear, "Quincy Mining Company," 525.

12   U.S. House, *Conditions in the Copper Mines*, 1458. J. L. Harris to Fish, March 7, 1904, MS-001, Box 337, Folder 9, MTU.

13   Murdoch, *Boom Copper*, 153.

14   A former employee of the Scotts Company sued his former employer, charging that he was fired because a drug test turned up nicotine. Joel Roberts, "Fired Smoker Sues Ex-Employer," November 30, 2006, www.cbsnews.com. Similarly, Jennifer Barrett, "Drop That Weight or You're Fired!" *Newsweek*, April 14, 2008, 18.

15   *The New Shorter Oxford English Dictionary* defines paternalism as, in part, "the claim or attempt by a government, company, etc., to take responsibility for the welfare of its people or to regulate their life for their benefit." Scranton, "Varieties of Paternalism," 237–38, 240. Crawford, *Building the Workingman's Paradise*, 15–18, discusses a particularly intrusive example.

16   Crawford, *Building the Workingman's Paradise*, 32, also pointed to a shift away from moral influence to an ideology of laissez-faire individualism as increasingly self-interested justifications were provided.

17   Richard T. Ely, "Pullman," 457, 461, 463. See also Buder, *Pullman;* Shuey, *Factory People and Their Employers,* 128; and Taylor, *Satellite Cities, 10.* "Fresh in the minds of all of us is the failure of the Pullman Company to maintain its authority over the village affairs of Pullman, Illinois," Buffington, "Making Cities for Workmen," 15.

18   Falconer, "What More than Wages?" 833. Discussion of "welfare work" in Nelson, *Managers and Workers,* 99. See also Brooks, "New Aspects of Employer's Welfare Work," 1–12. Tolman, *Industrial Betterment.* Budgett Meakin discussed "various industrial betterment schemes" in *Model Factories and Villages.* For historians' views of industrial betterment, see Brandes, *American Welfare Capitalism;* Crawford, *Building the Workingman's Paradise,* 46–53; Wright, *Building the Dream,* 177–92; and Tone, *The Business of Benevolence.* Ely, "An American Industrial Experiment," 40. Going, "Village Communities," 61. The government was also interested in this issue. See Gould, *The Housing of the Working People.* The Bureau of Labor also produced an exhibit for the St. Louis World's Fair on sixteen successful examples of the new corporate welfare, documenting these communities with 285 photographs and plans. Hanger, "Housing of the Working People," 1191–243.

19   Mulrooney, *A Legacy of Coal,* 65–73. Shifflett, *Coal Towns,* 33–66. Wolff, *Industrializing the Rockies,* 127–28, 164–65.

20   Alanen and Bjorkman, "Plats, Parks, Playgrounds, and Plants," 44–45. Crawford, *Building the Workingman's Paradise,* the best overview of these new company towns, cautions against being swayed by the aesthetic appeal of them and overlooking the issues of control that underlay them (8). Shifflett, *Coal Towns,* 148, points out that government reports similarly examined aspects of towns that were unimportant to the residents. Studies of new company towns include Alanen, *Morgan Park;* Mosher, *Capital's Utopia;* Garner, "Leclaire, Illinois," 219–27; and Alanen and Peltin, "Kohler, Wisconsin," 145–59. Older model towns are discussed in Garner, *The Model Company Town,* and Heath, "The Howland Mill Village," 64–111. Fortunately, there is a growing literature on worker houses *not* built by a company: Bigott, *From Cottage to Bungalow,* and Heath, *The Patina of Place,* which examines speculatively built three-deckers in New Bedford, Massachusetts, especially in part III.

21   Shifflett, *Coal Towns,* xv. Metheny, *From the Miner's Doublehouse.* I am also responding to the challenge laid out by Herbert Gutman, who charged that labor history emphasizes ways that capitalism transformed working people and that "too little attention has been given to the ways in which the behavior of working people affected the development of the larger culture and society in which they lived." Since he wrote that more than thirty years ago, the challenge has been taken up by others, but I still find it compelling. Gutman, *Work, Culture, and Society,* xii. Quincy built log houses at Swedetown in 1864; one-third of them were vacant by 1870. Fisher, "Quincy Mining Company Housing," 102–3. Prospective tenants for new houses at Quincy in 1918 demanded hot-air furnaces and three-fixture bathrooms (see chapter 4). Lawton to Parsons Todd, June 13, 1918, MS-001, Box 336, Folder 18, MTU. Backing off the rent increase also occurred at Quincy, in 1901, as shown in chapter 1. Harris to Todd, September 13, 1901, MS-001, Box 337, Folder 7, MTU.

22   Schlereth, "Material Culture and Cultural Research," 11–13.

23   One model of this is Heath, *Patina of Place.*

24   On beer, see "State to Rest in Seeberville Case at Session Today," *Daily Mining Gazette,* February 10, 1914. On wine, see Zimmerman, "From Paternalism to Privatization," 188–90. Quotation in Macfarlane, "The Issues at Calumet," 5.

25   Marcus and Segal, *Technology in America,* 193. Earlier examples include companies' control of workers' lives in boardinghouses in Lowell, Massachusetts. Gross, *The Course of Industrial Decline,* 83–84. MacNaughton to Lloyd, July 21, 1913, and MacNaughton to Shaw, August 26, 1913, MS-002, Box 47, Folder 495, MTU. Lloyd to MacNaughton, May 6, 1914, MS-002, Box 51, Folder 8, MTU.

26   Shifflett, *Coal Towns,* 33.

1. Saltboxes and T-Plans

1   Obituaries provided by Putrich family. Plan No. 2511 in Copper Range records, MS-028, Box 2, Folder 5, 2, Michigan Technological University Archives and Copper Country Historical Collections (hereafter MTU). Plan from Neg. No. 18837, State Archives of Michigan. U.S. Census, *Population,* 1910. Boarders listed *Daily Mining Gazette,* February 6, 1914.

2   Surviving houses date from ca. 1858 to 1918. Totals from U.S. Department of Labor, *Michigan Copper District Strike,* 113–16.

3   Hubka and Kenny, "Examining the American Dream," 55–58.

4   Hanson, "The Cultural Landscape and Social Composition of Ahmeek," 15. Another possibility for a construction date is 1874–80, when the land was owned by the Seneca Mining Company, which was undertaking exploratory work. My thanks to owner Mike Kezele, who permitted me entry in May 2000. In 1996 Mike had removed the clapboard siding, exposing the logs, and also removed all interior partitions and finishes. The original configuration of the interior could be determined from ghosting on the walls. Subsequent owners have painted the interior, destroying the evidence of the ghosting. The layout of the house is strikingly similar to another log house in Ahmeek at 11 First Street. This house, which was moved to its present site, still has its clapboard covering. The stairway is in the right-rear corner, although running to the left, unlike that in the house on U.S. 41, which runs to the right, and there is a hung chimney. Dennis Leopold and Matt Adair, Documentation of 11 First Street, Ahmeek (1997), MS-046, MTU.

5   Stephanie Atwood, Documentation of Central Mine House 25 (2006), MS-046, MTU.

6   These C&H drawings (6400), which are dated 1907, as well as those labeled "Osceola Consolidated Mining Co., North Kearsarge, Ahmeek, #7487" (undated), MS-005, MTU, accord with Karla Cross and Erica Hanson, Documentation of 26 First Street, Ahmeek (1997), MS-046, MTU.

7   Quincy Mining Co., *Annual Report for 1864.* Also McNear, "Quincy Mining Company," 519–21; Fisher, "Quincy Mining Company Housing," 62–63, 69–73; Michael Deegan, Documentation of 158 Limerick (2005), MS-046, MTU. Comparing Limerick house 62 (1027 square feet), a T-plan built in 1864, to House 25 at Central (893 square feet), a saltbox also built around 1864. Similarly, comparing 1899 T-plan in Mason (904 square feet on two floors) to 1917 saltbox in Mason (946 square feet on two floors). Mason T-plan QD 0063, MS-012, MTU. Mason saltbox QD 0162, QD 1479, MS-012, MTU.

8   Quincy drawings (Drawer 62, B-2, MS-012, MTU) are similar to drawings of 50802 Mesnard (formerly 251; after 1919, 720); Gary Kaunonen and Racheal Herzberg, Documentation

of Mesnard Company House (2004), MS-046, MTU. Two variations exist: one like the Mesnard house (QD 0062), dated June 1900, and one that is identical except a pantry addition to the corner of the T (QD 1486, MS-012, MTU).

9   Hanson, "The Cultural Landscape and Social Composition of Ahmeek," 40. C&H drawing collection, 7694, MTU. Another four-room dwelling in Copper Range, No. 3284, MS-028, Box 105, Folder 1, MTU. There, the stairway was placed similar to the one in Ahmeek.

10   C&H 6271, MS-005, MTU. Copper Range drawings, No. 671, Index L-284, MS-028, Box 105, Folder 1, MTU. Also *Engineering and Mining Journal,* December 28, 1912, 1231. Photo MTU 02406 unidentified, MTU. South Kearsarge photo in MS-002, Box 353, Folder 6H, MTU. LaSalle photo in RG 46, Box 3, Folder 6, State Archives of Michigan. Williams House, Trimountain, Image 05922, MTU.

11   Bjorkman, "Mine Worker Housing."

12   Bigott, "Bungalows and the Complex Origin of the Modern House," 34, notes that front hallways were the most expensive feature of a small house, prior to the introduction of bathrooms.

13   C&H drawing 6241, Drawer 115, MS-005, MTU. See also C&H 6220 (1899), with bathroom on second floor (Drawer 62, D-2, MTU), and 6242 (Drawer 62, D-3, MTU) and 6281 (Drawer 62, D-1, MTU), one-and-a-half-story versions. Kim Finch and Cristina Menghini, Documentation of 1769 Cemetery Street (2003), MS-046, MTU. Also, U.S. Census, *Population,* 1910.

14   C&H plans 6324 and 6325, both dated 1900, revised December 13, 1901, and Osceola plan July 15, 1907, Drawer 62, B-7 and B-8, MTU. Alicia Valentino, Documentation of 46454 Main Street, Dodgeville (2002), MS-046, MTU. Ahmeek reference from Hanson, "The Cultural Landscape and Social Composition of Ahmeek," 41–42. James Montney, Andrew Sewell, and William D. Updike, Documentation of House at Mandan (1998), MS-046, MTU. Isle Royale plans (C&H 6476), 1917, Drawer 62, C-7, MTU. Ahmeek plans (C&H 6438), 1916, do not have stairs to attic and are also slightly smaller, Drawer 62, C-6, MTU. Copper Range 2866, MS-028, Box 105, Folder 1. In addition, the Isle Royale plans appear with the Quincy Mining Co. title block, and nothing else changed, 1917, Drawer 62, C-8, MTU.

15   Papineau, *Old Victoria,* 106. U.S. Department of Labor, Michigan Copper District Strike, 116–17.

16   One building of this type, the barn boss's house, appears in a pre-1865 photograph reproduced in Monette, *Central Mine,* 83. These houses also had machine-cut nails, indicating a mid-nineteenth-century date. Don Durfee, Marco Meniketti, and Dorothy Quirk, Documentation of Barn Boss's House (1996), and Kevin O'Dell, Tim Tumberg, and Paul White, Documentation of House 61 (1996), MS-046, MTU.

17   QD 1479, MS-012, MTU.

18   *Daily Mining Gazette,* December 7 and 8, 1913.

19   Lawton to Todd, June 18, 1917, MS-001, Box 336, Folder 18, MTU. Todd to Lawton, June 21, 1917, MS-001, Box 336, Folder 18, MTU. McNear, "Quincy Mining Company," 530.

20   C&H drawings 6294, Drawer 62, E-4, MTU. Also, Drawers 115 and 342 for Colonial Revival renovation in 1926 and division into apartments in 1951. U.S. Census, *Population,* 1910.

21   S. B. Harris to Todd, August 7, 1901, MS-001, Box 337, Folder 6, 496, MTU.

22   S. B. Harris to Todd, June 30, 1900, Box 337, Folder 6, 304. Harris was apparently included in this change as well. Two years later, John L. Harris's demands for the superintendent position included a salary of $6,800, a house for which he would pay $1,800 a year, and the use of a team of horses. J. L. Harris to Todd, November 8, 1902, Box 337, Folder 9, 395. But Charles L. Lawton's employment contract of December 10, 1915, included, besides his $15,000 salary, a house with heat and light and furniture, as well as horses, carriages, and automobiles. Box 343, Folder 20. Todd to J. L. Harris, July 12, 1902, cited in Lankton and Hyde, *Old Reliable*, 57. J. L. Harris to Todd, July 12, 1902, Box 337, Folder 9, 329. Todd to J. L. Harris, January 17, 1905, Box 340, Folder 7. All in MS-001, MTU.

23   QD 0060, 0186, MS-012, MTU.

24   Todd to S. B. Harris, May 20, 1901, MS-001, Box 338, Folder 12, MTU. Todd to J. L. Harris, July 28, 1902, MS-001, Box 340, Folder 4, MTU. J. L. Harris to Todd, August 2, 1901, MS-001, Box 337, Folder 7, 218, MTU. Todd to J. L. Harris, August 18, 1902, MS-001, Box 338, Folder 14, MTU.

25   J. L. Harris to Todd, August 2, 1901, Box 337, Folder 7, 218, and Todd to J. L. Harris, August 18, 1902, Box 338, Folder 14. J. L. Harris to Todd, January 13, 1905, Box 337, Folder 11, 211. Todd to J. L. Harris, January 17, 1905, Box 340, Folder 7. All in MS-001, MTU.

26   Lawton to Todd, June 15, 1912, and Lawton to Todd, September 25, 1912, MS-001, Box 342, Folder 9, MTU.

27   Bennett, "Where the Bosses Lived," 81–83.

28   "Seen by the Search-Light," *Miner's Bulletin,* November 18, 1913.

29   Managers' detachment from housing assignments is somewhat belied by a letter from MacNaughton to Cake, acting superintendent of the stamp mills, May 21, 1902, MS-002, Box 159, Folder 4, 270, MTU: "In the future when making recommendations for houses for men in your department, will you not please make same to me direct and in writing. This will permit me to put applications on file, and they will receive due consideration and in the order in which they are made." These applications do not survive in MacNaughton's files, and it is likely that he passed them onto Brett, his land agent. Elsewhere, MacNaughton denied that he had anything to do with assigning houses. MacNaughton to Roehm, December 10, 1915, MS-002, Box 48, Folder 570, MTU.

30   J. L. Harris to Todd, August 7, 1902, 238, and J. L. Harris to Todd, September 11, 1902, MS-001, Box 337, Folder 7, 324, MTU. There was also an oblique reference in correspondence to "Mr. Pearce, Architect, failed to get up plans for houses as wanted," apparently for the doctor's house. Todd to S. B. Harris, May 20, 1901, MS-001, Box 338, Folder 12, MTU. Drawer 62, Folder I, MTU. For more on Eschweiler and Leibert, see www.social.mtu.edu/Copper CountryArchitects.

31   Charlton, Gilbert & Demar to Whiting, March 10, 1897, and March 29, 1897, MS-001, Box 114, Folder 16, MTU. Charlton, Gilbert & Demar said the charge for working drawings and specifications for one dwelling would be forty dollars; at 3 percent of cost of construction, that would mean the house would cost more than thirteen hundred dollars to build. Specifications and contract, MS-002, Box 208, Folder 25, MTU. "Building News," *Copper Country Evening News,* July 27, 1907. *Michigan Contractor and Builder* 6, no. 43 (April 19, 1913): 15. For more information on Charlton, Gilbert & Demar and Maass, see www.social.mtu.edu/Copper CountryArchitects.

32   The Sears houses are discussed further in chapter 4. Although Aladdin, another mail-order company, advertised C&H as a client, no record could be found that any of C&H's houses in the Copper Country were Aladdin's.

33   "Nationality of C&H Employees, Feb. 1910," MS-002, Box 211, Folder 036, MTU. "Statement of Employees and Householders at Mine, May 1st 1911," MS-028, Box 9, Folder 1, MTU. S. B. Harris to Todd, April 8, 1904, MS-001, Box 337, Folder 10, 400, MTU.

34   S. B. Harris to Mason, August 9, 1890, Box 337, Folder 1, 340. S. B. Harris to Todd, September 3, 1890, Box 337, Folder 1, 351. S. B. Harris to Todd, May 10, 1899, Box 337, Folder 6, 166. S. B. Harris to Todd, July 22, 1899, Box 337, Folder 6, 188. S. B. Harris to Anderson, August 3, 1899, Box 337, Folder 6. All in MS-001, MTU. "Twelve Houses Are Being Built," *Daily Mining Gazette*, September 30, 1899.

35   *Copper Country Evening News*, May 28, 1897. "Champion Mine Showing Good," *Daily Mining Gazette,* December 23, 1899. "Trimountain Looks as Well as Ever," *Daily Mining Gazette,* December 27, 1899. *Hancock Evening Journal,* August 15, 1901. Copper Range, *Annual Report for 1906,* 22. Denton to John Klas, February 10, 1913. Denton to Paine, September 4, 1915. Rashleigh Bros. to Denton, June 5, 1916. Rashleigh then charged $441.00 each for fifteen six-room houses. Rashleigh to Denton, July 3, 1916. All in CR-998, Box 8, Folder 11, MTU.

36   Cocking to MacNaughton, March 8, 1916, MS-002, Box 49, Folder 613, MTU.

37   Lawton to Todd, January 17, 1913, MS-001, Box 342, Folder 10. MacNaughton to Charlton & Kuenzli, January 16, 1906, MS-002, Box 43, Folder 152. Math. Mehrens[?] to Linden & Miller, November 2, 1897, MS-002, Box 128, Folder 10. Whiting to Linden & Miller, November 4, 1897, MS-002, Box 158, Folder 8. James M. Merton [?], Memo No. 590, October 26, 1898, MS-002, Box 128, Folder 10. James M. Merton [?], Memo No. 600, December 10, 1898, MS-002, Box 128, Folder 10. All in MTU.

38   The linkage of housing to captains' and foremen's areas is reflected in the reason Henry Brett gave for why someone (a railroad worker) could not get a house: "There has not been a house vacated by a RR man." Brett to MacNaughton October 20, 1913, attached to Mrs. Charles Walker to MacNaughton, October 17, 1913, MS-002, Box 47, Folder 501, MTU. This linkage is also seen in a letter from Robert Olander, a machine-shop worker: "I have made application to Mr. Brett, your land agent, a number of times, for a company house and was informed that there was a possibility of my getting a company house, some time in the next ten years or so, on account of hardly anyone seldom leaving the Machine Shop dept." Olander to MacNaughton, October 17, 1914, MS-002, Box 48, Folder 533, MTU. C&H, *Annual Report for 1891.* C&H, *Annual Report for 1893,* 9.

39   See, for example, Box 48, Folder 570. Charles L. Roehm to MacNaughton, n.d., Box 48, Folder 570. Emil Swanson to MacNaughton, August 15, 1914, Box 48, Folder 533. Rosa Dell'Acqua to MacNaughton, April 10, 1913, Box 47, Folder 501. Thomas F. Cocking to MacNaughton, November 16, 1914, Box 48, Folder 533. Frank Olson to MacNaughton, September 11, 1916, Box 49, Folder 613. All in MS-002, MTU.

40   Stephen Vertin to MacNaughton, June 22, 1917, and MacNaughton to Vertin, June 28, 1917, MS-002, Box 49, Folder 613, MTU. Cocking to MacNaughton, August 10, 1914, MS-002, Box 48, Folder 533, MTU. Anonymous to Agassiz, May 6, 1902, MS-002, Box 209, Folder 41, MTU.

41   MacNaughton to Brett, July 24, 1917, Box 172, Folder 64. "Employees Application for Company House," Box 112, Folder 22. Both in MS-002, MTU.

42   "Statement of Employees," 1905, 1907, 1910, MS-028, Box 9, Folder 1, MTU. U.S. Census, *Population*, 1910. Quincy rent books, MS-001, Box 39, Folders 1 and 2, MTU. Lankton and Hyde, *Old Reliable,* 152.

43   *Census of the State of Michigan*, 1904, 1: cix–cxiii. U.S. Department of Labor, *Michigan Copper District Strike,* 114–15.

44   Denton to Stimack, Taro, Wuorns, Aho, and Niku, September 11, 1914, MS-564, Box 8, Folder 22, MTU.

45   Taylor, "The Clash in the Copper Country," 135. See also Knowles, *Industrial Housing,* 371, and Streightoff, *The Standard of Living,* 84. Guilbault's peregrinations included one stint downstate. Guilbault interview.

46   Lankton, *Cradle to Grave,* 191–94. Denton to Paine, January 2, 1914, MS-028, Box 15, Folder 9, MTU.

47   DeSollar's Desk Spindle, Quincy Mining Company Collection, Keweenaw National Historical Park. Russell returned to Quincy five months later but was killed at work in February 1926, while unloading logs. Brian Cleven, Sarah Cowie, and Dan O'Rourke, Documentation of Pewabic Mining Co./Quincy Mining Co. House 117-503-222 (1995), MS-046, MTU. U.S. Census, *Population*, 1910 and 1920.

48   Rees, Robinson, and Petermann, *In the Matter of the Hearing before a Sub-Committee,* 49. In 1916, when C&H rewarded longtime employees at its fiftieth anniversary, the company honored 1,440 men with twenty-plus years of service, out of a total workforce of about 5,000. MS-002, Box 49, Folder 619, MTU. Thurner, *Strangers and Sojourners,* 224. C&H's aging workforce led to development of a retirement plan. Lankton, *Cradle to Grave,* 194. Veness-Randle, "The Social-Spatial Lifecycle of a Company Town," 74, examined C&H lease records, no longer extant. Michigan Office of the Commissioner of Mineral Statistics, *Mines and Mineral Statistics,* 277. Palmer to Commissioner of Labor Statistics, August 29, 1913, RG 280, Box 89, File 71/7Q, National Archives.

49   Quincy rent rolls, MS-001, Box 39, Folders 1 and 2, and Box 40, Folder 1, MTU. Stencel, "Worker Houses and Workers." "New Houses 1918," MS-001, Box 40, Folder 5, MTU. Lankton and Hyde, *Old Reliable,* 152–53.

50   Monkkonen, *America Becomes Urban,* 195. Chudacoff, *Mobile Americans,* 36.

51   Lawton to Todd, March 10–11, 18, 1909, and April 3, 1909, all in MS-001, Box 342, Folder 4, MTU, and May 19, 1910, MS-001, Box 342, Folder 6, MTU.

52   Lankton and Hyde, *Old Reliable,* 78–79. Mishkar and Hoagland, "Quincy Stamp Mills."

53   U.S. Department of Labor, *Housing by Employers,* 122. U.S. Department of Labor, *Michigan Copper District Strike,* 116. "Welfare Work of C&H," 576. Also in U.S. House, *Conditions in the Copper Mines,* 1441. Lawton to Todd, October 4, 1906, MS-001, Box 882, Folder 9, MTU. Lawton to Todd, October 26, 1909, MS-001, Box 342, Folder 5, MTU. Lawton to Todd, August 12, 1907, MS-001, Box 342, Folder 2, MTU.

54   For requests to MacNaughton, see chapter 4. S. B. Harris to Lynch, August 2, 1894, MS-001, Box 337, Folder 5, MTU. Denton to Santori, August 26, 1908, MS-028, Box 1, MTU.

55   U.S. Department of Labor, *Housing by Employers,* 246–47. Denton to Paine, April 14, 1916, CR-998, Box 342, Folder 11, MTU.

56   U.S. Department of Labor, *Michigan Copper District Strike,* 114.

57   "Statement of Employees and Householders at Mine, February 1, 1913," MS-028, Box 9, Folder 1, MTU.

58   Ibid. Also MacNaughton to Brett, July 24, 1917, MS-002, Box 172, Folder 64, MTU.

59   MacNaughton testimony, U.S. House, *Conditions in the Copper Mines,* 1442. U.S. Department of Labor, *Michigan Copper District Strike,* 114.

60   MacNaughton to Agassiz, September 7, 1901, MS-002, Box 159, Folder 3, 314, MTU. S. B. Harris to Todd, September 13, 1901, MS-001, Box 337, Folder 7, MTU.

61   U.S. House, *Michigan Copper District Strike,* 113. Grant to Lauck, February 27, 1914, U.S. Commission on Industrial Relations, Daily Reports. Rickard, *The Copper Mines of Lake Superior,* 20. U.S. House, *Conditions in the Copper Mines.* The absence of complaints was verified by Luke Grant, who reported that housing conditions were good, "no complaint being heard anywhere on that score." Grant to Lauck, March 3, 1914, U.S. Commission on Industrial Relations, Daily Reports.

62   During the shootings, with people running back and forth, no one ran out the front door. Antonia Putrich, baby in arms, ran out the back door, past the deputies, so close that her baby received powder burns on his face, and through the yard to the street, rather than run out the front door.

63   "Inventory of House #267, Mesnard Location, April 6, 1914," Quincy Mining Co. Collection, Keweenaw National Historical Park.

64   Clerk, Champion Copper Co., to Mrs. Maria Specciani (letter contains both spellings), August 3, 1909, same to Mrs. Barbara Gasparac, September 14, 1909, and same to Miss Elizabeth Mary Bartle, November 30, 1911, CR-998, Box 10, Folder 2, MTU.

65   On homeownership as an ideal, see Eisinger, "The Freehold Concept in Eighteenth-Century American Letters," 43; Wright, *Building the Dream,* xv; Upton, *Architecture in the United States,* 17; Kostof, *America By Design,* 10; Jackson, *Crabgrass Frontier,* 50; and Cullen, *The American Dream,* 136. On disadvantages of homeownership, see Streightoff, *The Standard of Living,* 84; Margaret F. Byington, *Homestead,* 62; Brody, *Steelworkers in America,* 87; Taylor, *Satellite Cities,* 16; Engels, *The Housing Question,* 50; Allen, *Industrial Housing Problems,* 26; Knowles, *Industrial Housing,* 371. Leftist historians have noted that working-class homeownership tended to tie up capital more than bestow social capital and eradicate inequality and that it had no advantage over renting. Luria, "Wealth, Capital and Power," 261, 268. Monkkonen, *America Becomes Urban,* 186, noted, "For the left, home ownership among the American working class continues to cause analytic conundrums." For evidence that the working class did aspire to homeownership, see Harris, "Working-Class Homeownership in the American Metropolis," 63, and Shuey, *Factory People and Their Employers,* 128. Mitchell quote from U.S. House, *Conditions in the Copper Mines,* 2307.

66   For discussions of boardinghouses, see Buder, *Pullman,* 78–79; Strasser, *Never Done,* 159; Jensen, "Cloth, Butter and Boarders," 20; Lauck and Sydenstricker, *Conditions of Labor in American Industries,* 293–97; Veiller, "Room Overcrowding and the Lodger Evil," 2: 59–61; Chapin, *The Standard of Living,* 80; Daunton, "Rows and Tenements: American Cities,

1880–1914," in *Housing the Workers*, 256–57; and Modell and Hareven, "Urbanization and the Malleable Household," 467–79. But by the early twentieth century, reformers already saw a greater evil: the lodging house, in which roomers did not take meals with the family. An urban phenomenon, the lodging house was thought to attract an anonymous, transient population at odds with the ideal of the home. By 1906, urban reformers already looked nostalgically at the "old-time boardinghouse," where the boarders knew each other and the landlady presided over the table. Wolfe, *The Lodging House Problem*, 46–47. Peel examines this phenomenon in "On the Margins," 813–34. Numbers of boarders are found in U.S. Senate, *Immigrants in Industries*, 46. In this sample, 35.3 percent of Croatian households had boarders, compared to 17.8 percent of all foreign-born households. In Michigan, Keweenaw and Houghton were also the counties with the second and third highest average number of people per dwelling—6.47 and 6.2, respectively. They also had the second and third highest family size. Luce County was first in both categories. *Census of the State of Michigan*, 1904, 1: 740.

67   Jacob Tijan was the only boarder present in both 1910 and 1913; he was the uncle of Albert and Alois. *Daily Mining Gazette*, February 6, 1914, 1. Testimony of Antonia Putrich, August 22, 1913, *The People vs. Thomas Raleigh et al.*, Case No. 4230, RG 89-465, MTU. Information on Albert and Josephine from Elaine and Joe Putrich, e-mail to author, August 3, 2002, who also note that Albert and Alois were sons of Joseph's sister, Catherine, who remained in Croatia. Information on Kalan from *Daily Mining Gazette*, February 7, 1914, 1, 8. The 1910 census indicates similar relationships. At that time, Joseph and Antonia had just one child, Mary, seven male boarders, and one female servant. Three of the boarders were surnamed "Fak," which is Joseph's mother's maiden name. And one of the boarders was Jacob Tijan, Joseph's brother-in-law, so possibly only three of the boarders were unrelated to the Putriches.

68   Denton attempted to identify occupants through a general notice to tenants, September 2, 1913, CR-998, Box 8, Folder 11, MTU. The number of boarders was apparently regulated in 1904, according to Trettin, "'Give Them Comfortable Quarters,'" 83, but Joseph Putrich did not pay any additional rent for his ten boarders, surely a situation that would be seen as excessive if the company were monitoring such a thing.

69   S. J. Kleinberg, "Seeking the Meaning of Life: The Pittsburgh Family and the Survey," 89, and Margo Anderson, "Does the Evidence Support the Argument? Margaret Byington's Cost of Living Survey of Homestead," 109–10, both in Greenwald and Anderson, eds., *Pittsburgh Surveyed*. Shergold, *Working-Class Life*, 277. Chapin, *The Standard of Living*. Reynolds, *The Housing of the Poor in American Cities*, 25. Pfeiffer, "From 'Bohunks' to Finns," 14, argued that the "so-called" Austrians pulled down the standard of living because they lived so cheaply. Kleinberg, *The Shadow of the Mills*, xviii. Land, "The Family Wage," 56–61. May, "The 'Good Managers,'" 353. May, "The Historical Problem of the Family Wage," 404. Jensen, "Cloth, Butter and Boarders," 19. Going, "Village Communities," 61. Bederman, *Manliness and Civilization*, 13.

70   Clerk, Champion Copper Co., to Mrs. Barbara Gasparac, September 14, 1909, CR-998, Box 10, Folder 12, MTU. When I published an article on this subject (Hoagland, "The Boardinghouse Murders," 1–18), I hadn't seen this letter; I subsequently revised upwards my estimates of what Antonia might have charged for board. In 1913 at Copper Range, company-run boardinghouses for workers imported during the strike charged $22 per month. Mendelsohn to

Denton, November 5, 1913, CR-998, Box 8, Folder 18, MTU. At another company, the "board bill" was $18 per month. U.S. House, *Conditions in the Copper Mines*, 1: 247. Rice, "Labor Conditions at Copper Range," 1232, puts it at $20 per month, including washing. In the anthracite coal fields the going rate for board, among Eastern Europeans, was $12 a month, according to Roberts, *Anthracite Coal Communities*, 106. Stofer, "An Examination of the Socio-Cultural Roles of Boardinghouses," 151, cites pay at a boardinghouse in Escanaba: $3 per week for a seven-day, seventeen-hour-per-day week. Food costs derived from "Cost of Living per Month for Average Family," MS-028, Box 1, Folder 9, MTU. A sociological study of the anthracite coalfields of Pennsylvania estimated an Eastern European's food expenditure to be much lower than average—only $5.85 a month—but food prices in the Copper Country appear to have been 50 percent higher than in eastern Pennsylvania. Roberts, *Anthracite Coal Communities*, 109. This is consistent with other estimates, such as Byington, *Homestead*, 45, who calculates the weekly expenditure on food of a Slavic family at $5.98, and Chapin, *The Standard of Living*, 137, who calculates the annual expenditure of an Austrian family in the $700–$799 income bracket at $321.97, or $6.19 per week. Bodnar, "Immigration and Modernization," 49, asserts that women were generally the "fiscal managers" in Slavic households. Kleinberg, "Technology," 66, points out how much harder housework was in working-class households than in middle-class establishments that had better services, machines, and servants.

71   Testimony of Humphrey Quick, August 21, 1913, *The People vs. Thomas Raleigh et al.*, Case No. 4230, RG 89-465, MTU. Croatians, or "Austrians" as they were termed, formed 23 percent of the workforce of 1,141 men at Champion, of which only 10 percent were American born. Immigrants in greater numbers were Finnish, 31 percent, and English, 18 percent. Champion Copper Co., "Statement of Employees and Householders at Mine, February 1, 1913," MS-028, Box 9, Folder 1, MTU. Painesdale was not unusual in its ethnic population. In the Copper Country, 80 percent of mine employees were foreign-born. Over a quarter of these were Finnish, and almost 15 percent were English. Most of the Croatians, and other immigrants from the Austro-Hungarian empire, came to Michigan after 1904. U.S. Senate, *Immigrants in Industries*, Part 17: Copper Mining and Smelting, part II, 85, 83. Rusich relationship described by Joe and Elaine Putrich, e-mail to author, July 26, 2002.

72   Neighboring households from *Daily Mining Gazette*, August 29, 1913, 2, and February 6, 1914, 2. Quote from testimony of Emilio Vittori, August 29, 1913, *The People vs. Thomas Raleigh, et al.*, Case No. 4230, RG 89-465, MTU.

73   Veness-Randle, "The Social-Spatial Lifecycle," 70. Veness-Randle had access to C&H lease records that are no longer available. Alanen and Franks, eds., *Remnants of Corporate Paternalism*, 13. Fisher, "Quincy Mining Company Housing," 309–12.

74   MacNaughton to commissioner of immigration, June 20, 1912, MS-002, Box 46, Folder 452, MTU. "Employees classified by nationality and department, January 27, 1908," and "Nationality of C&H Employees, Feb. 1910," MS-002, Box 211, Folder 36, MTU. "The Proposed Elimination of the Finns," 920. "Statement of Employees and Householders at Mine, February 1910," MS-028, Box 9, Folder 1, MTU.

75   Denton to Paine, April 14, 1916, CR-998, Box 8, Folder 11, MTU.

76   Among others who have made this argument are Williams and Young, "Grammar, Codes, and Performance," 40–51.

2. The Spaces of a Strike

1   Testimony of Antonia Putrich, August 22, 1913, *The People vs. Thomas Raleigh et al.*, Case No. 4230, Houghton County Circuit Court, RG 89-465, Michigan Technological University Archives and Copper Country Historical Collections (hereafter MTU). *Daily Mining Gazette,* August 23, 1913.

2   Lankton, *Cradle to Grave,* 230–31. "Work Pumps at One More Mine," *Boston Daily Globe,* July 29, 1913. In 1907, Socialists parading with red flags on Hancock's main street were restrained by the courts. Swaby Lawton, then Hancock's city attorney, was the prosecutor. S. Lawton to Kirchner, October 14, 1913, Acc. 06-087A, MTU. *Evening Copper Journal,* August 11, 1913.

3   On Quincy, U.S. House, *Conditions in the Copper Mines,* 931–32. A similar description is in S. Lawton to Otto Kirchner, October 14, 1913, Acc. 06-087A, MTU. On Copper Range, U.S. House, *Conditions in the Copper Mines,* 397. Denton to Paine, November 10, 1913, CR-998, Box 8, Folder 17, MTU.

4   The National Guard was down to 212 men by September 27. Beck, "Law and Order," 283. Lankton, *Cradle to Grave,* 231–32. MacFarlane, "The Issues at Calumet," 23.

5   Number of union members given in *Miners Magazine* 14, no. 527 (July 31, 1913): 5. In August, Walter Palmer of the Department of Labor concluded from statistics supplied by James MacNaughton that 15,483 had been employed on the eve of the strike; 8,078 worked for C&H and its subsidiaries. RG 280, Box 89, File 41/7-Qi, National Archives. In January, Swaby Lawton estimated that 8,724 men were back at work, compared to a workforce of 13,514 on the eve of the strike. Swaby Lawton to William Todd, January 8, 1914, Acc. 06-087A, MTU. Quincy Mining Co., *Annual Report for 1913,* 13. "Lake Superior Copper Mines," *Boston Daily Globe,* September 22, 1913. Thurner, *Rebels on the Range,* 236.

6   Lankton, *Cradle to Grave,* 235. S. Lawton to Todd, December 11, 1913, Acc. 06-087A, MTU. Thurner, *Rebels on the Range,* 127–28.

7   "Cost of Maintaining Militia Heavy," *Daily Mining Gazette,* September 9, 1913.

8   Fogelson, *America's Armories,* 41–44.

9   Quincy Mining Co., *Annual Report for 1913,* 12. Dodge to Ferris, August 2, 1913, Ferris Papers, RG 46, Box 1, Folder 11, State Archives of Michigan.

10   "Fairplay" to Ferris, August 14, 1913, Ferris Papers, RG 46, Box 1, Folder 4, State Archives of Michigan. Ferris to Vandercook, July 31, 1913, Vandercook Papers, Collection 11, Box 1, Folder 7, Michigan State University Archives. Ferris to Dodge, August 2, 1913, and Dodge to Ferris, August 2, 1913, Ferris Papers, RG 46, Box 1, Folder 11, State Archives of Michigan.

11   "Strength of M.N.G. on Duty in Copper Country," Abbey to Ferris, January 29, 1914, Ferris Papers, RG 46, Box 1, Folder 3, State Archives of Michigan. Vandercook to Ferris, August 31, 1913, Vandercook Papers, Collection 11, Box 1, Folder 9, Michigan State University Archives.

12   "New Armory Is Formally Opened," undated clipping, vertical files, MTU. "Quartermaster Dept. April 1903," MS-002, Box 327, Folder 8, MTU, lists all the members of the guard, what equipment they received, and where they lived and worked. Eighty-four men were listed; of the forty for whom places of work were given, twenty-nine worked for C&H or Tamarack mining companies. "Work Pumps at One More Mine," *Boston Daily Globe,* July 29, 1913.

13   Fogelson, *America's Armories,* 149. C&H drawings in Drawer 96, MS-005, MTU. The steel framework was provided by the Wisconsin Bridge & Iron Co. The opening event was a large ball—apparently, the first of many. Bennetts, "Industrial and Community Relations," *Mining Congress Journal,* 564. The armory served not only as the home of the local National Guard unit and the high school's ROTC program but also as the headquarters of the local chapter of the Red Cross, the Calumet Youth band, a Boy Scout troop, and a polling station for Calumet Township. All of these organizations lost possessions when the armory was destroyed by fire in 1942. Charles Stetter to Raymond Tiberg, June 15, 1984, Calumet Public School Library.

14   Harris to Todd, May 9, 1888, MS-001, Box 337, Folder 2, 446, MTU. It appears that the courthouse was not moved, however; it stayed on its original site until it was demolished in the 1950s. The Houghton Light Infantry shared quarters in a building at the corner of Huron and Montezuma with an ice rink and opera house.

15   "Topics in Wall Street," *New York Times,* September 5, 1913. *Miner's Bulletin,* August 21, 1913.

16   Lankton, *Cradle to Grave,* 237. Thurner, *Rebels on the Range,* 155.

17   Lankton, *Cradle to Grave,* 239. Grant to Lauck, U.S. Commission on Industrial Relations, March 3, 1914.

18   *Daily Mining Gazette,* February 6, 1914, 1–2. Testimony of John Stimac, August 29, 1913, and Humphrey Quick, August 21, 1913, *The People vs. Thomas Raleigh et al.*, Case No. 4230, RG 89-465, MTU. Richard Flannigan, "Statement of Circuit Judge," *People vs. Cooper et al.,* Case No. 4231, RG 89-465, MTU. One boarder who went to South Range that morning testified that they went by rail, which meant they rode Copper Range's own train. Transcript of trial, 111, based on S. Lawton's notes, Acc. 06-087A, MTU.

19   Testimony of Humphrey Quick, August 21, 1913, and Richard Flannigan, "Statement of Circuit Judge," *People vs. Cooper et al.,* Case No. 4231, RG 89-465, MTU. Lawton, "In the matter of the petition," August 7, 1915, RG 46, Box 4, Folder 12, State Archives of Michigan, 13. Search described in Testimony of Albert Tijan, August 21, 1913, *People vs. Thomas Raleigh, et al.,* Case No. 4230, RG 89-465, MTU.

20   Testimony of Antonia Putrich, August 22, 1913, *People vs. Thomas Raleigh,* Case No. 4230, RG 89-465, MTU.

21   Raleigh's bail of $5,000 was posted by Frederick Denton, the manager of Copper Range, and John C. Mann, who was the proprietor of Douglass House and who also ran boardinghouses at the mines during the strike. Galbraith to Denton, June 6, 1914, Wilbert Anderson Collection, Houghton County Historical Society.

22   Thirty-five hundred was the figure given by the newspaper. *Daily Mining Gazette,* August 19, 1913. A. O. Sarell, "The Copper Country Strike," October 23, 1913, gave the figure at 12,576. Sarell was a unionist. Finlandia University Archives.

23   Foner, *History of the Labor Movement,* 5: 189.

24   Ibid., 198. Wolff, *Industrializing the Rockies,* 235–37.

25   C&H and Copper Range leases in RG 46, Box 2, Folder 10, State Archives of Michigan; Quincy's dwelling house lease in MS-001, Box 27, Folder 1, and ground lease in MS-001, Box 28, Folder 1, MTU. Copper Range's ground lease was worded slightly differently, with the number of days left blank, to be filled in.

26   Harris to Bailey, May 5, 1892, MS-001, Box 337, Folder 4, MTU. Harris to Lynch, August 2, 1894, MS-001, Box 337, Folder 5, MTU. Denton to Santoni, August 26, 1908, MS-028, Box 1, MTU.

27   *Walter Dokmonovich et al. v. Baltic Mining Co. et al.,* Case No. 4220, RG 89-465, MTU. Similar eviction notice quoted in "A Landlord's Agreement," *Miner's Bulletin,* September 6, 1913, and in *Miners Magazine* 14, no. 540 (October 30, 1913): 11.

28   "List of those on whom notice was served October 14, 1913," CR-998, Box 8, Folder 11, MTU. Calendar, Volume 14, RG 89-465, MTU. The commissioner's book that would include most of these cases has been lost, although the subsequent volume, Volume 59, beginning on January 31, 1914, is in RG 89-465, MTU. Putrich decision in 59: 104.

29   *Evening Copper Journal,* August 11, 1913. U.S. House, *Conditions in the Copper Mines,* 1443.

30   S. Lawton to C. Lawton, March 24, 1914, Acc. 06-087A, MTU.

31   Lawton to Todd, September 6, 1913, MS-001, Box 342, Folder 11, MTU. Eviction notice in *Quincy Mining Co. vs. Oscar Pelto, et al.,* Case No. 4379, RG 89-465, MTU. Lawton to Todd, September 10, 1913, MS-001, Box 342, Folder 11. Lawton to Todd, October 4, 1913, MS-001, Box 343, Folder 17. Lawton to Todd, September 22, 1913, MS-001, Box 342, Folder 11, MTU.

32   Lawton to Todd, October 20, 1913. Lawton to Todd, October 24, 1913. Lawton to Todd, October 25, 1913. Lawton to Todd, November 1, 1913. Lawton to Todd, November 3, 1913. Lawton to Todd, November 7, 1913. All in MS-001, Box 342, Folder 11, MTU.

33   Lawton to Todd, December 15, 1913, and December 18, 1913, MS-001, Box 342, Folder 11, MTU. S. Lawton to C. Lawton, November 29, 1913, and S. Lawton to Kirchner, December 18, 1913, Acc. 06-087A, MTU.

34   Todd to Lawton, December 16, 1913, MS-001, Box 344, Folder 3, MTU. S. Lawton to Todd, December 19, 1913, Acc. 06-087A, MTU.

35   S. Lawton to Kirchner, December 18, 1913, S. Lawton to Todd, December 19, 1913, S. Lawton to C. L. Lawton, January 19, 1914, S. Lawton to Kirchner, March 28, 1914, S. Lawton to C. L. Lawton, March 24, 1914, Acc. 06-087A, MTU. Denton to Paine, March 24, 1914, CR-998, Box 8, Folder 17, MTU. C. Lawton to Todd, January 20, 1914, and March 24, 1914, MS-001, Box 342, Folder 12, MTU. S. Lawton said that Robinson, C&H's lawyer, had originated the consent decree. S. Lawton to Kirchner, December 18, 1913, Acc. 06-087A, MTU.

36   Kerr and LeGendre to Western Federation of Miners, Statement of Account, Box 1, Folder 2, Papers of WFM/IUMMSW, University of Colorado at Boulder Archives. Grant to Lauck, U.S. Commission on Industrial Relations, Daily Reports on Congressional Hearings, February 21, 1914.

37   U.S. House, *Conditions in the Copper Mines,* 1028–57. Also evicted at this time were Theodore Bissonnette, Andrew P. Kangas, John Kempinnen, and Elmer Holappa and their families.

38   Denton to Paine, January 23, 1914, CR-998, Box 8, Folder 17, MTU. "Statement of Employees and Householders at Mine, February 1, 1913," MS-028, Box 9, Folder 1, MTU.

39   Quincy Mining Co., *Annual Report for 1913,* 14. Lawton to Todd, November 20, 1914, Todd to Lawton, November 7, 1913, and Todd to Lawton, January 5, 1914, MS-001, Box 344, Folder 3, MTU. "Nationalities of all men employed December 1st, 1919," MS-001, Box 344, Folder 10, MTU.

40   U.S. House, *Conditions in the Copper Mines,* 265. Alfred Haddy, who built his own house on his own land in Ahmeek Village, also noted that mining companies had deputies patrolling his village. U.S. House, *Conditions in the Copper Mines,* 176.

41   U.S. House, *Conditions in the Copper Mines,* 1852. Lawton to Todd, July 10, 1913, Folder 11, and Lawton to Todd, January 16, 1914, Folder 12. Both in MS-001, Box 342, MTU.

42   Lawton to Todd, July 29, 1908, Folder 3, and Lawton to Todd, April 4, 1914, Folder 12, both in MS-001, Box 342, MTU.

43   Committee, *Strike Investigation,* 1–2. Lawton to Todd, September 18, 1913, MS-001, Box 342, Folder 11, MTU.

44   Committee, *Strike Investigation,* passim.

45   Ibid., 30–32.

46   Ibid., 84.

47   Lawton to Todd, October 25, 1913, Acc. 001, Box 342, Folder 11, MTU. Todd to Lawton, October 27, 1913, MS-001, Box 343, Folder 19, MTU. Denton to Paine, October 23, 1913, CR-998, Box 8, Folder 17, MTU.

48   Nordberg, "Company Houses along the Picket Line," 66. Thurner, "Western Federation of Miners," 43. LeGendre to Moyer, October 21, 1926, WFM Box 1, and Moyer to LeGendre, November 17, 1926, WFM Box 1, Folder 12, Papers of WFM/IUMMSW, University of Colorado at Boulder Archives

49   U.S. House, *Conditions in the Copper Mines,* 1331. Quincy Mining Co., Labor Attendance and Salary, June 1851–March 1855, MS-001, Box 51, MTU. Charges for board began in August 1853; doctor's charges were also instituted at this time. McNear, "Quincy Mining Company," 516, citing QMC annual report for 1862. *Quincy Mining Co. Journal for 1864–66,* 599 (December 1865) and 630 (January 1866), MS-001, Box 522 (mislabeled), MTU.

50   Adams, "Memories of a Copper Country Childhood," unpaginated.

51   S. Lawton to Todd, February 26, 1914, Acc. 06-087A, MTU.

52   Denton to Prof. H. S. Munroe, December 17, 1913, CR-998, Box 8, Folder 20, MTU. This was written during the strike but clearly pertained to prestrike buildings. Lawton to Todd, April 28, 1906, MS-001, Box 342, Folder 1, MTU.

53   Abbey to Ferris, September 22, 1913, RG 46, Box 1, Folder 3, State Archives of Michigan. "Lake Superior Copper Mines," *Boston Daily Globe,* September 22, 1913. U.S. House, *Conditions in the Copper Mines,* 1466. Denton to Paine, October 23, 1913, CR-998, Box 8, Folder 17, MTU. C&H Drawings that survive, undated but probably from this period, depict a two-story building with bunk rooms accommodating four men each. Several options were offered: 24 by 62 feet, 24 by 76 feet, and 24 by 80 feet. It is not clear if any bunkhouses were built to these plans, which were signed by "E.[?] Ulseth," probably Edward Ulseth, the building contractor. C&H Dr. 116, MS-005, MTU. S. Lawton to Todd, February 26, 1914, Acc. 06-087A, MTU.

54   Lawton to Todd, September 6, 1913, and Lawton to Todd, September 25, 1913, MS-001, Box 342, Folder 11, MTU.

55   Lawton to Todd, November 14, 1913, November 24, 1913, and December 3, 1913, MS-001, Box 342, Folder 11, MTU. McNear, "Quincy Mining Company," 527, citing Mann to Lawton, November 21, 1913. Lawton to Todd, January 24, 1914, noting "shortly after Mr. Mann left," MS-001, Box 342, Folder 12, MTU.

56   Denton to Paine, January 26, 1914, MS-028, Box 15, Folder 8, MTU.

57   Denton to Paine, October 23, 1913, CR-998, Box 008, Folder 17, MTU.

58   Lawton to Todd, November 14, 1913, MS-001, Box 343, Folder 17, MTU.

59   U.S. House, *Conditions in the Copper Mines,* 2343.

60   Quincy Mining Co., *Annual Report for 1916,* 15 and 17. Photo of drawing in Historic American Engineering Record, MI-2-250, Library of Congress.

61   Lawton to Parsons Todd, April 13, 1917, MS-001, Box 336, Folder 18, MTU. McNear, "Quincy Mining Company," 527, citing Todd to Lawton, May 4, 1917. McNear, "Quincy Mining Company," 528, citing Lawton to Todd, September 27, 1920.

62   Denton to Paine, September 4, 1915, Acc. 564, Box 8, Folder 11, MTU. Todd to Lawton, June 8, 1917, MS-001, Box 336, Folder 18, MTU.

3. "Home for the Working Man"

1   Obituaries provided by Putrich family. U.S. Census, *Population,* 1920 and 1930. Sale of house in Deed Book 333:435, Fulton County Courthouse, Lewistown, Illinois. Garden recollection from Joe Putrich, written communication, July 2003.

2   Zunz, *The Changing Face of Inequality,* 152–54. *Daily Mining Gazette,* March 24, 1914.

3   Whitaker, "The Relation of Agriculture to Mining," 24–25. Alanen and Raker, "From Phoenix to Pelkie," 58.

4   *Calumet and Red Jacket News,* May 1, 1890. "Calumet-Laurium: Big Building Boom for Season of 1900," *Daily Mining Gazette,* March 20, 1900. Monkkonen, *America Becomes Urban,* 200. U.S. Census, *Population,* 1910. *Daily Mining Gazette,* May 17, 1903. U.S. House, *Conditions in the Copper Mines,* 1774.

5   Quincy Mining Co., *Annual Report for 1890,* 12. Water pipes, grading, bridge, mentioned in Quincy Mining Co., *Annual Report for 1892,* 16. Plat recorded March 4, 1891, Harris to Todd, March 16, 1891, MS-001, Box 337, Folder 2, Michigan Technological University Archives and Copper Country Historical Collections (hereafter MTU). Land contract agreements, MS-001, Box 31, Folder 1, MTU.

6   The extent of owner building has been debated by Richard Harris and Thomas Hubka. See Harris, *Unplanned Suburbs,* chapter 8, and Hubka, "Just Folks Designing," 428.

7   Todd to Hanchette, October 24, 1899, MS-001, Box 344, Folder 10, MTU. Harris to Mason, January 3, 1895, MS-001, Box 337, Folder 5, 82. In laying out the neighborhood, Quincy claimed a civic benefit: "Our chief object in view, although we expect to realize what the lots are worth, is to improve the general appearance of the property north of Hancock and in that way also add value and beauty to the village itself." Mason? or Todd? to Hanchette, October 24, 1899, McNear notes, Acc. 03-008A, Box 1, Folder 2, MTU. Lankton and Hyde, *Old Reliable,* 152. Quincy Mining Co., *Annual Report for 1899* and *1900.* Quincy leased land in Coburntown, for example, platted in 1896.

8   Another problem encountered with the platting was the topography of the hillside. When Timothy Binane purchased a house and lot, he noted that "the water-course . . . is now in

such a condition that the water runs through the cellar." Dunstan & Hanchette to Quincy Mining Co., May 22, 1901, MS-001, Box 339, Folder 17, MTU. This "water-course" shows up on the plat. Indentures, MS-001, Box 32, Folder 6, MTU.

9   Mason? Or Todd? to Hanchette, October 24, 1899, and Dunstan & Hanchette to Todd, July 23, 1900, McNear notes, Acc. 03-008A, Box 1, Folder 2, MTU.

10   Dunstan & Hanchette to Todd, July 23, 1900, McNear notes, Acc. 03-008A, Box 1, Folder 2, MTU. Only one buyer can be linked to the shantytown neighborhood—Gabriel Moreau, who was listed on Ravine Street, Hancock Twp. Todd to Dunstan & Hanchette, August 2, 1900, MS-001, Box 339, Folder 15, MTU. Dunstan & Hanchette to Harris, October 15, 1900, MS-001, Box 339, Folder 17, MTU. These houses were all in Block E, lots 16–22, 24–26; 413, 409, 405, 401, 331, 327 (or 329), 325, 317, 313, 309 Wright Street.

11   For more information on Pearce, see www.social.mtu.edu/CopperCountryArchitects.

12   444 White Street, Block G, Lot 1, in Quincy Hillside Addition. Deed and installment purchase in MS-001, Box 29, MTU. Mortgage books EE:252 and LL:89, Houghton County Courthouse. Sanborn Map Co., *Hancock,* 1907. The Arvolas sold the house to Matti and Helma Norko, who obtained a $500 mortgage from Northern Michigan Building & Loan and gave the Arvolas a promissory note. Deed book 70:70, Houghton County Courthouse.

13   Correlation of Quincy Mining Co. sales (MS-001, Boxes 32 and 33), *Polk Directories,* Sanborn maps, deed books. The numbers are: lots laid out, ninety-three; lots with houses on them, seventy-two; lots with commercial buildings, six; lots never built on, eight; lots never sold, seven (in Quincy Hillside Addition, excluding block 12). Of lots with houses, fifty-nine owner occupied at some point in first decade. Of them, thirty-three skilled workers, twelve laborers. Non–blue collar were two white collar, two merchants, one management. The rest had no occupation given.

14   J. L. Harris to Todd, July 12, 1902, MS-001, Box 337, Folder 7, MTU. Quincy Mining Co. sales, MS-001, Box 33, MTU. Sanborn Map Co., *Hancock,* various years. *Polk Directories.* In Quincy Second Hillside Addition, 150 lots laid out, 54 had houses built on them, 1 church, 9 lots sold but not built on. In July 1905 the newspaper noted, "A large number of the men employed in these mines [Quincy and Franklin] have purchased property on the side hill within the past year and they are now building homes. The Quincy Mining company has also assisted the boom by erecting a large number of up to date houses on the side hill, which they dispose of to private families when completed. A large number of these houses have already been completed and are now being occupied." "Building Boom on Quincy Hill," *Daily Mining Gazette,* July 14, 1905. "Hancock Department: Building Season Opens with a Rush," *Daily Mining Gazette,* April 30, 1905.

15   "Hancock Department: Building Season Opens with a Rush," *Daily Mining Gazette,* April 30, 1905. Smaller houses were block 4, lot 2 (49231 Hillside); block 8, lot 13 (19570 Sampson); and block 8, lot 15 (19604 Sampson). Larger houses were block 13, lot 8 (49142 Roosevelt); block 6, lot 6 (311 White); and block 6, lot 8 (317 White).

16   Hanchette's lots were block 8, lot 7 (19547 McKinley); block 8, lot 9 (19529 McKinley); block 12, lot 12 (19642 Sampson); block 12, lot 13 (gone); block 12, lot 14 (19644 Sampson); and block 8, lot 1 (19583 McKinley). Spear's house was 19642 Sampson. Peterson's house was 19644 Sampson. U.S. Census, *Population,* 1910.

17   Hanchette & Lawton to Quincy Mining Co., December 8, 1905, MS-001, Box 342, Folder 1, MTU.

18   Ethnic groups had varying attitudes towards boarders as well. Modell and Hareven, "Urbanization and the Malleable Household," 471. U.S. Senate, Immigration Commission, *Immigrants in Industries,* 46.

19   *Portage Lake Mining Gazette,* October 10, 1889. Michel, *Visions to Keep,* 10.

20   Properties with no mortgages: 24. The breakdown of mortgages in Quincy Hillside Addition: Northern Michigan Building & Loan, 36; Superior SB, 12; Copper Country Building & Loan, 4; private mortgages, 12. This counts multiple mortgages for the same property and from the same agency as one; but multiple mortgages for the same property from two lenders are counted as two. Salfenauer house was 49292 Roosevelt, B3 L2. Quincy Mining Co. land contracts, MS-001, Box 29, MTU. Mortgage Books LL: 85 and KK: 235, Houghton County Courthouse. U.S. Census, *Population,* 1910. In the Hillside Additions, mortgagees other than building and loan associations included Superior Savings Bank as well as private individuals. The Toomey house was Lot 5, block H, Quincy Second Hillside Addition. Mrs. Mary Toomey to Charles A. Wright, October 17, 1902, Mortgage Book FF: 503, Houghton County Courthouse.

21   I defined installments as more than two payments. In Quincy Hillside Addition, forty-eight chose this option; twenty-four paid in one lump sum or in two payments. In Quincy Hillside Second Addition, twenty-two paid by installment plan versus thirty-one who did not. Brisson house was 311 White, Lot 6 Block 6. Quincy Mining Co. land contracts, MS-001, Box 29, MTU. U.S. Census, *Population,* 1910.

22   Quincy Mining Co. Land Contracts, MS-001, Box 29, MTU. Mortgage Books, EE: 252 and Deed Books, 70: 70, Houghton County Courthouse. Quincy Mining Co. employment cards, MS-001, Box 287, MTU. U.S. Census, *Population,* 1910.

23   331 Wright, L20 Block E. U.S. Census, *Population,* 1900, 1910, and 1930. Quincy Mining Co. land contracts, MS-001, Box 29, MTU. *Polk Directories.*

24   Harris to Todd, August 18, 1896, MS-001, Box 337, Folder 5, MTU.

25   Streightoff, *The Standard of Living,* 84. Engels, *The Housing Question,* 50. Allen, *Industrial Housing Problems,* 26. Luria, "Wealth, Capital, and Power," 268. *Daily Mining Gazette,* March 24, 1914. Wright, *Building the Dream,* xv. Monkkonen, *America Becomes Urban,* 187.

26   Gates, *Michigan Copper,* 232. Deed Book 112: 505 and Mortgage Book C4: 78, Houghton County Courthouse. Arvola paid $3,153.45, including interest (MS-001, Box 29, MTU). Also, note that he went on strike (as did everyone) July 23, 1913 but didn't return until July 1, 1914 (per employee cards MS-001, Box 288, MTU; his employee number was 3839, then 3426). His $25 per month payments stopped after July 1913 and didn't resume until June 1915. The Seppalas bought the house for a nominal $1; its true selling price is unknown.

27   Hayward and Belfoure, *The Baltimore Rowhouse,* 12–14. Lord proprietors established the system in several British–American colonies; ground rents found particular usage in Philadelphia and Baltimore. Thanks to Larry Lankton for suggesting the parallel to mineral rights to me, November 15, 2007. Pewabic Mining Co., *Annual Report for 1862,* 13. Harris to Haggerty, September 19, 1892, MS-001, Box 336, Folder 15, MTU. In another case, lawyers' correspondence from 1882 refers to a house that Gustav Johnson had built on Allouez Mining Company land "with the understanding with agent that the house was to be his to do therewith as he pleased."

Apparently, the company claimed ownership of the house. T. F. Powers to Thomas L. Chadbourne, October 4, 1882, and Chadbourne to Fred Smith, October 19, 1882, RG 76-83, Lot 1, Acc. B448, Folder 18, State Archives of Michigan.

28   Pewabic Mining Co., *Annual Report for 1862*, 13. *Engineering and Mining Journal* (September 5, 1885): 169. Sanborn Map Co., *Red Jacket*, 1893. *Calumet and Red Jacket News*, August 5, 1890.

29   Harris to Mason, August 8, 1896, MS-001, Box 337, Folder 5, MTU.

30   Copper Range's lease extended for twenty-one years. There seems to have been some latitude in the requirement that they be employees: "Our invariable rule (and the rule of all neighboring mines) is to charge, in such cases, $5 per year ground rent if the owner of the house is an employee of the Quincy, and ten dollars a year if he is not such an employee." Harris to Dunstan, May 21, 1901, MS-001, Box 337, Folder 6, 449, MTU. Copper Range banned the sale of merchandise as well as alcohol. C&H and Quincy required good morals, not Copper Range. C&H and Quincy forbade transfer of lease, not Copper Range. Permission to install toilets and electricity in MacNaughton to Joseph Matthews, MS-002, Box 48, Folder 574, and Goulet to MacNaughton, 1915, MS-002, Box 48, Folder 572, MTU.

31   C&H deeds, Acc. 03-050A, MTU. RG 46, Box 2, Folder 10, State Archives of Michigan.

32   Quincy ground lease in MS-001, Box 27, Folder 1, MTU. Copper Range 1913 lease in RG 46, Box 2, Folder 10, State Archives of Michigan. Harris to Todd, August 18, 1896, MS-001, Box 337, Folder 5, 262, MTU. U.S. Department of Labor, *Michigan Copper District Strike*, 119.

33   C&H deeds, Acc. 03-050A, MTU. Brett to Whiting, December 12, 1895, MS-002, Box 101, Folder 4, MTU.

34   *Copper Country Evening News*, April 24, 1903; C&H deeds, Acc. 03-050A, MTU.

35   *Copper Country Evening News*, May 4, 1897.

36   *Calumet and Red Jacket News*, July 25, 1890. "Calumet-Laurium: Building Boom Soon To Be On," *Daily Mining Gazette*, March 15, 1905. Calumet & Hecla Mining Co., *Annual Report for 1894–95*.

37   Shannon Bennett and James A. Rudkin, Documentation of Blue Jacket Dwelling 566/568 (2006), MS-046, MTU. Kantor and Silvola first appear in the 1888 tax roll. The house did not appear in the 1886 tax roll, when there were only seventeen houses in Blue Jacket. Kantor and Silvola do not show up in the 1900 census or in the *Polk Directories*.

38   The surnames were difficult to read on the manuscript census. Basso, for instance, is listed as such in the 1899–1900 *Polk Directory* but appears as "Bassi" in the census. The others were not listed in the *Directory*. Further, the census taker appears to have Americanized their first names. U.S. Census, *Population*, 1900.

39   U.S. Census, *Population*, 1910. Ponsetti also rendered as Ponsetto and Poncetto. Bennett and Rudkin, Documentation of Blue Jacket Dwelling 566/568.

40   U.S. Census, *Population*, 1920 and 1930. Bennett and Rudkin, Documentation of Blue Jacket Dwelling 566/568.

41   Tax Assessment Book, Calumet Township, 1900, RG 77-105, MTU. *Polk's Directory* for 1901–2.

42   U.S. Census, *Population*, 1900, listed these 92 households on Cedar Street, but it obviously included much more than just Cedar Street, which had about 25 houses at this time. Second and Third streets were not indicated in the census, so it appears that "Cedar Street"

included them too. While the extent of "Cedar Street" is not clear, it appears to have been confined to Blue Jacket. The census was cross-referenced with information in Merritt, Morin, Deegan, and Kotlensky, Survey of Blue Jacket.

43   Seth Depasqual and Marc Henshaw, Documentation of 25125 (3122) Tunnel Street (2008), and Andrew Mueller and Yolanda Bertran, Documentation of 25260 (3117) Tunnel Street (2008), MS-046, MTU.

44   C&H employment card for Edgar Richards, MS-002, Box 382, MTU. Marriage License No. 48 (1929), 6:231, Houghton County Courthouse. Jail Records, County of Houghton, inmate No. 2775, RG 77-105, MTU. Although the 1930 census listed Minnie as Urbon, the 1930 *Polk Directory* listed her as Richards. Urbon was not living with her at the time of the 1930 census. His jail record shows no discharge information. Primeau interview. Nuottila interview. *Polk Directories.* U.S. Census, *Population,* 1920 and 1930. Sanborn Map Co., *Laurium,* various years.

45   *Polk Directories.* Tax Assessment books, RG 77-105, MTU. U.S. Census, *Population,* 1910 and 1920.

46   Universal Oil Products, Inc., to Edgar Richards and Ann M. Richards, his wife, and Marcia A. Primeau, lot 7, October 14, 1980, Deed Book 65/469, Houghton County Courthouse.

47   U.S. Department of Labor, *Michigan Copper District Strike,* 119 and 122, citing *Daily Mining Gazette,* October 24, 1913. Taylor, "Clash in the Copper Country," 135. Primeau interview.

48   U.S. House, *Conditions in the Copper Mines,* 2307.

49   Numbers according to U.S. Department of Labor, *Michigan Copper District Strike,* 117. According to Calumet & Hecla Mining Co., *Annual Report for 1913,* 969 leased lots at $5 per year. Quincy had 300 company houses and 200 ground-rent houses in 1901. Harris to Todd, August 1, 1901, MS-001, Box 337, Folder 6, 490, MTU.

50   Jennifer Bollen, David Hayes, and Kevin Schofield, Documentation of 108 7th Street, Calumet (1998), MS-046, MTU.

51   Bollen, Hayes, and Schofield, Documentation of 108 7th Street, Calumet. U.S. Census, *Population,* 1910.

52   U.S. Census, *Population,* 1910.

53   Ibid.

54   Bollen, Hayes, and Schofield, Documentation of 108 7th Street, Calumet. U.S. Census, *Population,* 1920 and 1930.

55   Some of the few multiunit houses included the three-unit house at 595-97-99 Bluejacket (57397 Waterworks Street) and a ten-unit building on 9th Street in Calumet, identified by Jeremiah Mason. Neither building is extant.

56   Calumet & Hecla Mining Co., *Annual Report for 1938,* 4.

57   Adams in July 1946, 6; Wilson in July 1946, 5; Marcotte in September 1948, 8, *C&H News and Views.* Goldstein, *Do It Yourself,* 31–32.

58   Koupus, July 1946, 6, Kauppila, August 1947, 5, and Tolonen, June 1948, 8, *C&H News and Views.*

59   Hall in September 1947, 3, Bracco same, 7, Larson in July 1946, 4, and Notario same, 5, *C&H News and Views.*

60   Karna in September 1948, 3, Michaud in July 1946, 4, and Anderson and Geshel in July 1946, 4, *C&H News and Views.* Zimmerman, "From Paternalism to Privatization," 135.

61   Larry Mishkar, Documentation of Destrampe House (2002), MS-046, MTU.

4. Acquiring Conveniences

1   Photograph of kitchen, Neg. No. 18835, and yard, Negs. 18840 and 18841, State Archives of Michigan. No coal purchases were deducted from Putrich's paycheck, as they were for Dally and others. CR-879, Box 61, Michigan Technological University Archives and Copper Country Historical Collections (hereafter MTU). Candle mentioned in Grubesich testimony, Case No. 4230, *People vs. Thomas Raleigh, et al.,* 40, CR-89-465, MTU.

2   Cowan, *More Work for Mother.* Lankton, *Beyond the Boundaries,* 89–105, discusses household conveniences in the Copper Country before 1875, a situation that was largely unchanged for the working class in the early twentieth century.

3   U.S. Department of Labor, *Michigan Copper District Strike,* 113. Lawton to Parsons Todd, July 8, 1918, MS-001, Box 336, Folder 18, MTU. Zimmerman, "From Paternalism to Privatization," 107–8.

4   Zimmerman, "From Paternalism to Privatization," 103–4, 147.

5   U.S. Department of Labor, *Michigan Copper District Strike,* 126. C&H Drawing 6401, MS-005, MTU.

6   U.S. Department of Labor, *Michigan Copper District Strike,* 114. C&H drawing 6401, MS-005, MTU.

7   Mary Grentz Butina remembered the men of her household chopping wood on company land, then paying someone to haul it home. This was in the 1920s and 1930s, though. Butina interview. Workers also took out stumps from company land, which is ostensibly why they needed blasting powder outside of work, or so they argued to the congressional investigators. U.S. House, *Conditions in the Copper Mines,* 890. U.S. Department of Labor, *Michigan Copper District Strike,* 123. These chimneys were found in the log house in Ahmeek as well as in frame houses at Central and Quincy. U.S. Department of Interior, *Houses for Mining Towns,* 26, 28.

8   U.S. Department of Labor, *Michigan Copper District Strike,* 114.

9   Caron to MacNaughton, June 29, 1915, MS-002, Box 48, Folder 572, MTU. MacNaughton to Jess, June 15, 1915, MS-002, Box 48, Folder 570, MTU. Boyd to MacNaughton, August 7, 1916, and reply August 8, MS-002, Box 49, Folder 613, MTU.

10   Joe and Elaine Putrich, e-mail to author, August 2, 2003.

11   Philip Miller, May 5, 1914, MS-002, Box 47, Folder 517, MTU.

12   Worst spelled: "Ma we ave a tolet put in the saler plas." John Ellis, 1915, MS-002, Box 48, Folder 572, MTU.

13   Two hundred seventy-eight letters regarding toilets survive; eighty-five of them were written in response to requests that do not survive. They date between 1912, when the head plumber requested that a policy be outlined, and 1917. "Occupant . . . wants to buy a water closet for same. Are you willing that he should put one in, if so, what are to be the conditions?" Wm. Phillips on behalf of Samuel Jordan, September 27, 1912, Box 47, Folder 487. John Hicks, April 2, 1914, Box 4, Folder 517. Mrs. John N. Brown, February 16, 1914, Box 47, Folder 517. Thomas Ellis, December 2, 1915, Box 48, Folder 572. William Becker, March 19, 1914, Box 47, Folder 501. Fred Cudlip, April 21, 1914, Box 47, Folder 517. Peter Sterk, May 14, 1915, Box 48, Folder 572. James H. Berryman, March 30, 1914, Box 47, Folder 517. Alex A. Brown, May 11, 1914, Box 47, Folder 517. William Taylor, August 7, 1915, Box 48, Folder 572. All in MS-002, MTU.

14   Mrs. George Gipp, May 1, 1914, Folder 517. Daniel Macdonald, May 2, 1914, Folder 517. Thomas F. Cocking, May 5, 1914, Folder 517. Mrs. Fred Lebeau, March 14,1913, Folder 487. All in MS-002, Box 47, MTU.

15   Mrs. John N. Brown, February 16, 1914, Box 47, Folder 517. Louis Nadeau, February 23, 1914, Box 47, Folder 517. "There are sewer connection and stone foundation and the putting in of it would be all that is required." Charles Laechel, October 10, 1916, Box 48, Folder 594. John Bracco, May 13, 1916, Box 48, Folder 594. All in MS-002, MTU.

16   A hundred and fifty-three letters concern the introduction of electricity into houses. A hundred and forty-five of these come from householders; there are eight responses to requests that do not survive. Another fifty-nine requests came from the stamp mills, routed through the stamp mill superintendent on a form. Steven Kestner, September 27, 1915, Box 48, Folder 574. Mrs. James Moyle, November 12, 1913, Box 46, Folder 457A. Henry Peck, November 12, 1915, Box 48, Folder 574. John Vertin, August 30, 1916, Box 48, Folder 595. James Collie, August 13, 1912, Box 46, Folder 457. John German, May 26, 1917, Box 48, Folder 595. Mrs. Charles Nelson, January 8, 1917, Box 48, Folder 595. Oscar J. Larson, December 1, 1915, Box 48, Folder 574. All in MS-002, MTU.

17   Alex Kerr, November 16, 1912, Folder 457. W. A. Sullivan, September 9, 1912, Folder 457. Mrs. James Moyle, November 12, 1913, Folder 457A. All in MS-002, Box 46, MTU.

18   M. M. Morrison on behalf of Chas. Fien, December 26, 1912, MS-002, Box 46, Folder 457, MTU.

19   R. T. Bennetts, September 28, 1915, MS-002, Box 48, Folder 574, MTU.

20   "C&H Starts a Day Service," *Daily Mining Gazette,* August 31, 1900. A steam line ran down Calumet Avenue. Samuel Jess, December 4, 1913, Box 47, Folder 501. Mathias Kauth, May 14, 1917, Box 49, Folder 613. Paul Le Chevalier, July 27, 1916, Box 49, Folder 613. Letters in MS-002, MTU.

21   Benedict, *Red Metal,* 89, quotes an 1893 description: "Lake Superior Water Works, steam operated, pumps and boilers all in duplicate to avoid any possibility of failure, and with a capacity of 2,000,000 gallons per day. An 18 inch intake pipe extends 1200 feet into the lake and a 12 inch pipe conveys the water 4-1/2 miles to a standpipe at the mine, a rise of 700 feet and an elevation ample for gravity distribution to the whole location." Vaughan to Mac-Naughton, July 1, 1907, MS-002, Box 44, Folder 230, MTU. A second intake pipe was added in the winter of 1906–7. U.S. Department of Labor, *Michigan Copper District Strike,* 114. U.S. House, *Conditions in the Copper Mines,* 442.

22   *Calumet and Red Jacket News,* August 30, 1890. Population of Calumet village was 3,073 in 1890. Thurner, *Calumet Copper,* 106. MacNaughton to Agassiz, May 29, 1905, Box 53, Folder 18. Agassiz to Whiting, August 1, 1898, Box 102, Folder 14. MacNaughton to Agassiz, June 13, 1908, and Agassiz to MacNaughton, June 17, 1908, Box 53, Folder 3. Letters in MS-002, MTU.

23   Benedict, *Red Metal,* 89. *Hancock Evening Journal,* July 10, 1901. Vaughan to MacNaughton, July 1, 1907, MS-002, Box 44, Folder 230, MTU. "List of Company Houses with Inside Closets, October 1911," MS-002, Box 54, Folder 2, MTU. U.S. Department of Labor, *Michigan Copper District Strike,* 114. *Calumet and Red Jacket News,* October 23, 1891.

24   *Copper Country Evening News,* March 5, 1897. *Portage Lake Mining Gazette,* August 5, 1897. Completed 1899. Busch, "Laurium Historic District." This was replaced by a new system in 1901. "Sewers Finished," *Hancock Evening Journal,* November 1, 1901.

25   "Guarding against Typhoid," *New York Times,* March 12, 1904. Vaughan to MacNaughton, July 1, 1907, MS-002, Box 44, Folder 230, MTU.

26   Vaughan to MacNaughton, July 1, 1907, Box 44, Folder 230. MacNaughton to Agassiz, July 6, 1907, Box 53, Folder 5. Agassiz to MacNaughton, July 11, 1907, Box 53, Folder 5. All in MS-002, MTU.

27   Mrs. Mary Muretic, MacNaughton response, July 17, 1916, MS-002, Box 48, Folder 594, MTU.

28   Thirty-nine petitioners requested that the toilet be put in their basement (thirty-three of them using that word; the other six, "cellar"). Nels E. Olsen, April 20, 1914, Box 47, Folder 517. Michael Sullivan, May 1, 1914, Box 47, Folder 517. After asking MacNaughton to have the company carpenters enlarge his barn's doors in order to accommodate an automobile that his son won in a voting contest, John Caron added, "Would also appreciate installing of toilet in cellar, as present outhouse is very inconvenient in winter, and the odor is disagreeable in warm weather." MacNaughton suggested that he hire his own carpenter to build the garage, but that the toilet could be added. John Caron, June 29, 1915, Box 48, Folder 572. The head carpenter, J. S. Cocking, reported that carpenters had built rooms to enclose the 162 toilets that had been installed in 1915. J. S. Cocking to MacNaughton, March 8, 1916, Box 49, Folder 613. All in MS-002, MTU.

29   John Messner, May 16, 1914, MS-002, Box 47, Folder 517, MTU. C&H notebook, House 149/151, Keweenaw National Historical Park.

30   John Rock was a typical householder; a French Canadian carpenter, he lived in 1690 with his wife Minnie and their three children. MacKenzie et al., 1914, MS-002, Box 48, Folder 533, MTU.

31   Geshel interview. This is in front-gable side-entrance house, C&H 6271, Dr. 62, C-2, MTU. C&H 6281, Dr. 62, D-1, MTU.

32   C&H never considered retrofitting bathrooms in company houses, but it did consider the construction of clubhouses for its workers. Agassiz dismissed the idea of equipping them with baths, preferring a central bathhouse. Agassiz to MacNaughton, November 19, 1906, MS-002, Box 53, Folder 7, MTU. *Portage Lake Mining Gazette,* July 16, 1862. R. L. Polk and Co., *Polk's Houghton Directory,* 1910. Alanen and Raker, "From Phoenix to Pelkie," 62.

33   February 24, 1912, MS-002, Box 211, Folder 35, MTU. U.S. House, *Conditions in the Copper Mines,* 1441. Dyer, "The Truth about the Copper Strike," 249. The Peninsula Electric Light & Power Company, a home-grown company, sold out in 1902 to the national firm of Stone & Webster, who reorganized the local office as the Houghton County Electric Light Company. Peninsula had begun lighting Calumet, Red Jacket, and Lake Linden in 1887 from its plant at the head of Torch Lake. *Torch Lake Times,* June 11, 1887.

34   W. H. McGrath, Houghton County Electric Light Co., to MacNaughton, February 10, 1906, Box 43, Folder 153. William Berryman, MacNaughton to Bosson, November 1, 1911, Bosson to MacNaughton, November 2, 1911, MacNaughton to Bosson, November 20, 1911, Box 46, Folder 438. All in MS-002, MTU.

35   Frederick Bosson, December 11, 1913, Box 46, Folder 457A. Fred Williams, MacNaughton to James Collie, October 17, 1916, Box 49, Folder 613. Richard John Nottle, March 9, 1917, Box 48, Folder 595. All in MS-002, MTU.

36   Wm. J. Bennetts, December 6, 1911, Box 46, Folder 438. Also Alex MacDonald, December 6, 1911, Box 46, Folder 438. Joseph Matthews, October 22, 1915, Box 48, Folder 574. All in MS-002, MTU.

37   William Berryman, October 30, 1911, MS-002, Box 46, Folder 438, MTU.

38   William Moore, March 21, 1913, Box 46, Folder 457A. James Collie, August 13, 1912, Box 46, Folder 457. James Berryman, September 5, 1912, Box 46, Folder 471. Thomas R. Eddy, January 16, 1913, Box 46, Folder 471. M. M. Morrison on behalf of William Marcham, September 15, 1910, Box 45, Folder 405. All in MS-002, MTU.

39   Henry Brett was given the job of assigning houses in 1891. This had previously been handled by foremen, and certain houses remained connected to certain jobs, so perhaps MacNaughton didn't want to interfere in this historic relationship but felt more justified with new technologies that had no such precedent.

40   Copper Range, *Annual Report for 1899*. Copper Range, *Annual Report for 1907*, 33. In 1903–4 the company built a second water tank holding two hundred thousand gallons near Shaft B. "Painesdale Waterworks," *Daily Mining Gazette*, November 14, 1903. In 1912 Champion replaced its previous water source southeast of Painesdale with one on the southwest, a concrete-lined reservoir for domestic and industrial uses. Copper Range, *Annual Report for 1912*, 32. Butina interview. Butina was born in 1905, moved to 48 Second Street, Seeberville, in 1921, and lived there until her death in 2006. Sergey interview. Sergey was born in 1923 in the house he lived in into the twenty-first century, 25 Second Street. Jane Nordberg, "Township Awaits Sewer System," *Daily Mining Gazette*, October 23–24, 2004. Baltic and Trimountain still do not have sewers. Laura Kirby, "Adams Township Grapples with Sewage Issue," *Daily Mining Gazette*, January 27, 2006.

41   QD0059, MS-012, MTU. "A large stone cistern, 20' x 20' x 10' was partly built back of the old hospital to replace old wood one entirely worn out." Harris to Todd, August 3, 1888, MS-001, Box 337, Folder 3, 470, MTU. Buildings near No. 8 shaft drew water from that shaft, where it was piped to a thirty thousand-gallon tank on a thirty-four-foot tower. Quincy Mining Co., *Annual Report for 1916*, 15. Lawton to Todd, November 4, 1915, and November 24, 1915, MS-001, Box 342, Folder 15, MTU. Parsons Todd to Lawton, November 16, 1917, MS-001, Box 336, Folder 18, MTU. Quincy Mining Co., *Annual Report for 1918*, 18. In fact, Quincy's water supply problems persisted into the 1960s, and Quincy continued to shut off water at 10 a.m. Raasio interview.

42   Quincy Mining Co., *Annual Report for 1918*, 18, and *1919*, 17. Lawton to Parsons Todd, April 27, 1918, MS-001, Box 336, Folder 10, and Lawton to Parsons Todd, July 17, 1918, Folder 18, MTU.

43   Gary Kaunonen and Racheal Herzberg, Documentation of Mesnard Company House, MS-046, MTU. In 1946 this house had no bathroom or toilet. Office of Price Administration Rent Control cards, MS-001, Box 40, Folder 8, MTU. The rent, $4.50 per month in 1946, rose to $5.50 by the 1960s, to $10.50 in 1970, to $29 in 1975, and to $49 in 1980. It is possible the bathroom was added in the 1970s but more likely after the house went into private ownership after 1983. The first tenant, Thomas Maunder, who was captain of the No. 8 shaft, later moved into one of the Sears houses built in 1917–18. In 1912 he became captain of South Quincy, supervising three shafts, and in 1920 he became chief mining captain. This house's next tenant was William J. Sampson, who became a shift captain at No. 8. He lived here until 1918, when he also moved

into a Sears house. Gary Kaunonen and Racheal Herzberg, Documentation of Mesnard Company House, MS-046. Quincy Mining Co., *Annual Report for 1912*, 20.

44 Lawton to Todd, June 15, 1912, and September 25, 1912, MS-001, Box 342, Folder 9, MTU. Chris Merritt, Documentation of Quincy House 172 (2005), MS-046, MTU, and undated drawings in Quincy file labeled "Berryman House" in pencil, MS-012, MTU. Dwelling repairs (1906–13), Folder 2; (1913–19), Folder 4; (1919–28), Folder 18. All in MS-001, Box 44, MTU.

45 Interviews with former resident who wished to remain anonymous. Husband George was born in the house in 1921. Her father-in-law's father (George's grandfather) lived there before them, 1912–58. She said, "It was a sad forty years when I look back."

46 Stoker interview.

47 Lawton to Todd, March 23, 1917, and May 30, 1917, MS-001, Box 336, Folder 18, MTU.

48 Todd to Lawton, June 4, 1917, Folder 19. Lawton to Todd, June 13, 1917, Folder 18. Quincy Drawing 1820-F, MS-012, MTU. Todd to Lawton, June 21, 1917, Folder 18. Lawton to Todd, June 26, 1917, Folder 18. Letters all in MS-001, Box 336, MTU.

49 Quincy Mining Co., *Annual Report for 1917*, 16. Lawton to Todd, April 2, 1917, MS-001, Box 336, Folder 18, MTU.

50 Todd to Lawton, July 23, 1917, MS-001, Box 336, Folder 18, MTU.

51 Lawton to Todd, July 25, 1917, MS-001, Box 336, Folder 18, MTU.

52 Lawton to Verville, August 27, 1917, Box 337, Folder 37. Todd to Lawton, July 25, 1917, Box 336, Folder 18. Lawton to Todd, August 24, 1917, Box 336, Folder 18. Parsons Todd to Lawton, August 28, 1917, Box 336, Folder 18. All in MS-001, MTU.

53 Exact cost was $2,687.58 and $4,882.56. Lawton to Todd, July 25, 1917, Box 336, Folder 18. Further discussion of costs in Lawton to Todd, July 27, 1917, Box 344, Folder 18. Lawton to Todd, July 28, 1917, Box 336, Folder 18. Todd to Lawton, September 4, 1917, Box 344, Folder 9. Lawton to Todd, September 7, 1917, Box 344, Folder 9. Todd to Lawton, September 11, 1917, Box 344, Folder 9. "List of New Numbers for Company Houses," June 1, 1919, author's collection. House rent cards, 1915–20, Box 42, Folders 1, 2, and 3. All in MS-001, MTU.

54 Lawton to Parsons Todd, October 25, 1917, Lawton to Todd, December 26, 1917, and Lawton to Parsons Todd, June 10, 1918, MS-001, Box 336, Folder 18, MTU.

55 Lawton to Parsons Todd, June 13, 1918, Parsons Todd to Lawton, June 14, 1918, Parsons Todd to Lawton, July 20, 1918, and Lawton to Parsons Todd, July 29, 1918, MS-001, Box 336, Folder 18, MTU.

56 Lawton to Todd, September 12, 1918, MS-001, Box 336, Folder 18, MTU. "New Houses August 1918," MS-001, Box 40, Folder 5, MTU. Ore, *The Seattle Bungalow*, 157 n. 26 mentions that in 1915 hot-water heat cost 65 percent more to install but was 50 percent cheaper to operate than hot-air furnaces.

57 Lawton to Todd, November 7, 1906, MS-001, Box 342, Folder 1. Quincy Mining Co., *Annual Report for 1919*, 17.

58 "New Houses August 1918," Box 40, Folder 5. House rent cards 1915–20, Box 42, Folders 1, 2, and 3, and 1921–26, Box 42, Folder 5. "Nationalities of all Men Employed," December 1, 1919, Box 344, Folder 10. QMC employment clerk to Fred Nuttall, QMC master mechanic, October 10, 1921, Box 344, Folder 10. All in MS-001, MTU.

59 Atlas Powder Company apparently built catalog houses at Senter. An Aladdin ad that claimed C&H as a client could not be verified.

5. Churches, Schools, Bathhouses

1   *Daily Mining Gazette,* February 6, 1914. John Stimac's testimony mentions Mrs. Stimac's store, *People vs. Thomas Raleigh, et al.,* Case No. 4230, 139, RG 89-465, MTU. Another reference to the store run by Mrs. Antonija Stimac in CR-998, Box 8, Folder 22, Michigan Technological University Archives and Copper Country Historical Collections (hereafter MTU).

2   U.S. Department of Labor, *Michigan Copper District Strike,* 124–26. Lankton, *Cradle to Grave,* 189.

3   Lankton, *Cradle to Grave,* 188.

4   At Painesdale most of the institutions clustered in the heart of the community. Because all of them were on company land, this was obviously the company's intention. The elementary school was located on the block bounded by Goodell, Hulbert, Kearsarge, and Iroquois streets. To the west was the Albert Paine Methodist Church, donated by the Paine family in 1907–8 and named in honor of William Paine's father, a Congregational minister. Southwest of the school was a Finnish hall. Southeast of the school was the Sarah Sargent Paine Memorial Library, dedicated in 1904 to William Paine's mother. East of the school was the high school, an impressive Jacobean Revival sandstone structure. Schools, churches, libraries, and fraternal buildings helped foster community in their own ways but under the watchful eye of company management. Other institutions, seen as less vital, were located out of the core. Siller's hotel and store were situated on the main road into town from the north, near the Sacred Heart Catholic Church, built in 1905. Goodell's store and the post office were located down near the railroad tracks, and other stores were scattered around the community, accommodated in houses.

5   Lankton, *Cradle to Grave,* 166. Quincy Mining Co., *Annual Report for 1866,* 15. Denton to Mrs. Antonija Stimach [spelled with an h in this letter], Mr. Isaac Taro, Mr. Isaac Wuorns, Mrs. Joel Aho, and Mrs. Maria Niku, September 11, 1914, CR-998, Box 8, Folder 22, MTU. Thurner, *Strangers and Sojourners,* 179. U.S. Department of Labor, *Michigan Copper District Strike,* 123.

6   First Congregational Church destroyed by fire January 23, 1949, according to *C&H News and Views* (February 1949), 7.

7   Stetter, *The Central Mine M.E. Church,* 5.

8   Wendy Nicholas, "Central Mine Methodist Episcopal Church," HABS No. MI-421, Historic American Buildings Survey, Library of Congress. Monette, *Central Mine,* 39–49.

9   Mason *donated* a lot to Hancock Baptist Church, Harris to Todd, September 25, 1891, Box 4, 43. Quincy *sold* property to St. Joseph's Church for a thousand dollars for the purposes of building a church and school. Harris to Todd, August 5, 1885, Folder 3, 40. Harris to Ed Perso, Treas., St. Joseph's Church, August 14, 1888, Folder 3, 477. Harris to Mason, July 29, 1892, Folder 3, 206 (re: Baptist Church). Harris to Todd, July 19, 1899, Folder 6, 187 (re: Methodist Church). Harris to Todd, December 19, 1900, Folder 6, 368 (re: Norwegian Lutheran Congregation of Quincy). Quote from Harris to Todd, January 4, 1893 (should be 1894), Folder 4, 462. Also, Harris to Mason, April 8, 1893, Folder 4, 354. Harris to Mason, July 14, 1893, Folder 4, 397. Harris to Todd, July 24, 1893, Folder 4, 401 and again 402. Harris to Mason, August 5, 1895, Folder 5, 146. All in MS-001, Box 337, MTU.

10   MacNaughton to Pederson, June 26, 1913, MS-002, Box 47, Folder 506, MTU. U.S. Department of Labor, *Michigan Copper District Strike,* 1445. Calumet & Hecla, *Annual Report for 1893,* 9. Committee of the Copper Country, *Strike Investigation,* 41. MacNaughton to Pennanen, November 7, 1910, MS-002, Box 45, Folder 415, MTU.

11   MacNaughton to Agassiz, August 3, 1905, and Agassiz to MacNaughton, August 6, 1905, MS-002, Box 53, Folder 17, MTU. Lankton, *Cradle to Grave,* 179. Agassiz also disliked supporting parochial schools.

12   Rezek, *History of the Diocese,* 2: 280–82. Dimensions from "St. Louis Church," *Copper Country Evening News,* June 12, 1900.

13   Kevin Harrington, "St. Anne's Church," HABS No. MI-417, Historic American Buildings Survey, Library of Congress, saw the construction contract, dated March 22, 1900, for $28,000. Rezek says it was $28,300, probably due to change orders (or to architect's fee?), and also says the total cost was $43,000. Rezek, *History of the Diocese,* 282. The main altar cost $1,126. "St. Louis Church," *Copper Country Evening News,* June 12, 1900. "Interior Finish Well Under Way," *Daily Mining Gazette,* April 11, 1901. "New French Church," *Copper Country Evening News,* May 3, 1901. "The New Church," *Copper Country Evening News,* June 10, 1901. "Sunday, June 16," *Copper Country Evening News,* May 16, 1901. "St. Anne's Church," *Copper Country Evening News,* December 12, 1900. "Artists' Work," *Copper Country Evening News,* June 14, 1901. "St. Anne's Church," *Copper Country Evening News,* June 1, 1901. An organ was not installed until 1920. It was furnished by the Estey Organ Company of Brattleboro, Vermont, at a cost of $5,150. Rectory built in 1909 for $9,000. New roof in 1928. In 1938–39, grotto built in basement. In 1939 basement ceiling covered with Celotex, walls painted. All from "Calumet French Parish," 76A.

14   Thurner, *Calumet Copper,* 22, 76. "New Sandstone Church," *Copper Country Evening News,* March 7, 1899. "Contract Is Let," *Copper Country Evening News,* March 15, 1900. The $10,000 debt figure repeated in "St. Anne's Church," *Copper Country Evening News,* June 1, 1901. "Calumet French Parish," 76A. The church interior has been repainted, perhaps as early as 1939, and again in the early 1960s. Little of the original decorating scheme remains.

15   Rezek, *History of the Diocese,* 276–77, 287. "Will Part," *Copper Country Evening News,* June 10, 1901. In 1966 several ethnic parishes consolidated. St. Anne's, St. John's, and St. Mary's joined St. Joseph's, which was renamed St. Paul the Apostle.

16   U.S. House, *Conditions in the Copper Mines,* 1475–76. Atkinson, *The Church and Industrial Warfare,* 42.

17   *Copper Country Evening News,* September 16, 1898.

18   Cost from U.S. House, *Conditions in the Copper Mines,* 1451. Shaw & Hunnewell drawings, Drawer 94, MS-005, MTU. *Copper Country Evening News,* September 16, 1898. My thanks to Lynn Bjorkman, who is preparing a history of this building for Keweenaw National Historical Park, for sharing her research with me.

19   Army posts also located baths and libraries in the same building. Hoagland, *Army Architecture in the West,* 195. Agassiz to Whiting, October 22, 1898, MS-002, Box 102, Folder 14, MTU.

20   "Calumet Library," *Copper Country Evening News,* June 13, 1903. "New Reading Room for the Children," *Daily Mining Gazette,* January 10, 1904. Van Slyck, *Free to All,* 175–77. 1905 drawings in Drawer 95, and drawings dated January 3, 1911, in Drawer 94, MS-005, MTU.

21   *Copper Country Evening News,* September 16, 1898. Doubts about the workers' willingness to use the new library also appeared in "The New Public Library," *Copper Country Evening News,* August 8, 1896. The Calumet Board of Education had established the Calumet Public Library in 1894, consolidating a township library and a school library and opening

it to the public. Trebilcock, "History of the Public Schools." Agreement between C&H and School Board, May 7, 1898, MS-002, Box 210, Folder 24, MTU. Calumet & Hecla, *Annual Report for 1898.*

22   Briggs to Agassiz, May 10, 1898, MS-002, Box 102, Folder 15, MTU. *Copper Country Evening News,* September 16, 1898. *C&H News and Views* (November 1943), 1. "Mrs. M. F. Grierson, former librarian, is taken by death," *Daily Mining Gazette,* June 19, 1944. "'Mrs. E. S. Grierson Day' is held here by business women," *Daily Mining Gazette,* November 8, 1939. *Library Journal* 23 (1898): 190; 27 (1902): 260; 28 (1903): 235, 620; 29 (1904): 377; 31 (1906): 296; 32 (1907): 40; 38 (1913): 574. *Copper Country Evening News,* September 16, 1898.

23   Grierson, "Calumet and Hecla Library," 561–62. "C&H Library," *Hancock Evening Journal,* October 24, 1903. Calumet population figure included Red Jacket Village and Laurium. Library report for year ending September 30, 1910, MS-002, Box 210, Folder 24, MTU. Figures for 1915 from untitled typescript on welfare work, MS-002, Box 213, Folder 36, MTU.

24   Van Slyck, *Free to All,* 32. Rice, "Labor Conditions at Calumet & Hecla," 1238.

25   Grierson, "Calumet and Hecla Library," 562. Van Slyck, *Free to All,* 135. Fiske, "The Human Interest," 30, 33–35. On plantings, see Merrill to Grierson, May 12, 1899, MS-002, Box 101, Folder 13, MTU.

26   Fond memories of the library appear, for example, in Arthur Thurner, "A Tradition of Excellence," paper delivered at the opening of the Library Museum, July 6, 1975, Keweenaw National Historical Park. "Welfare Work of the C&H," *Miner's Bulletin,* August 28, 1913. Benedict, *Red Metal,* 233–34. *C&H News and Views* (November 1943), 1.

27   Calumet & Hecla, *Annual Report for 1899. Copper Country Evening News,* September 16, 1898. Grierson to MacNaughton, February 19, 1907, and November 17, 1909, MS-002, Box 45, Folder 351, MTU.

28   Grierson to MacNaughton, February 19, 1907, and MacNaughton to Charlton, February 23, 1907, MS-002, Box 45, Folder 351, MTU. C&H may have put the bathhouse project on hold while the YMCA was under construction. U.S. House, *Conditions in the Copper Mines,* 1452.

29   New York and Boston usually included pools in their public bathhouses, Baltimore and Philadelphia usually included public laundries, and Chicago neither. Williams, *Washing "The Great Unwashed,"* 35. Grierson to MacNaughton, February 19, 1907, MS-002, Box 45, Folder 351, MTU.

30   Charlton to MacNaughton, February 25, 1907, MS-002, Box 44, Folder 187, MTU. "New Bathhouse Is Ready," *Daily Mining Gazette,* December 10, 1911.

31   Grierson to MacNaughton, November 17, 1909, MS-002, Box 45, Folder 351, MTU. Carter to MacNaughton, May 1, 1911, and December 18, 1913, and bath reports, MS-002, Box 212, Folder 33, MTU. Bruce Norden, interviewed by Jo Urion, January 14, 2003, and John and Eleanor Buckett, interviewed by Jo Urion, March 27, 2002, Oral History Collection, Keweenaw National Historical Park. One reformer, Mayor Josiah Quincy of Boston, thought that the need for bathing suits discouraged poor people from using pools, so his city provided bathing suits to children for free and to adults for a small charge. Others thought that removing the requirement for bathing suits entirely was a neater solution and, one reformer noted, it "adds extensively to the interest that is taken in the amusement and perhaps even to its benefits." Quincy, "Playgrounds, Baths, and Gymnasia," 146. Calumet Baths, for years 1913 and 1915, MS-002, Box 212, Folder 33, MTU.

32   Adams Township's population was 8,419 in 1910, while Calumet Township's was 32,000 or so (not counting Red Jacket Village and Laurium). Adams Township's population in 1900 was 3,253 (Lucchesi, *History of Sarah Sargent Paine Memorial Library,* 3 and 10). Library was built by Prendergast and Clarkson. "Sarah Sargent Paine Memorial Library Day," *Daily Mining Gazette,* November 14, 1903.

33   Drawings in Collection 01, Number 1148, Wisconsin Architectural Archives. Rice, "Labor Conditions at Copper Range," 1229. Charlotte Hubbard Goodell, "Annual Report to the Board of Trustees of the Sarah Sargent Paine Memorial Building" (1905), Vertical Files, MTU.

34   Rice, "Labor Conditions at Copper Range," 1229. Goodell, "Annual Report," Vertical Files, MTU.

35   "Painesdale Library Has 75th Birthday," *Daily Mining Gazette,* July 20, 1978. Lucchesi, *History of Sarah Sargent Paine Memorial Library.* One sad aspect is that when the library moved out in 1962, it stored all of its papers and books in the former dispensary, which burned down several months later, destroying its history. The new library, built in 1962, also named for Sarah Sargent Paine, was reorganized as a nonprofit organization, whose president was William P. Nicholls, vice president of Copper Range. Construction was partly funded by members of the Paine family as well as the Copper Range Foundation. "New Paine Library to Open Sunday," *Daily Mining Gazette,* December 14, 1962. Today the township owns the building and runs the library. Gondek interview.

36   Lawton to Todd, November 24, 1915, and Lawton to Todd, November 30, 1915, Box 342, Folder 15, MS-001, MTU. Maass Bros. drawings, November 23, 1915, QD0152-5, MS-012, MTU. Todd to Lawton, December 22, 1915, Box 336, Folder 18. Lawton to Todd, December 2, 1915, Box 342, Folder 15. Both in MS-001, MTU.

37   Todd to Lawton, March 17, 1916, MS-001, Box 366, Folder 9, MTU. Todd saw no need for women to use the second floor, but he apparently was not thinking about the library, which had a female attendant. March 4, 1917, drawings, QD0156, MS-012, MTU.

38   Todd to Lawton, August 30, 1918, MS-001, Box 366, Folder 9, MTU. Quincy Mining Co., *Annual Report for 1918,* 18. McNear, "Quincy Mining Company," 565.

39   Telegram, MacNaughton to Agassiz, September 1, 1905, MS-002, Box 53, Folder 10, MTU.

40   "School Houses on Calumet & Hecla property, May 1905," MS-002, Box 211, Folder 4, MTU. Trebilcock, "History of the Public Schools," 4. *History of the Upper Peninsula,* 300. This school was destroyed by fire in 1929 and rebuilt.

41   "School Houses on Calumet & Hecla property, May 1905," MS-002, Box 211, Folder 4, MTU. Trebilcock, "History of the Public Schools," 6, 10, 14. U.S. House, *Conditions in the Copper Mines,* 1444.

42   Agassiz to Whiting discussing plans of high school, September 13 and October 14, 1900, MS-002, Box 102, Folder 13, MTU. "Last Night's Fire Loss in Calumet Officially Stated to Be $100,000," *Copper Country Evening News,* September 1, 1905. "Cost of Manual Training and High Schools and Miscowaubik Club, September 1905," MS-002, Box 211, Folder 4. A. E. Winship, *Journal of Education,* April 4, 1904, cited in Arthur W. Thurner, "A Tradition of Excellence," paper delivered at opening of Library Museum, July 6, 1975, 9, Keweenaw National Historical Park.

43   Charlton to MacNaughton, September 2, 1905, Box 43, Folder 152. Agassiz to MacNaughton, September 2, 1905, and MacNaughton to Agassiz, September 7, 1905, Box 53, Folder 10. All in MS-002, MTU.

44   MacNaughton to Agassiz, September 30, 1905, Folder 10, and Agassiz to MacNaughton, October 3, 1905, MS-002, Box 53, Folder 9, MTU.

45   Charlton to MacNaughton, October 10, 1905, Box 43, Folder 152. MacNaughton to Agassiz, October 7, 1905, and Agassiz to MacNaughton, October 10, 1905, Box 53, Folder 9. Telegram, Agassiz to MacNaughton, October 11, 1905, Box 53, Folder 10. All in MS-002, MTU.

46   MacNaughton to Agassiz, November 8, 1905, Agassiz to MacNaughton, November 13, 1905, and MacNaughton to Agassiz, November 29, 1905, Box 53, Folder 12. I was surprised to discover that the building in which I work (MTU's Administration Building and Library, now Academic Office Building), designed by Charlton & Kuenzli in 1908, also has an internal downspout in its flat roof. MacNaughton to Charlton & Kuenzli, January 16, 1906, and Charlton & Kuenzli to C&H, April 28, 1906, Box 43, Folder 152. Calumet & Hecla, *Annual Report for 1906.* "Cost of School Buildings and Equipment, 26 October 1911," Box 211, Folder 4. All in MS-002, MTU.

47   Drawings in Collection 11, Number 11, Wisconsin Architectural Archive. Photos of interior in MS-003, Box 9, Folder 13, MTU. Trebilcock, "History of the Public Schools," 30. "Will Begin Shop Work Tomorrow," *Daily Mining Gazette,* September 22, 1907.

48   Trebilcock, "History of the Public Schools," 30.

49   Ibid., 42. MacNaughton to Agassiz, September 7, 1905, MS-002, Box 53, Folder 10, MTU.

50   As recounted by MacNaughton to F. W. Cooley, Superintendent of Schools, Calumet, October 8, 1901, MS-002, Box 159, Folder 3, 362, MTU.

51   *General Rules,* 56–59. Stetter to Tiberg, June 15, 1984, Calumet Public School Library.

52   Thurner, *Calumet Copper,* 64–65. Wiltse, *Contested Waters,* 30, argues that YMCAs, which had a membership fee, were inherently middle class. In 1907 the membership fee was two dollars. YMCA Constitution attached to Westerman to MacNaughton, December 1, 1911, MS-002, Box 46, Folder 442. By 1921 this YMCA had a sliding scale of membership fees, ranging from two dollars for "preparatory boys" to fifteen dollars for "business men." "Young men" paid five dollars. YMCA, *27th Annual Report. Copper Country Evening News,* February 8, 1898, cited in Engel and Mantel, *Calumet,* 11. *The Senior,* 48 and 51. Westerman, general secretary of the YMCA, to MacNaughton, December 9, 1911, MS-002, Box 46, Folder 442, MTU. Brisson, "D. Fred Charlton," 159. The attribution comes from the Marquette *Daily Mining Journal* in a summary article about Charlton's career (August 31, 1918) and could have been referring to the earlier YMCA, but it is the latter one that looks more like Charlton's work. Shaw to Ulseth, August 19, 1908, MS-002, Box 107, Folder 4, copy in Box 53, Folder 70, MTU.

53   Skating rink drawings in Drawer 96, MS-005, MTU. By 1931 C&H also provided assistance to a golf club and built tennis courts at various sites and a recreational camp on the lakeshore. Bennetts, "Industrial and Community Relations," 564. Other athletic facilities included bowling alleys, such as the one built by Champion Copper Company in Painesdale.

54   Copper Range, *Annual Report for 1908,* 33. Rice, "Labor Conditions at Copper Range," 1229.

55   Collection 01, Number 816, Wisconsin Architectural Archives.

56   "Painesdale High School an Efficient Institution," *Daily Mining Gazette,* March 21, 1912.

57   Drawings dated July 3, 1933 in 87U, Acc. 05-003A, MTU. Some correspondence in RG 69, A3112, roll 2525, reel 629, National Archives. "Death Takes Mrs. Jeffers," *Daily Mining Gazette,* March 30, 1949.

58   Harris to Mason, August 19, 1890, MS-001, Box 337, Folder 2, MTU. Quincy Mining Co., *Annual Report for 1895,* 14. McNear, "Quincy Mining Company," 547–48.

59   Lawton to Todd, June 15, 1912, MS-001, Box 342, Folder 9, MTU.

60   Harris to Todd, September 5, 1892, 233, Harris to W. C. Watson, Osceola Mine, August 31, 1892, 225, and Harris to Watson, September 3, 1892, 233, MS-001, Box 337, Folder 4, MTU.

61   Agassiz to MacNaughton, October 3, 1905, MS-002, Box 53, Folder 9, MTU. Trebilcock, "History of the Public Schools," 11.

62   "Hospital Opens Saturday Night," *Daily Mining Gazette,* April 20, 1906.

63   "C&H Hospital Staff," *C&H News and Views* 3, no. 3 (January 1945): 4.

64   Lankton, *Cradle to Grave,* 184, quoting Mineral Statistics for 1899, 276–77.

65   Charlton, Gilbert & Demar to Whiting, June 23, 1897, MS-002, Box 114, Folder 16, MTU.

66   Rosenberg, *The Care of Strangers,* 342. Simonson to MacNaughton, June 10, 1908, MS-002, Box 45, Folder 267, MTU. In addition, wood-frame hospitals, once favored in the theory that they would become "poisoned" and need to be replaced, were discarded in favor of antiseptic and fireproof masonry buildings. Hoagland, *Army Architecture in the West,* 161.

67   Shaw to MacNaughton, July 29, 1912, MacNaughton to Charlton, August 20, 1912, Charlton to MacNaughton, August 24, 1912, and MacNaughton to Charlton, August 29, 1912, MS-002, Box 47, Folder 478, MTU.

68   Shaw to MacNaughton, September 5, 1912, E. S. Grierson to MacNaughton, September 13, 1912, and Shaw to MacNaughton, November 21, 1912, MS-002, Box 47, Folder 478, MTU. Haven & Hoyt's drawings have not been found.

69   MacNaughton to Shaw, May 16, 1913, MS-002, Box 47, Folder 478, MTU.

70   Gates, *Michigan Copper,* 138.

71   The hospital received large additions in 1964 and 1998. *Keweenaw Memorial.* By 1931 and perhaps much earlier, this public hospital took all of C&H's obstetrical cases. Bourland, "The Medical Department," 556.

72   This hospital built a nine-story structure with a capacity of 170 patients in 1951. The hospital, renamed Portage View in 1995, moved to new quarters up on Quincy Hill in 2000. It is now known as Portage Health. "Portage Health Celebrates 110 Years of Caring," *Daily Mining Gazette,* December 14, 2006. Harris to Todd, October 23, 1899, 224, Harris to Todd, October 31, 1899, 225, and Todd to Harris, July 24, 1900, 327, MS-001, Box 337, Folder 6, MTU. There was also a Finnish hospital in Hancock, which operated from 1917 until about 1929.

73   Todd to Harris, September 26, 1895, MS-001, Box 338, Folder 9, MTU.

74   Harris to Todd, July 12, 1895, Todd to Harris, July 14, 1895, and Mason to Harris, August 7, 1895, Box 338, Folder 9. Harris to Todd, August 19, 1895, Box 337, Folder 5, 152. All in MS-001, MTU.

75   Rae and Rae, *Morristown's Forgotten Past*, 43, 85, 161, 165. "Robert C. Walsh," [obituary] *Jerseyman*, October 6, 1911, 5. My thanks to Lynn Bjorkman for sharing these documents with me.

76   Harris to Mason, September 5, 1895, 158. Harris to Mason, October 17, 1895, 165. Harris outlined the costs: "At the quarry . . . $3.00 per cord, towing 50 [cents], unloading and teaming to mine, $2.50 total, for rubble, $6.00 per cord. Drawing, or dressing will be 23 cents per square foot." Harris to Mason, May 4, 1896, 232. Harris to Todd, January 4, 1897, 302. All in MS-001, Box 337, Folder 5, MTU.

77   Photos of drawings in HAER collection, HAER No. MI-2-223 and -224, Historic American Engineering Record, Library of Congress.

78   Harris to W. F. Crane, General Auditor, Copper Queen Cons. Mining Co., N.Y., September 13, 1904, Folder 12, 122. Todd, in New York, initially asked to countersign all checks, but Harris managed to dissuade him. Harris to Todd, February 1, 1900, and February 9, 1900, Folder 6, 272 and 276. Paying by check was also the recommendation of a 1901 audit. Harris to Todd, January 28, 1901, Folder 6, 386. All in MS-001, Box 337, MTU. Quincy Mining Co., *Annual Report for 1913*, 10. Hyde, "An Economic and Business History," 226. Lawton to Todd, June 13, 1913, MS-001, Box 342, Folder 11, MTU. There were 968 employees in 1895 and 1,993 in 1912. Lankton and Hyde, *Old Reliable*, 152.

79   Hyde, "An Economic and Business History," 226. Lawton to Todd, March 4, 1913, Folder 10, and Lawton to Todd, November 4, 1915, Folder 15, MS-001, Box 342, MTU. Undated drawings from Keweenaw National Historical Park.

80   *Calumet and Red Jacket News*, July 29, 1887, cited in Bjorkman, "Draft Historic Structure Report," 11.

81   *Calumet and Red Jacket News*, July 29, 1887, cited in Bjorkman, "Draft Historic Structure Report," 11.

82   Bjorkman, "Draft Historic Structure Report," 20–22.

83   Copper Range, *Annual Report for 1899* and *1900*.

84   Agassiz to Whiting, August 21, 1895, MS-002, Box 101, Folder 8, MTU.

85   C&H's use of D. Fred Charlton is instructive. The company first hired Charlton, Gilbert & Demar in 1897 for the remodeling of the hospital. With a change in general manager, though, Charlton seems to have been forgotten until he reintroduced himself to MacNaughton after the high school burned down. MacNaughton hired his firm, Charlton & Kuenzli, to design the new high school, and was so pleased with their work that he immediately put them on the design of a bathhouse. That project was interrupted while the YMCA was built, which Charlton & Kuenzli designed. In 1909 MacNaughton hired the firm to design an addition to C&H's office building and to complete the design of the bathhouse. When those were completed, he hired the firm to design a new hospital, but then fired them when Agassiz began working with Boston architects on that project. Charlton to MacNaughton October 2, 1905, MS-002, Box 43, Folder 152, MTU.

86   Atkinson, *The Church and Industrial Warfare*, 43.

87   For example, in 1915, 28,795 men took baths, compared to only 11,409 women (also 14,816 boys and 7,060 children). "Calumet Baths, for year 1915," MS-002, Box 212, Folder 33, MTU. In a sampling of copper-mining households, investigators found that 94 percent of foreign-born males spoke English, but only 57.6 percent of foreign-born females. U.S. Senate, *Immigrants in Industries*, part 1, 73.

6. Preservation and Loss

1   Erin Alberty, "Murder Victims at Rest," *Daily Mining Gazette,* May 22–23, 2004.

2   "Verdict Is In," *Daily Mining Gazette,* January 1, 1914.

3   Grant to Lauck, March 2–3, 1914, U.S. Commission on Industrial Relations, "Daily Reports."

4   Molloy, *Italian Hall,* 146.

5   Ibid., passim. "A Harvest of Death," *Miner's Bulletin,* December 28, 1913.

6   Molloy, *Italian Hall,* 142 and 146.

7   Thurner, *Rebels on the Range,* 141. R. C. Peterson and Carl Peterson, "Italian Hall Confession," *Daily Mining Gazette,* March 16, 1982. Steve Lehto investigated and dismissed the Chapman story. Lehto, *Death's Door,* 190–92.

8   Molloy, *Italian Hall,* 81, 95, 28–29. "A Harvest of Death," *Miner's Bulletin,* December 28, 1913.

9   "Eighty-three Murdered!" *Tyomies (The Workman),* December 26, 1913; typescript translation in RG 46, Box 2, Folder 2, State Archives of Michigan. "Tyomies Office Raided," *Daily Mining Gazette,* December 28, 1913. "A Harvest of Death," *Miner's Bulletin,* December 28, 1913. J. E. Ballinger, "Christmas Festivities End in Carnage of Death," *Miners Magazine,* January 1, 1914. Molloy, *Italian Hall,* 142.

10   Benedict, *Red Metal,* 229. "80 Perish in Christmas Eve Tragedy at Calumet," *Daily Mining Gazette,* December 25, 1913.

11   "The Italian Hall," *Calumet and Red Jacket News,* September 4, 1891. "Italian Hall a Mass of Ruins," *Calumet News,* January 2, 1908. *Daily Mining Gazette,* March 3, 1904, 6.

12   Measurement of foyer from Taipalus, who measured the space in 1980. Ted Taipalus, "Memories of Italian Hall," *Copper Miner's Journal* 7, no. 41 (October 11, 1984), B-1 and B-8, Vertical Files, Michigan Technological University Archives and Copper Country Historical Collections (hereafter MTU). Measurement of stairs from U.S. House, *Conditions in the Copper Mines,* 2098. Other descriptive material in Kevin Harrington, "Italian Hall," HABS No. MI-425, Historic American Buildings Survey, Library of Congress. "The Italian Benevolent Society's New Home," *Calumet News,* October 13, 1908. The exterior set of doors is on exhibit at the Coppertown Museum in Calumet. The five-panel doors, although evidencing alterations to the locking mechanism, open outwards.

13   My thanks to Jeremiah Mason and Scott See for the folding door explanation and to Larry Lankton for helping me articulate it. The same situation, of sheer numbers of people preventing egress, occurred in February 2003 in a nightclub in Chicago. There, twenty-one people died in a stampede to the exits. Although the case is not yet settled, the exit doors were apparently operable, but the capacity of the nightclub was more than the exits could handle. Mike Robinson, "Chicago Nightclub Owners Could Face Criminal Charges in Stampede Deaths," *Daily Mining Gazette,* February 18, 2003.

14   "Xmas Tree Panic Costs 80 Lives," *New York Times,* December 25, 1913. It is worth noting that these stereoviews bore the "union label" of the Allied Printing Trades Council of Houghton. Postcard collection donated to MTU Archives by Louis Koepel. *Miners Magazine,* January 8, 1914. Lankton, *Cradle to Grave,* 238.

15   Taipalus, "Memories of Italian Hall," *Copper Miner's Journal,* Vertical Files, MTU.

16   Bloor, *We Are Many*. Lyric from liner notes in Woody Guthrie, *Struggle*. Arlo Guthrie's concert at the Calumet Theatre on September 24, 2004, sold out immediately, enabling organizers to schedule an additional concert. He played to a sold-out theater again on October 16, 2007.

17   A radio program discussing the event aired in 1975. "1913 Calumet Disaster to Be Recalled," *Tech Topics* December 18, 1975, Vertical Files, MTU. John Beem wrote a play called "The Mother Lode," which opened in Detroit in 1980. Barbara Hoover, "Playwright Explores the 1913 Calumet Tragedy," *Daily Mining Gazette*, June 9, 1980, reprinted from *Detroit News*, May 29, 1980. A song by Larry Penn called "Frozen in Time" argues that Italian Hall may be gone, but it lives in Woody Guthrie's song. There is also a film in production about the tragedy; the filmmakers note that it was Guthrie's song that attracted them to the subject matter. Filmmakers Ken Ross and Louis V. Galdieri, advertisement in *Daily Mining Gazette*, November 12, 2002. They also note that Bob Dylan performed Guthrie's song in Carnegie Hall in 1961. www.1913massacre.com. Seitz and Masterson quoted in Zerbel, *An American Opera: The Children of the Keweenaw*, 82–90, 11.

18   Maurice Halbwachs distinguished between collective memory and history, the latter beginning when the former ends. Collective memory is personal and experiential, while history is intellectual and rationalizing. *The Collective Memory*, 52, 78. Perhaps the memorial marks the evolution from collective memory into history. See also Norkunas, *Monuments and Memory*, 43–44. Sue Cone, Clerk of Calumet Village, personal interview, August 15, 2002. Peggy Germain, Friends of the Italian Hall, Inc., telephone interview, November 10, 2002. Robert Pieti, "C&H's Paternalism a Simmering Cauldron," *L'Anse Sentinel*, December 20, 1989.

19   "Save Italian Hall Organization Forms," *Daily Mining Gazette*, June 25, 1980. "Friends Seeking Deadline Extension," *Daily Mining Gazette*, July 16, 1980. "Razing of Italian Hall Is Advised," *Daily Mining Gazette*, July 21, 1988. "Italian Hall," *Daily Mining Gazette*, April 6, 1983. Jane Nordberg, "Meeting Held to Plan Strike Centennial," *Daily Mining Gazette*, January 30, 2008.

20   Peggy Germain, "Italian Hall Is Destroyed," *Daily Mining Gazette*, October 8, 1984. "Park Work Begins," *Daily Mining Gazette*, July 21, 1988. "Italian Hall Project," *Daily Mining Gazette*, September 19, 1989. Germain interview. The Coppertown Museum in Calumet, which displays the doors, also interprets the event in a small exhibit.

21   Germain, *Tinsel and Tears*. Maki, *Stairway to Tragedy*. Edwards, *Tragedy on Seventh Street*. Molloy, *Italian Hall*. Germain, *False Alarm*. Lehto, *Death's Door*.

22   Murdoch, *Boom Copper*, 225–26. Benedict, *Red Metal*, 229. Thurner, *Rebels on the Range*, 138–74. Lankton, *Cradle to Grave*, 236–39. Munch, "1913 Massacre at Italian Hall," 20–21. There were also more literal depictions of the event. Photographer Eric Munch documented the building before its demolition. These photographs appeared in the *Chronicle* and again in an exhibit, *Italian Hall: Beyond the Bricks*, at Omphale Gallery, Calumet, August 2004. See also Michael F. Wendland, "The Calumet Tragedy," *American Heritage* (April–May 1986): 39–48.

23   Dan Roblee, "Italian Hall Disaster," *Daily Mining Gazette*, August 5, 2000. I sat on the board of the Keweenaw Heritage Center, the organization that asked that the mural be removed, and although I was not privy to discussions at the time, I did hear later that the objections were due to the artwork's irreverence toward its subject matter. Board members cited the feelings of people who had survived the tragedy and were still alive.

24   Milder statements include the Houghton County Board of Commissioners' "In memory of the people who perished in the Italian Hall Disaster, December 24, 1913" and the Calumet Women's Club's "In Memory of the Italian Hall: Gone but not forgotten."

25   Jane Nordberg, "Italian Hall Filmmakers Preview Work," *Daily Mining Gazette,* July 9, 2004. "Beautiful New Italian Building Is Dedicated," *Daily Mining Gazette,* October 11, 1908. "Hall Dedication Brilliant Event," *Calumet News,* October 12, 1908.

26   RG 46, Box 4, Folder 12, and Box 5, Folders 2 and 3, State Archives of Michigan.

27   Organizations meeting in Italian Hall mentioned in U.S. House, *Conditions in the Copper Mines,* 2098. "Italian Hall a Mass of Ruins," *Calumet News,* January 2, 1908.

28   Kevin Harrington, "Red Jacket Theatre and Town Hall," HABS No. MI-415, Historic American Buildings Survey, Library of Congress. "New City Fire Hall," *Copper Country Evening News,* August 16, 1898.

29   Red Jacket Village Council Minutes, 3 (November 15, 1898): 443; 3 (December 6, 1898): 446; 3 (March 11, 1899): 462; 4 (June 6, 1899): 5–6; 4 (July 12, 1899): 10; 4 (August 3, 1899): 14, Calumet Village Hall. *Copper Country Evening News,* November 2, 1898, November 16, 1898, and November 28, 1898.

30   Murdoch, *Boom Copper,* 151. Quoted by Monette, *The Calumet Theatre,* 18. "Financial Statement," *Copper Country Evening News,* March 9, 1899. "Red Jacket Lost Money in Its Water Department," *Calumet News,* March 1, 1910. "Annual Statement," *Copper Country Evening News,* March 3, 1898. Red Jacket Village Council Minutes 5 (April 11, 1910): 167, Calumet Village Hall.

31   *Copper Country Evening News,* January 7, 1899, and October 2, 1899.

32   Red Jacket Village Council Minutes, 3 (March 11, 1899): 461, Calumet Village Hall. Exact figures reported in the village's financial statement of March 8, 1901, are theater, $65,119.19, and town hall, $23,150.60, total, $88,269.79. *Copper Country Evening News,* March 9, 1901. "Blaze of Glory," *Copper Country Evening News,* March 21, 1900. " 'The Highwayman' Captured the Town," *Daily Mining Gazette,* March 21, 1900.

33   Red Jacket Village Council Minutes 3 (September 8, 1897): 379, Calumet Village Hall. *Copper Country Evening News,* November 2, 1898. "A New Opera House," *Copper Country Evening News,* November 28, 1898.

34   "Red Jacket Will Acquire Lots from the C.&H. Co.," *Calumet News,* May 3, 1910. "Red Jacket Purchases Four Lots from C.&H.," *Calumet News,* May 4, 1910. Red Jacket Village Council Minutes, 5 (May 3, 1910): 176–77, Calumet Village Hall. Kevin Harrington, "Red Jacket Theatre and Town Hall," HABS No. MI-415, Historic American Buildings Survey, Library of Congress, identifies the deed as Deed Book 88: 140, September 9, 1910.

35   Village officials seem to have neglected to name their new building, resulting in varied names and spellings. The ad for the opening called it "The New Opera House, Red Jacket" (*Daily Mining Gazette,* March 20, 1900), another ad at that time called it the "Calumet theater" (Facsimile program, Vertical Files, MTU), and a year later an ad called it the "Calumet Theatre" (*Copper Country Evening News,* March 4, 1902). "The Rise and Fall of the Calumet Theatre, 1900–1930," typescript in Vertical Files, MTU.

36   Monette, *The Calumet Theatre,* 56–72. Facsimile of 1901 program, Vertical Files, MTU. "Blaze of Glory," *Copper Country Evening News,* March 21, 1900. Ann Satterthwaite, who is writing a book on opera houses, has identified many municipal opera houses, for example, Londonderry, N.H., in 1889, Hudson, N.Y., in 1880, Brattleboro, Vt., in 1895, Vergennes, Vt., in 1897, Barre, Vt., in 1886, Claremont, N.H., in 1897, Camden, Maine, in 1894, Biddeford, Maine,

in 1894, and Northampton, Mass., in 1892. E-mails to author, August 10, 2007, and January 25, 2008.

37 Monette, *The Calumet Theatre*, 82–92.

38 Stanton, *The Lowell Experiment*, chapter 5, examines a more successful post-industrialist shift to historic preservation in Lowell, Massachusetts. Sabo, *Coppertown USA*. James L. Kerwin, "Calumet's Goal: Coppertown USA," *Detroit News*, March 1976. Cynthia Beaudette, "Labor of Love," *Daily Mining Gazette*, August 2, 1993.

39 James L. Kerwin, "Calumet's Goal: Coppertown USA," *Detroit News*, March 1976. Cynthia Beaudette, "Labor of Love," *Daily Mining Gazette*, August 2, 1993.

40 Lidfors, "Calumet Historic District." "Save the Theatre," *Daily Mining Gazette*, August 29, 1992. The park also acquired another building at Quincy, the former Mesnard street-car station, but its importance to the park was more because of its location in an enclave surrounded by park lands than as an historic site.

41 The park does have some interpretation, including wayside signs in the C&H industrial core, walking tour booklets of Calumet village and industrial core, and seasonal rangers leading tours. So far, this interpretation does not shrink from relating excesses of paternalistic domination, but it does not always look at the situation from the worker's point of view.

42 Funding for these organizations is tenuous. Most sites charge a small entrance fee and rely on grants from government agencies or downstate foundations. Local support in a deindustrialized region is meager. The Calumet Theatre Company, for instance, relies on membership dues and grants from the Michigan Council for the Arts and Cultural Affairs. www.calumettheatre.com. The Keweenaw National Historical Park Advisory Commission, which I chair, worked with the park on the designation of the Heritage Sites and continues to work with them. Ethnographer Cathy Stanton, *The Lowell Experiment*, 21, identifies places interpreted to the public as "cultural performance." If buildings perform, or function, in a certain way, then their rehabilitation as a preserved and interpreted building is a cultural performance, one in which identities are reexamined.

43 Amy K. Lavin, "Why Local Museums Matter," 13, and Elizabeth Vallance, "Local History, 'Old Things to Look At,'" and "Sculptor's Vision: Exploring Local Museums through Curriculum Theory," 28, all in Lavin, ed. *Defining Memory*.

Bibliography

"About." *The Calumet Theatre.* www.calumettheatre.com (accessed April 14, 2008).

Adams, Julia Hubbard. "Memories of a Copper Country Childhood." Privately printed, no date [accessioned 1973].

Alanen, Arnold R. *Morgan Park: Duluth, U.S. Steel, and the Forging of a Company Town.* Minneapolis: University of Minnesota Press, 2007.

Alanen, Arnold R., and Lynn Bjorkman. "Plats, Parks, Playgrounds, and Plants: Warren H. Manning's Landscape Designs for the Mining Districts of Michigan's Upper Peninsula, 1899–1932." *IA: Journal of the Society for Industrial Archeology* 24, no. 1 (1998): 41–60.

Alanen, Arnold R., and Thomas J. Peltin. "Kohler, Wisconsin: Planning and Paternalism in a Model Industrial Village." *AIP Journal* (April 1978): 145–59.

Alanen, Arnold R., and Suzanna E. Raker. "From Phoenix to Pelkie: Finnish Farm Buildings in the Copper Country." In *New Perspectives on Michigan's Copper Country,* edited by Alison K. Hoagland, Erik C. Nordberg, and Terry S. Reynolds. Privately printed, 2007.

Alanen, Arnold R., and Katie Franks, eds. *Remnants of Corporate Paternalism: Company Housing and Landscapes at Calumet, Michigan.* Calumet: Keweenaw National Historical Park, 1997.

Allen, Leslie H. *Industrial Housing Problems.* Boston: Aberthaw Construction Co., 1917.

"An Interior Ellis Island: Immigrants and Ethnicity in Michigan's Copper Country." Web exhibit, www.ethnicity.lib.mtu.edu. 2006. Michigan Technological University Archives and Copper Country Historical Collections (accessed July 17, 2008).

Atkinson, Henry A. *The Church and Industrial Warfare: A Report on the Labor Troubles in Colorado and Michigan.* Federal Council of the Churches of Christ in America, Commission on the Church and Social Service, 1914.

Beck, William. "Law and Order during the 1913 Copper Strike." *Michigan History* 54, no. 4 (Winter 1970): 275–92.

Bederman, Gail. *Manliness and Civilization: A Cultural History of Gender and Race in the United States, 1880–1917.* Chicago: University of Chicago Press, 1995.

Benedict, C. Harry. *Red Metal: The Calumet and Hecla Story.* Ann Arbor: University of Michigan Press, 1952.

Bennett, Shannon A. "Where the Bosses Lived: Managerial Housing of Three Companies in Michigan's Copper Country." Master's thesis, Michigan Technological University, 2007.

Bennetts, John G. "Industrial and Community Relations." *Mining Congress Journal* (October 1931): 563–64.

Bigott, Joseph C. "Bungalows and the Complex Origin of the Modern House." In *The Chicago Bungalow,* edited by Dominic A. Pacyga and Charles Shanabruch. Chicago Architectural Foundation, Arcadia, 2003.

———. *From Cottage to Bungalow: Houses and the Working Class in Metropolitan Chicago, 1869–1929*. Chicago: University of Chicago Press, 2001.

Bjorkman, Lynn. "Draft Historic Structure Report: Calumet and Hecla General Office." Part I: Developmental History. Keweenaw National Historical Park, 2001.

———. "Mine Worker Housing in Calumet, Michigan 1864–1950: Historic and Architectural Survey." Calumet: Keweenaw National Historical Park, 2000.

Bloor, Ella Reeve. *We Are Many: An Autobiography of Ella Reeve Bloor*. New York: International Publishers, 1940.

Bodnar, "Immigration and Modernization: The Case of Slavic Peasants in Industrial America." *Journal of Social History* 10, no. 1 (Fall 1976): 44–71.

Bourland, P. D. "The Medical Department of the Calumet and Hecla Consolidated Copper Company." *Mining Congress Journal* (October 1931): 555–57.

Brandes, Stuart D. *American Welfare Capitalism, 1880–1940*. Chicago: University of Chicago Press, 1976.

Brisson, Steven C. T. "D. Fred Charlton's Architectural Practice and Design in the Upper Peninsula of Michigan, 1887–1918." Master's thesis, State University of New York, Oneonta, 1992.

Brody, David. *Steelworkers in America: The Nonunion Era*. Cambridge: Harvard University Press, 1960. Reprint, New York: Russell and Russell, 1970.

Brooks, John Graham. "New Aspects of Employer's Welfare Work." *Journal of Social Science* 42 (1904): 1–12.

Buder, Stanley. *Pullman: An Experiment in Industrial Order and Community Planning, 1880–1930*. New York: Oxford University Press, 1967.

Buffington, Eugene J. "Making Cities for Workmen." *Harper's Weekly* 53 (May 8, 1909): 15–17.

Busch, Jane C. "Laurium Historic District." National Register of Historic Places Registration Form. 2004.

Butina, Mary Grentz. Personal interview. Painesdale, July 24, 2002.

Byington, Margaret F. *Homestead: The Households of a Mill Town*. New York: Russell Sage Foundation, 1910. Reprint, Pittsburgh: University of Pittsburgh Press, 1974.

"Calumet French Parish of St. Ann Started in 1884." *Our Sunday Visitor*. August 30, 1953.

Census of the State of Michigan, 1904. Volume 1: Population. Lansing: Wynkoop, Hallenbeck, Crawford Co., 1906.

Chapin, Robert Coit. *The Standard of Living among Workingmen's Families in New York City*. New York: Charities Publication Committee, 1909.

Chudacoff, Howard P. *Mobile Americans: Residential and Social Mobility in Omaha, 1880–1920*. New York: Oxford, 1972.

Committee of the Copper Country Commercial Club of Michigan. *Strike Investigation*. Privately printed, 1913.

Cone, Sue. Clerk of Calumet Village. Personal interview. Calumet, August 15, 2002.

"Copper Country Architects." Web exhibit, www.social.mtu.edu/CopperCountryArchitects. 2008. Michigan Technological University Social Sciences Department.

Cowan, Ruth Schwartz. *More Work for Mother: The Ironies of Household Technology from the Open Hearth to the Microwave*. New York: Basic Books, 1988.

Crawford, Margaret. *Building the Workingman's Paradise: The Design of American Company Towns*. London and New York: Verso, 1995.

Cullen, Jim. *The American Dream: A Short History of an Idea that Shaped a Nation*. New York: Oxford, 2003.

Daunton, M. J., ed. *Housing the Workers, 1850–1914: A Comparative Perspective*. London: Leicester University Press, 1990.

Dyer, Francis John. "The Truth about the Copper Strike." *National Magazine* 40, no. 2 (May 1914): 235–51.

Edwards, Michael. *Tragedy on Seventh Street*. Video. Washington Middle School, Sixth-Grade North Team Reading Classes, 2003.

Eisinger, Charles E. "The Freehold Concept in Eighteenth-Century American Letters." *William and Mary Quarterly*, 3rd ser., 4, no. 1 (January 1947): 42–59.

Ely, Richard T. "An American Industrial Experiment." *Harper's Monthly Magazine* 105, no. 625 (June 1902): 39–45.

———. "Pullman: A Social Study." *Harper's New Monthly Magazine* 70, no. 417 (February 1885): 452–66.

Engel, Dave, and Gerry Mantel. *Calumet: Copper Country Metropolis*. Privately printed, 2002.

Engels, Frederick. *The Housing Question*. 1872. Reprint, New York: International Publishers, 1935.

Falconer, Kenneth. "What More than Wages?" *Engineering Magazine* 38, no. 6 (March 1910): 833–40.

Fields, Richard A. *Range of Opportunity: A Historic Study of the Copper Range Company*. Privately printed, 1997.

Fisher, Nancy Beth. "Quincy Mining Company Housing, 1840s–1920s." Master's thesis, Michigan Technological University, 1997.

Fiske, Anna J. "The Human Interest in Library Work in a Mining District." *Proceedings of the Michigan Library Association*. Lansing: Wynkoop Hollenbeck Crawford, 1907.

Fogelson, Robert M. *America's Armories: Architecture, Society, and Public Order*. Cambridge: Harvard University Press, 1989.

Foner, Philip S. *History of the Labor Movement in the United States, Volume V: The AFL in the Progressive Era, 1910–1915*. New York: International Publishers, 1980.

Galdieri, Louis V., and Ken Ross. *1913 Massacre*. www.1913massacre.com (accessed February 7, 2003).

Garner, John S. "Leclaire, Illinois: A Model Company Town (1890–1934)." *Journal of the Society of Architectural Historians* 30, no. 3 (October 1971): 219–27.

———. *The Model Company Town: Urban Design through Private Enterprise in Nineteenth-Century New England*. Amherst: University of Massachusetts, 1984.

Gates, William B. Jr. *Michigan Copper and Boston Dollars: An Economic History of the Michigan Copper Mining Industry*. Cambridge: Harvard University Press, 1951.

General Rules and Course of Study of the Public Schools of Calumet. September 1926.

Germain, Peggy. *False Alarm: 1913 Italian Hall Disaster and Death Certificates*. Privately printed, 2005.

———. Telephone interview. November 10, 2002.

———. *Tinsel and Tears*. Privately printed, 1984.

Geshel, Brian. Personal interview. Houghton, October 3, 2005.

Going, Charles Buxton. "Village Communities of the Factory, Machine Works, and Mine." *Engineering Magazine* 21 (1901): 59–74.

Goldstein, Carolyn M. *Do It Yourself: Home Improvement in 20th-Century America*. New York: Princeton Architectural Press for National Building Museum, 1998.

Gondek, Jim. Telephone interview. January 16, 2008.

Gould, E. R. L. *The Housing of the Working People*. U.S. Commissioner of Labor, 8th Special Report. Washington: GPO, 1895.

Greenwald, Maurine W., and Margo Anderson, eds. *Pittsburgh Surveyed: Social Science and Social Reform in the Early Twentieth Century*. Pittsburgh: University of Pittsburgh Press, 1996.

Grierson, Marie F. "Calumet and Hecla Library." *Mining Congress Journal* (October 1931): 561–62.

Gross, Laurence F. *The Course of Industrial Decline: The Boott Cotton Mills of Lowell, Massachusetts, 1835–1955*. Baltimore: The Johns Hopkins University Press, 1993.

Guilbault, Frieda Durocher. Personal interview. Houghton, November 5, 2003.

Guthrie, Woody. *Struggle*. Smithsonian/Folkways SF 40025, released 1976.

Gutman, Herbert G. *Work, Culture, and Society in Industrializing America: Essays in American Working-Class and Social History*. New York: Alfred A. Knopf, 1976.

Halbwachs, Maurice. *The Collective Memory*. Translated by Francis J. Ditter Jr. and Vida Yazdi Ditter. New York: Harper and Row, 1980.

Hanger, G. W. W. "Housing of the Working People in the United States by Employers." *Bulletin of the Bureau of Labor,* no. 54, U.S. Department of Commerce and Labor (Washington, D.C.: GPO, 1904), 1191–243.

Hanson, Erica L. "The Cultural Landscape and Social Composition of Ahmeek Location and Ahmeek Village, 1902–1932." Master's thesis, Michigan Technological University, 1998.

Harris, Richard. *Unplanned Suburbs: Toronto's American Tragedy, 1900 to 1950*. Baltimore: The Johns Hopkins University Press, 1999.

———. "Working-Class Homeownership in the American Metropolis." *Journal of Urban History* 17, no. 1 (November 1990): 46–69.

Hayward, Mary Ellen, and Charles Belfoure. *The Baltimore Rowhouse*. New York: Princeton Architectural Press, 1999.

Heath, Kingston Wm. "The Howland Mill Village: A Missing Chapter in Model Workers' Housing." *Old-Time New England* (1997): 64–111.

———. *The Patina of Place: The Cultural Weathering of a New England Industrial Landscape*. Knoxville: University of Tennessee Press, 2001.

History of the Upper Peninsula of Michigan. Chicago: Western Historical Co., 1883.

Hoagland, Alison K. *Army Architecture in the West: Forts Laramie, Bridger, and D. A. Russell, 1849–1912*. Norman: University of Oklahoma Press, 2004.

———. "The Boardinghouse Murders: Housing and American Ideals in Michigan's Copper Country." *Perspectives in Vernacular Architecture* 11 (2004): 1–18.

Hubka, Thomas. "Just Folks Designing: Vernacular Designers and the Generation of Form." In *Common Places: Readings in American Vernacular Architecture*, edited by Dell Upton and John Michael Vlach, 426–32. Athens: University of Georgia Press, 1986.

Hubka, Thomas, and Judith T. Kenny. "Examining the American Dream: Housing Standards and the Emergence of a National Housing Culture, 1900–1930." *Perspectives in Vernacular Architecture* 13, no. 1 (2006): 49–69.

Hyde, Charles K. "An Economic and Business History of the Quincy Mining Company." HAER MI-2. U.S. Department of the Interior, National Park Service, Historic American Engineering Record, 1978.

Jackson, Kenneth T. *Crabgrass Frontier: The Suburbanization of the United States*. New York: Oxford, 1995.

Jensen, Joan. "Cloth, Butter, and Boarders: Women's Household Production for the Market." *Review of Radical Political Economics* 12, no. 2 (Summer 1980): 14–24.

Keweenaw Memorial: The First 100 Years. Six Productions video, 2003.

Kleinberg, S. J. *The Shadow of the Mills: Working-Class Families in Pittsburgh, 1870–1907*. Pittsburgh: University of Pittsburgh Press, 1989.

———. "Technology and Women's Work: The Lives of Working Class Women in Pittsburgh, 1870–1900." *Labor History* 17 (1976): 58–72.

Knowles, Morris. *Industrial Housing*. New York: McGraw-Hill, 1920.

Kostof, Spiro. *America by Design*. New York: Oxford, 1987.

Land, Hilary. "The Family Wage." *Feminist Review* 6 (1980): 56–77.

Lankton, Larry. *Beyond the Boundaries: Life and Landscape at the Lake Superior Copper Mines, 1840–1875*. New York: Oxford, 1997.

———. *Cradle to Grave: Life, Work, and Death at the Lake Superior Copper Mines*. New York: Oxford, 1991.

Lankton, Larry, and Charles K. Hyde. *Old Reliable: An Illustrated History of the Quincy Mining Company*. Privately printed, 1982.

Lauck, W. Jett, and Edgar Sydenstricker. *Conditions of Labor in American Industries: A Summarization of the Results of Recent Investigations*. New York: Funk and Wagnalls, 1917.

Lavin, Amy K., ed. *Defining Memory: Local Museums and the Construction of History in America's Changing Communities*. Lanham, Md.: Alta Mira Press, 2007.

Lehto, Steve. *Death's Door: The Truth behind Michigan's Largest Mass Murder*. Privately printed, 2006.

Lidfors, Kate. "Calumet Historic District." National Historic Landmark Nomination Form, 1988.

Lucchesi, Jane C. *History of Sarah Sargent Paine Memorial Library*. Privately printed, 1978.

Luria, Daniel D. "Wealth, Capital, and Power: The Social Meaning of Home Ownership." *Journal of Interdisciplinary History* 7, no. 2 (Autumn 1976): 261–82.

Macfarlane, Peter Clark. "The Issues at Calumet." *Collier's* 52, no. 21 (February 7, 1914): 5+.

Maki, Wilbert. *Stairway to Tragedy*. Privately printed, 1983.

Marcus, Alan I., and Howard P. Segal. *Technology in America: A Brief History*. 2nd ed. Orlando, Fla.: Harcourt Brace, 1999.

May, Martha. "The 'Good Managers': Married Working Class Women and Family Budget Studies, 1895–1915." *Labor History* 25, no. 3 (Summer 1984): 351–72.

———. "The Historical Problem of the Family Wage: The Ford Motor Company and the Five-Dollar Day." *Feminist Studies* 8, no. 2 (Summer 1982): 399–424.

McNear, Sarah. "Quincy Mining Company: Housing and Community Services, c. 1860–1931." HAER MI-2. U.S. Department of the Interior, National Park Service, Historic American Engineering Record, 1978.

Meakin, Budgett. *Model Factories and Villages: Ideal Conditions of Labour and Housing*. London: T. Fisher Unwin, 1905. Reprint, New York: Garland, 1985.

Merritt, Chris, Bode Morin, Michael Deegan, and Arron Kotlensky. "Survey of Blue Jacket." Term paper. 2005.

Metheny, Karen Bescherer. *From the Miner's Doublehouse: Archaeology and Landscape in a Pennsylvania Coal Town*. Knoxville: University of Tennessee Press, 2007.

Michel, Sandra Seaton. *Visions to Keep: The D&N Story*. Privately printed, 1990.

Michigan Office of the Commissioner of Mineral Statistics. *Mines and Mineral Statistics*. Lansing: Robert Smith and Co., 1900.

Mishkar, Larry, and Alison K. Hoagland. "Quincy Stamp Mills Historic District." National Register of Historic Places Registration Form, 2006.

Modell, John, and Tamara K. Hareven. "Urbanization and the Malleable Household: An Examination of Boarding and Lodging in American Families." *Journal of Marriage and the Family* 35 (August 1973): 467–79.

Molloy, Larry. *Italian Hall: The Witnesses Speak*. Privately printed, 2004.

Monette, Clarence J. *The Calumet Theatre*. Privately printed, 1979.

———. *Central Mine: A Ghost Town*. Privately printed, 1985.

Monkkonen, Eric H. *America Becomes Urban: The Development of U.S. Cities and Towns, 1780–1980*. Berkeley: University of California Press, 1998.

Mosher, Anne E. *Capital's Utopia: Vandergrift, Pennsylvania, 1855–1916*. Baltimore: The Johns Hopkins University Press, 2004.

Mulrooney, Margaret M. *A Legacy of Coal: The Coal Company Towns of Southwestern Pennsylvania*. Washington, D.C.: Historic American Buildings Survey/Historic American Engineering Record and America's Industrial Heritage Project, National Park Service, U.S. Department of the Interior, 1989.

Munch, Eric. "1913 Massacre at Italian Hall." *Chronicle: Quarterly Magazine of the Historical Society of Michigan* 19, no. 4 (Winter 1983/84): 20–21. And subsequent letters to the editor, *Chronicle* 20, no. 2 (Summer 1984), and 20, no. 4 (Winter 1984/85).

Murdoch, Angus. *Boom Copper*. 1943. Reprint, privately printed, 1964.

Nelson, Daniel. *Managers and Workers: Origins of the Twentieth-Century Factory System in the United States, 1880–1920*. 1975; 2nd ed. Madison: University of Wisconsin Press, 1995.

Nordberg, Erik. "Company Houses along the Picket Line: A Photographic Essay on the Michigan Copper Strike of 1913." *Mining History Journal* (1998): 63–75.

Norkunas, Martha. *Monuments and Memory: History and Representation in Lowell, Massachusetts*. Washington: Smithsonian, 2002.

Nuottila, Craig. Personal interview. Calumet, September 17, 2007.

Ore, Janet. *The Seattle Bungalow: People and Houses, 1900–1940*. Seattle: University of Washington Press, 2007.

Papineau, Joseph R. *Old Victoria, Forest Queen of Copper Mines, 1841–1991*. Privately printed, 1998.

Peel, Mark. "On the Margins: Lodgers and Boarders in Boston, 1860–1900." *Journal of American History* 72, no. 4 (March 1986): 813–34.

Penn, Larry. "Frozen in Time." *1913*. www.angelfire.com (accessed February 7, 2003).

Pfeiffer, C. Whit. "From 'Bohunks' to Finns: The Scale of Life among the Ore Strippings of the Northwest." *Survey* 36, no. 1 (April 1, 1916): 8–14.

Polk, R. L. and Co. *Polk's Houghton Directory*. Detroit: Polk Publishing Co., multiple years.

Primeau, Tom and Marcia. Personal interview. Calumet, April 28, 2007.

"The Proposed Elimination of the Finns." *Engineering and Mining Journal* 97, no. 18 (May 2, 1914): 920.

Putrich, Joe and Elaine. Interview. Numerous communications.

Quincy, Josiah. "Playgrounds, Baths, and Gymnasia." *Journal of Social Science* 36 (December 1898): 139–47.

Raasio, Clyde. Personal interview, Quincy Hill, January 22, 2008.

Rae, John W., and John W. Rae Jr. *Morristown's Forgotten Past: "The Gilded Age."* Privately printed, 1981.

Rees, Robinson, and Petermann, et al. *In the Matter of the Hearing before a Sub-committee of the Committee on Mines and Mining*. Brief of Counsel for the Mining Companies. Privately printed, 1914.

Reynolds, Marcus T. *The Housing of the Poor in American Cities*. 1893. Reprint, College Park: McGrath, 1969.

Rezek, Antoine Ivan. *History of the Diocese of Sault Ste. Marie and Marquette*. 2 vols. Chicago: M. A. Donahue, 1907.

Rice, Claude T. "Labor Conditions at Calumet & Hecla." *Engineering and Mining Journal* 92 (December 23, 1911): 1235–39.

———. "Labor Conditions at Copper Range," *Engineering and Mining Journal* 94, no. 26 (December 28, 1912): 1229–32.

Rickard, T. A. *The Copper Mines of Lake Superior*. New York: Engineering and Mining Journal, 1905.

"Robert C. Walsh" [obituary]. *Jerseyman*. October 6, 1911, 5.

Roberts, Peter. *Anthracite Coal Communities*. New York: Macmillan, 1904.

Rosenberg, Charles E. *The Care of Strangers: The Rise of America's Hospital System*. New York: Basic Books, 1987.

Sabo, Randy. *Coppertown USA: A Copper Country Happening*. Privately printed, 1974.

Sanborn Map Co. *Fire Insurance Maps*. Various years.

Satterthwaite, Ann. E-mails. August 10, 2007, and January 25, 2008.

Schlereth, Thomas J. "Material Culture and Cultural Research." *Material Culture: A Research Guide*. Edited by Thomas J. Schlereth. Lawrence: University Press of Kansas, 1985.

Schutz, Irene. Telephone interview, November 11, 2003; personal interview, Painesdale, November 15, 2003.

Scranton, Philip. "Varieties of Paternalism: Industrial Structures and the Social Relations of Production in American Textiles." *American Quarterly* 36, no. 2 (Summer 1984): 235–57.

Seitz, Paul. *The Children of the Keweenaw: An American Opera*. Libretto by Kathleen Masterson. Privately printed, 2001.

The Senior. Yearbook of Calumet High School. 1907.

Sergey, Joseph. Personal interview. Painesdale, July 24, 2002.

Shergold, Peter R. *Working-Class Life: The 'American Standard' in Comparative Perspective, 1899–1913*. Pittsburgh: University of Pittsburgh Press, 1982.

Shifflett, Crandall A. *Coal Towns: Life, Work, and Culture in Company Towns of Southern Appalachia, 1880–1960*. Knoxville: University of Tennessee Press, 1991.

Shuey, Edwin L. *Factory People and Their Employers: How Their Relations Are Made Pleasant and Profitable*. New York: Lentilhon, 1900.

Stanton, Cathy. *The Lowell Experiment: Public History in a Postindustrial City*. Amherst: University of Massachusetts Press, 2006.

Stencel, Craig. "Worker Houses and Workers at the Mason Stamp Mill during 1900 and 1910." Term paper. 1999.

Stetter, R. Charles. *The Central Mine M.E. Church*. Privately printed, 1981.

Stofer, Paula. "An Examination of the Socio-Cultural Roles of Boardinghouses and the Boarding Experience on the Michigan Mining Frontier, 1840–1930." Ph.D. diss., Michigan State University, 1997.

Stoker, Kim. Personal interview. Houghton, December 10, 1996.

Strasser, Susan. *Never Done: A History of American Housework*. New York: Pantheon, 1982.

Streightoff, Frank Hatch. *The Standard of Living among the Industrial People of America*. Boston: Houghton Mifflin, 1911.

Taylor, Graham Romeyn. "The Clash in the Copper Country: The First Big Strike in Fifty Years in the Industrial Backwoods of Upper Michigan." *The Survey* (November 1, 1913): 127–49.

———. *Satellite Cities: A Study of Industrial Suburbs*. New York: Appleton, 1915.

Thurner, Arthur W. *Calumet Copper and People: History of a Michigan Mining Community, 1864–1970*. Privately printed, 1974.

———. *Rebels on the Range: The Michigan Copper Miners' Strike of 1913–1914*. Privately printed, 1984.

———. *Strangers and Sojourners: A History of Michigan's Keweenaw Peninsula*. Detroit: Wayne State University Press, 1994.

———. "Western Federation of Miners in Two Copper Camps: The Impact of the Michigan Copper Miners' Strike on Butte's Local No. 1." *Montana: Magazine of Western History* (Spring 1983): 30–45.

Tolman, William Howe. *Industrial Betterment*. New York: Social Science Press, 1900.

Tone, Andrea. *The Business of Benevolence: Industrial Paternalism in Progressive America*. Ithaca: Cornell University Press, 1997.

Trebilcock, W. E. "History of the Public Schools of Calumet." 1943? Typescript in MTU Archives.

Trettin, Lillian. "'Give Them Comfortable Quarters': Tied Housing and Homeownership in the Lake Superior Copper District." *Michigan: Explorations in its Social History*. Edited by Francis X. Blair Jr. and Mars A. Vinovskis. Ann Arbor: Historical Society of Michigan, 1987.

Upton, Dell. *Architecture in the United States*. Oxford: Oxford University Press, 1998.

U.S. Census. *Population Schedules*. 1880, 1900, 1910, 1920, and 1930.

U.S. Commission on Industrial Relations. Daily Reports on Congressional Hearings, Copper Strike, Hancock, Michigan, February–March, 1914.

U.S. Department of the Interior. Bureau of Mines. *Houses for Mining Towns*. Bulletin No. 87. Washington, D.C.: GPO, 1914.

U.S. Department of Labor. Bureau of Labor Statistics. *Housing by Employers in the United States*. Bulletin No. 263. Washington, D.C.: GPO, 1920.

U.S. Department of Labor. Bureau of Labor Statistics. *Michigan Copper District Strike.* Bulletin No. 139. Washington, D.C.: GPO, 1914.

U.S. House, Subcommittee of the Committee on Mines and Mining. *Conditions in the Copper Mines of Michigan.* 63rd Cong., 2nd sess. Washington, D.C.: GPO, 1914.

U.S. Senate. Immigration Commission. *Immigrants in Industries.* 61st Cong., 2nd sess., Senate Doc. 633. Washington, D.C.: GPO, 1911. Part 17 (of 25 parts): Copper Mining and Smelting.

Van Slyck, Abigail A. *Free to All: Carnegie Libraries in American Culture, 1890–1920.* Chicago: University of Chicago Press, 1995.

Veiller, Lawrence. "Room Overcrowding and the Lodger Evil." *Housing Problems in America: Proceedings of the National Housing Association, Volume 2.* Cambridge, Mass.: University Press, 1912.

Veness-Randle, April René. "The Social-Spatial Lifecycle of a Company Town: Calumet, Michigan." Master's thesis, Michigan State University, 1979.

Wallace, Kim E. *Brickyard Towns: A History of Refractories Industry Communities in South-Central Pennsylvania.* Historic American Buildings Survey/Historic American Engineering Record, National Park Service, 1993.

"Welfare Work of C&H," *Engineering and Mining Journal* 98, no. 13 (September 26, 1914): 575–77.

Wendland, Michael F. "The Calumet Tragedy." *American Heritage* (April–May 1986): 39–48.

Whitaker, J. Russell. "The Relation of Agriculture to Mining in the Upper Peninsula of Michigan." *Journal of Geography* 25 (1926): 21–30.

Williams, Marilyn Thornton. *Washing "The Great Unwashed": Public Baths in Urban America, 1840–1920.* Columbus: Ohio State University Press, 1991.

Williams, Michael Ann, and M. Jane Young. "Grammar, Codes, and Performance: Linguistic and Sociolinguistic Models in the Study of Vernacular Architecture." In *Gender, Class, and Shelter: Perspectives in Vernacular Architecture, V.* Edited by Elizabeth Collins Cromley and Carter L. Hudgins. Knoxville: University of Tennessee Press, 1995.

Wiltse, Jeff. *Contested Waters: A Social History of Swimming Pools in America.* Chapel Hill: University of North Carolina, 2007.

Wolfe, Albert Benedict. *The Lodging House Problem in Boston.* Cambridge: Harvard University Press, 1913.

Wolff, David A. *Industrializing the Rockies: Growth, Competition, and Turmoil in the Coalfields of Colorado and Wyoming, 1868–1914.* Boulder: University Press of Colorado, 2003.

Wright, Gwendolyn. *Building the Dream: A Social History of Housing in America.* Cambridge: MIT Press, 1981.

Young Men's Christian Association of Calumet. *27th Annual Report.* May 1, 1921–April 30, 1922. Privately printed, 1922.

Zerbel, Scott R. (producer). *An American Opera: The Children of the Keweenaw.* Six Productions video, 2001.

Zimmerman, Donna. "From Paternalism to Privatization: The Evolution of a Corporate Mining 'Location' in the Copper District of Michigan's Keweenaw Peninsula." Master's thesis, University of Wisconsin-Madison, 2000.

Zunz, Olivier. *The Changing Face of Inequality: Urbanization, Industrial Development, and Immigrants in Detroit, 1880–1920.* Chicago: University of Chicago Press, 1982.

Archives

Bentley Historical Library, University of Michigan, Ann Arbor
    Lucius Lee Hubbard Collection
Calumet Public School Library, Calumet, Michigan
    History Files
Calumet Village Hall, Calumet, Michigan
    Red Jacket Village Council Minutes
Clarke Historical Library, Central Michigan University, Mount Pleasant, Michigan
    Aladdin Collection
Finlandia University Archives, Hancock, Michigan
Fulton County Courthouse, Lewistown, Illinois
    Deed and mortgage books
Houghton County Courthouse, Houghton, Michigan
    Deed and mortgage books
    Marriage licenses
Houghton County Historical Society, Lake Linden, Michigan
    Wilbert Anderson Collection
Keweenaw National Historical Park, Calumet, Michigan
    Oral History Collection
    Photographic Collections
    Quincy Mining Company Collection
Library of Congress, Washington, D.C.
    Historic American Buildings Survey
    Historic American Engineering Record
Michigan State University Archives, East Lansing, Michigan
    Vandercook Papers (Collection 11)
Michigan Technological University Archives and Copper Country Historical Collections,
    Houghton, Michigan
    Acc. 03-008A Quincy and Michigan Copper Mining Research Collection
    Acc. 03-050A Calumet & Hecla Collection
    Acc. 05-003A Gundlach Map Collection
    Acc. 06-087A Seeberville Court Files
    Acc. CR-879 Copper Range Labeled Books
    Acc. CR-998 Copper Range Inmet
    MS-001 Quincy Mining Company Collection
    MS-002 Calumet & Hecla Mining Company Collection
    MS-003 Calumet & Hecla Photograph Collection
    MS-005 Calumet & Hecla Engineering Drawings Collection
    MS-012 Quincy Mining Company Engineering Drawings
    MS-028 Van Pelt Copper Range Collection
    MS-046 Historic Districts and Buildings of the Upper Peninsula
    RG 77-105 Houghton County Tax Books
    RG 89-465 Houghton County Circuit Court Records

National Archives, College Park, Maryland
 RG 69 Work Projects Administration
 RG 280 Federal Mediation and Conciliation Service
State Archives of Michigan, Lansing, Michigan
 RG 46 Ferris Papers
 RG 76-83 Erastus Clement Jarvis Collection
University of Colorado at Boulder Archives, Boulder, Colorado
 Papers of WFM/IUMMSW
Wisconsin Architectural Archives, Milwaukee, Wisconsin
 Charlton & Kuenzli Collection
 Eschweiler Collection

Newspapers

Boston Daily Globe
C&H News and Views (Calumet)
Calumet and Red Jacket News
Calumet News
Copper Country Evening News (Calumet)
Daily Mining Gazette (Houghton)
Detroit News
Evening Copper Journal (Hancock)
Hancock Evening Journal
L'Anse Sentinel
Library Journal
Michigan Contractor and Builder (Detroit)
Miner's Bulletin (Hancock)
Miners Magazine (Boulder, Colorado)
New York Times
Portage Lake Mining Gazette (Houghton)
Torch Lake Times (Lake Linden)

Mining Company Annual Reports

Calumet & Hecla
Copper Range
Pewabic
Phoenix
Quincy

Index

Page numbers in italics refer to illustrations.

Alison K. Hoagland is professor emerita of history and historic preservation at Michigan Technological University. She is the author of *Buildings of Alaska* and *Army Architecture in the West: Forts Laramie, Bridger, and D. A. Russell, 1849–1912.*

Made in the USA
Coppell, TX
29 July 2021